The Visual Basic Coach

Jeff Salvage
DREXEL UNIVERSITY

Boston San Francisco New York
London Toronto Sydney Tokyo Singapore Madrid
Mexico City Munich Paris Cape Town Hong Kong Montreal

Executive Editor	Susan Hartman Sullivan
Associate Editor	Elinor Actipis
Executive Marketing Manager	Michael Hirsch
Production Services	Daniel Rausch/Argosy Publishing
Composition	Susannah Cahalane
Copyeditor	Kate Givens
Technical Art	Chuck Larson
Proofreader	Kim Cofer
Interior Design	Gina Hagen and Joyce Cosentino
Cover Design	Night & Day Design and Joyce Cosentino
Design Manager	Gina Hagen
Prepress and Manufacturing	Caroline Fell

Access the latest information about Addison-Wesley titles from our World Wide Web site:
http://www.aw.com/cs

Library of Congress Cataloging-in-Publication Data

Salvage, Jeff.
    The Visual Basic coach : Jeff Salvage.
        p. cm.
        ISBN 0-201-74549-6 (pbk.)
    Microsoft Visual Basic for applications 2. Visual BASIC (Computer program language) I. Title.

QA76.73.B3 S245 2002
005.26'8—dc21   2001041265
                                                                                            CIP

12345678910- CRK-04030201

This book is dedicated to my angelic niece Ally.

PREFACE

With the many Visual Basic 6.0 books on the market, why write another one? Our approach addresses the needs of information systems professionals. Unlike many texts that are more scientifically and mathematically based, *The Visual Basic Coach* targets those developers most likely to learn Visual Basic. Visual Basic 6.0 already has a huge installed base, and more and more people are learning it every day. While a new version of Visual Basic, Visual Basic .NET, is on the horizon, it is a huge departure from the development environment of version 6.0. History shows that when a radically different version of a language is introduced, its acceptance will take longer than a simple upgrade. Therefore, this book targets the many people still wanting to learn Visual Basic 6.0 with an eye toward converting to Visual Basic .NET in the future.

Target Audience

Although I was trained as a computer science major, I have done most of my consulting in the Information Systems field. While some computer scientists are striving to become hard-core applications developers who will write the latest operating system from Microsoft, many more programmers are studying to become the information systems professionals of tomorrow. A computer science professional most likely will go on to develop operating systems and application programs like Microsoft Word or Excel. However, information systems professionals may move on to develop database applications, or become network administrators or even database administrators.

The "Coach" series of textbooks is designed specifically for information systems professionals. Their needs are unique in that they require non-mathematical and non-scientific examples. They need examples that relate to topics they already know. Therefore, *The Visual Basic Coach* is comprised of business, humorous, and sports examples so that readers can relate to the problems they are trying to solve.

The Visual Basic Coach is perfect whether you intend to program for the rest of your life, are required to take a course in school, or wish to merely gain an appreciation for programming. This text is designed to be a standalone volume for students who are not majoring in computer science learning Visual Basic. It also may function as a bridge between your current level of understanding and more advanced Visual Basic texts.

Author's Approach

Because the audience for *The Visual Basic Coach* is different from most programming texts, I have taken a unique approach by applying many techniques learned from coaching athletes to the teaching of computer programming. I have competed as an international athlete representing the United States and currently am coaching Olympic hopefuls in the sport of race walking. In many ways the teaching of race walking is similar to that of computer programming.

Race walking is a complex sport that requires combining Olympian endurance with a very complicated technique. In order to master it, it requires a great deal of practice and attention to the details of proper technique. Coaches do not start athletes by sending them into competition on the first day of practice. Instead, many coaches require athletes to repeat drills over and over again until they have mastered the techniques of the sport.

Similarly, instead of beginning with problem solving, this text teaches sound Visual Basic syntactical fundamentals first. While learning the basic building blocks of Visual Basic, we will perform programming drills repeatedly until readers understand the fundamentals and subtleties of Visual Basic. This approach contrasts with many other texts trying to be more of a complete reference manual instead of an instructional textbook. They introduce too many constructs of Visual Basic before solidifying a mastery of the most required Visual Basic syntax. While we do not focus on these additional features, we have added some of the important ones at the end of each chapter in a special section that can be skipped by novice programmers.

Throughout the text we will present new features of Visual Basic, explain their syntax, and present drills that explore the subtleties of the syntax. We supplement these drills with real-world examples of programming problems and build on the knowledge gained from these drills. Because there are so many options in Visual Basic, topics deemed optional are added at the end of each chapter in a Coach's Corner so that more advanced students can learn them, while students looking for a basic understanding of the language can skip over them.

While writing the proper programs is important, so is motivating the people around you to get the job done. The idea is the same, whether it is breaking up the monotony of a long racewalk by joking around or breaking up the dryness of a computer text. *The Visual Basic Coach* finds different ways to motivate and amuse you as you read through the text.

Scope of Coverage

The Visual Basic Coach covers Visual Basic as though readers have never learned a programming language before. Starting with a brief introduction to computer languages and where Visual Basic fits in, we get students rolling immediately with an example that illustrates the reason Visual Basic has the word "Visual" in its title. Students are introduced to the development environment and how to create an application with images and text.

Once a basic understanding of the environment is mastered, a basic understanding of programming constructs follows: variables, operators, conditional statements, loops, and functions. These constructs are used to develop programs that solve relatively simple but useful problems. Interweaved between learning these constructs are the introduction of many of the basic controls used regularly by Visual Basic developers. Instead of just listing these controls, examples are given that motivate the benefit of one control over the other based on the goal of the application.

Once the students have gained a firm understanding of basic Visual Basic, we'll concentrate on additional features of Visual Basic such as arrays, user-defined types, and files. While many introductory classes in Visual Basic do not cover extensive advanced topics, we have made it easy to select the ones that an instructor wishes to add to his or her course. Both simple and advanced coverage of databases are covered in two separate chapters. Also included are sections on drag and drop interfaces, graphic routines, multiform applications, Menus and basic object-oriented programming.

Rounding out the text is a chapter highlighting the issues with developing in Visual Basic .NET. It is meant to be used as a primer to prepare developers who are familiar with Visual Basic for programming in Visual Basic .NET.

Pedagogy
Drills

The Visual Basic Coach has many strengths that separate it from other Visual Basic texts. We all know that you cannot learn to program by merely reading a textbook in a narrative format. *The Visual Basic Coach* combats this with around 100 drills that provide students with immediate feedback on their understanding of what they just learned. The drills are presented as questions and their complete solutions with detailed explanations are included at the end of each chapter.

The following is a sample of a few drills from the conditional statements chapter. It shows how a student can get immediate feedback with variations of the same problem, changed slightly, so he or she can master all aspects of the concept being taught.

DRILL 7.8

What is the value in `txtOutput's` `Text` property after the following code has been executed?

```
Private Sub cmdOutput_Click()
Dim intCounter As Integer

For intCounter = 2 To 10 Step 5
   txtOutput.Text = txtOutput.Text + Str(intCounter) + " "
Next intCounter

txtOutput.Text = txtOutput.Text + Str(intCounter)
End Sub
```

(continues)

DRILL 7.8 (continued)

The output is as follows:

```
2  7  12
```

When the command button is clicked, the code executes as follows: First the `For` loop is entered and the `intCounter` variable is initialized to 2. Since 2 is less than or equal to 2, the body of the `For` loop executes. This appends a "2" and a space to the `txtOutput` text box. Then the loop counter, `intCounter`, is incremented by 5 to 7.

Since 7 is less than or equal to 10, the body of the `For` loop executes again. This time a "7" and a space are appended to `txtOutput`. Once again, `intCounter` is incremented by 5 to 12.

Since 12 is not less than or equal to 10, the loop terminates. However, in this case our processing is not complete. The value 12 contained in the variable `intCounter` remains and is appended to `txtOutput` as the last statement of the command button's code.

Tips

Throughout the chapters frequent tips highlight key programming issues.

TIP

A `Long` variable can hold any value that an `Integer` variable can, but not vice versa.

Warnings

Commonly made mistakes are highlighted with a Warning Box.

WARNING

When you list a range of numbers for a `Case` statement, you must list the smaller number first.

VB .NET Alerts

There are many instances in which an application developed in a Visual Basic 6.0–oriented way will experience problems in Visual Basic .NET. Wherever these issues exist, we will point out how to avoid them. For example:

Visual Basic .NET Alert

While Visual Basic Version 6.0 will allow the developer to declare more than one variable on a line even if they are of different types, this will not be supported in VB .NET and should be avoided. Another good reason to declare variables on their own line is that the developer can add a comment for each variable.

End-of-chapter Material
Key Terms
At the end of each chapter all new terms introduced within the chapter will be listed with a condensed definition of the word.

Case Studies
In each chapter you will find a case study that focuses on the skills developed in the chapter in a practical, real-world example. Throughout most of the text, the case studies focus on a business-owner creating a system that will process payroll for his company. It is simple and clear to follow. We provide the problem statement, discuss its solution, and then provide the coded solution. By immediately reinforcing the skills learned in the chapter, retention will be greatly improved.

Coach's Corner
At the end of each chapter, optional topics are included to round out students' knowledge of the topics introduced in each chapter.

Additional Exercises
Finally, each chapter is ends with a series of short-answer questions and programming assignments for students to practice what they have learned in the chapter.

Different Course Options
This book is designed for a one or two semester introductory programming sequence for non-computer science majors. In general, each chapter builds on the last and is designed to follow sequentially. However, the text was designed with the idea that many topics are optional. Many of these optional topics are presented at the end of each chapter in the Coach's Corners. These topics can be added or removed without adding dependency issues. Additionally, while chapters 1–7 are fairly mandatory for any programming sequence, many of the additional chapters can be skipped based on the preferences of the instructor.

To The Students
So you're taking a computer course. Odds are you'll either love it or hate it. It's the job of this text to help you through it. Regardless of why you are taking the course you need to learn the material presented by your teacher. If you follow my advice, the process will be a lot easier. This book is designed to be interactive. DO NOT just read the drills. Try them. You will learn much more that way. While some of the examples are dry and simply there to help with your mastery of the Visual Basic syntax, many more are colorful statements from things I enjoy. The sports theme shows up in many examples, but I have also included many names and quotes from movies. Try to see if you can figure then out. Hopefully I am not dating myself too badly.

Supplements
The following supplements will be made available on-line for qualified instructors only through your Addison-Wesley sales representative: the instructors manual, complete answers to the exercises in the chapters, source code to all programs, test banks of sample exams, and lecture notes in a Microsoft PowerPoint™ format. Source code and PowerPoint™ slides are available to all readers at *www.aw.com/cssupport*.

Acknowledgments

Many people's efforts go into the creation of a textbook in addition to the author's. Obvious thanks go to my editors Susan Hartman Sullivan and Elinor Actipis without whose efforts *The Visual Basic Coach* would not have reached publication, Patty Mahtani and Daniel Rausch for their assistance in the production cycle of the text, and Michael Hirsch for making sure the world knows about this text. Additional thanks goes to Eric Smith and Charley Shuman, who helped proof early versions of the text.

Along the way many people helped with the many stages my manuscript went through. Additional thanks go to my reviewers:

Tammy L. Ashley, *New Hampshire Community Technical College at Manchester*
Chris Beaumont, *Queens College*
Bruce W. Mielke, *University of Wisconsin, Green Bay*
Steve Robischon
Alfred J. Seita, *Kapiolani Community College*
Edward J. Williams, *University of Michigan*
Jeff Yeley, *Houston Community College*

A special thanks goes to Dr. Nira Herrmann who continues to make teaching at Drexel a pleasure.

CONTENTS

CHAPTER 1
Introduction to Computing

CHAPTER 2
Your First Visual Basic Applications

CHAPTER 1
Introduction to Computing

CHAPTER
OBJECTIVES

◆ Introduce a perspective on computing

◆ Discuss the evolution of computer programming

◆ Introduce Visual Basic and its motivations

◆ Discuss the commonalities of Visual Basic and other environments

◆ Introduce the characteristics of a quality computer program

◆ Explain the difference between sequential/top-down algorithms and event-driven algorithms

◆ Introduce the basic concept of an object

It wasn't that long ago that people thought of computers as tools for the scientist or something out of a science fiction movie. Times have certainly changed. Today our daily lives are inundated with computerized devices wherever we go. We do not feel complete without our cell phone, access to email and an Internet connection, and the list goes on.

A scant five years ago, I gave a talk at a non-computer-related conference where I told people that an email address would soon be as commonplace as a fax number. I was laughed at. Two years later, at the same conference, almost everyone in the room had one. Technology has changed dramatically and at an ever-increasing pace that seemingly has no end.

All of this technology starts with people writing computer programs.

1.1 Types of Languages and Why They Are Useful

As there are many different computer applications so are there many different programming languages to create those applications. Before we can compare and contrast programming languages and the concepts behind them, we must first decide what a programming language is.

A **programming language** is an agreed-upon format of symbols that enables a programmer to instruct a computer to perform certain predefined tasks.

Symbols are used to communicate a programmer's intent to a computer; how understandable these symbols are determines the level of the programming language. Some languages are written in an English-style prose that is very readable by the programmer, but more difficult for the computer to understand. These languages are often referred to as high-level languages. In contrast, other languages are easy for the computer to understand, but very difficult for the programmer to comprehend. These languages are known as low-level languages.

The earliest computers really didn't have much of a programming language. To instruct these computers to accomplish tasks, early computer programmers entered a series of numbers by manually flipping switches. Programming these machines was also difficult because these numbers were not entered in the common decimal form, but in an encoding scheme called binary numbers. Binary numbers are an encoding scheme where values are represented by a series of 1's and 0's. By combining 1's and 0's, different numbers can be represented. These machines were extremely difficult to program and thus were used only to solve simple problems that were repeated over and over again.

It didn't take long for computer scientists to realize that in order for computers to be more useful, they would require a programming environment that was a bit more robust than manually flipping switches.

Two major leaps forward were the creation of an **assembly language** and the introduction of **punch cards**. An **assembly language** utilizes a series of mnemonics to represent commonly used instructions. Additionally, to increase the readability of the program, numbers could be entered in our commonly used decimal notation instead of the cryptic binary format previously used.

Another milestone was the creation of **punch cards** to facilitate the entry and storage of these programs. A punch card was a cardboard card in which a machine popped holes, thereby allowing the representation of an instruction and its operators. These punch cards could be assembled into a program by piling the cards in the proper order and placing them in the card reader to be read in sequence.

While punch cards and the associated assembly language were a monumental leap forward, they still provided immense problems when dealing with non-trivial programs.

One big issue was that assembly language programs written for one computer system would not work on another computer system. This meant that when your company upgraded its computer system, you would be forced to rewrite many of your applications. Additionally, you might have to spend time learning the new assembly language required for the new computer system.

Another issue was that while the assembly languages available were easy for the computer to understand and better than dealing with the 1's and 0's of a pure machine language, they didn't map themselves well to real-world problems.

Two popular computer languages were developed to combat these problems: **COBOL** and **FORTRAN**. These languages were developed to meet the different needs of computer users. COBOL, which stands for Common Business Oriented Language, was used primarily for business processing. For example, it was used to write programs such as handling a company's payroll or maintaining a company's inventory. In contrast FORTRAN, which stands for formula translator, was designed primarily to perform mathematical calculations extremely quickly.

Both these languages were a major improvement over the existing assembly language in terms of the time required to develop applications. These languages raised the level of the machine to the programmer. By providing built-in commands for commonly used operations, the language allowed programmers to solve their problems by writing less, and more understandable, code.

Aside from reducing the time it would take to solve a problem, another big advantage is that standards were developed so that the language was the same from computer system to computer system. This meant that programs written for one computer system could be run on another computer system without having to be rewritten.

Although humans wrote these programming languages so they were more understandable, they required translation into a language the computer system could understand. As new computer systems were developed, they would include a translator for these standard languages that would convert the standard language into a language the computer could understand.

Controversy arose over whether these languages produced programs that were slower to execute than handwritten assembly-language programs. While one camp of computer system developers was trying to improve the efficiency of the machine code generated by these new languages, other camps were developing new "better" computer languages. The quest for the Holy Grail of computer languages began. Almost with a religious fervor, languages were developed to deal with all types of situations. Languages were produced for business applications, mathematical applications, artificial intelligence applications, and then the quest to develop a single universal language that would meet all users needs.

The quest for a single programming language cycles into popularity from time to time. One of the most ambitious attempts was PL/1. It was IBM's attempt at combining the best of FORTRAN and COBOL. What IBM got was a language that many feel was very complex and not as useful as either FORTRAN or COBOL for their respective tasks.

As computer technology, capacity, and speed increased, the need for better and more diverse languages developed. Even teaching languages were developed such as Pascal, which were only intended to teach sound programming principles, and not intended for business or scientific applications.

While many of these languages addressed the needs of the programmers writing applications, they didn't address the needs of the programmers developing the operating systems of the day. Today we are familiar with operating systems such as Windows NT and UNIX, which are written for more than one type of computer system. This way when Microsoft wants to develop a version of Windows NT for another computer platform, it only needs a program that translates the language in which Microsoft developed the operating system to the machine on which it wishes it to run. The most popular of these languages was **C**.

Because of C's popularity, it became much more than a language used for developing operating systems. Programmers quickly started to use C to write applications for many different needs. The programs produced were efficient and rivaled the performance of handwritten assembly-language programs. Indeed, with today's efficient compilers and complex computer systems, the C compiler may generate machine code that runs faster than hand-developed assembly language.

As C increased in popularity and a large group of reusable programs was developed, new issues arose. How could programs be reused more effectively?

A new methodology was developed for creating reusable programs. The concept was to create objects that closely wrapped a computer program and the data on which it operated. It would only allow programmers access to the data in ways intended by the original programmer, so that programmers with less knowledge could not damage the data.

Languages like Smalltalk were developed on this approach, but more importantly, programmers wanted to be able to leverage their existing programs and therefore, object-oriented extensions to languages that previously existed were developed. Object-oriented Pascal and **C++** were two of these. Because they were not created from scratch, the object-oriented extensions sometimes required kludgey language syntax.

Recently a new language has come on the scene: **Java**. Java is an object-oriented language that is very similar to C++. It has many of the same features as C++, but without the awkwardness of some of the syntax. Additionally, Java is made so that it can be run on any computer without having to recompile your code for that machine. This is a huge advantage when dealing with Internet-based applications, but has disadvantages as well. One big problem with Java is that its performance is much slower than C++'s performance. Its simpler syntax removes some of the power C++ gives the programmer. It also is inherently slower because the program must be translated into machine language by the computer executing it. This added step is acceptable in small applications that are run from the Web, but for enterprise-wide application development, this presents a performance issue.

1.2   Where Does Visual Basic Fit In?

So where does **Visual Basic** fit into the overabundance of computer languages available? Visual Basic has its roots in the language called **BASIC**. But Visual Basic isn't your mother's BASIC.

BASIC was developed in 1964 by John Kemeny and Thomas Kurtz (at Dartmouth College) as a language for the rest of us. BASIC (Beginner's All-purpose Symbolic Instruction Code) was a language written to help non-scientists develop computer programs. Indeed, it was the first computer language I learned. My experience with it was dramatically different from what your experience with Visual Basic will be.

The original BASIC was a great start, but very limited. While I was successful writing small programs as a high school student, trying to write large integrated systems with it would prove difficult to write and even more difficult to maintain. My high school classmates were enthralled with a simple text adventure game I created, which by today's standards of adventure games would be laughed at. It allowed a player to navigate by typing simple two word sentences and the program responded with a text display. Today's adventure games allow for interactive 3D graphics and Internet connections to allow multiple player games. Was it my lack of skill that limited my game? In a word, no. The world of BASIC and other programming languages has changed dramatically to allow games to have capabilities we did not even dream of at the beginning of the home computer revolution.

Microsoft got its start writing BASIC compilers. However, the BASIC it developed bears little resemblance to Visual Basic. When the original BASIC compilers were developed, there were no graphical user interfaces (GUI) to program, databases to interface with, or objects to develop. So, while Visual Basic has BASIC in its name, it is a completely different world than the one I programmed in during high school.

Today's Visual Basic requires understanding many modern programming concepts. Its use varies greatly from C++ and many of the traditional languages. Visual Basic can be used to solve many programming problems, but the most popular uses in the business world are to develop **front ends** for **databases** and to develop **prototypes** of applications.

Both of these uses have arisen due to the strengths and weaknesses inherent in Visual Basic. Visual Basic makes developing GUI very easy. However, this ease comes with the price of performance. The two types of applications that benefit from Visual Basic's strengths are not victims of its weaknesses.

Applications developed to be prototypes show how an application works. If the application works slowly, it is not important since prototypes will be discarded and the application will be developed in a more efficient language when it goes to production.

Applications that are front ends for databases may perform slightly slower than if they are developed in another language. However, the majority of time that the program executes it will be waiting for information from a database. Requesting information from a database is not significantly slower in Visual Basic than other applications.

Therefore, the ease in creating the front end and connecting to the database outweighs any performance issues Visual Basic introduces.

1.3 What Makes a Quality Program?

What features are embodied in quality programs? Beginning students often argue that since their program functions properly, they should receive an 'A.' A program that meets the specifications dictated to the programmer only meets the first criterion of a quality program. A quality program should have all of the following characteristics.

- Readability
- Modularity
- Efficiency
- Robustness
- Usability

Readability

In the real world, specifications for a program constantly change. After a programmer meets the initial requirements, users often see the value of their new application and desire additional features. This maintenance phase of a computer project can actually be more expensive than the original development process. Therefore, it is imperative that the program be written so that it can be understood by other programmers as well as the original programmer.

To improve readability, a key method a programmer can employ is to add comments to the program. Comments are statements in a program that explain the program's purpose and any unclear pieces of code along the way. These comments should be written into the code at the time that the code is written, not after the entire program is completed. Sometimes comments within the code are not enough and it is often necessary to produce external documentation to round out the explanation of a project.

Beginning programmers, as well as some seasoned professionals, will jokingly argue that they do not comment their code to ensure job security. In reality, a programmer who develops readable, reliable code is far more valuable to a company than one who hoards knowledge in cryptic code. Additionally, a programmer who becomes the sole person to understand the code often ends up maintaining that code instead of moving on to more exciting and lucrative projects.

Additionally, having a programming standards document is extremely important. In the corporate programming environment, many programmers work together as a team to develop a single program. It is imperative that everyone follows the same conventions. These can include indenting your code in a consistent manner, capitalizing the first letter of each word in a variable name, and using the same abbreviations each time you abbreviate a long word.

Modularity

To reduce the cost of maintenance, code must be modularized. This requires that programs be written in an orderly fashion with problems divided into smaller subproblems and then assembled in a logical order. Each piece of code should accomplish one task and be capable of standing on its own.

Efficiency

The next issue is the tradeoff between writing compact, super-efficient code versus writing clear, readable code that may run a little more slowly and take up slightly more room. Which is more desirable? Well, that depends on the situation. If the code is being written for an air-to-air combat system, speed of execution and size are the most important issues. However, as stated earlier, Visual Basic is not used when high performance is the key design criteria. Therefore, you are adding complexity without a true increase in the goals of the application. Size of the program is not usually an issue with Visual Basic applications either. In order to execute a Visual Basic application, additional files must be installed on a computer that make the size of an individual application irrelevant. Coupled with the fact that computer memory prices have rapidly been declining, reducing the size of most applications is not overly important.

It is important to realize that the number of characters you write in your program does not necessarily relate to program size. Sometimes small amounts of code require far more space than the remainder of the program.

If you do decide to add lines of code that are cryptic for the purposes of speed or size, you should do two things. First, explain the intricacies of the code in full detail. Second, if a simpler way exists to implement the code, indicate so in the comments. This will assist future programmers in modifying your code, even if they do not understand your shortcut.

Robustness

If a program is written to accomplish a task, how does it handle cases when the input to the program is not as expected? Does it crash? Does it go into an infinite loop? Or does it display a message indicating the information entered is incorrect and gracefully allow the user to exit or continue? A program should never crash. A robust program will handle all of these situations in a graceful manner.

Usability

Usability is probably the most difficult issue to master. A program must be correct to be useful. Whether the project is an assignment in class or a task given by your boss at work, if the project does not meet the needs of the end user, regardless of the elegance of your solution, it may never be used.

These are all issues that should be considered while programming. Following them will lead to a successful program and will require a lot less stress in getting there.

1.4   Understanding Algorithms

While we have introduced you to the concept of different programming languages, we have not introduced you to the concept behind giving instructions to a computer that will perform tasks that you wish.

Instead of jumping right into a programming example, let's practice by first trying to understand the concept of an **algorithm**. An algorithm is the sequence of steps required to solve a problem. Instead of thinking about algorithms in terms of a computer program, let's try to understand the algorithm behind a process that you are already familiar with. It is important to learn how to understand a process completely and then be able to explain it in simple steps before we try to write a program to accomplish a task. This is often easier said than done.

Algorithms can be represented in a graphical format called a **flowchart**.

Observe the following algorithm to listen to the radio station 610 WIP on the AM band on your stereo.

Step 1: Turn the stereo on.
Step 2: If the band is set to FM, switch it to AM.
Step 3: If the station is set to a station greater than 610, turn the station to the left until 610 is reached.

Flow Chart Symbol	Symbol Meaning
Process	Used to represent calculations and data manipulation.
Decision	Used to represent a comparison with either a Yes/True result or a No/False result.
Data	Used to represent the input or output of data.
Terminator	Used to indicate the beginning or ending of a task.
——→ —— No ——→ —— Yes ——→	These connector lines are used to join the other symbols within the flowchart. The 2nd and 3rd ones are used in conjunction with a Decision Box.

Step 4: If the station is set to a station less than 610, turn the station to the right until 610 is reached.

Step 5: Listen to the best sports talk station in the country.

Here is the algorithm represented as a flowchart.

Figure 1.1
Radio Station Flowchart

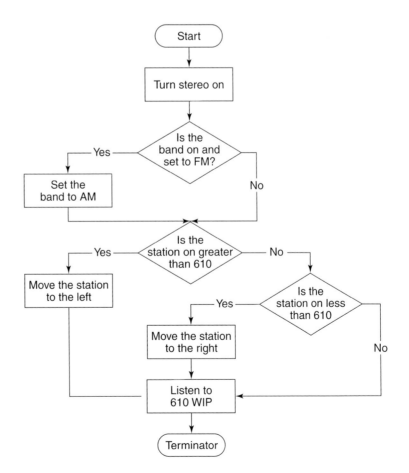

You can see that a simple algorithm can lead to a large flowchart very easily. Even though they can be large, they are often useful. We will use flowcharts to graphically represent new programming constructs as we introduce them.

1.5   Top-down versus Event–driven Algorithms

One can classify algorithms into two categories. The first, top-down or sequential, are the types of problems that are solved by traditional programming languages. They lend themselves to problems that have a starting point, a predetermined series of steps, and an ending point. The other type of algorithm solves a problem, but not as a straight-line solution. Algorithms that respond to external stimuli are considered event-driven.

Top-Down/Sequential Algorithm

Consider the steps required to boil an egg.

Step 1:   Open closet door.
Step 2:   Remove pot.
Step 3:   Close closet door.
Step 4:   Place pot under sink faucet.
Step 5:   Turn on the cold water.
Step 6:   Wait until the pot is full.
Step 7:   Turn off the cold water.
Step 8:   Place pot on stove burner.
Step 9:   Turn burner on high heat.
Step 10:   Open refrigerator door.
Step 11:   Take out the egg carton.
Step 12:   Open the egg carton.
Step 13:   Remove an egg from the carton.
Step 14:   Close the egg carton.
Step 15:   Place the egg carton back in the refrigerator.
Step 16:   Close the refrigerator door.
Step 17:   Open the silverware drawer.
Step 18:   Remove a large spoon.
Step 19:   Close the silverware drawer.
Step 20:   Wait until the water is boiling
Step 21:   When the water is boiling, place the egg in the pot using the spoon.
Step 22:   Wait three minutes until the egg is cooked.
Step 23:   Shut the stove off.
Step 24:   Remove the egg from the pot.

The preceding steps follow a sequential nature. You may not have believed so many steps are required to properly give instructions; however, giving good directions requires details so that ambiguous situations do not occur.

DRILL 1.1

Write down the steps required to describe how you would brush your teeth in the morning.

DRILL 1.2

Write down the steps required to parallel park a car.

Event-Driven Algorithms

Consider the steps required for playing tennis (for simplicity's sake, let's assume that you are the one serving). These steps are not as straightforward as the steps involved in cooking the egg. The key difference is that the steps required to play tennis cannot be predicted in advance. They must be listed in what-if prose.

Step 1:   Walk up to the serving line.
Step 2:   Toss the ball up in the air.
Step 3:   Swing the racket so that you hit it to the other player in the opposite box.
Step 4:   Wait for the ball to strike the tennis court.
Step 5A: If the ball lands legally in the box, wait to see if the opponent hits your serve back toward you.
Step 5B: If the ball lands outside the box, you must serve again. Go to step 1.
Step 6A: If the ball is hit back, and it is hit to your right, move toward the right so you are in position to hit it back.
Step 6B: If the ball is hit back, and it is hit to your left, move toward the left so you are in position to hit it back.
Step 6C: If the ball is hit back and it is hit directly at you, wait for it to arrive.
Step 7A: If the ball is hit back and it is hit in front of you, move forward.
Step 7B: If the ball is hit back and it is hit behind you, move backward.
Step 8A: If the ball is hit outside the lines, do not hit it and let it pass. Go to step 1.
Step 8B: If the ball is hit so that it is a legal shot, hit it in a place the opponent is not. Go to step 6A.

The answer given for the exercise is obviously incomplete. To document every event that could happen in a game of tennis would take many pages. However, it should be obvious that there is a difference in nature of the algorithm of cooking an egg and the algorithm of playing tennis.

DRILL 1.3

Write down the steps to drive an Audi S4 with an automatic transmission around a block with lights at each corner. Assume that the car is parked on the street.

1.6   Concept of an Object

You may be wondering if you are ready to talk about **objects** when you haven't even left the first chapter. Don't worry, this won't be a detailed discussion of the intricacies of object-oriented design and all of the implementation problems associated with it. We'll enter into a more detailed discussion when we reach Chapter 12. Instead, we are going to start to think about everyday objects and try to document their properties and behaviors. This is motivated by the fact that programming with Visual Basic quite often entails using objects with properties and behaviors associated specifically with it. To create an application that solves a problem or mimics a real-world object, we must first understand how to describe such an object. Therefore, we are going to practice documenting the properties and behaviors of a few real-world objects.

DRILL 1.4

Describe in detail the properties of a simple household phone and the actions that can be performed upon it. Assume that the person reading your document has never seen a phone before.

DRILL 1.5

Describe in detail the properties of a simple digital alarm clock and the actions that can be performed upon it. Assume that the person reading your document has never seen an alarm clock before.

1.7 Interpreters and Compilers

Applications written in languages like Visual Basic must be converted into a language the machine understands before the computer can execute the application. There are two main methods for accomplishing this: interpreting and compiling.

An **interpreter** is a program that converts the language the developer writes to a language the computer understands at the time the application is executed. As each line of code written by the developer is executed it is converted on the fly. While this is convenient, it leads to slow executing applications.

A **compiler**, on the other hand, will perform all of the translations at once. The results are stored in a file called an **executable**. By performing all of the translations ahead of time, the executable will run faster than the application would if it were run on an interpreter.

So which is Visual Basic? Actually, it is both. When you are developing your applications, your code will be interpreted. While it will run slower, it is an easier environment to develop in. Then when you are ready to give your application to others, you will compile your application for distribution.

Key Words and Key Terms

Algorithm
The steps required to solve a problem.

Assembly Language
A low-level programming language utilizing a series of mnemonics to represent commonly used instructions.

BASIC
An early beginning programming language developed to be easy to program.

C
A computer language created in order to develop operating systems like UNIX.

C++
A computer language that evolved from C to include object-oriented extentions.

COBOL
One of the early computer languages developed for business transactions.

Compiler A program that converts all of the source code of a programming language to a language the computer understands at once.

Database
A computer system designed to optimize the storing and accessing of large amounts of data.

Event-driven algorithm
An algorithm that responds to external stimuli.

Executable
A program produced by a compiler that was translated from a programming language into a language the computer can understand.

Flowchart
A graphical representation of an algorithm.

FORTRAN
One of the early computer languages developed for mathematical calculations.

Front end

A computer program that acts as an interface to display information coming from another computer system.

Interpreter

A program that converts a single line of source code at a time into a language that the computer understands.

Java

A new computer language that is object-oriented and portable to run on any machine.

Object

An object in computer terms is a programming construct that encompasses both the data and procedures that act upon that data in one unit.

Programming language

A standardized format of symbols that allow a programmer to instruct a computer to perform certain predefined tasks.

Prototype

A program designed to test a concept and show a user how a program will be developed in another more efficient language.

Punch cards

A mechanism to enter a program into a computer that stores the program on cardboard cards with holes punched out to represent the program.

Sequential algorithm

An algorithm that follows a series of steps in its execution.

Visual Basic

Mircosoft's modern version of the BASIC computer language.

Answers to Chapter's Drills

Drill 1.1

In giving instructions to brush one's teeth, one should assume that the person receiving the instructions would take nothing for granted. This is the way a computer operates. A computer does exactly what you tell it, not what you meant to tell it. The following is our teeth brushing solution—my dentist would be so proud!

1. To brush one's teeth, one must first get out of bed.
2. Remove your blanket and swing your legs over the edge of the bed.
3. Stand up and walk toward the bathroom.
4. If the door is closed, open it.
5. Walk into the bathroom.
6. Turn on the light.
7. Walk toward the sink.
8. Turn on the cold water faucet.
9. Pick up a cup and fill it with water.
10. Place the cup down on the counter.
11. Pick up the toothpaste.
12. Unscrew the cap.
13. Pick up the toothbrush.
14. Place the head of the toothbrush under the running water.
15. Remove the toothbrush from the water.
16. Point the toothpaste, open end down, toward the head of the toothbrush.

17. Squeeze the tube lightly so that a little of the paste is squeezed onto the toothbrush.
18. Stop squeezing the toothpaste.
19. Put the toothpaste down.
20. Bring the toothbrush up to your mouth.
21. Move the toothbrush back and forth across your teeth.
22. Repeat until all teeth are well cleaned.
23. Pick up the cup of water.
24. Pour some of the water in your mouth.
25. Place cup down.
26. Swoosh the water around your mouth.
27. Spit the water out.
28. Repeat if necessary until all the toothpaste is out of your mouth.
29. Rinse the toothbrush off.
30. Place the toothbrush back where you got it.
31. Put the cap back on the toothpaste.
32. Shut the water off.
33. Shut the light off.
34. Exit the bathroom.
35. Close the door behind you.

If we dissect this solution, you will see that I have not left much to chance. When programming a computer, this is essential. You will also see that steps like 4 involve decisions to make. Most computer programs will make decisions along the way as to whether or not to take additional steps. In step 22 we see another concept of programming, the concept of looping. Often it is required to repeat a step a number of times before moving to the next step.

A final issue to notice is that I did not end the algorithm with the completion of the brushing of my teeth, but with the returning of the bathroom to its initial conditions. It will be important when we program to make sure that we do not leave resources that we use unreturned to the computer when our programs finish executing.

Drill 1.2
There is no easy answer to this drill. The question was asked to stress an important point. Make sure that you get complete instructions about what you are supposed to be solving.

If you were asked to write instructions to parallel park a car, you should immediately think of other questions to ask before attempting to solve the problem: Is the car an automatic or manual transmission? If it is a manual transmission, where is reverse?

Only by fully specifying a problem may programmers be sure that they are solving the right problem. All too often programmers develop applications that, although they function without error, do not solve the problem they were intended for.

Drill 1.3
In order to solve this problem, we needed to specify exactly the type of car that we are going to use. If we did not, it would be impossible to specify steps on how to drive. Imagine if we did not specify that it was an automatic transmission. Would you have specified that the steps were for an automatic transmission or manual? Obviously a manual transmission would require many more steps.

Step 1:   Unlock the car door.
Step 2:   Open the driver's side door.
Step 3:   Sit down in the driver's seat.
Step 4:   Close the car door.
Step 5:   Put on the safety belt.
Step 6:   Put the key in the ignition.
Step 7:   Turn the key.
Step 8:   Place foot on the brake.
Step 9:   Release the emergency brake.
Step 10:   Put the car in drive.
Step 11:   Place the left turn signal on.
Step 12:   Look to see if any cars are coming.
Step 13:   If a car is coming, wait.
Step 14:   When no cars are coming, turn the steering wheel to the left and release your foot from the brake and gently press the gas pedal.
Step 15:   When the car has pulled out, turn the steering wheel to straighten the car out.
Step 16:   Continue driving down the street.
Step 17:   If a car in front of you slows down, press the brake gently so that you are not too close to it.
Step 18:   If a car to your left has a turn signal on, slow down and let it pass.
Step 19:   As you approach the light, turn on your right turn signal.
Step 20A: If you reach the light and it is red, come to a complete stop.
Step 20B: If you reach the light and it is yellow, slow down and come to a complete stop.
Step 20C: If you reach the light and it is green, slow down and turn to the right.
Step 21:   If you stopped at the light, and there is no sign stating you cannot turn on red and there is no oncoming traffic, make a right turn, otherwise you must wait until the light turns green.

This process would continue around the block and conclude when the car reaches the original starting point.

Drill 1.4

We can divide our documentation into two sections: properties and behaviors. The properties will describe the physical makeup of the phone while the behaviors will describe what actions can be performed using the phone.

A phone is used by entering a series of numbers called a phone number into the phone on its buttons. The phone number must be obtained from an external source and must be valid in order for the phone call to go through. A phone number is either seven or 10 digits. With 10 digits, phone numbers must be preceded with a one before entering the 10 digits. Each digit should be entered by pressing the button corresponding to the digit for a brief time. Wait a brief time before the next digit is entered. When all the digits are entered, a connection is made to the party you dialed.

Properties:
◆ Button with the number 1 on it.
◆ Button with the number 2 and the letters ABC on it.
◆ Button with the number 3 and the letters DEF on it.
◆ Button with the number 4 and the letters GHI on it.
◆ Button with the number 5 and the letters JKL on it.
◆ Button with the number 6 and the letters MNO on it.
◆ Button with the number 7 and the letters PQRS on it.
◆ Button with the number 8 and the letters TUV on it.
◆ Button with the number 9 and the letters WXYZ on it.

◆ Button with the number 0 on it.
◆ Button with an * on it.
◆ Button with a # on it.
◆ Button with the word REDIAL on it.
◆ Large button with no wording on it.

Behaviors:

◆ Button 1: If pushed it enters the 1 digit of a phone number.
◆ Button 2: If pushed it enters the 2 digit of a phone number.
◆ Button 3: If pushed it enters the 3 digit of a phone number.
◆ Button 4: If pushed it enters the 4 digit of a phone number.
◆ Button 5: If pushed it enters the 5 digit of a phone number.
◆ Button 6: If pushed it enters the 6 digit of a phone number.
◆ Button 7: If pushed it enters the 7 digit of a phone number.
◆ Button 8: If pushed it enters the 8 digit of a phone number.
◆ Button 9: If pushed it enters the 9 digit of a phone number.
◆ Button 0: If pushed it enters the 0 digit of a phone number.
◆ Button *: Used to interact with computer systems that the phone may connect to.
◆ Button #: Used to interact with computer systems that the phone may connect to.
◆ REDIAL Button: If pushed, it dials the last phone number entered into the phone.
◆ Large Button: This hangs up the phone, which ends the phone call and resets the phone.

Drill 1.5

We can divide our documentation into two sections: properties and behaviors. The properties will describe the physical makeup of the alarm clock while the behaviors will describe what actions the alarm clock can perform.

An alarm clock is used to tell the time of day. It also can be set to sound an alarm at a given time of day. The time of day may be set or the time the alarm will sound can be set. Both are set in the same way. Exact times are not punched in; instead the time is moved forward at a quick or slow pace until the time desired is displayed.

Properties:

◆ Hour Display: An LCD output to display the hour of the time being displayed. It can be a number from 1 to 12.
◆ Minute Display: An LCD output to display the current minute of the time being displayed. It can be a number from 0 to 59.
◆ Second Display: An LCD output to display the current second of the time being displayed. It can be a number from 0 to 59.
◆ A.M./P.M. Display: An LCD output to display an indicator of whether the current time is in the A.M. or P.M. for the time being displayed.
◆ Current Hour: The hour of the current time. It can be a number from 1 to 12.
◆ Current Minute: The minute of the current time. It can be a number from 0 to 59.
◆ Current Second: The second of the current time. It can be a number from 0 to 59.
◆ Current A.M./P.M.: an indicator of whether the current time is in the A.M. or P.M.
◆ Alarm Hour: the hour of the time the alarm will go off if it is set to go off. It can be a number from 1 to 12.
◆ Alarm Minute: the minute of the time the alarm will go off if it is set to go off. It can be a number from 0 to 59.
◆ Alarm Second: the second of the time the alarm will go off if it is set to go off. It can be a number from 0 to 59.
◆ Alarm A.M./P.M.: an indicator of whether the alarm will go off in the A.M. or P.M., if the alarm is set.

Behaviors:

1. Set Alarm: Set the hour, minute, and A.M./P.M. of the alarm.

2. Set Time: Set the hour, minute, and A.M./P.M. of the actual time.

3. Fast Button: If the switch is either in Set Alarm or Set Time position, increment the Alarm Time or Actual Time at a fast pace. As long as the button is depressed the time will continue to increment.

4. Slow Button: If the switch is either in Set Alarm or Set Time position, increment the Alarm Time or Actual Time at a slow pace. As long as the button is depressed the time will continue to increment.

5. Activate Alarm: If the button is pressed, the alarm is set to go off at the time indicated by the Alarm Time.

6. Deactivate Alarm: If the button is pressed and the alarm is on, shut it off.

7. Increment Time: The clock will automatically increment the time by a second every second and display it. If the new time is equal to the Alarm Time and the alarm is set on, the alarm will sound.

INTERVIEW
An Interview with Patrick Meader

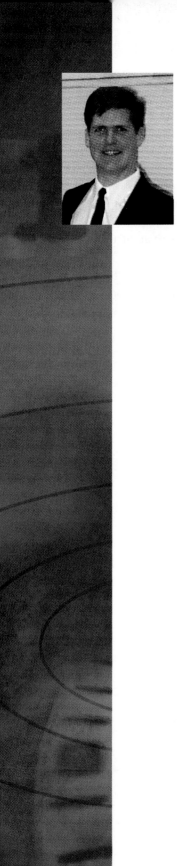

Patrick Meader is editor-in-chief of Visual Studio Magazine. He has spent more than nine years editing technical journals, covering the Windows development market for the last five.

Where is VB most widely used?

VB is the workhorse of corporate businesses that depend on Windows, from banks to insurance companies, hospitals to power companies. It is used in businesses large and small and for projects large and small. Some people may be more familiar with VB in its Microsoft Office form, VBA, where it serves as the scripting language that underpins Microsoft Office. Whenever you record a macro, Office is converting the tasks to VB-based code. Most businesses use Visual Basic in conjunction with other tools, such as Microsoft Access or SQL Server. Note that Visual Basic runs only on Windows, to date, with a subset (VBA) available on the Mac.

What are some of the new features to Visual Basic .NET?

VB .NET is a ground-up rewrite of VB, and incorporates a wide range of new features, including implementation inheritance, a more robust threading model, a new Forms package (Windows Forms), and the ability to write Web applications in much the same way that you write traditional Windows desktop applications. VB .NET is a powerful tool, but the changes from the previous version are extensive, and Microsoft broke backward compatibility in several cases to achieve its goals. VB .NET is built on top of Microsoft's .NET framework, and it is that framework and its plethora of base classes that give Visual Basic .NET most of its power.

How will upcoming changes in VB affect the industries that use it?

That's a tough question to answer at this point. VB .NET is aimed at writing scalable corporate applications. It enables you to do some kinds of tasks better and more efficiently, and often faster.

Implementation inheritance and the improved threading support will mean you can write some higher-end applications with fewer lines of code and maintain it more easily. At the same time, VB .NET's new feature set will require learning a significant number of new techniques and approaches. Still, VB .NET appears easier to learn than C++, C#, Java, or even many of the narrowly focused 4GLs.

As a result of the new version and changes, which industries do you see using it more and in what ways?

VB .NET is aimed primarily at large scale, enterprise-oriented (read: Fortune 500) businesses. It is intended to enable Microsoft to make headway into the kinds of businesses that have traditionally been the domain of big iron.

What are some of the special features of your magazine?

Visual Studio Magazine (recently renamed from Visual Basic Programmer's Journal) is a how-to, technical magazine for programmers who use the Visual Studio programming suite (of which Visual Basic is a large part).

Please tell us about how you got involved with VB?

I came to the Visual Basic Programmer's Journal from a magazine on piano teaching, Keyboard Companion. I saw an ad for an entry-level editor while perusing the job board at my alma mater, UCLA. I had no previous computer-related publishing experience, but I didn't know anything about teaching piano before joining Keyboard Companion, and that had been a fun and engaging experience. So, I called the number, interviewed, and was offered the job. I accepted, of course.

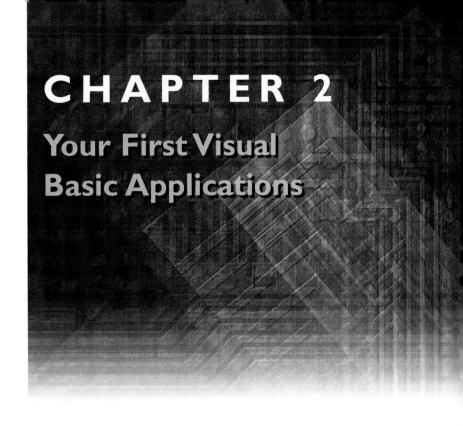

CHAPTER 2
Your First Visual Basic Applications

In this chapter we will introduce the Integrated Development Environment and create your first application. While this application is more fun than a real-world example, it will demonstrate Visual Basic's versatility in creating applications with text, graphics, and user-interaction.

You will learn development standards from the very first application and continue to use these standards throughout the text. It is important to follow these standards, because they will improve the readability of all the applications you develop and reduce the effort it takes to maintain them.

There's an old expression that a book is often judged by its cover. This holds true for the applications you develop as well. In the first few seconds users view your application, they will develop an initial evaluation of its quality. Therefore, the aesthetic nature of your application is important. We will spend a good portion of this chapter familiarizing you with the tools Visual Basic provides to assist your developing aesthetically pleasing applications. It only takes a few more minutes to make your applications look professional. It's time well spent.

2.1 What Is a Project?

In order to develop an application in Visual Basic you must start by creating a **project**. A project in Visual Basic is its way of grouping all of the components that make up your application in one package.

New Project Tab

When you start Visual Basic you will be presented with the New Project screen that allows you to create a new project or open an existing project. It even provides an option to allow you to quickly access the most recently used projects. This is shown in the following figure:

Figure 2.1
New Project Screen

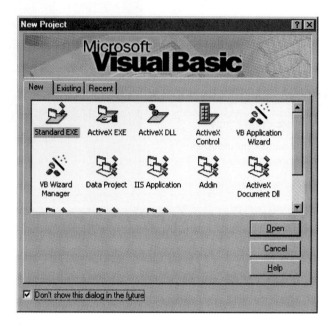

To create a new project, simply click on the `Standard EXE` icon shown in Figure 2.1.

Existing Project Tab

To open an existing project, first click on the Existing Project tab to display a dialog box with a directory tree. This is shown in the following figure:

Figure 2.2
Existing Project Screen

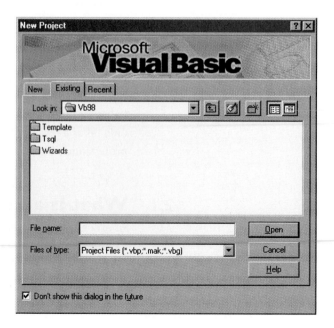

You probably noticed that no projects are visible. This is normal. You haven't created any yet. With the Existing Project tab, you can navigate to any project file stored on your computer in the same manner that you search for a document to open.

Recent Project Tab

After you have created a few projects you may want to be able to access them easily in the same way that you can access recently used documents in Microsoft Word. Although you haven't created any projects yet, I have. The following figure shows the Recent Project tab with many projects being displayed:

Figure 2.3
Recent Project Screen

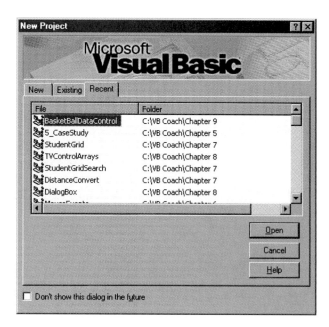

To open a recent project, just double-click on the one you wish to open.

2.2   Introduction to the Integrated Development Environment

Unlike older computer languages that forced programmers to develop their applications in a completely disjointed manner, Visual Basic provides a complete environment to assist the developers with creating their applications.

This environment may vary slightly from computer to computer. However, the majority of the key items are essentially the same. Variation in the environment may happen because your computer's display may be smaller or larger than the one I used to develop the examples in the text, or it may be that someone may have modified the environment before you used it…you get the idea.

The typical Integrated Development Environment is displayed in the following figure:

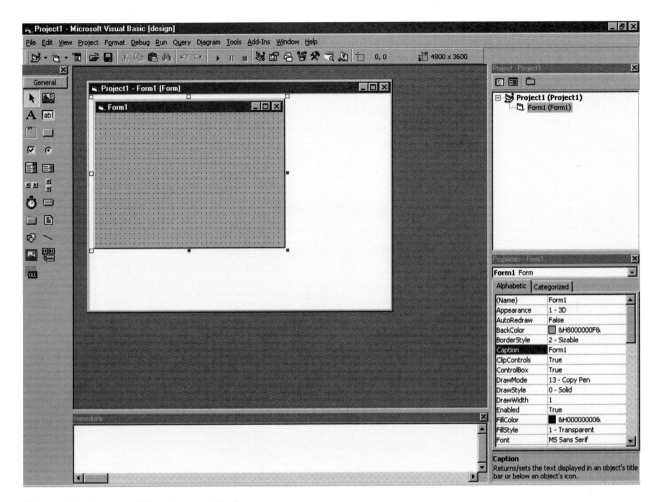

Figure 2.4   Integrated Development Environment

Project Explorer Window

In section 2.1 we demonstrated that you could create a new project or open an existing one. In either case, the components of the project are organized in the Project Explorer window. Currently you only have a single form included in your project. Later when you create projects with multiple forms you will learn how to select which form you wish to work on. You will add additional objects as you learn them.

Figure 2.5
Project Explorer Window

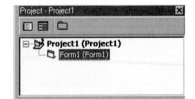

Standard Toolbar

Just as Microsoft Word has a main toolbar as well as additional formatting toolbars, Visual Basic has a main or Standard toolbar as well as additional toolbars to give the developer easy access to commonly used operations.

Figure 2.6
Standard Toolbar

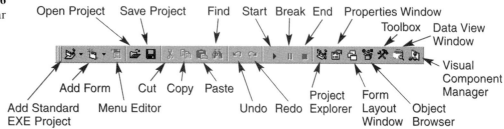

Form Window

You can imagine the Form window like a painter's canvas. It is where you will lay out the design of a form for your application. It is where you will place the components of a form and it will be the interface for placing the code associated with the components.

Figure 2.7
Form Window

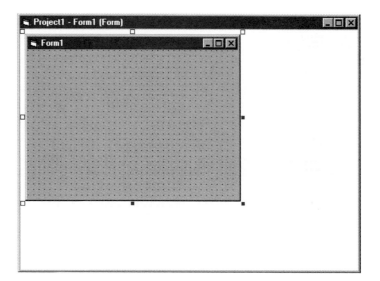

Toolbox Window

Visual Basic's Toolbox window can be thought of as similar to the additional toolbars that come with Microsoft Word. When you install Visual Basic, the initial setup of the Toolbox window contains 21 commonly used controls that are placed on a form to create an application.

Figure 2.8
Toolbox Window

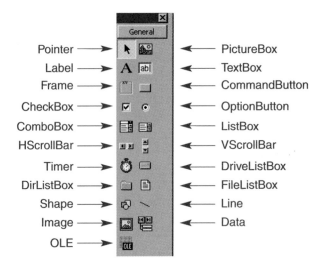

Pointer ———→ ←——— PictureBox
Label ———→ ←——— TextBox
Frame ———→ ←——— CommandButton
CheckBox ———→ ←——— OptionButton
ComboBox ———→ ←——— ListBox
HScrollBar ———→ ←——— VScrollBar
Timer ———→ ←——— DriveListBox
DirListBox ———→ ←——— FileListBox
Shape ———→ ←——— Line
Image ———→ ←——— Data
OLE ———→

Properties Window

Components of Visual Basic have many properties associated with them. A property is a way of specifying different constructs in Visual Basic. Among other properties, the Properties window allows the developer to control the color, font, and size of Visual Basic constructs. The Properties window is an interface to these properties, enabling developers to click on the property that they wish to set and then allow that property to be typed in.

The control pull-down menu indicates for which control the Properties window is displaying the properties. This is selected by single-clicking on a control on the Form window. You can also select the control by clicking on the pull-down menu and selecting the control that you wish to work with.

The current property selected is highlighted and additional information explaining the purpose of that property is displayed at the bottom of the window.

Figure 2.9
Properties Window

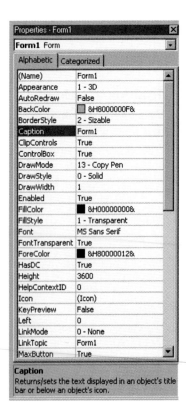

Menu Bar

The Visual Basic menu bar is located just below the title bar. It contains shortcuts to commonly used commands.

Figure 2. 10
Menu Bar

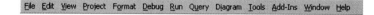

2.3   Creating Your First Application

VB Applications start with a basic form to which you add controls that come with Visual Basic and code that you write to make the controls work in the way that you wish.

For your first application, you are going to create a form that acts out the classic tale of "The Lady or the Tiger" by Frank R. Stockton. If you are unfamiliar with this tale, blame your English teachers. A brief synopsis of the story is:

> In ancient times there was a king who would not allow anyone but royalty to love his daughter. However, as fate would have it a peasant from the village fell in love with the princess and the princess fell in love with him. When the king discovered this, he subjected the peasant to a trial of guilt or innocence. The peasant would be placed in front of two doors. Behind one door is a tiger, behind another is a beautiful young maiden. If the peasant picks the door with the tiger behind it, then he is obviously guilty and would be eaten by the tiger. If he picks the door with the young maiden, he would be assumed innocent and would get to marry the young maiden.
>
> When the time to pick the door came, the peasant looked up at the princess and asked which door. The princess replied the right. The question is, is the princess telling the truth? If she is, would she not be jealous that her love would marry another? Would she lie?

We do not answer the question, but we can create an application to simulate it. When the application is complete, it will appear as follows:

TIP

When developing an application it is always a good idea to sketch how the application looks before you begin to code it.

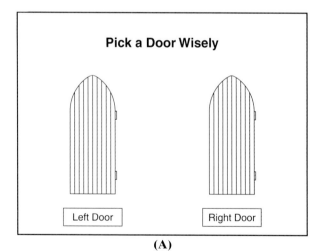

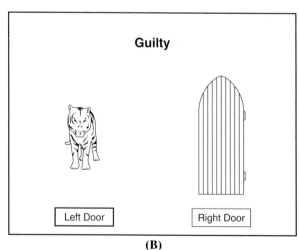

Figure 2.11   (A) Sketch of the Application; (B) Sketch of Left Door Selected. *(continues)*

Figure 2.11 *(continued)*
(C) Sketch of Right
Door Selected

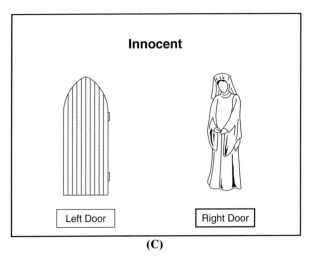

(C)

You will develop this application in a stepwise fashion.

Setting the Project and Form Name   The first step in coding any application is to name the project and the form. Both the form name and the project name should represent the purpose of each. You might think that it is redundant to have to name both; however, in the future, you will create applications with multiple forms.

As your application will simulate the story of "The Lady or the Tiger," you should name your project so that it reflects that. Therefore, call your project `LadyOrTiger`.

Step 1:   When a project is created, it has the default name `Project1`. You can see the default name in the title bar of the application. To change this, click on the Project Properties... menu item of the Project menu.

Figure 2.12
Project Properties Window

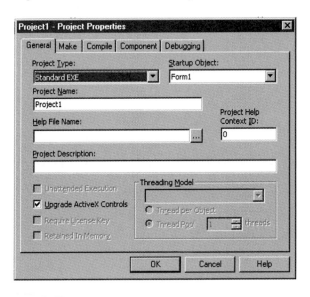

TIP

When using three-letter prefixes you should use the standard prefixes set forth by Microsoft. All of Microsoft's prefixes are lowercase. We will be introducing each one as necessary when we introduce new constructs.

By changing the name in the Project Name text box to `LadyOrTiger` and clicking on the OK button, you have changed the name of the application. Notice the new name of the project in the title bar.

Step 2:   You also must rename the default form of the application. The default name for a form is `Form1`. You can see the default name in the title bar of the Form window as well as in the Properties window for the form. You need to give the form a new name that represents the actions that will occur on the form. However, when naming forms in Visual Basic, your name should follow Microsoft's naming convention. The prefix identifies what type of object you are naming. In this case, use the prefix `frm` to indicate that your name is associated with a Form object.

By double-clicking on the window containing the name `Form1`, it will become highlighted as in Figure 2.13.

Figure 2.13
Highlighted Name in
Properties Window

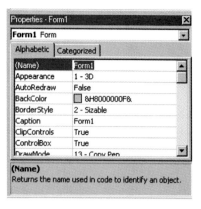

Step 3: Now you can type the new name, `frmLadyOrTiger`, in the Properties window as shown in Figure 2.14.

Figure 2.14
New Name in Properties
Window

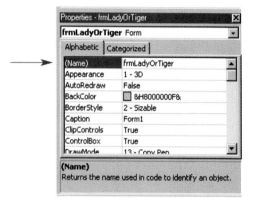

Notice that once the name has been changed to `frmLadyOrTiger`, the new name appears in the Properties window as well as in the Project title bar.

Figure 2.15
New Name in Project
Window

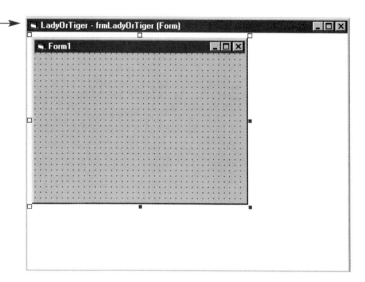

Setting the Caption Property of the Form   While the previous steps you followed set the name of the form as it appears to the developer in the code, you also should change the name of the form that appears in the title bar of the form. You can see this in Figure 2.15, where the default name is set to Form1.

Step 4:   For your application, you will change the displayed name to Lady Or The Tiger. This is accomplished by setting the Caption property.

Figure 2.16
New Name in Properties
Window

Once the name has been changed in the Caption property, you will see the change in the form as shown in Figure 2.17, where the new caption is visible in the title bar of the form:

Figure 2.17
Empty Form with New
Caption Property

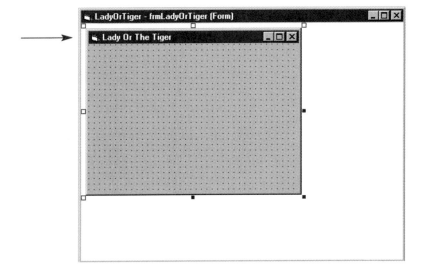

Changing the ScaleMode Property   You are used to measuring a physical object with a ruler. The ruler displays inches and centimeters to measure objects with both the English and Metric systems. While both systems work, usually an individual has a preference to work in one system or the other.

Similarly, Visual Basic has multiple measuring systems to indicate the size and location of a control. The default system of measurement is called a **twip**. There are 1440 twips contained in an inch. We find it easy to work in a measurement system that you are more familiar with, **pixels**. A pixel is a single point on the screen.

Step 5: By changing the `ScaleMode` property for the form in the Properties window, you can set Visual Basic to use pixels as your form of measurement for this project.

Figure 2.18
`ScaleMode` Property Set to 3-Pixel

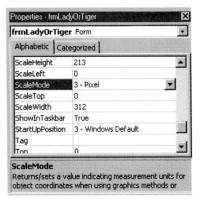

Placing a Label Control on the Form   You are now ready to build your application by adding controls to the form. Your first step is to add a **label control** to the form. A label control allows you to add **static text** to a form. Static text is text that typically will not change when the application runs. The text that you wish to place on the form is `Pick a Door Wisely`.

Place a label control on this form so that you can add the text you wish onto the form.

Step 1: Select the label control by single-clicking on the **icon** for the label control. This can be seen in the following figure:

Figure 2.19
Select Label Control

Step 2: Place the label in the desired position on the form. You want the text to appear across the top of the form, so point the mouse near the upper-left corner of the form. While holding the mouse button down, move the mouse cursor to the right end of the form and a little lower than the previous clicked location. This can be seen in the following figure:

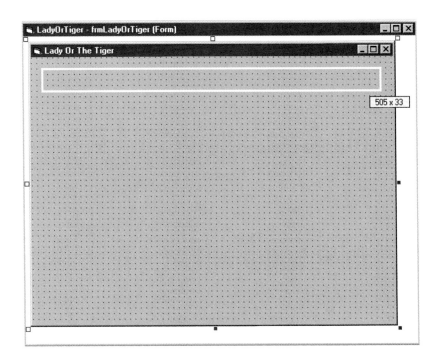

Figure 2.20
Placing Label Control

Step 3: Release the mouse button, thereby completely specifying the location, width, and height of the text box. You can see the outline of the label control in the following figure:

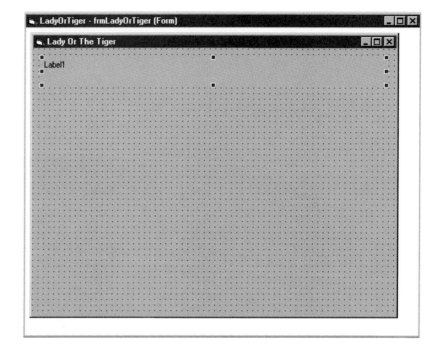

Figure 2.21
Label Control
Placed on Form

Step 4: Make sure that your label control is roughly the same size as ours. If it is not, there are two ways that you can modify your control so that it matches your size.

    The first method is to adjust it visually. You can point to any of the small outline boxes that define the border of your control, and by clicking on a box and holding the mouse button down, you can stretch the control in whatever direction you wish. When the control is the size that you want, you release the mouse button and it resizes. You can repeat this process for any of the sizing handles until the label control is the size that you wish.

    The second method is more precise. By modifying the properties of the label control, you can set the `Height`, `Width`, `Left`, and `Top` properties to the exact values that we have set ours to. In this example they are set to 33, 505, 16, and 16 respectively.

    To set the properties, make sure the label control is selected. This is accomplished by clicking once on the control. When the control is selected, you will see the outline boxes appear around the border of the label control. You will also see the label control's name appear in the Properties window. In this case, the name is `Label1`.

    Although there are many other properties, set only the four that we mentioned. To set each one, select the property by clicking on it in the Properties window and type the new value in it.

Step 5: Although not required, it is a good practice to name your controls. Therefore, set the `Name` property of the label to `lblTitle`.

Step 6: Set the label to display the text value you wish it to display for the title. This is extremely easy. Click the `Caption` property and type `Pick a Door Wisely`.

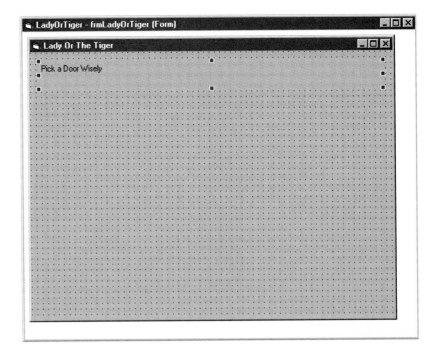

Figure 2.22
Label Control with
Caption Set

Step 7: While you now have the desired text displayed, you may notice that the text is not as large as you may like. This can easily be remedied by changing the Font property to a large font style. However, a font is not made up of a simple numerical property. A font is composed of a type face, size, and style. Visual Basic allows you to specify all of these with a single screen. By clicking on the Font property in the Properties window, the Font property window will change to display a button that contains three dots. This button can be clicked to reach the window with all of the font properties displayed. See the following figures, which show the button and the associated window that is displayed when the button is clicked.

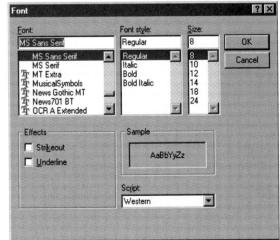

Figure 2.23 Properties Window   **Figure 2.24** Font Specification Window

By setting the Font Style to Bold and the Size to 18 and then clicking on the OK button, you will see the changes to the form in the following figure:

Figure 2.25
Label Control with
Reset Font

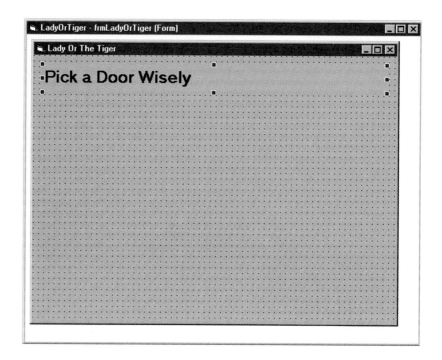

TIP

When you first set the size of a control, it is not always the correct size. In this case it was, but if the original size for the label control was not sufficient, you could increase the size of the label by either setting the `Height` and `Width` properties of the label, or pulling the bottom right corner of the form to the size that you desire.

Step 8: The final step is to align the text so that it is centered in the form. There are two ways of doing this. The first is to try to align it visually using the cursor. By clicking on it and dragging it from side to side one can align the text as desired. However, it is often easier to set the alignment of the text to Center and the text will automatically be centered within the label control. Clicking on the `Alignment` property and selecting Center from the pull-down menu can do this.

2.4 Picture Box Control

Visual Basic allows you to easily add pictures to your form. In our example, you wish to add a picture of a door twice. To display a picture, you will use the **picture box control**.

Step 1: You start by clicking on the picture box control in the Control toolbar. This is shown in the following figure:

Figure 2.26
Select the Picture Box
Control

Step 2: Now you want to place the picture box control in a similar manner as you did with the label control. Click just below and to the left of the text in the label control you previously placed. Hold the mouse button down and release it with the mouse pointer near the bottom of the form and aligned with the c of the label control. Another way to set the size of the control that you want is to hold the cursor in one place while the mouse button is still held down. A small box will appear with the coordinates of the lower-right corner. In your case you wish it to be 161, 153. This is shown in the following figure:

Figure 2.27
Outline when Selecting
Picture Box

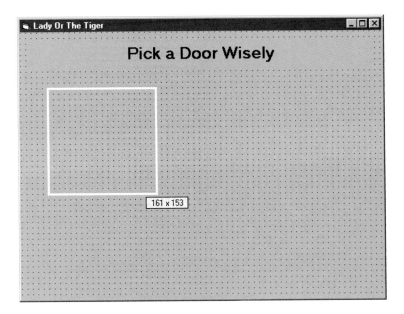

Step 3: Set the Name property of the picture box to pctLeftDoor.

Step 4: Next you need to select the picture that you wish to display within the box. You must click on the Picture property. Once clicked, the Picture property will display a command button with an ellipsis (...) as did the Font property in your label control example. By clicking on the button, a dialog box will appear to select the graphic file to display within the picture box control. This is shown in the following figure:

Figure 2.28
Load Picture Dialog Box

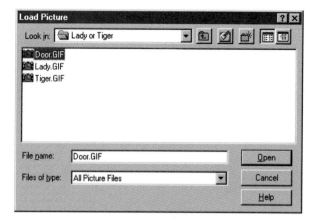

By selecting the file that you want and clicking on the Open button, the graphic file is displayed in the picture box control. This is shown in the following figure:

Figure 2.29
Picture Box Control with
Picture Displayed

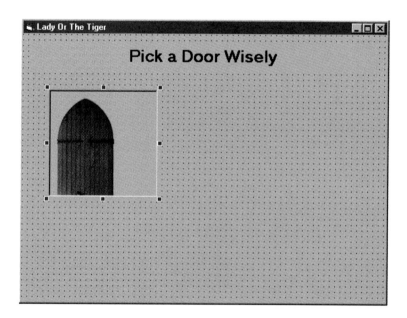

Step 5: You should immediately notice that the entire picture is not displayed. This is because you did not make the picture box control large enough. Additionally, you may have a problem in that the form is not large enough to hold a larger picture box control. This is not a problem for long. You can simply increase the size of the picture box, and if necessary, the form.

To increase the size of the picture box you can either set the `Height` and `Width` properties of the picture box, or pull the bottom right corner of the picture box to the size that you desire. See the following figure showing the resized picture box:

Figure 2.30
Resized Picture Box

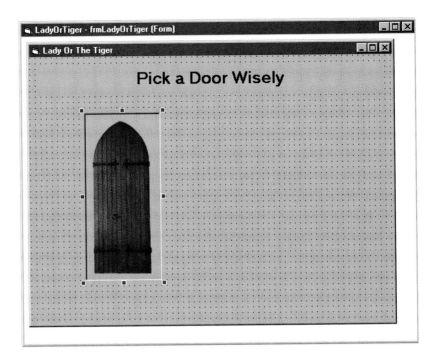

Step 6: Do you notice that there is a border around the picture box? So that your application will appear as if the door is just sitting on the form without a border surrounding it, set the `BorderStyle` property to `0 - None`.

Step 7: The last step is to repeat the process and create another picture box, `pctRightDoor`, with the same picture. Your form should now look like Figure 2.31.

Figure 2.31
Both Doors Showing

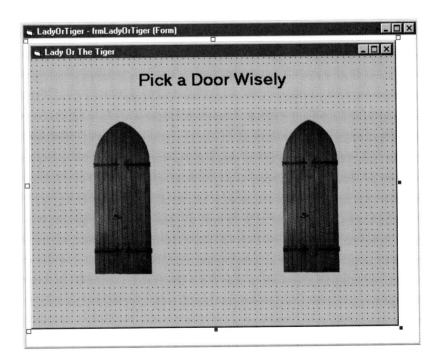

2.5 **Text Box Control**

Often you require a method to gather text from the user. By using a text box control you can place an area on the form where the users of the application may enter any text they wish. Anyone who has filled out a form on the Internet is already familiar with this type of control. Conceptually there is no difference between the text box that you use in a Web page and one that is placed on a Visual Basic form. You are going to add a text box to your application so the peasant can ask which door he should choose.

Step 1: Select the text box control from the Control toolbar:

Figure 2.32
Select Text Box Control

Step 2: Once the text box control is selected, place a text box on the form in the same manner as the other controls. See the following figure where we placed it in between the two picture box controls:

Figure 2.33
Text Box Added to Form

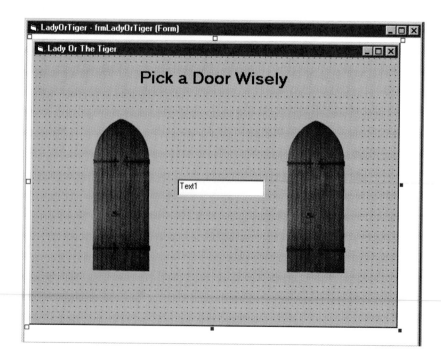

Step 3: Set the `Name` property of the text box to `txtQuestion`.

Step 4: You can see that Visual Basic automatically inserts the default text `"Text1"`. Usually, you do not wish this default text to be the value initially displayed. As with almost every control Visual Basic provides a property that allows us to change the default characteristics. You can even set it to nothing at all. You can do this by clicking on the `Text` property erasing `"Text1"`. This is shown in the following figures:

Figure 2.34
Text Box with Text Empty

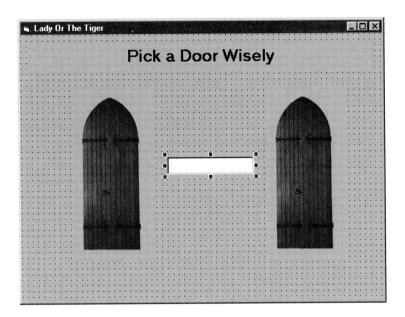

Figure 2.35
Text Box Property Window

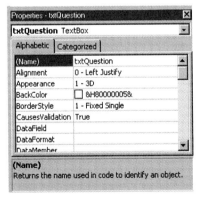

Step 5: While you know the text box is used to enter the peasant's question to the princess, the user of the application might not, so you will add a label control above the text box to indicate that. The label should be created in a similar manner as the previous label. You need to set the `Name` of the label to `lblQuestion`, the `Font Style` is set to `Bold`, and the `Caption` is set to `Question`. This is shown in Figure 2.36.

Figure 2.36
Question Label Added

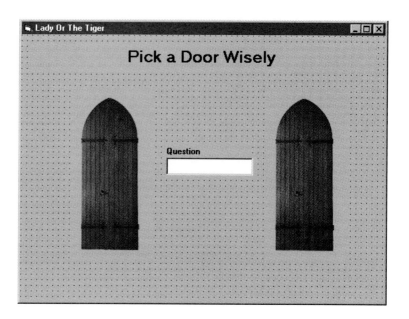

2.6 Command Button Control

Until now, you have provided very little interactivity to your form. This is about to change with the addition of the command button control. If you have filled out a form on the Internet, you are already familiar with command buttons. When you are done filling out a form on a Web page, you must click on a button to submit the form to the Web site for processing. A command button in Visual Basic is no different conceptually.

Step 1: Select the command button control from the Control toolbar:

Step 2: Once the command button control is selected, place a command button on the form in the same manner as the other controls. See the following figure where you placed it directly under the picture box control:

Figure 2.37
Select
Command
Button
Control

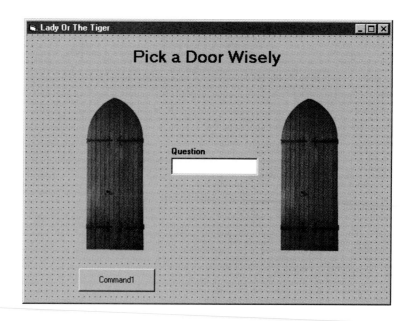

Figure 2.38
Form with Command
Button Control Added

Step 3: Set the Name property of the command button to cmdLeftDoor.

Step 4: You can see that Visual Basic automatically inserts the default text Command1 on the command button control. As with the text box control, you usually do not wish this default text to the displayed. It is a better practice to identify a command button control by setting the Caption property to indicate what its function will be. So far we haven't discussed what the function of the command button is, so we'll give you a little insight. In the next section you are going to modify the command button so that when it is clicked, the form changes the items it is displaying. It will change the form so that it displays either the Tiger or Lady picture.

For now, let's just change the command button control so that it displays the caption Left Door. This is done by clicking on the Caption property and typing Left Door.

Step 5: The last step is to repeat the process and create another command button, cmdRightDoor. Your form should now look like Figure 2.39.

Figure 2.39
Both Command
Buttons Added

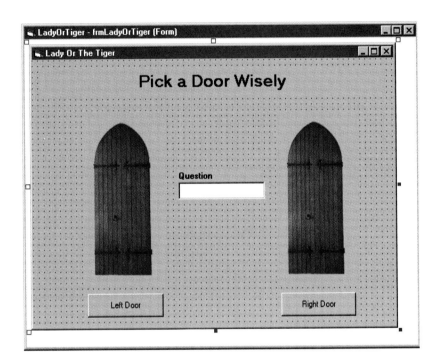

If you ran the application now and clicked on the command button, you would see that the button depresses and comes back up, however no action is executed. In the next section, you will add the capability to cause actions when the command button is depressed.

2.7   Basic Event Handling

You now will add functionality so that clicking on your command button will cause the form to display either a young maiden or a tiger. Also, if the young maiden is displayed, the label should change to Innocent. However, if the tiger appears, the label should change to Guilty. You will also notice whatever text is in the text box is erased. This involves your first real coding. In this case, your coding will be triggered by an event. Visual Basic makes it easy to code for events. Built in to controls are pre-defined events that have no action attached to them.

By double-clicking on the command button when the application is not running, the following code snippet is displayed:

Figure 2.40
Empty Code for Click
Event

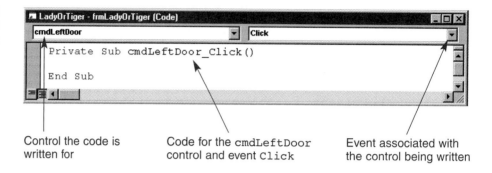

Control the code is
written for

Code for the cmdLeftDoor
control and event Click

Event associated with
the control being written

Events in Visual Basic are coded within the boundaries of the text shown. It may look a little cryptic, but once you understand the pattern, it is easy to understand. The first two words `Private Sub` indicate that the event that you are coding is private (only available in the current form) and a subroutine (a small piece of code that accomplishes a given task). The next text `cmdLeftDoor_Click()` indicates that this code is attached to the `cmdLeftDoor` command button and will be executed when a `Click` event occurs. The final text `End Sub` indicates the ending of the event.

Predefined words like `Private`, `Sub`, and `End` are considered **keywords** in the Visual Basic language. They have a special meaning and cannot be used for other purposes.

TIP

Notice that keywords like `Private`, `Sub`, and `End` will appear in blue while the rest of the code appears in black. This will help differentiate the keywords from the rest of your code.

Your code belongs in between these two lines. It will be executed whenever the command button `cmdLeftDoor` is clicked.

First, let's remove any text that is placed in the `txtQuestion` text box.

In order to change the text box programmatically, you need to indicate that you want to change the `Text` property of the `txtQuestion` text box control. Visual Basic is "smart" in the way it allows you to type information in a code snippet. If you type a control name like `txtQuestion` and then type a period, it will display all of the available properties that you may access. By typing a `T` for `Text`, the pull-down menu displays and the first property starting with the letter `T` is displayed. You have the option of typing out the word `Text` or scrolling down to the `Text` property. When the `Text` property is selected, press the spacebar for the code `txtQuestion.Text` to be displayed. This is shown in the following two figures:

Figure 2.41
Pull-down Menu for
Properties

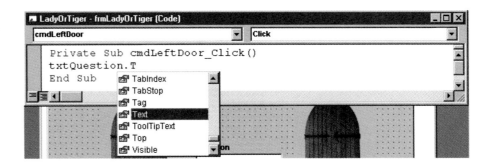

Figure 2.42
Filled in Property Text

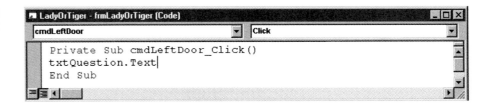

TIP

If you type a period and a drop-down menu does not appear, you probably have typed the name of the control incorrectly.

To cause a text box's `Text` property to change, you simply type an equal sign followed by the new value you want to display in quotation marks. This is shown in Figure 2.43.

To change a picture, you must programmatically change properties that previously you had changed interactively.

Figure 2.43
Code to Change Label's
Caption

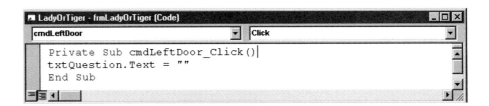

Visual Basic .NET Alert

In Visual Basic Version 6.0, it is possible to assign the default property of a control without actually listing the property.

```
txtQuestion = ""
```

However, this will not work in VB .NET and should be avoided!

Let's see what happens when we run the application. Click on the Start button (), in the Standard toolbar to run the application.

Type a question into the text box like `Which Door?` Click on the command button `cmdLeftDoor`, and the text in the text box will be removed. This is shown in the following figures:

Figure 2.44
Before Command Button is
Clicked

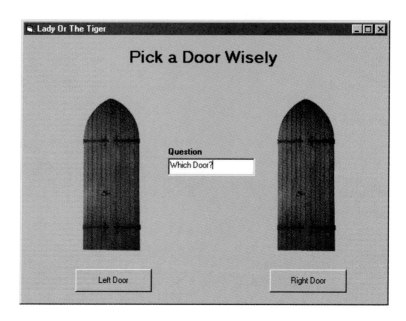

Figure 2.45
After Command Button is
Clicked

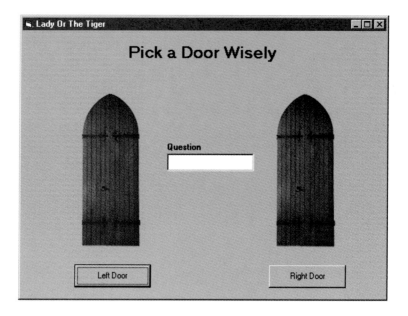

To make the additional changes, you follow a similar process. You need to set the `Picture` property in `pctLeftDoor` to the new graphic. However, because a picture is a little more complicated than a text message, you must type `LoadPicture(` *"Picture name and path goes here"*) to the right of the equal sign. In your case the picture name and path are `"C:\VB Coach\Chapter 2\Code\Lady Or Tiger\Tiger.jpg"`. This can be seen below along with the changing of the label control `lblTitle` to `Guilty`:

```
LadyOrTiger - frmLadyOrTiger (Code)                              _ □ ×
cmdLeftDoor                      ▼   Click                           ▼
    Private Sub cmdLeftDoor_Click()
    txtQuestion.Text = ""
    pctLeftDoor.Picture = LoadPicture("C:\VB Coach\Chapter 2\Code\Lady or Tiger\Tiger.gif")
    lblTitle.Caption = "Guilty"
    End Sub
```

Figure 2.46 cmdLeftDoor's Complete Code

Here is the final result of clicking the cmdLeftDoor command button:

Figure 2.47
After cmdLeftDoor
Command Button is Clicked

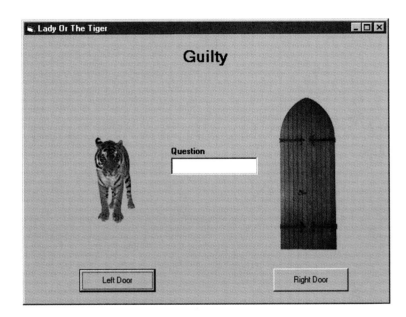

Finally, you need to set the code for the cmdRightDoor command button in a similar fashion. The code follows in Figure 2.48.

```
LadyOrTiger - frmLadyOrTiger (Code)                              _ □ ×
cmdRightDoor                     ▼   Click                           ▼
    Private Sub cmdRightDoor_Click()
    txtQuestion.Text = ""
    pctRightDoor = LoadPicture("C:\VB Coach\Chapter 2\Code\Lady or Tiger\Lady.gif")
    lbltitle.Caption = "Innocent"
    End Sub
```

Figure 2.48 cmdRightDoor's Complete Code

Here is the final result of clicking the cmdRightDoor command button:

Figure 2.49
After `cmdRightDoor`
Command Button is Clicked

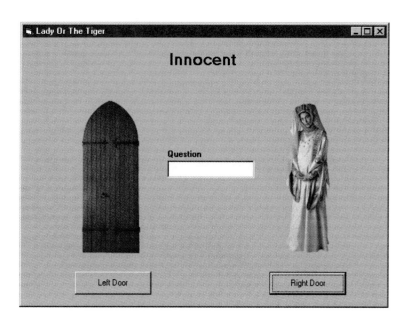

TIP

It is possible to assign most of a control's properties programmatically. Observe how you can set the text box `txtQuestion`'s properties in the following code.

```
Private Sub cmdChangeFont_Click()
txtQuestion.Font.Bold = True
txtQuestion.FontSize = 20
End Sub
```

The code sets the text box `txtQuestion` to be displayed with a bold font and a size of 20.

2.8   Saving the Project

You wouldn't want to do all this work and not have your project saved! It is important to save your work regularly. A good habit is to actually save your work when you first start your application and then save it again periodically.

You can save your project by either clicking on the Save icon in the Standard toolbar, or selecting File and Save from the menu bar.

The first time that you save a project or a form, you will be presented with a dialog box requesting a filename. If a form was created without being saved, you will be presented with the following dialog box:

Figure 2.50
Save File As Dialog Box for
Forms

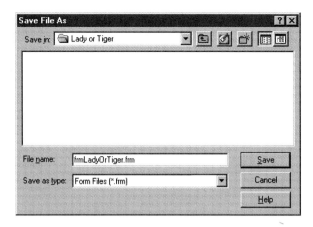

You can save the file in the directory that appears, or navigate to a directory where you would rather store the file. Either way, you should replace the default name with a more descriptive one.

Then, if you have not yet saved the project, you will be presented with a dialog box requesting the name of the project. This is shown in the following figure:

Figure 2.51
Save File Dialog Box
for Projects

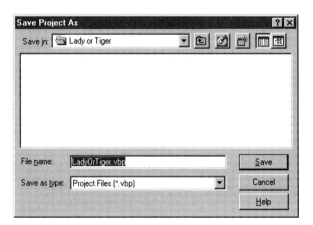

Again, you can save the file in the directory that appears, or navigate to a directory that you would rather store the file. Either way, you should replace the default name with a more descriptive one.

2.9 Cleaning It All Up

Right now you are probably feeling pretty good. You've just finished creating your first Visual Basic application. However, you're really not finished. While your application basically works, is it really as polished as you would like it? You might be asking, What do you mean by polished?

Applications that work are not enough when you enter the real world of programming. How many times have you gone to a Web page and been knocked out by the presentation of the information on the page? How many times have you gone to a page and been unimpressed by the color selection, alignment of the information, or general artistic flair of the page?

While we are not going to give you a lesson in art and color palette selection, because that would be beyond the scope of this text, there is one property of proper design that is important to discuss: alignment.

The alignment of the objects that you place on your form is important. If you look at the example you will see that there is no pattern as to how your objects line up with one another or the form itself. This is bad form design.

While one can try to visually line up each control so they look aesthetically appealing, this is not recommended. It is better to use the built-in alignment features of VB.

Left, Center, and Right Alignment

The first step is to decide how you want your form to look. Would it make sense to align everything to the left, right, center, or some combination of alignments? Look at the following four figures. Which one looks the most aesthetically pleasing?

Figure 2.52   Unaligned Controls

Figure 2.53   Center Aligned Controls

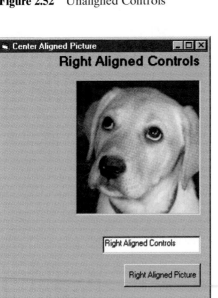

Figure 2.54   Right Aligned Controls

Figure 2.55   Left Aligned Controls

While there is no accounting for taste, I think most of us would agree that the figure with all of the controls aligned to the center is the most aesthetically pleasing. Because there are different times that you want items aligned as is shown in each of those figures, we will show you how to align controls with each method.

The first step in aligning text is the same regardless of the alignment option you choose. You must select all of the controls that you want to align. There are a few ways to do this.

TIP

If you are selecting all of the items on the form, you can use the keyboard shortcut <CTRL>–<A>. By pressing the <CTRL> key and the <A> key simultaneously, all the items on the form will be selected.

To select a group of controls at once, you can draw a box around the controls you wish to select. You must select the pointer from the Control toolbar. Then click on the upper-left corner of the area from which you wish to select the controls. While holding the mouse button down, drag the pointer to the lower-right corner of the area from which you wish to select. You will see a dashed box form around the area as you select it. Then release the mouse button and you will see the controls within the box highlighted with boxes around them (see Figure 2.56).

Figure 2.56
More Than One Control
Selected

To select each individual control, one at a time, you can hold either the <SHIFT> key or <CTRL> key down and click on each control that you wish to select. When all of the controls are selected that you desire, release the key <SHIFT> or <CTRL> key.

Once the controls are selected, the next step is to decide whether you want to align to the left, center, or right. In either case, you will click on the Format menu, and then the Align option. A pull-down menu will appear, with the options for Left, Center, and Right among others (see the following figure). Select the appropriate choice and your controls will align accordingly.

Figure 2.57
Aligning Controls to the
Center

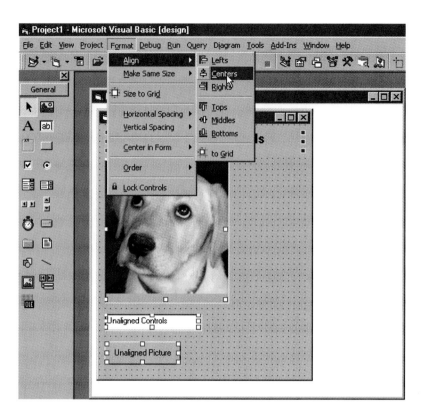

One final step may be necessary. If you aligned the text in a label as you did in Section 2.3, you may have to change it to the same alignment that you just selected in the previous example.

Sometimes controls need to be aligned vertically. You can do this with Tops, Middles, or Bottoms menu items from the Align submenu of the Format menu. Visual Basic will also allow you to automatically resize controls to the same size. Options to make the selected controls the same width, height, or width and height. These options are available from the Make Same Size option of the Format menu.

2.10 Use of Color

You've now learned how to create a neat looking form; however, we have neglected to talk about the use of color within the form. Your applications had color, but only in the sense that you used a color photograph. All of the controls were black with a gray background.

Visual Basic gives us the capability to set the color of almost every control. However, how you use color should follow some rhyme or reason. When programmers are given the capability to use color, often they set controls to different colors just because they can. The appropriate use of color should have meaning. It should be used with some form of artistic style. Certain color schemes go well together, others do

WARNING

True artistic style is sometimes beyond the grasp of some programmers. If this is you, get assistance from someone with a little style to help spruce up your application.

not. This book is not meant to teach you artistic style, its meant to teach you the techniques to develop applications and give you basic guidelines of style.

While the `Lady or the Tiger` application was an excellent first application, there is little need for adding color to it. Instead, imagine if you had a travel application. The application will be very simple, since you have not learned much of Visual Basic's power yet. Your application will display a picture box, label, text box and command button. The application will show two possible vacations for a travel company. One location will be Ireland, the other Egypt. To enhance the application, you will set the color scheme of the application slightly differently for each location. For Ireland, you will use a green color scheme, while the Egyptian scheme will be set to gold.

For demonstration purposes, we will not show you step-by-step directions to create this application. Instead, focus on the use of color.

So where should you add color? The question is how much green or gold should be displayed. There is no "right" answer to this question. Observe the following pictures.

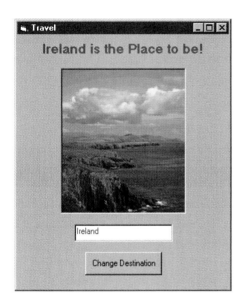

Figure 2.58 Label and Text Box in Pink

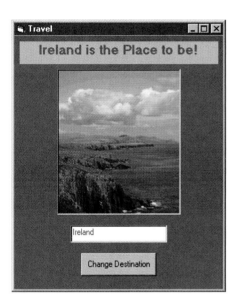

Figure 2.59 Label, Text Box, and Background in Green

Figure 2.60
Label and Form
Backgrounds
in Green

Which application looks the best is a matter of preference. Personally, I like the third one the best. While the first one is aesthetically pleasing, it is not emphasizing the green enough. The second application has the label's background color left as its default value, which just looks wrong.

WARNING

Clearly the second choice looks poorest. I showed it because it is common to change the foreground color of a label, but not the background color. The background color, if not set, remains to the default. In this case, it's set to gray.

The two properties that were used in the previous applications were `ForeColor` and `BackColor`. Each can be set interactively or programmatically.

To set the color interactively use the following steps:

Step 1: Click on the control for which you wish to change the color.
Step 2: Click on the property you wish to change (`ForeColor` or `BackColor`).
Step 3: Click on the drop-down arrow to get the Pallete window to appear.
Step 4: Click on the Palette tab of the pop-up window.
Step 5: Click on the color you wish to select.

The Palette pop-up window can be seen in the following figure:

Figure 2.61
Palette Pop-up Window

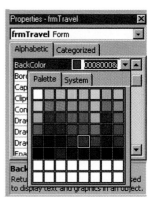

WARNING

If you set the `ForeColor` of a form, the entire form will not turn color until you run the application. Instead, small dots in the color you selected will appear in the background of the form.

To change the color of a control programmatically, you can use one of the following predefined Visual Basic colors:

```
vbBlack
vbRed
vbGreen
vbYellow
vbBlue
vbMagenta
```

```
vbCyan
vbWhite
```

Although we stated that we were going to use a gold scheme for Egypt, there is no constant for gold. The easiest way around this is to use the closest color that exists. Later you will learn how to pick specific colors. To change the green colors in the application to yellow, you will use `vbYellow` and the following code when the command button is clicked:

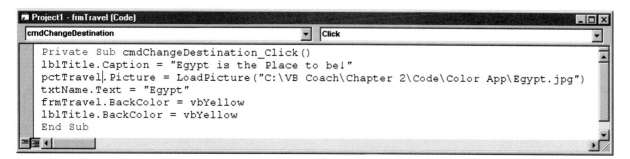

```
Private Sub cmdChangeDestination_Click()
lblTitle.Caption = "Egypt is the Place to be!"
pctTravel.Picture = LoadPicture("C:\VB Coach\Chapter 2\Code\Color App\Egypt.jpg")
txtName.Text = "Egypt"
frmTravel.BackColor = vbYellow
lblTitle.BackColor = vbYellow
End Sub
```

Figure 2.62   Code for Command Button

Figure 2.63
Egypt Application

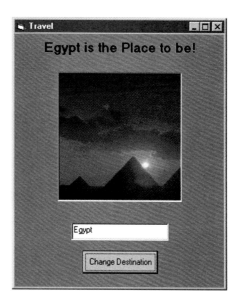

If you do not wish to use one of the predefined colors, you may select any color from your color palette. A color in Visual Basic is considered a normal RGB (Red, Green, Blue) color. It is composed of three numbers, one for Red, one for Green, and one for Blue. Each has a range from 0 to 255. By combining different values for Red, Green, and Blue you can select any color from the palette.

If you just try to guess what numbers represent which colors, you will have a difficult time. By using an application like the Microsoft Paint that comes with Windows, you can graphically select the color and then the application will provide the RGB values needed. Just select Edit Colors from the Colors menu.

Selecting a color is complicated by the fact that specifying an RGB color must be done in an encoding scheme called **hexadecimal** numbers. For instance, if you wanted to select a color closer to gold, its decimal RGB values would be (206, 143, and 43). It's hexadecimal value would be (CE, 8F, and 2B).

Instead of using the hexadecimal values that you do not understand, you can use a built-in function of Visual Basic called RGB. By placing the decimal values in the RGB function as follows, you can select the colors you desire.

```
frmCuteGirl.ForeColor = RGB(206, 143, 43)
```

WARNING

You may be wondering why we didn't change the command button's color. Unfortunately, Visual Basic does not give us an easy way to change the color properties of a command button.

◆ 2.11 Case Study

Problem Description

A company that sells products on the Internet, Walking Promotions, wants to develop an application to track its financial data. Create an application that allows the entry of the names of the employees, how many hours they worked that week, and a place to display their payment for the week as well as a total cost of payroll. In addition, beautify the form by adding the company's logo to the form as well as a title.

Discussion

While you do not know enough to create an application that will actually process the payroll, you can at least set up the user interface of the application. It will require using text boxes, picture boxes, and labels controls.

In order to make your form look professional you should also use the alignment and spacing options to space your controls evenly.

To make programming easier in the future, it is a good idea to name all of the controls something a little more specific than the default values. This will make them more discernible later.

Solution

The project requires a single form and a graphic file containing the logo. The graphic file will be called `WalkingPromotionsLogo.jpg`. While you have many options in how you lay out your solution, we have created a simple, intuitive solution. Your completed application should look as follows:

Figure 2.64
Sketch of Application

> **Payroll Accounting System**
>
> Walking Logo
>
> **Employee Name**   **Hours Worked**   **Weekly Pay**
>
> **Total Payroll**

You may add the controls to your form in any order that you wish. However, we recommend that you follow the order given in the solution.

TIP

It is often useful to change the name of your controls to something more meaningful than the default value. In the following controls you will set the `Name` property so that you can refer to the controls by fitting names.

WARNING

Many novice programmers will confuse the `Name` property with the `Caption` property. The `Name` property identifies the control to the programmers, while in contrast the `Caption` property identifies the control to the user of the application. The `Name` property is not visible when the application is running.

Change Screen Units to Pixels

By changing the `ScaleMode` property for the form in the Properties window, you can set Visual Basic to use pixels as your form of measurement for this project. All measurements and locations for controls are given in pixels.

Adding the Logo

To add the Walking Promotions logo to a blank form, follow the steps that you used when adding a picture box control in Section 2.4.

Step 1: Select the picture box control from the Control toolbar.
Step 2: Place the mouse over the area of the form you wish to be the upper-left corner of the logo.
Step 3: Hold the mouse button down and drag the pointer to the lower-right corner where the logo will be placed.
Step 4: Release the mouse button and the picture box control will be placed on the form.

Step 5: Click on the `Picture` property in the Properties window and click on the `WalkingPromotionsLogo.jpg` to select the appropriate graphic.

Step 6: Set the `Border` property in the Properties window to `0 - None`, so that a border is not drawn around the logo.

Step 7: Click on the `Name` property and change the `Name` property to `pctLogo`.

Adding the Labels

You need to add a total of five labels to the form. However, it makes sense to add the first four now and then after you add the text box controls to come back and add the last one so that they line up appropriately.

To add a label control, follow the steps that you performed in Section 2.3. You can follow the same steps for each label, and the properties of each label are shown.

Step 1: Select the label control from the Control toolbar.

Step 2: Place the mouse over the area of the form you wish to be the upper-left corner of the label control.

Step 3: Hold the mouse button down and drag the pointer to the lower-right corner where the label control will be placed.

Step 4: Release the mouse button and the label control will be placed on the form.

Step 5: Click on the `Caption` property in the Properties window and type `Payroll Account System`.

Step 6: Click on the `Font` property in the Properties window and set the Font Size to 14 and the Font Style to Bold.

Step 7: Click on the `Name` property and change the `Name` property to `lblTitle`.

In addition, you must place three more label controls on the form. The following are the properties to each control that must be placed:

Name: lblEmployeeName	Name: lblHoursWorked	Name: lblWeeklyPay
Caption: Employee Name	Caption: Hours Worked	Caption: Weekly Pay
Font: Size = 14, Style = bold	Font: Size = 14, Style = bold	Font: Size = 14, Style = bold
Left: 16	Left: 129	Left: 137
Top: 96	Top: 96	Top: 96
Height: 25	Height: 25	Height: 25
Width: 137	Width: 232	Width: 368

Adding the Text Boxes

You need to add a total of thirteen text box controls on the form. You will follow the same steps that you followed in Section 2.9. You can place them in any order that you wish, but remember that they all need to be lined up when you are finished. You can line up the text boxes either manually or with the alignment options we demonstrated in Section 2.5.

The following steps are required to place the first text box control on the form:

Step 1: Select the text box control from the Control toolbar.

Step 2: Place the mouse over the area of the form you wish to be the upper-left corner of the text box control.

Step 3: Hold the mouse button down and drag the pointer to the lower-right corner of where the text box control will be placed.

Step 4: Release the mouse button and the text box control will be placed on the form.

Step 5: Click on the `Name` property in the Properties window and type `txtEmployee1`.

Step 6: Click on the `Text` property in the Properties window and clear the default text so that nothing is displayed in the text box when you run the application.

The remaining text boxes are placed the same way, but with the following properties:

Name: txtEmployee2	Name: txtEmployee3	Name: txtEmployee4
Text:	Text:	Text:
Left: 16	Left: 16	Left: 16
Top: 168	Top: 208	Top: 248
Height: 25	Height: 25	Height: 25
Width: 185	Width: 185	Width: 185
Name: txtHours1	Name: txtHours2	Name: txtHours3
Text:	Text:	Text:
Left: 232	Left: 232	Left: 232
Top: 128	Top: 168	Top: 208
Height: 25	Height: 25	Height: 25
Width: 73	Width: 73	Width: 73
Name: txtHours4	Name: txtWeeklyPay1	Name: txtWeeklyPay2
Text:	Text:	Text:
Left: 232	Left: 368	Left: 368
Top: 248	Top: 128	Top: 168
Height: 25	Height: 25	Height: 25
Width: 73	Width: 129	Width: 129
Name: txtWeeklyPay3	Name: txtWeeklyPay4	Name: txtTotalPay
Text:	Text:	Text:
Left: 368	Left: 368	Left: 368
Top: 208	Top: 248	Top: 288
Height: 25	Height: 25	Height: 25
Width: 129	Width: 129	Width: 129

Adding the Final Label

There is no difference in adding the last label. The reason we waited to add it at the end was so that we could determine the proper location to place it. Here are the properties for the last label:

Name: lblTotalPay
Caption: Total Pay
Font: Size = 14, Style = bold
Left: 256
Top: 296
Height: 17
Width: 105

The final application will look as follows:

Figure 2.65
Final Application

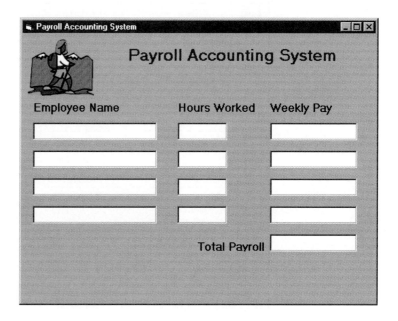

Tab Index

When you create applications, you often add controls in the order you think about them, not necessarily in the order the user wishes to enter data. When you place controls on a form, they receive a default tab index that follows the order they are added to the form.

Create a form using the following instructions exactly in the same order that they are listed:

Step 1: Create a command button at the bottom of the form.
Step 2: Create a text box in the lower right side of the form, but above the command button.
Step 3: Create a text box directly above the text box in step 2.
Step 4: Create a text box to the left of the text box step 2.
Step 5: Create a text box to the left of the text box created in step 3.

Observe the following diagram showing how you should create your form. Notice that the text boxes have their default text values displayed. It should clarify which text boxes were created first:

Figure 2.66
Form with Text Boxes

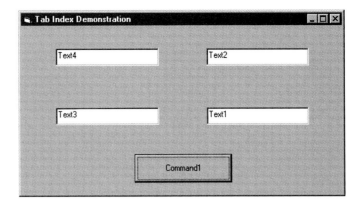

Step 6: Run the application. Notice the focus of the application is on the command button.
Step 7: Press the <TAB> key. Notice the focus changes to the text box with `Text1` showing.
Step 8: Press the <TAB> key. Notice the focus changes to the text box with `Text2` showing.
Step 9: Press the <TAB> key. Notice the focus changes to the text box with `Text3` showing.
Step 10: Press the <TAB> key. Notice the focus changes to the text box with `Text4` showing.
Step 11: Exit the application.

A well-designed program should start with the focus in the upper-left corner. When the <TAB> key is pressed, you should move to the next logical control. This may be to the right or just below the current one. The order is not important as long as you choose an order that makes logical sense in your application and is consistent throughout your application.

Fortunately Visual Basic allows us to control the tab index of the application. One of the properties of every control is the tab index property.

Observe the tab index of the text box in the upper-left corner of the form. It is set to 4. By setting it to 0, you can make it the first control in the tab order of the application. Then you can set the remaining controls to 1, 2, 3, and 4, so that the application's tab order behaves in an intuitive manner.

Tab Stop

Often you do not wish a control to be in the tab order at all. Label controls function this way. If you run an application that contains labels, observe that they are not tabbed on as you repeatedly press the <TAB> key.

Visual Basic provides us with a property, `TabStop`, to control this behavior for other controls. In your `Lady or the Tiger` application, you have no reason to tab over to the picture box control. Therefore, you should set the `TabStop` property of the picture box to `False`. A `False` setting will remove the control from the tab loop. A `True` setting will place it in the tab loop. Most controls will have this property.

 TIP

Be aware not all controls have a `TabIndex` and a `TabStop`.

Key Words and Key Terms

Caption
Sets the name that will be displayed for a control when the program is executed.

Command button control
A control that acts as an action button. When depressed, code can be attached to execute.

Control toolbar
A window with icons that link to commonly used controls that may be added to the form by the programmer.

Icon
A small graphic that represents a larger purpose. In this case you use an icon to represent actions that can be followed if the icon is selected.

Font
Sets the various typeface and style properties for the font of the control.

Form window
A window that allows a programmer to create an application's form by attaching code and controls.

Height
Controls the vertical size of a control.

Keyword
A special word that is predefined by Visual Basic with a special meaning.

Label control
A control that displays static text. This text can be changed programmatically.

Left
Controls the horizontal placement of a control. It indicates the leftmost location of the control.

Menu bar
A series of text shortcuts to commonly used routines in the development of an application.

Name
Sets the name by which the control can be referenced programmatically.

New Project window
A window that displays the options for creating a new project.

Picture box control
A control that displays a picture.

Project Explorer window
A window that shows the major components of a project.

Standard toolbar
A shortcut to commonly used actions that affect the project. The actions are represented by small icons associated with actions.

Properties window
A window that allows the programmer to change the properties of a control.

Static text
Text that cannot be changed by the user of the application.

TabIndex
Sets the order of the control as the user tabs from control to control.

TabStop
Determines whether a control will be in the tab order.

Text box control
A control that allows text to be entered into it.

Top
Controls the vertical placement of a control. It indicates the topmost location of the control.

Width
Controls the horizontal size of a control.

Additional Exercises

1. The Name of a form is a _____.

   a. Control   b. Event   c. Property   d. Picture

2. Click is a(n) _____ on a Command button.

   a. Control   b. Event   c. Property   d. Picture

3. A TextBox is a _____.

   a. Control   b. Event   c. Property   d. Picture

4. A caption is a(n) _____ on a command button.

   a. Control   b. Event   c. Property   d. Picture

5. Explain when you would use a text box, label, picture box, and command button control.

6. Explain the difference between the `Caption` property and the `Name` property.

Assume for the next five questions that a command button `cmdButton1`, a label `lblLabel1`, and a text box `txtText1` are on a form `frmForm1`.

7. Is there an error in the following code? If so, correct it.

```
Private Sub cmdButton1_Click()
    txtText1.Caption = 'Will This Work?'
End Sub
```

8. Is there an error in the following code? If so, correct it.

```
Private Sub cmdButton1_Click()
    txtText1.Capton = "Will This Work?"
End Sub
```

9. Is there an error in the following code? If so, correct it.

```
Private Sub cmdButton1_Click()
    Label1.txtText1 = "Will This Work?"
End Sub
```

10. Is there an error in the following code? If so, correct it.

```
Private Sub cmdButton1_Click()
    frmForm1.BackColor = LightBlue
End Sub
```

11. Is there an error in the following code? If so, correct it.

```
Private Sub cmdButton1_Click()
    frmForm1.BackColor = vbLightBlue
End Sub
```

12. Does changing the `TabIndex` of a control change the way it is displaying in any manner? If so, indicate how.

13. Will the following code change the `Picture` property of the picture box `pctPicture` so that it will display the photo `ExamplePicture.jpg`?

```
pctPicture.Picture = "ExamplePicture.jpg"
```

14. Write the code required to change the height and width of the text box `txtText1` to double its current size when the command button `cmdButton1` is clicked.

15. Write an application that contains a label, a text box, and a command button. When the command button is clicked, have the label move to the right the number of pixels entered in the text box. If a negative number is entered, have the label control move to the right that many pixels.

16. Write an application that displays a label and two command buttons. Display the text `How large will I go?` in the label. Set the caption of the first command button to `Reduce` and set the code to decrease the size of the font of the label by one each time it is clicked. Set the caption of the second command button to `Enlarge` and set the code to increase the size of the font of the label by one each time it is clicked. Make sure that the label is set to a True Type font.

17. Write an application that contains one label control and four command buttons. Each command button should have a different caption and message associated with it. When the command button is clicked, the associated message should be displayed in the label control. You may pick the captions and messages for each Command button.

18. Enhance your application from exercise 18 so that the last command button clicked the message is displayed in a bold font.

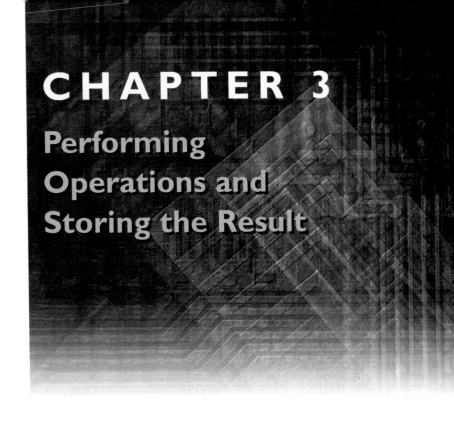

CHAPTER 3

Performing Operations and Storing the Result

So far you have learned how to enter and display values in a various number of forms. In this chapter you will learn how to perform operations on these values and store them in the computer's memory. You will also learn when it is important to set values so they cannot be modified. Finally you will learn how to inspect a program to see where possible errors may occur.

3.1 Variables

In Chapter 2, you saw that you can store values in controls such as a text box. If done repeatedly, this can be extremely inefficient. Often you wish to store values without having to create an object. Visual Basic allows you to store values in a **variable**.

Variables and objects share similar properties, although you create them differently. To create an object, you selected it from a toolbar and dragged it onto the form. This gave it a default name and datatype. Dragging and dropping cannot create a variable, but creating a variable requires the same specifications as creating an object. In order to use a variable, you must have a method to allocate the appropriate amount of space and associate a name and datatype for it. You must give the variable a valid **variable name** so that you may reference the stored value throughout the program. Additionally, you must select from a list of **variable datatypes** indicating to Visual Basic how much space to allocate and how to process and display the variable when it is used within the program.

Variables of different datatypes exist so that you can store different types of values. One datatype is the **Integer**. An integer is a whole number. Typically you represent integers as a number following the pattern:

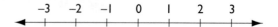

You can see that positive numbers, negative numbers, and the number zero are all included. Visual Basic provides the variable datatype `Integer` to allow the creation of variables of this type.

Selecting the Proper Datatype

However, selection of `Integer` as a variable's datatype requires some thought. The maximum and minimum size of a variable must be taken into account. Does the program you are writing require storing a grade on an exam with a maximum value of 100 and a minimum value of 0? Does the program you are writing require storing the total number of people in the United States? That number would be upwards of 280 million people.

Visual Basic provides two `Integer` datatypes depending upon the range of values the integer variable you are declaring requires. If you require an integer that will always remain between –32,768 and 32,767 you can use the `Integer` datatype. However, if your variable must store an integer of greater or less than the extremes indicated, you must use the **Long** datatype. A `Long` variable can store a value from –2,147,483,648 to 2,147,483,647.

What happens if you use the wrong datatype? Well, that depends upon which datatype you choose. Beginner programmers might decide to use the `Long` datatype in all cases because it would safeguard against guessing wrong. However, while it will not cause an error in the execution of the program (commonly known as a **run-time error**), it will waste memory. A `Long` variable takes double the space of an `Integer` variable.

If, on the other hand, you choose a variable to be an `Integer` and then set it to a value out of the range of the variable, you will get an execution error. Observe the following code and the error message you receive when you execute it.

```
Private Sub cmdOverFlow_Click()
 Dim IntegerVariable As Integer

 IntegerVariable = 32767
 IntegerVariable = IntegerVariable + 1
End Sub
```

If you ignore the statement declaring the variable for now, you can see how you can set the variable `IntegerVariable` to 32767 because 32767 is a value within the range of an `Integer`. However, when you execute the next line, the variable should contain the value 32768. Because an integer cannot store a value that large, you get an execution error, shown in the following figure:

Figure 3.1
Overflow Error

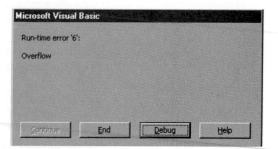

An **overflow** is the term used to describe when you try to store a value in a variable that is too big. When you learn a bit more of the Visual Basic language you will learn ways of preventing this type of error.

Other Variable Datatypes   Not all values you store are whole numbers. Often you are required to store decimal numbers. Visual Basic provides multiple options for selecting the datatype of the variable to use when storing decimal numbers. Each datatype for numerical values has different precisions and storage requirements. A programmer can select from **Single**, **Double**, **Decimal**, or **Currency** when creating a decimal variable.

The first three decimal datatypes allow the storage of decimal numbers. They are listed in increasing order of precision and storage requirements. The fourth, `Currency`, is used for storing values when they are listed in dollars and cents.

Another simple datatype is a **string**. Visual Basic provides the `String` datatype to allow the storage of characters. A `String` can store a series of characters together. It is very versatile in that you are not required to define how much space is required. A `String`'s storage requirement is directly related to the length of a string that you wish to store.

You may remember that you have already used `Strings` in your earlier applications. A `String` is specified as a double quote, `"`, a series of characters, and another double quote.

Rounding out the simple datatypes is the **Date** datatype. Although you could store a date as a `String`, storing it in the `Date` datatype will give you additional functionality. In order to store a `Date` you need to enclose the date in # signs. See the following example, which assigns the date January 28th 2001.

```
Dim SuperBowl As Date
SuperBowl = #1/28/2001#
```

By using a `Date` datatype, you can increment the date by simply adding one. Therefore `SuperBowl + 1` would equal `1/29/01`.

There are many other datatypes, but we will introduce them in later chapters, as they are required.

DRILL 3.1

In each real-world situation, list the variable type that would be most appropriate:

1 A variable to store an hourly wage of an employee.
2 A variable to store the average score on an exam that has the lowest possible grade of 0 and highest grade of 100.
3 A variable to store the sum of 50 test scores on an exam that has the lowest possible grade of 0 and highest grade of 100.
4 A variable to store the sum of 500 test scores on an exam that has the lowest possible grade of 0 and highest grade of 100.
5 A variable to store the sum of 5,000 test scores on an exam that has the lowest possible grade of 0 and highest grade of 100.
6 A variable to store the expression "The 76'ers are looking great this year!"
7 Tomorrow's date.

DRILL 3.2

If the following code were executed, would an overflow occur? If so, why?

```
Private Sub Command1_Click()
 Dim IntegerVariable As Integer

 IntegerVariable = -32768
 IntegerVariable = IntegerVariable + 1
End Sub
```

DRILL 3.3

If the following code were executed, would an overflow occur? If so, why?

```
Private Sub Command1_Click()
 Dim IntegerVariable As Integer

 IntegerVariable = 10000
 IntegerVariable = IntegerVariable * 3
End Sub
```

DRILL 3.4

If the following code were executed, would an overflow occur? If so, why?

```
Private Sub Command1_Click()
 Dim IntegerVariable As Integer

 IntegerVariable = 32767
 IntegerVariable = IntegerVariable - 5
 IntegerVariable = IntegerVariable + 5
 IntegerVariable = IntegerVariable + 1
End Sub
```

Chart Summarizing Datatypes

Datatype	Description	Range
Boolean	Logical data	True or false
Currency	Monetary values	15 digits to the left of the decimal, four digits to the right of the decimal
Date	Date and time data	January 1, 0100 to December 31, 9999
Double	Large or high precision floating point numbers	Floating point number with up to 14 digits of accuracy
Integer	Small integer numbers	–32,768 to 32,767
Long	Large integer numbers	–2,147,483,648 to 2,147,483,647
Single	Small floating point numbers	Floating point number with up to six digits of accuracy
String	Character data	Varies based on size of string
Variant	Stores any datatype	Dependent upon what is being stored, should not be used under normal circumstances

Variable Names

A variable name in Visual Basic begins with a letter and may be followed by any number of letters, underscores, or digits. A variable name can be as small as one letter or as large as 255 letters, underscores, and digits. However, when picking a variable name, it should be representative of the value that you are storing. Try to stay away from variable names like X. If the represented value is the number of students in a class, a good variable name might be `NumberStudents`. As your programs get larger, more readable variable names will make the program easier to follow.

Letters used in variable names can be either lowercase or uppercase. Visual Basic will use the capitalization of the variable when it is declared as the proper capitalization. This means that if you refer to the variable with a different capitalization later in the program, it will convert the capitalization to the one used earlier in the program. For example, if you declare a variable as `NUMBERstudents` and then refer to it in the program as `numberSTUDENTS`, Visual Basic will automatically convert the variable name back to the way it was initially declared as in `NUMBERstudents`.

TIP

Often programmers do not remember exactly how to spell a variable. Since Visual Basic will allow you to declare a variable just by using it, this can cause problems. If you misspell a variable name, it will just create another one. To combat this, follow a consistent naming scheme like capitalizing the first letter of each word. You can be sure that you're using the correct variable name by spelling it in all lowercase after the initial declaration. Visual Basic will automatically capitalize the variable name when you finish the line. If the variable name does not capitalize the way you expect it, you have a spelling mistake on the previous line.

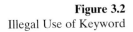

TIP

Variable names may contain a keyword as part of the name of a variable.

Visual Basic does not differentiate between two variable names that are identical except for the case of the letters in their names. If a language does, it is considered **case sensitive**. Therefore, Visual Basic is not case sensitive.

A variable name cannot be a keyword already used by Visual Basic. Therefore, variable names like `Private`, `Dim`, or `Integer` are illegal.

Visual Basic will immediately provide feedback that you have violated the rules of declaring a variable. See the following example of a message that you will receive when you declare a variable name improperly.

Figure 3.2
Illegal Use of Keyword

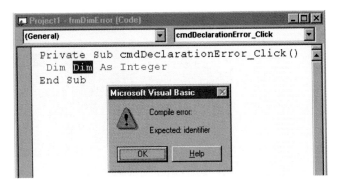

DRILL 3.5

Determine which of the following variable names are valid:

1 `Moira`
2 `Ben`
3 `Moira&Ben`
4 `Moira_Ben`
5 `_MoiraBen`
6 `IsThisLegal`
7 `HowAboutThis?`
8 `PrivateDancerWasTheNameOfASong`
9 `Private`

Declaring a Variable

In order to use a variable in Visual Basic, you should indicate to the compiler that the variable exists before you actually access it. This is called declaring a variable. Declaring or allocating a variable means that you are indicating to the computer the type of variable that you wish to use as well as the name that you are going to reference it from within the program.

Always Use Option Explicit   While Visual Basic will allow you to use a variable that you have not declared, this is a very dangerous practice. If you use a variable that has not been declared, Visual Basic will assign it a `Variant` datatype. While this will not cause your application to operate improperly, it is one of the least efficient datatypes and will most probably waste resources.

Often beginning developers will wish to skip the step of declaring a variable to save time. In the end, usually it will cost time. When variables are not declared, if you misspell the variable, your program will continue to execute, assuming that you created the misspelled variable on the fly. You will believe your program is working properly, but a subtle error will most probably creep into your application.

Visual Basic allows you to set it so that you can force yourself to declare variables. By adding the code `Option Explicit` to your form, you can enforce this very valuable standard.

Setting Option Explicit

Step 1:   Right-click on the form to which you wish to add the `Option Explicit` statement. The following pop-up menu will appear:

Figure 3.3
Pop-Up Menu to View Code

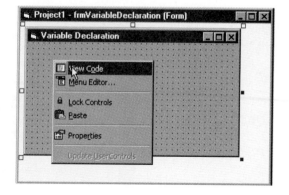

Step 2: Select the `View Code` item. The General Declarations section will appear.

Figure 3.4
General Declarations
Section

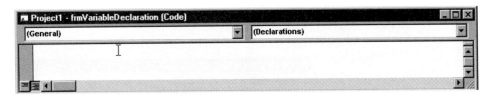

Step 3: Type `Option Explicit`.

That's it, now whenever you attempt to use a variable that isn't declared, you will receive an error message like the one shown in Figure 3.5.

Figure 3.5
Declaration Error

If you want to ensure that you are always in `Option Explicit` mode, you can configure Visual Basic so that it automatically adds the `Option Explicit` statement to your forms as you create them. Click on the Options item from the Tools menu. Then click on the Module tab and select the Require Variable Declaration check box.

The Dim and Public Keywords

There are two statements that you can use to declare a variable: **Dim** and **Public**. Which you choose depends on whether you wish the variable to be used solely within the code you declared it within or by other areas of code throughout your application. The degree of visibility to which a variable can be seen by other areas of code is known as the **scope** of a variable.

When a variable is declared with the `Dim` keyword, its scope is within the set of code in which the `Dim` statement is contained. So if a variable is defined in a control's `Click` event, then that variable may only be referenced within that `Click` event. Any attempt to reference the variable elsewhere will result in an error.

While a variable should be declared as locally as possible, a variable can be declared so that it is visible to the entire form. This should only be done when absolutely necessary. This is accomplished by declaring the variable in the General Declarations section of a form's code. This method will be shown shortly.

The last method of declaring a variable is to use the `Public` keyword. This will allow a variable to be visible to the entire application. As we will not discuss applications with multiple forms until Chapter 11, we will skip this option for now.

So, we will stick to using the `Dim` keyword when declaring a variable. To actually declare the variable, you need to first type the word `Dim`, followed by a space, followed by the variable name, followed by the word `As`, followed by the datatype of variable. The syntax for declaring a variable using the `Dim` keyword is shown in the following code:

```
Dim VariableName As Datatype
```

The following is an example of declaring three variables called intStudentGrade, sngStudentAverage, and curStudentWage in the Click event's code for a command button. They are declared as the datatypes Integer, Single, and Currency, respectively.

Figure 3.6
Code for Declaring Variables

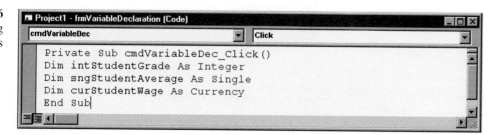

Adding a Comment It is always a good idea to add a comment on the same line indicating the purpose of the variable. A comment may be added to a line by typing a single quote and then the comment that you wish to make. Comments are not part of the actual code, but a way of documenting the code so that it is more understandable.

The following code will demonstrate documenting the previous example:

Figure 3.7
Comments Added to Code

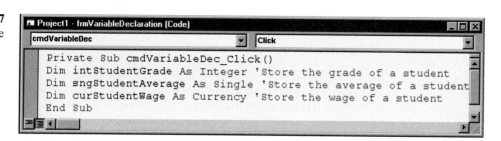

Visual Basic .NET Alert

While Visual Basic Version 6.0 will allow the developer to declare more than one variable on a line even if they are of different types, this will not be supported in VB .NET and should be avoided. Another good reason to declare variables on their own line is so that the developer can add a comment for each variable.

TIP

The comments in your code will appear in green as in Figure 3.7.

Many beginning programmers may wish to use a dash in a variable name. There is a very good reason why Visual Basic does not allow you to do this. Can you guess what it is? Maybe the following bit of code will help illustrate the problem with using a dash.

Figure 3.8
Illegal Use of Dash

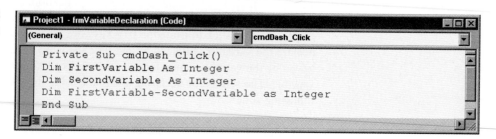

If Visual Basic allowed you to declare a variable called `FirstVariable-SecondVariable`, it couldn't distinguish between the operation `FirstVariable` minus `SecondVariable` and the variable `FirstVariable-SecondVariable`. It is important when writing computer programs that you do not create ambiguous conditions. If there is no clear indication of what you intend the computer to accomplish, the computer will not be able to guess what you intend.

Naming Conventions

Although not a rule imposed by the Visual Basic language, it is a good practice to use a naming convention when declaring variables.

Visual Basic users follow a simple standard used throughout the industry for Visual Basic applications. All variable names should start with a three-letter abbreviation indicating the variable's datatype.

After the three-letter abbreviation a variable should be described in enough detail so that its purpose is self-explanatory. Another good standard is to capitalize the first letter of each word used in the variable name. It allows the reader of the code to easily differentiate the words in a variable name.

A final convention that will improve your code's readability is to be consistent with any abbreviations that you might use repeatedly through your code. For instance if you wish to abbreviate the word Number, you could abbreviate it as Num or Nbr. It really doesn't matter which you choose, as long as you use the same one throughout your code.

Chart Summarizing Datatype Prefixes	
Datatype	**Prefix**
Boolean	bln
Currency	cur
Date	dte
Double	dbl
Integer	int
Long	lng
Single	sng
String	str
Variant	vnt

DRILL 3.6

What would happen if you tried to write code as follows:

```
Private Sub cmdDrill_Click()
DrillValue = 10
Dim DrillValue As String
DrillValue = "What will be the output?"
MsgBox DrillValue
End Sub
```

3.2 Simple Operators

If computers could only allow the entry, storage, and display of values, our society would not be so heavily dependent upon them. A programmer begins to tap a computer's power by writing simple programs that perform calculations.

Visual Basic allows the user to perform all the numerical operations you are familiar with. A computer uses symbols called **operators** to indicate that an operation is to be performed. You are already familiar with the operator for assignment, the equal sign (=). Addition, subtraction, multiplication, and division are all supported, using operators that you are already familiar with as well. They are **+**, **–**, *****, and **/** operators, respectively. The values that operators perform their actions upon are known as **operands**.

Visual Basic can use these operators in many ways; however, the only way that you have been taught so far is in the command button `Click` event. You'll start by creating a form with a text box `txtOutput` and a command button `cmdAdd`. In the command button's `Click` event you will declare a variable `intTotal`, add one plus one together, and stores the result in `intTotal`. Finally, you will copy the value to the text box for output in the form.

Create Form

Step 1: Create a new project.
Step 2: Set the `Name` property of the form to `frmAdd`.
Step 3: Set the `Caption` property to `Addition Operator`.

Add Output Text Box

Step 1: Place a text box control in the middle of the form.
Step 2: Set the `Name` property to `txtOutput`.

Add Command Button

Step 1: Place a command button control below the `txtOutput` text box.
Step 2: Set the `Name` property to `cmdAdd`.
Step 3: Set the `Caption` property to `Add`.
Step 4: Double-click on the `cmdAdd` command button and add the following code:

Figure 3.9
Command Button Code

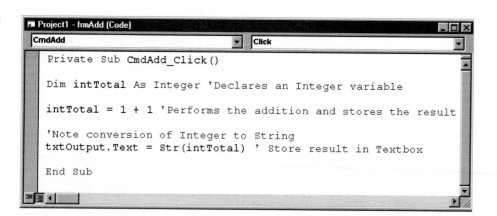

The code within the event `cmdAdd_Click` introduces two operators, both of which you are already familiar with and operate in the manner you would expect. The operator, +, takes two values and adds them together. The result, 2, is then assigned using the equals operator, =, to the `txtOutput` text box. This is shown in the following figure:

Figure 3.10
Application after Command
Button Is Clicked

Expressions may contain more than just values and operators. They may also contain parentheses. Parentheses tell the computer to calculate the operations inside the parentheses before performing the rest of the calculations. The order in which the operations are performed is referred to as the **order of precedence** of the operations. So far, the operations learned follow the same precedence learned in elementary school mathematics. Therefore, when reading from left to right, you perform all the operations in the parentheses first, and then the exponentiations, and then all the multiplication and divisions, finally all the additions and subtractions.

DRILL 3.7

The following code snippets are designed to test your order of precedence knowledge. Try working out each example first, and then type in the snippet and execute it. Compare your results to the answers found at the end of the chapter.

```
Private Sub cmdDrill_Click()
    txtOutput.Text = 4+5*6-3/3+6
End Sub

Private Sub cmdDrill_Click()
    txtOutput.Text = (4+5)*6-(3/3+6)
End Sub

Private Sub cmdDrill_Click()
    txtOutput.Text = (4+5)/(1+2)
End Sub

Private Sub cmdDrill_Click()
    txtOutput.Text = 4*5*(3+3)
End Sub

Private Sub cmdDrill_Click()
    txtOutput.Text = 2-2/2+2*2-3
End Sub
```

The examples in Figure 3.9 and Drill 3.7 were all selected with one thing in common. All the calculations produced results that were whole numbers.

Using the same application, you can change the operation from 1 + 1 to 1 / 3. What do you think the result would be? If you were familiar with Visual

(continues)

DRILL 3.7 (continued)

Basic, you would know the answer is 0.333333333333333. However, programmers already familiar with other languages might not be so quick to guess that. Visual Basic is not as strict in enforcing the use of proper datatypes as some other languages are. Other languages do not produce results of one datatype when the calculation is performed on operands of another datatype. In this example the operands are integers while the result is a decimal.

Example: Counter Application

You now know enough to create an application that acts as a counter. A counter should start at zero and increment by one each time a button is pressed. It is also useful to have an additional button that will reset the counter to zero. The application will look as follows:

Figure 3.11
Sample Counter Application

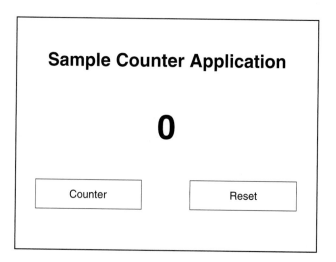

You can attach code to the command button for the counter, cmdCounter, to add one to the value stored as the caption in the Label that represents the counter, lblCounter. You can then attach similar code to the command button to reset the counter, cmdReset, to set the caption for lblCounter back to 0.

To develop this application, start with a blank form and perform the following steps:

Create Form

Step 1: Create a new project.
Step 2: Set the Name property of the form to frmCounter.
Step 3: Set the Caption property to a Sample Counter Application.

You need a variable to store the current value of the counter. Because this variable will be accessed from multiple controls' Click events, you need to declare it in the General Declarations section.

Add intCounter Variable

Step 1: Right-click on the form.
Step 2: Click on the View Code item of the pop-up menu.
Step 3: Your code should default to the General Declarations section. The pull-downs of your code should look as follows:

Figure 3.12
General Declarations
Section

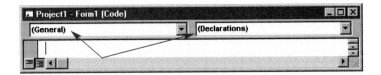

Step 4: Type `Dim intCounter as Integer`.

For the remaining steps, you must switch back to the object view of the application.

Add Title Label

Step 1: Place a label control across the top of the form.
Step 2: Set the `Name` to `lblTitle`.
Step 3: Set the `Caption` to `Sample Counter Application`.
Step 4: Set the `Font` property to a Size of 14 and a Style of Bold.
Step 5: Set the `Alignment` property to Center.

Figure 3.13
Application with
Title Label Placed

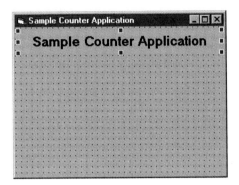

Add Counter Label

Step 1: Place a label control across the top of the form.
Step 2: Set the `Name` property to `lblCount`.
Step 3: Set the `Caption` property to `0`.
Step 4: Set the `Font` property to a Size of 24 and a Style of Bold.
Step 5: Set the `Alignment` property to Center.

Figure 3.14
Application with Counter
Label Added

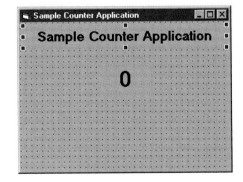

Add Counter Button

Step 1: Place a command button control in the bottom-left side of the form.

Step 2: Set the `Name` property to `cmdCounter`.

Step 3: Set the `Caption` property to `Counter`.

Step 4: Double-click on the command button.

Step 5: Attach the code to add 1 to the counter label, `lblCount`, to the command button's `Click` event.

Figure 3.15
Application with
`cmdCounter` Command
Button Placed

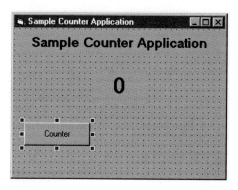

Figure 3.16
Code for `cmdCounter`
Command Button

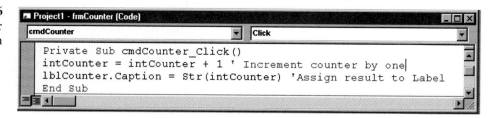

Add Reset Button

Step 1: Place a command button control in the bottom-right side of the form.

Step 2: Set the `Name` property to `cmdReset`.

Step 3: Set the `Caption` property to `Reset`.

Step 4: Double-click on the command button.

Step 5: Attach to the command button the code to reset the counter label, `lblCounter`, to 0.

Figure 3.17
Application with `cmdReset`
Command Button Added

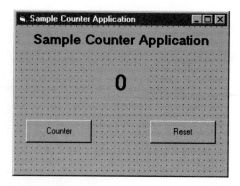

Figure 3.18
Code for `cmdReset`
Command Button

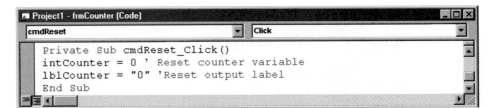

```
Private Sub cmdReset_Click()
intCounter = 0 ' Reset counter variable
lblCounter = "0" 'Reset output label
End Sub
```

TIP

A variable should always be initialized to a value before it is used. While Visual Basic automatically initializes numerical variables to 0, it is not a good practice to depend upon it.

3.3 Local and Global Variables

In the previous examples we have demonstrated variables declared in different locations within the applications. When a variable is declared within an event, it is only visible within the code for that event. Variables of this nature are known as local in scope. When a variable is declared within the General Declarations section of a form, it is visible to the entire form and known as a global in scope.

Scope Drills

For the following three drills assume that a form has been created with three command buttons: `cmdInitialize`, `cmdAdd`, and `cmdOutput`.

DRILL 3.8

If the following three `Click` events are coded, what would the output be if the command buttons were clicked in the following order: `cmdInitialize`, `cmdAdd`, and `cmdOutput`?

```
Private Sub cmdInitialize_Click()
Dim intDrillValue As Integer
intDrillValue = 10
End Sub

Private Sub cmdAdd_Click()
intDrillValue = intDrillValue + 10
End Sub

Private Sub cmdOutput_Click()
MsgBox Str(intDrillValue)
End Sub
```

DRILL 3.9

If the following three Click events are coded, and the variable intDrillValue is declared in the General Declarations section, what would the output be if the command buttons were clicked in the following order: cmdInitialize, cmdAdd, and cmdOutput?

```
Dim intDrillValue As Integer

Private Sub cmdAdd_Click()
intDrillValue = intDrillValue + 10
End Sub

Private Sub cmdInitialize_Click()
intDrillValue = 10
End Sub

Private Sub cmdOutput_Click()
MsgBox Str(intDrillValue)
End Sub
```

DRILL 3.10

If the following three Click events are coded, and the variable intDrillValue is declared in the General Declarations section, what would the output be if the command buttons were clicked in the following order: cmdAdd and cmdOutput?

```
Dim intDrillValue As Integer

Private Sub cmdAdd_Click()
intDrillValue = intDrillValue + 10
End Sub

Private Sub cmdOutput_Click()
MsgBox Str(intDrillValue)
End Sub
```

Review of Arithmetic Operators

Operators	Operations
( )	Parentheses
^	Exponentiation
* /	Multiplication and Division
+ –	Addition and Subtraction

3.4 Constants

Often in programming you want to represent values that will not change during the execution of the program. These values are called **constants**. They are added to the program for two purposes.

First, by adding a name to associate with the value, your program will become more readable. Imagine if you wrote a program that computed sales tax. While you could type the tax amount directly into the equations using it, a person reading the program would not immediately understand the purpose of the value .06 without reading a comment. By adding a constant called `SalesTax` and setting it to .06, you accomplish this.

In addition, another benefit occurs if the value .06 appeared in the program many times. If the sales tax was increased, let's say to pay for a new football stadium, you would have to change it in many places, thus increasing your risk of adding an error to the program. With the use of constants you only have to change the value in a single place.

You may be wondering why you just do not use a variable instead of coming up with a new way to define a constant. Simple, a variable has the ability to change within the program. You wouldn't want to risk the chance that you could inadvertently change a value that shouldn't be changed. With a constant, there is no way to change it.

In order to declare a constant, you type the keyword **Const**, a space, followed by the name of the constant, followed by a space, followed by an equals sign, followed by the value to set the constant to. This can be seen in the following code that illustrates the syntax of assigning a constant:

```
Const ConstantName = Value
```

In addition to the format given, you may include a datatype for the constant. You may also use an expression instead of the value shown previously.

Here is the a more descriptive way of assigning a constant:

```
Const ConstantName As DataType = Expression
```

TIP

The rules for naming a constant are the same as those for naming a variable.

Example: Sales Tax Calculation

Let's create a very simple application to calculate the sales tax for a purchase. It will use a constant in order to indicate the sales tax percentage. In a program this small you might not think a constant is worthwhile, however it is good practice, especially if your program may grow in size.

Start by placing a label "Sales Tax Calculation" across the top of the form.

Create Form

Step 1: Create a new project.
Step 2: Set the `Name` property of the form to `frmCounter`.
Step 3: Set the `Caption` property to a `Sample Counter Application`.

Add Title Label

Step 1: Click on the label control in the Control toolbar.
Step 2: Draw a label control on the form.
Step 3: Change the `Caption` property to `Sales Tax Calculation`.
Step 4: Change the `Font` property to Bold and 14 point size.

Figure 3.19
Label Added to Application

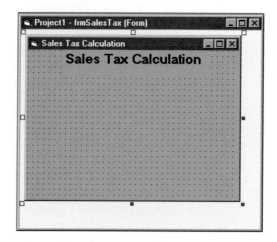

Next, Add three more labels, `Purchase Price`, `Sales Tax`, and `Final Price`.

Add Purchase Price Label

Step 1: Click on the label control in the Control toolbar.
Step 2: Draw a label control on the form.
Step 3: Change the `Name` property to `lblPurchasePrice`.
Step 4: Change the `Caption` property to `Purchase Price`.
Step 5: Change the `Font` property to Bold and a Size of 10.

Add Sales Tax Label

Step 1: Click on the label control in the Control toolbar.
Step 2: Draw a label control on the form.
Step 3: Change the `Name` property to `lblSalesTax`.
Step 4: Change the `Caption` property to `Sales Tax`.
Step 5: Change the `Font` property to Bold and a Size of 10.

Add Final Price Label

Step 1: Click on the label control in the Control toolbar.
Step 2: Draw a label control on the form.
Step 3: Change the `Name` property to `lblFinalPrice`.
Step 4: Change the `Caption` property to `Final Price`.
Step 5: Change the `Font` property to Bold and a Size of 10.

Figure 3.20
Additional Labels Added to
Application

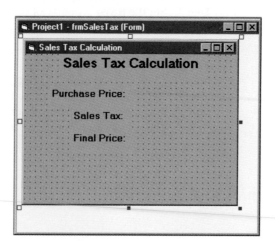

Next you need to add three text boxes: `txtPurchasePrice`, `txtSalesTax`, and `txtFinalPrice`.

Add Purchase Price Text Box

Step 1: Click on the text box control in the Control toolbar.
Step 2: Draw a text box control on the form.
Step 3: Set the `Name` property of the control to `txtPurchasePrice`.
Step 4: Erase the value in the `Text` property.

Add Sales Tax Text Box

Step 1: Click on the text box control in the Control toolbar.
Step 2: Draw a text box control on the form.
Step 3: Set the `Name` property of the control to `txtSalesTax`.
Step 4: Erase the value in the `Text` property.

Add Final Price Text Box

Step 1: Click on the text box control in the Control toolbar.
Step 2: Draw a text box control on the form.
Step 3: Set the `Name` property of the control to `txtFinalPrice`.
Step 4: Erase the value in `Text` property.

Figure 3.21
Text Boxes Added to
Application

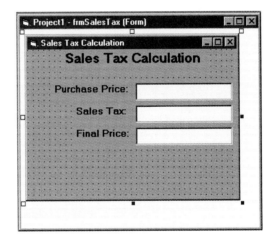

Next you must add a command button to perform the calculation.

Add Calculation CommandButton

Step 1: Click on the command button control in the Control toolbar.
Step 2: Draw a command button control on the form.
Step 3: Set the `Name` property of the control to `cmdCalculate`.
Step 4: Change the `Caption` property to `Calculate`.

Figure 3.22
Calculate Command Button
Added to Application

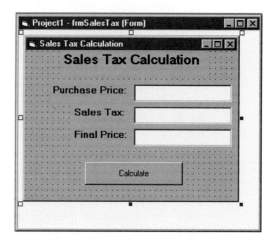

The final step is to add the code to perform the calculations.

Add Code to Command Button

Step 1: Double-click on the `cmdCalculate` command button.

Step 2: Type the declaration to define a constant called `curSalesTaxRate` as a `Currency` datatype and set it equal to 0.06.

Step 3: Declare three variables: `curSalesTaxAmount`, `curFinalPrice`, and `curPurchasePrice`. Although you could use the text box values directly, this is a dangerous practice and should be avoided!

Step 4: Convert the value stored in the `txtPurchasePrice` text box to a numerical value and store it in the `curPurchasePrice` variable.

Step 5: Calculate the `curSalesTaxAmount` by multiplying the `curSalesTaxRate` by `curPurchasePrice`.

Step 6: Calculate the `curFinalPrice` by adding the amount stored in the `curPurchasePrice` and `curSalesTaxAmount`.

Step 7: Store the `SalesTaxAmount` in the `txtSalesTax` text box.

Step 8: Store the `FinalPrice` in the `txtFinalPrice` text box.

Figure 3.23
Code for Command Button

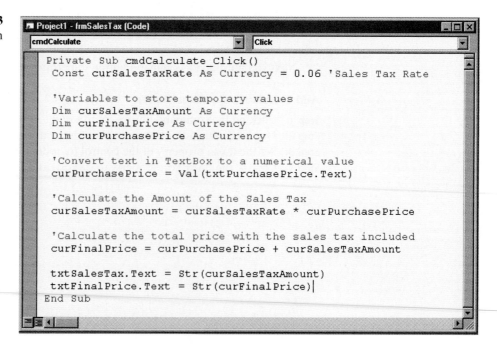

Try clicking on the `Calculate` command button when no value has been entered into the `txtPurchasePrice` text box. You will receive an error. This is because you have not coded your application to be robust. A robust program is one that handles improper input. As you learn more about the Visual Basic language you will learn how to handle these situations.

3.5   Using the Debugger

So far the programs you have written have been simple enough that if you did not write them correctly the first time, it was easy enough to figure out the source of any errors that occurred.

However, as your programs become more complex, you will need more sophisticated ways of determining the source of errors. Therefore, we are going to introduce a tool in Visual Basic called the **Debugger**.

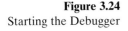

T I P

The idea of finding and removing errors in your application is known as debugging. You may be wondering how the process got such a non-technical name. In the early days of computers, a problem developed with a computer's execution. It turned out that an insect had flown into the computer and broken it. The discovery of the problem led to the term debugging a computer problem.

As we introduce more features of the Visual Basic language we will introduce more features of the Visual Basic Debugger. Our goal for this chapter is to introduce the Debugger and show you how you can step through the execution of your program while watching how objects and variables change.

To demonstrate this, we will use the previous example and show you how to step through its execution.

Instead of running the application in the normal manner, click on the Debug menu and then click on Step Into. Notice that the <F8> key can be used to shortcut this step. In the future you will use the <F8> key instead.

Figure 3.24
Starting the Debugger

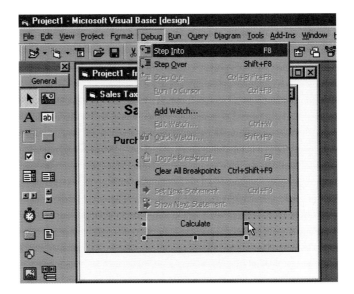

Next, enter a value for the purchase price. In this example you will enter $49.95. Notice that you do not have to enter the dollar sign.

Figure 3.25
Application Executing with
Purchase Price Entered

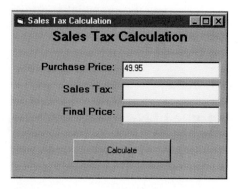

Then click on the cmdCalculate command button. Notice that instead of executing the code, the actual code is displayed. You are now in the Visual Basic Debugger. The yellow highlight indicates what line you are about to execute. As you can see from the following figure, you are about to enter the code to execute for the cmdCalculate command button.

Figure 3.26
Code Being Stepped Into

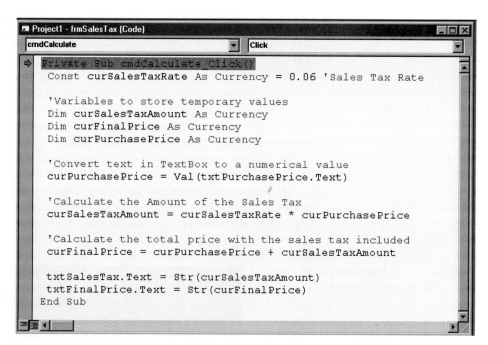

The Visual Basic Debugger allows you to do much more than just step through the code. If you move the mouse pointer over objects and variables and then pause, the object or variable's value will be displayed in a mini pop-up window. See the following figure as you mouse over the txtPurchasePrice text box to see the value, 49.95, contained within.

Figure 3.27
Control Being Moused Over
to Show Value

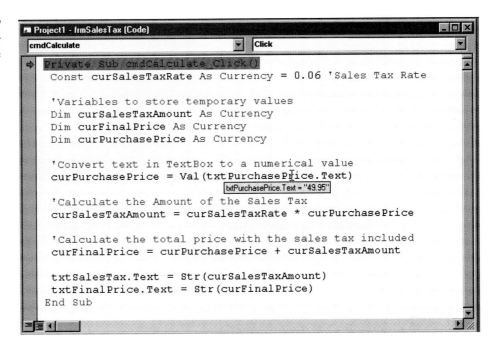

Notice that if you mouse over the variable `curSalesTaxAmount` its initial value is 0.

Figure 3.28
Variable Being Moused
Over to Show Initial Value

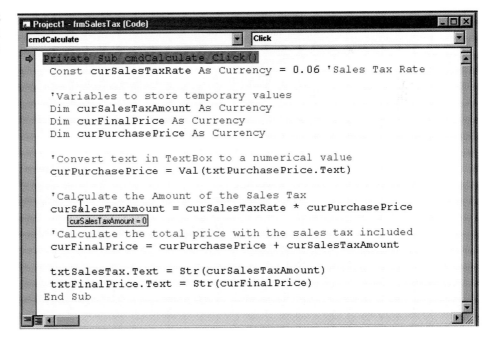

However, if you press the `<F8>` key a few times, you can see that you execute the statements one at a time. If you mouse over the `curSalesTaxAmount` variable after it is calculated, the new value, `2.997`, appears. If you press `<F8>` a few more times, the rest of the code is executed and you arrive at the final screen of the application.

Figure 3.29
Final View of the
Application

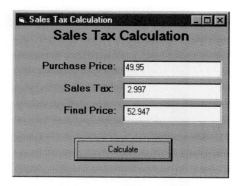

WARNING

Notice that the values are not exactly currency values, as you would like. You need to round the result to two decimal places. There are a few ways of doing this that will be shown in Chapter 6.

◆ 3.6 Case Study

Problem Description You wish to modify the Case Study from Chapter 2 and add the computational functionality that was missing. Now, instead of only allowing the entry of a person's name, hours worked, and weekly pay, you need to add a `cmdCalculate` command button that will automatically calculate a person's weekly pay as well as the total payroll cost. A person's weekly pay will be calculated by multiplying the number of hours a person worked by a fixed hourly rate of $9.50/hour. After all of the employees' weekly pay has been calculated, you must calculate the Total Payroll.

The following figure will demonstrate what the input to your application may look like:

Figure 3.30
Sketch of Application

```
┌─────────────────────────────────────────────────────────┐
│  ┌───────────┐                                            │
│  │  Walking  │       Payroll Accounting System            │
│  │   Logo    │                                            │
│  └───────────┘                                            │
│                                                            │
│   Employee Name        Hours Worked        Weekly Pay      │
│   ┌──────────────┐     ┌─────────┐      ┌──────────────┐   │
│   │              │     │         │      │              │   │
│   └──────────────┘     └─────────┘      └──────────────┘   │
│   ┌──────────────┐     ┌─────────┐      ┌──────────────┐   │
│   │              │     │         │      │              │   │
│   └──────────────┘     └─────────┘      └──────────────┘   │
│   ┌──────────────┐     ┌─────────┐      ┌──────────────┐   │
│   │              │     │         │      │              │   │
│   └──────────────┘     └─────────┘      └──────────────┘   │
│   ┌──────────────┐     ┌─────────┐      ┌──────────────┐   │
│   │              │     │         │      │              │   │
│   └──────────────┘     └─────────┘      └──────────────┘   │
│                                                            │
│        ┌────────────────┐              ┌──────────────┐   │
│        │   Calculate     │ Total Payroll│              │   │
│        └────────────────┘              └──────────────┘   │
└─────────────────────────────────────────────────────────┘
```

After the `cmdCalculate` command button is clicked, the following would be sample output for the input shown in the previous figure:

Figure 3.31
Sketch of Application and
How It Will Work

Walking Logo	**Payroll Accounting System**	
Employee Name	**Hours Worked**	**Weekly Pay**
Jeff Salvage	60	570
John Nunn	40	380
Eric Smith	20	190
Elizabeth Paxton	10	95
Calculate	**Total Payroll**	1235

Problem Discussion   The solution to the problem will entail two basic steps. You must compute the values for Weekly and Total Pay and then you must assign those values to the text box controls for display. Both of these functions can be performed from within the code to process a click from the cmdCalculate command button.

Problem Solution   Fortunately, almost all of the controls for your application were placed on the form in Chapter 2's case study. You need only add one control, cmdCalculate. This control will be a command button that will perform the calculations necessary for the application.

Although it is not required, the use of a constant in this solution is desirable. You should code a constant to indicate the Pay Rate. This way you can change the Pay Rate once and have it affect the entire application.

Set the Constant

Step 1: Right-click the mouse and click on View Code.
Step 2: Type Const sngPayRate as Single = 9.5.

Your code should look as follows. Notice that the two pull-down menus indicate General and Declarations:

Figure 3.32
Code to Set the Constant

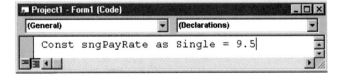

Place a Command Button

Step 1: Click on the command button control in the Control toolbar.
Step 2: Draw a command button control on the form.
Step 3: Change the Name property to cmdCalculate.
Step 4: Change the Caption property to Calculate.
Step 5: Add the code for the command button.

The command button's code must calculate each employee's weekly pay. It computes it by multiplying the number of hours worked by a pay rate of $9.50. Note that the code does not reference the value $9.50 directly; instead it uses the constant that you defined, sngPayRate.

Once the weekly pay is computed, it is converted to a string and output in the person's Weekly Pay text box.

Additionally, you must track the total pay of all four employees. When the first employee's weekly pay is computed, you assign the computed value to the total pay variable because this is the intialization of the variable. For the second, third, and fourth employees, you add their weekly pay to the total of the previously computed employee pay.

The final total is copied to the text box control for display. The code follows:

Figure 3.33
cmdCalculate
Command Button Code

```
Private Sub CmdCalculate_Click()
'Temporary Variables to Store Calculations
Dim curTotalPay As Currency
Dim curWeeklyPay As Currency

'First Person's Calculations
'Compute weekly pay of 1stw person
curWeeklyPay = Val(txtHours1.Text) * sngPayRate
'Convert weekly pay to String and output
txtWeeklyPay1.Text = Str(curWeeklyPay)
'Initialize total pay to first person's weekly pay
curTotalPay = curWeeklyPay

'Second Person's Calculations
'Compute weekly pay of 2nd person
curWeeklyPay = Val(txtHours2.Text) * sngPayRate
'Convert weekly pay to String and output
txtWeeklyPay2.Text = Str(curWeeklyPay)
'Add to total pay 2nd person's pay
curTotalPay = curTotalPay + curWeeklyPay

'Third Person's Calculations
'Compute weekly pay of 3rd person
curWeeklyPay = Val(txtHours3.Text) * sngPayRate
'Convert weekly pay to String and output
txtWeeklyPay3.Text = Str(curWeeklyPay)
'Add to total pay 3rd person's pay
curTotalPay = curTotalPay + curWeeklyPay

'Fourth Person's Calculations
'Compute weekly pay of fourth person
curWeeklyPay = Val(txtHours4.Text) * sngPayRate
'Convert weekly pay to String and output
txtWeeklyPay4.Text = str(curWeeklyPay)
'Add to total pay 4th person's pay
curTotalPay = curTotalPay + curWeeklyPay

'Convert Total Pay to a string and copy to TextBox
txtTotalPay.Text = Str(curTotalPay)
End Sub
```

Converting Datatypes

The code in Figure 3.33 presents two new problems. When the values for the number of hours each employee works are entered, they are stored in a text box. When a value is stored in a text box it is stored as a string. However, in order to perform mathematical calculations, you need to convert it to a numerical value. This is accomplished with a built-in function called `Val`. When you place `Val` in your code, as you did, it will return the numerical value for the string placed within the parentheses.

The second problem is that once you have calculated the Weekly and Total pays, you need to store them back in the `Text` property of the text boxes. Therefore, you use the `Str` function to convert a numerical value to a `String` datatype. While a text box will allow a numerical value to be assigned to its `Text` property, it is good programming practice to convert the type directly.

You will learn more about functions in Chapter 6.

Figure 3.34
Final Application

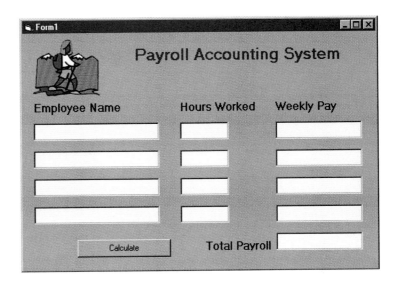

CORNER

Throughout this and the previous chapter you have seen that you can display information in a text box control. However, often you may wish to display information to the user of the application but not take up space on your form for it. A message box is an excellent way to solve this dilemma.

The following code illustrates the syntax of a simple call to a message box:

```
MsgBox "Message"
```

`MsgBox` is the keyword that indicates to Visual Basic that you wish a message to be displayed in a small window. Small windows like the one used for a message box are commonly referred to as dialog boxes. By placing any text you want displayed within a series of double quotes a message can be displayed.

Creating a Message Box

Follow these simple steps to create your first message box.

Step 1: Add a command button to a blank form.

Step 2: Assign the code `MsgBox "Don't Forget To Pay Your Taxes"` to the command button.

Step 3: Run the application.

Step 4: Click on the command button.

Step 5: The message box appears.

The application and the associated code should look as follows:

Figure 3.35
Application and Code
Demonstrating a
Message Box

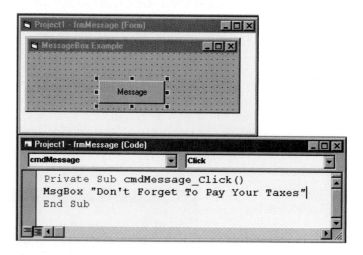

When the application runs, the following message box appears:

Figure 3.36
Message Box Displayed
from the Application

The message box we just demonstrated is the simplest of the ones provided by Visual Basic. You may have noticed that when you typed `MsgBox` and then a space, additional information appeared. This information serves as a guide for you to provide additional options to the `MsgBox` command. The first option is for the `Prompt`. The `Prompt` is the value that you typed to be displayed. The other items are optional ways of further modifying the message box displayed.

TIP

Items listed with [ ] around them are optional, while items like `Prompt` are mandatory because they are listed without brackets surrounding them.

There are too many options to list here, but by selecting different values, you can change the way your message box is displayed.

Figure 3.37
Message Box `Prompt`

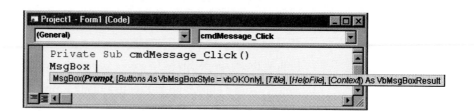

For instance, imagine if someone entered data that would cause a number to be divided by zero. Because computers cannot divide by zero, a good developer would check to see if this was about to occur. If it was, a good procedure is to indicate that a critical error has occurred in the execution of the application. This is preferable to actually attempting the illegal operation and getting an error message that is native to Visual Basic. You could use the following code:

```
MsgBox "Division By Zero Occurred", vbCritical
```

The following message box would be displayed:

Figure 3.38
Critical Message Box
Displaying Division By Zero
Message

Another option is to display a message box with an exclamation mark in the window. If you used the following code:

```
MsgBox "You Had Better Pay Your Taxes Now", vbExclamation
```

the following message box would be displayed:

Figure 3.39
Exclamation Message Box
Displaying Taxes Message

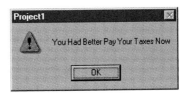

TIP

Notice that the message box automatically adjusts its size so that it holds the entire message. Just another useful feature Visual Basic has built in for you.

These are just a few examples. You should explore more options by checking the MSDN or by exploring the type ahead feature. Notice that if you have typed your commands up to and including the **vb** for the type of message box, a list appears from which you may choose. Try them out and see what happens. Most are self-explanatory.

Figure 3.40
Message Box Type Ahead
Showing Different Types of
Message Boxes

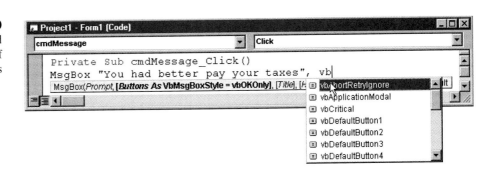

Adding a Title to the Message Box

You may not have noticed, but the previous message boxes had a title of `Project1` in the window's title bar. This is poor application development. By adding an additional parameter to the `MsgBox` statement, you can specify a title for the title bar of the message box. Observe the following code that will place the title `"Tax Message"` in your message box:

```
MsgBox "Don't Forget To Pay Your Taxes", vbOKOnly, "Tax
Message"
```

Figure 3.41
Message Box with Title

Key Words and Key Terms

Case sensitive
A language that considers variables spelled with different capitalization as separate variables.

Constant
A value that does not and cannot change during the execution of the program.

Currency
A variable datatype that stores a monetary value 15 digits to the left of the decimal and 4 digits to the right of the decimal.

Date
A variable datatype that stores a date.

Debugger
A utility in Visual Basic that allows programmers to step through their program and determine the source of an error.

Dim
Defines a variable with a scope local to the code it's declared within.

Double
A variable datatype that allows the storing of a decimal value with up to 14 digits of accuracy.

Integer
A variable datatype that allows the storing of an integer value between –32,768 and 32,767.

Long
A variable datatype that allows the storing of an integer value between –2,147,483,648 and 2,147,483,647.

Operator
A representation of an action that will be performed upon whatever operands are placed next to it.

Order of Precedence
The order in which the operations are performed when evaluating an expression.

Overflow
A run-time error occurs when one attempts to assign a value to a variable that is outside of the acceptable range for that variable type.

Public
Defines a variable that is visible throughout the entire application.

Run-time error

An error caused by the execution of the application.

Scope

The extent a variable or object is visible to the rest of the application.

Single

The smallest variable datatype that allows the storing of a decimal value with up to six digits of accuracy.

String

A variable datatype that allows the storing of a series of characters.

Variable

A way the computer stores a value in memory.

Variable name

The name to which a variable is referred from within the source code of the program.

Variable type

The classification of a variable so that Visual Basic knows how much space to allocate and how to operate upon it.

Variant

A datatype that allows any type of variable to be stored.

Answers to Chapter's Drills

Drill 3.1

1. The most appropriate variable datatype to store an hourly wage of an employee is a `Currency`. `Currency` is designed to store values that contain dollars and cents. An hourly wage would be specified in dollars and cents.

2. The most appropriate variable datatype to store an exam that has the lowest possible grade of 0 and highest grade of 100 would be an `Integer`. An `Integer`'s range is from –32,768 to 32,767. All the values between 0 and 100 are within the range of an `Integer`.

3. In order to figure out the answer for this, you need to calculate the range of the values the sum may be. The lowest possible sum would be if everyone got a zero; therefore the lower bound is 0. The highest possible sum is if everyone got a 100. Therefore, the upper bound is 5,000. Since all the values between 0 and 5,000 are within the range of an `Integer`, an `Integer` can be used to store this value.

4. In order to figure out the answer for this, you need to calculate the range of values the sum may be. The lowest possible sum would be if everyone got a zero; therefore the lower bound is 0. The highest possible sum is if everyone got a 100. Therefore, the upper bound is 50,000. Since all the values between 0 and 50,000 are not within the range of an `Integer`, an `Integer` cannot be used to store this value. However, a `Long` can be used, since its range is from –2,147,483,648 to 2,147,483,647.

5. In order to figure out the answer for this, you need to calculate the range of the values the sum may be. The lowest possible sum would be if everyone got a zero; therefore the lower bound is 0. The highest possible sum is if everyone got a 100. Therefore, the upper bound is 500,000. Since all the values between 0 and 500,000 are not within the range of an `Integer`, an `Integer` cannot be used to store this value. However, a `Long` can be used, since its range is from –2,147,483,648 to 2,147,483,647.

6. The expression you wish to store is non-numeric. It is a series of characters; therefore you would use a `String` variable.

7. Any day can be stored in a `Date` variable.

Drill 3.2

The code indicated would execute without an overflow error. The range of an `Integer` is –32,768 to 32,767. When you add 1 to –32,768 you get –32767, which is in the range.

Drill 3.3

The code indicated would execute without an overflow error. The range of an `Integer` is –32,768 to 32,767. The value you store in `IntegerVariable` is 30,000, which is within the bounds of an `Integer`.

Drill 3.4

The code indicated would produce an overflow error on the last assignment to `IntegerVariable`. You can add and subtract from an `Integer` as many times as you like as long as you do not exceed the lower or upper bounds of the `Integer`.

The initial value of `Integer` is 32,767. This is a valid value. Then you subtract 5 so the value assigned is 32,762. This is valid, so you continue. You then add 5 to get back to the original value. It's as if the two lines of code were never executed.

However, when you add 1 in the last line of code, you attempt to set the value to 32,768. This is out of range and you get an overflow error.

Drill 3.5

Determine which of the following variable names are valid:

1. `Moira` is a valid variable name. It starts with a letter and is followed by letters.
2. `Ben` is a valid variable name. It starts with a letter and is followed by letters.
3. `Moira&Ben` is not a valid variable name. It contains the `&` character, which is not allowed in variable names.
4. `Moira_Ben` is a valid variable name. It starts with a letter and is followed by a combination of letters and underscores.
5. `_MoiraBen` is not a valid variable name. It starts with an underscore, which is not allowed in variable names.
6. `IsThisLegal` is a valid variable name. It starts with a letter and is followed by only letters.
7. `HowAboutThis?` is not a valid variable name. It contains a question mark, which is not allowed in variable names.
8. `PrivateDancerWasTheNameOfASong` is a valid variable name. It contains only characters and although it is long, it does not contain more than 255 characters. Remember it is okay to use a keyword as part of a larger variable name.
9. `Private` is not a valid variable name. Although it contains only letters, it is one of the keywords defined in Visual Basic and may not be used as a variable name.

Drill 3.6

If `Option Explicit` were specified, the developer would have received an error message when he or she used the variable `DrillValue` without declaring it. Otherwise, if `Option Explicit` was not specified, when `DrillValue` was first used it would be declared as a `Variant`. Then when it was declared as a `String`, Visual Basic would produce an error `"Duplicate Declaration in current space"`, since it was trying to declare the same variable as a different type.

Remember that variables should always be declared before they are used.

Drill 3.7
4+5*6–3/3+6

The first calculation is **4+5*6–3/3+6**. Reading from left to right, the first calculation you compute is 5*6, because there are no parentheses and it is the first multiplication or division.

By replacing the 5*6 with 30, you rewrite the expression as **4+30–3/3+6**. Since there are no parentheses you evaluate the next multiplication or division that you see when reading from left to right. Reading from left to right, the next part of the expression to compute is 3/3.

By replacing 3/3 with 1, you rewrite the expression as **4+30–1+6**. Since no parentheses, multiplications, or divisions remain, the solution to the problem is a simple matter of adding and subtracting the numbers from left to right until you get the answer of 39.

(4+5)*6–(3/3+6)

The second calculation is **(4+5)*6–(3/3+6)**. Reading from left to right, the first calculation you compute is (4+5) because 4+5 is in the first set of parentheses found.

By replacing (4+5) with 9, you rewrite the initial expression as **9*6–(3/3+6)**. Reading from left to right, you must continue to compute the values in the remaining parentheses. Therefore, you must compute the entire expression (3/3 + 6) before you evaluate 9*6–. You start by computing 3/3 since it is the first multiplication or division inside the parentheses. Then you can rewrite the expression inside the parentheses as **(1+6)**. Adding the 1 to the 6 you get 7.

By replacing (3/3+6) with 7, you rewrite the initial expression as **9*6–7**. Since no more parentheses exist, you continue with the evaluation by computing the first multiplication or division found when reading from left to right. Therefore, the next calculation evaluated is 9*6.

By replacing (9*6) with 54, you rewrite the expression as **54–7**. The final answer is then calculated with a result of 47.

(4+5)/(1+2)

The third calculation is **(4+5)/(1+2)**. Reading from left to right you must compute the values in the parentheses first. The first expression evaluated is (4+5).

By replacing (4+5) with 9, you rewrite the expression as **9/(1+2)**. Since there still exists a set of parentheses, you must compute the expression inside the remaining parentheses, (1+2).

By replacing the (1+2) with 3, you rewrite the initial expression as 9/3. This leaves you with a simple division to calculate the final answer, 3.

4*5*(3+3)

The fourth calculation is 4*5*(3+3). Reading from left to right, you must compute the values in the parentheses first. You compute (3+3).

By replacing (3+3) with 6, you rewrite the initial expression as **4*5*6**. This is a simple series of multiplication that can be computed to get your final answer of 120.

2–2/2+2*2–3

The fifth calculation is **2–2/2+2*2–3**. Reading from left to right, since there are no parentheses, you compute the first multiplication or division you see. This would be 2/2.

By replacing 2/2 with 1, you rewrite the initial expression as **2–1+2*2–3**. You continue evaluating the expression by finding the next multiplication or division. This would be 2*2.

By replacing 2*2 with 4, you rewrite the initial expression as **2–1+4–3**. The remaining problem is a simple series of additions and subtractions to reach the final answer of 2.

Drill 3.8

The answer to the drill depends on whether you set the `Option Explicit` feature of Visual Basic. If `Option Explicit` is turned on, you will receive an error when you enter the `cmdAdd`'s `Click` event because `intDrillValue` has not been declared yet.

If the `Option Explicit` option is not turned on, Visual Basic will ignore that the variable has not been declared in the `Click` events of `cmdAdd` and `cmdOutput`. Because the variable was declared within the `cmdInitialize Click` event, it is only visible to the `cmdInitialize Click` event. Therefore, the other `Click` events do not see that you have initialized `intDrillValue` to 10. Instead, it uses Visual Basic's default initialization value of 0. This is a bad practice and should be avoided!

Drill 3.9

Unlike Drill 3.8, this drill declares `intDrillValue` in the General Declarations section of the form. Therefore, `intDrillValue` is visible to the entire form. When `cmdInitialize` is clicked, the value of `intDrillValue` is set to 10. This value is still 10 when `cmdAdd` is clicked. 10 is added to `intDrillValue` and stored back in `intDrillValue`. The value of `intDrillValue` is then 20. When `cmdOutput` is clicked, the value of `intDrillValue`, still 20, is displayed.

Drill 3.10

This drill is similar to Drill 3.9, however, the value of `intDrillValue` is never initialized. Therefore, the default value of `intDrillValue` is set to 0. This is a very bad practice and should be avoided. While the value 10 will be output, it is not the desired result.

Additional Exercises

1. Which of the following are valid variable names?
   a. `IsThisZValid?`
   b. `IfNotThisMustBeValid`
   c. `Go_Sixers!`
   d. `123456`
   e. `Dim`
   f. `HOW_ABOUT_ALL_CAPS`
   g. `Dimension`

2. True or False
   a. A variable is considered an operand.
   b. Basic operations in Visual Basic follow a different precedence than traditional mathematics.
   c. The user of the application can change a constant if extreme circumstances exist.
   d. A variable called `COOLNESS` and a variable called `coolness` are considered different variables due to the rules of case sensitivity in Visual Basic.
   e. An `Integer` datatype can store the value 0.
   f. An `Integer` datatype can store the value 50,000.
   g. An `Integer` datatype can store the value –1.1.
   h. The value 1234 is the same thing as the value "1234".

3. What is the value of the following expressions:
   a. $(1 + 8 / 2 + ((1 * 4) + (5 * 4)) / 4)$
   b. $((1 + 1 + 1 + 1) / 2 + (1 + 1 + 1) / 3)$
   c. $(5 * 5 + 5 / 5 + 6)$
   d. $(((3 + 4) + (4 * 7)) / 5)$
   e. $((3 * 6 * 7 * 2) + 12 / 2)$

4. Are the following expressions valid?

    a. $(3 + 4)$
    b. $(3 + 4) * 1$
    c. $4 (5 + 6)$
    d. $(5) * (5) * ((10))$
    e. $)(1 + 1)($
    f. $(5)(5)$

5. Which of the following datatypes will allow the storing of the number 40,000? List all the datatypes that apply:

    a. `Integer`   b. `Long`   c. `Single`   d. `Currency`   e. `Date`

6. By using `Option Explicit`, Visual Basic will enforce the industry standard naming conventions mentioned in this chapter. (True/False, if False, explain why.)

7. Declaring a variable with the _____ keyword will allow the entire application to use it and should be avoided.

    a. `Dim`   b. `Public`   c. `Variable`   d. `Constant`

8. A _____ is a useful tool to determine what is wrong with your application.

    a. Control   b. Debugger   c. Toolbox   d. Window

9. What is the value of `ExampleValue` after the following code is executed?

```
Dim ExampleValue As Date
ExampleValue = #1/31/01#
ExampleValue = ExampleValue + 5
```

10. Is there a difference between the value `#1/5/01#` and `"#1/5/01#"`? If so, what is it?

11. Write an application that will contain one text box, three labels, and a command button. The text box will allow the initial investment to be entered by the user. When the command button is clicked, have the application calculate the value of the investment after five years, assuming a 12% return on investment, and place it in one of the labels. The remaining label controls should indicate the purpose of the text box and result storing label.

12. Write an application that calculates a person's interest payment for a year. The application should contain three text boxes and a command button. The first text box should accept the amount of a person's debt. The second should accept the interest rate. When the command button is clicked, the third text box should output the amount of interest the person will pay in a year.

13. Write an application that will compute the volume of a pool. Include three text boxes to enter the height, width, and length of the pool. Include a command button that will compute the volume and store the result in a fourth text box. Finally label all of the text boxes. Volume is computed by multiplying the height, width, and length together.

14. Write an application that will compute the square footage of a home by allowing the user to enter the length and width of up to 10 rooms. Create a text box for each length and width to be entered. Also add labels so that the user of the application understands what the text boxes are used for. Finally add a command button that will calculate the square footage of each room and then sum the results to get the total square footage. This result should be displayed in another text box.

15. Write an application that calculates a student's GPA for a semester. The application should store up to five class grades (each has the same number of credits),

each in a separate text box. A grade can be a 0, 1, 2, 3, or 4. Output the student's overall average. Make sure that the program remembers decimal places in its calculation.

16. Write an application that calculates the discount amount for a store's products. The application should accept five sale prices and five retail prices for products that a store carries. Create a text box for each price. Also create a text box for each set of prices to store the discount amount of each product. Finally, create a command button that when clicked computes the discount of each item and places the result in the appropriate text box.

17. Modify the Counter application in this chapter so that it has an additional command button cmdDecrement. When clicked, cmdDecrement should reduce the value of the counter by one.

18. Modify the Counter application developed in assignment 17 so that it has an additional text box, txtValue. When the command buttons are clicked, instead of incrementing or decrementing by one, have it increment or decrement by the value stored in txtValue.

19. Write an application that displays the standings of a sport's team and all of the statistics that are associated with it. The application should have text boxes for five teams. Each team should have a text box for the Team's Name, Number of Wins, Number of Losses, and Winning Percentage. The first place team should have a text box for the Magic Number, while the remaining teams should have a text box for Games Back. Also include a command button to compute the necessary values.

   The application should allow the user to enter the Team's Name, Wins, and Losses. They should enter the First Place team first, Second Place team second, and so on. When the user clicks on the command button, it should compute the Winning Percentage, Games Back, and Magic Number.

   The Winning Percentage value is computed by dividing the number of wins by the total number of games played.

   The Games Back value is computed by subtracting the current team's wins from the first place team's wins and multiplying it by .5. Then subtract the number of losses of the first place team from the current team and multiply the result by .5. Add both results together to get the Games Back value.

   The Magic Number is the number of victories by the 1st place team or losses by the 2nd place required for the 1st place team to clinch the playoffs. In order to perform the calculation you must establish the total number of games. This should be a constant declared at the beginning of your application. In basketball, for instance, it's 82 games. You can compute the Magic Number by subtracting the number of Games Back of the 2nd place team from the number of games remaining for the first place team.

   Below is a sample of what the calculations might be:

Team	Wins	Losses	Winning Pct		
Sixers	31	10	0.756	36	Magic #
Knicks	26	15	0.634	5	Games Back
Heat	25	16	0.609	6	Games Back
Magic	22	18	0.55	8.5	Games Back
Hawks	20	20	0.5	10.5	Games Back

20. Write an application that contains four command buttons. Each command button should correspond to a direction: Up, Down, Left, and Right. When a command button is clicked, all the command buttons should move one space in the direction associated with that command button. Therefore, if the Left command button is clicked, each command button's `Left` property should have one subtracted from it.

INTERVIEW

An Interview with Adam Wartell

Adam Wartell is the Development Engineer for Pep Boys of Philadelphia, PA, an automotive retail and service company with centers nationwide. His responsibilities include Visual Basic programming, mentoring of lower-level programmers, and design and implementation of technical architecture. Adam also teaches part-time for Executrain of Philadelphia.

What brought you to Pep Boys?

I actually studied and trained to be an auto mechanic during my junior and senior years of high school. After working full-time in that field, I realized that getting greasy wasn't for me, so I worked toward a management position, went to school, and earned a degree in Specialized Computer Technology. My first position after graduating was as a software tester. It wasn't long before I decided that I wanted to program, so I worked hard, proved myself competent in programming, and got promoted to a programmer position. Since then, I've worked as a consultant on numerous projects for various clients, and now as a Development Engineer for Pep Boys. Ironic that I started my working career on one side of the auto service industry, now I'm on the other.

What kinds of projects are you currently working on?

I am currently working on a pricing system. It allows the user to store, view, edit and report on pricing of products. It is a three-tier application with the user interface and the business and data logic COM components all written in VB. The data is stored in a DB2 database running on a OS/390 mainframe. There are also stored procedures that handle some of the business & data logic.

How do you like working with VB?

Visual Basic 6.0 is the version of VB I have been using for over two years now. I have found it to be very powerful and easy to work with. For someone that does not know anything about programming, learning programming using VB makes it very easy. The context-sensitive help system is fantastic. A lot of what I have learned about VB came from reading the help documents. Features new to VB 6.0, such as the 'Auto List Members' that helps you enter code faster, and the Data Environment help make application development even easier.

How do you see VB evolving in your industry over the next few years?

I would have to say that Visual Basic will stay one of the top two development environments for a very long time. Because of its ease of use, and because it gets more powerful with each new version, it may become the top programming environment.

What advice do you have for students entering the computer field using VB?

Focus on COM and COM+. Also, as .NET becomes widely accepted, your focus should include it as well. Stay on top of the latest VB technologies, subscribe to a magazine or two that focus on VB and/or programming so you can keep up on what's hot.

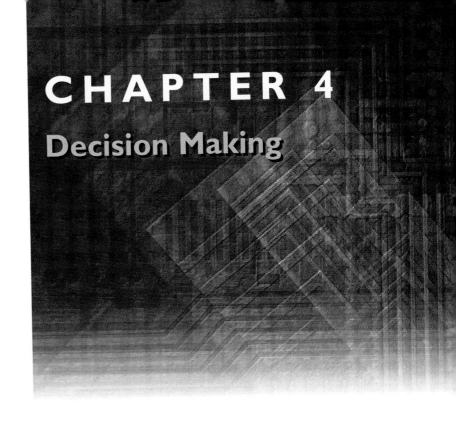

CHAPTER 4
Decision Making

Currently, your computer consists of a glorified calculator with simple input and output operations. A useful computer requires the capability to make decisions. The key to programming the computer to make correct decisions is making sure you understand how to represent and evaluate the expression representing the decision properly. Therefore, you will inspect the evaluation of the truthfulness of an expression in great detail. You will practice syntax by performing many non–real-world drills that are designed to reinforce the syntax of their evaluation and then introduce real-world applications to show their usefulness. Mastery of the evaluation of conditional expressions will also pay dividends when you study looping statements in future chapters, so your time will be well spent.

4.1   If Statements

You are all familiar with the concept of making a decision. When driving a car, you have to make decisions all the time. When you drive up to a light, you decide if it is red to stop the car.

Graphically it would look as follows:

Figure 4.1
Graphical Representation of
Driving a Car

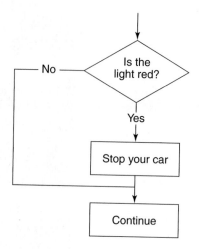

Visual Basic offers more than one way for decisions to be made. Each has its purpose in modeling the way a decision is made. The simplest, which matches the idea of a single decision to a single result, is the **If** statement.

You can program an `If` statement by using the following code that illustrates its syntax:

```
If (Expression) Then
    Program statements to execute if expression is true
End If
```

An `If` statement consists of an expression that determines whether a program statement or statements execute. An expression can be the comparison of two values. To compare values you may use any of the following operators:

<	Less than
>	Greater than
<=	Less than or equal to
>=	Greater than or equal to
=	Equal to
<>	Not equal to

By placing either a variable or constant value on both sides of the operator, an expression can be evaluated to either **True** or **False**. Here are some sample expressions that evaluate to `True`:

```
1 = 1
2 >= 1
2 >= 2
1 <= 2
1 < 2
1 <> 2
"a" <> "c"
"A" <> "a"
"D" = "D"
```

Here are some sample expressions that evaluate to `False`:

1 = 2
2 <= 1
2 < 2
3 > 4
1 >= 2
1 <> 1
"a" = "A"
"D" <> "D"

When the condition in an `If` statement evaluates to `True`, the statement(s) immediately following it is executed until an **End If** statement is reached. If the `If` statement evaluates to `False`, the statements immediately after it, until the `End If`, are not executed.

DRILL 4.1

Indicate whether each expression evaluates to `True` or `False`.

```
1  (5 >= 4)
2  (-3 < -4)
3  (5 = 4)
4  (5 <> 4)
5  (4 >= 4)
6  (4 <= 4)
```

Example: Check for Yes Entered By User

By using an `If` statement, you can determine if the value that is entered in a text box is equal to the value you desire. See the following code as an example that compares the text box contents to the `String` `"Yes"`. The code assumes that a command button `cmdIf` has been created to place the code and two text boxes `txtInput` and `txtOutput` (both with their `Text` property empty) were created to hold the input and output.

```
Private Sub cmdIf_Click()

If (txtInput.Text = "Yes") Then
    txtOutput.Text = "This will output, because the user entered Yes"
End If

End Sub
```

What do you think would be contained in `txtOutput`:

1 If the user enters "Yes" in the `txtInput` text box?
2 If the user enters "No" in the `txtInput` text box?

Example with "Yes" Entered in txtInput   When the program is executed and the command button is clicked, the `If` statement is evaluated. If the user enters `"Yes"`, the `If` statement evaluates the expression by comparing `"Yes"` to `"Yes"`, and the conditional expression will evaluate to `True`. Therefore, all the statements until the `End If` are executed. So, the text `"This will output, because the user entered Yes"` is placed in the `txtOutput` text box.

Example with "No" Entered in txtInput   When the program is executed and the command button is clicked, the `If` statement is evaluated. If the user enters `"No"`, the `If` statement evaluates the expression by comparing `"No"` to `"Yes"`, and the conditional expression will evaluate to `False`. Therefore, none of the statements before the `End If` are executed. So, no action is taken by the application and the `txtOutput` text box remains empty. It is important to note that any value other than `"Yes"` will produce no output in the `txtOutput` text box.

Example: Simple If with Code Following It

Here is another example using the same application. The only change that you have made is that you have added a concatenation statement after the `If` statement. The code follows:

```
Private Sub cmdIf_Click()

If (txtInput.Text = "Yes") Then
    txtOutput.Text = "This will output, because the user
entered Yes"
End If

txtOutput.Text = txtOutput.Text & " and this is here as well"

End Sub
```

What do you think would be contained in `txtOutput`:

1 If the user enters "Yes" in the `txtInput` text box?
2 If the user enters "No" in the `txtInput` text box?

Example with "Yes" Entered in txtInput   If the user enters a `"Yes"` in the `txtInput` text box, the output would be as follows:

```
This will output, because the user entered Yes and this is
here as well
```

> **TIP**
>
> The & operator will concatenate strings together so they combine to be one string containing both values.

Both expressions are concatenated; the statement within the `If` statement is executed because (`txtInput.Text = "Yes"`) evaluates to `True` as before and the second statement executed because it is not in the `If` statement, and therefore always executes.

Drills 4.2, 4.3, 4.4, and 4.5 use the sample application as in the previous example.

Example with "No" Entered in txtInput   However, if the user enters a value other than `"Yes"` in the `txtInput` text box, the output would be as follows:

```
and this is here as well
```

When the value stored in `txtInput` is anything other than `"Yes"`, then (`txtInput.Text = "Yes"`) evaluates to `False` and the first assignment to the `txtOutput` text box is not performed. However, since the second statement has nothing to do with the `If` statement, it is executed as before.

DRILL 4.2

Given the following code:

```
Private Sub cmdIf_Click()
Dim intUserValue As Integer

intUserValue = Val(txtInput.Text)

If (intUserValue > 2) Then
    txtOutput.Text = "The first statement prints"
End If
txtOutput.Text = txtOutput.Text & " and the second statement prints"
End Sub
```

What do you think would be contained in txtOutput:

1 If the user enters 1 in the txtInput text box?
2 If the user enters 2 in the txtInput text box?
3 If the user enters 3 in the txtInput text box?

DRILL 4.3

Given the following code:

```
Private Sub cmdIf_Click()
Dim intUserValue As Integer

intUserValue = Val(txtInput.Text)

If (intUserValue < 2) Then
    txtOutput.Text = "The first statement prints"
End If
txtOutput.Text = txtOutput.Text & " and the second statement prints"
End Sub
```

What do you think would be contained in txtOutput:

1 If the user enters 1 in the txtInput text box?
2 If the user enters 2 in the txtInput text box?
3 If the user enters 3 in the txtInput text box?

DRILL 4.4

Given the following code:

```
Private Sub cmdIf_Click()
Dim intUserValue As Integer

intUserValue = Val(txtInput.Text)

If (intUserValue >= 2) Then
    txtOutput.Text = "The first statement prints"
End If
txtOutput.Text = txtOutput.Text & " and the second statement prints"
End Sub
```

What do you think would be contained in txtOutput:

1 If the user enters 1 in the txtInput text box?
2 If the user enters 2 in the txtInput text box?
3 If the user enters 3 in the txtInput text box?

DRILL 4.5

Given the following code:

```
Private Sub cmdIf_Click()
Dim intUserValue As Integer

intUserValue = Val(txtInput.Text)

If (intUserValue <= 2) Then
    txtOutput.Text = "The first statement prints"
End If
txtOutput.Text = txtOutput.Text & " and the second statement prints"
End Sub
```

What do you think would be contained in txtOutput:

1 If the user enters 1 in the txtInput text box?
2 If the user enters 2 in the txtInput text box?
3 If the user enters 3 in the txtInput text box?

Example: In Stock?

Now that you understand the basic operations of If statements, let's write your first application where a decision is required. The application will ask the user to enter the amount of a product a company has on hand. If the number is greater than 0, the program outputs that the item is "In Stock". Otherwise, it outputs that the item is "Sold Out".

It will require creating a form with a text box, txtStockAmount, to store the amount of a product a company has; a label with the Caption property set to

"Amount in Stock", another label lblInStock to hold a message, and a command button with the Caption property set to "Calculate". This can be seen in the following figure:

Figure 4.2
In-Stock Application

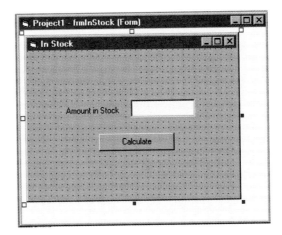

Attached to the command button is the following code.

Figure 4.3
Code for In-Stock
Application

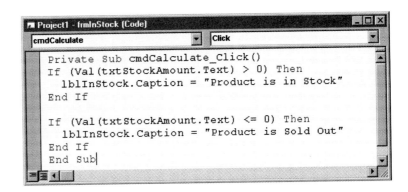

```
Private Sub cmdCalculate_Click()
If (Val(txtStockAmount.Text) > 0) Then
    lblInStock.Caption = "Product is in Stock"
End If

If (Val(txtStockAmount.Text) <= 0) Then
    lblInStock.Caption = "Product is Sold Out"
End If
End Sub
```

The code of the program compares the number entered by the user to zero. If it is greater than zero, the message "Product is in Stock" is displayed. Then the value is compared to see if it is less than or equal to zero. If so, then the message "Product is Sold Out" is displayed.

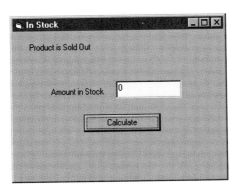

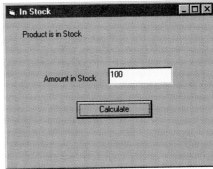

Figure 4.4   Sold-Out Output   **Figure 4.5**   In-Stock Output

Visual Basic .NET Alert

While variables could be declared within the `If` statement and still function properly, this will not be true in Visual Basic .NET and should be avoided. All variables should be declared at the beginning of the routine they are used in.

Example: Expenses?

Let's write a program that outputs the difference between the amount of your income versus the amount of your expenses, as well as printing a message that indicates whether or not you are spending more than you are making.

First, you must create a form that has three text boxes: `txtIncome`, `txtExpenses`, and `txtDifference`. Each should have a label above it indicating what is stored in the text box: `Income`, `Expenses`, and `Difference`, respectively. Additionally, you need a label above the other controls large enough to hold your output message. Finally, you need a command button to calculate the difference and output the message. This can be seen in the following form:

Figure 4.6
Income/Expense Form

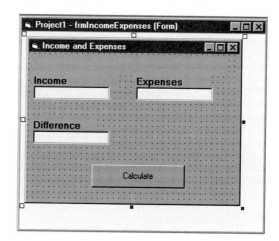

The code for the `Calculate` command button is as follows:

Figure 4.7
Code for Income/Expense
Command Button

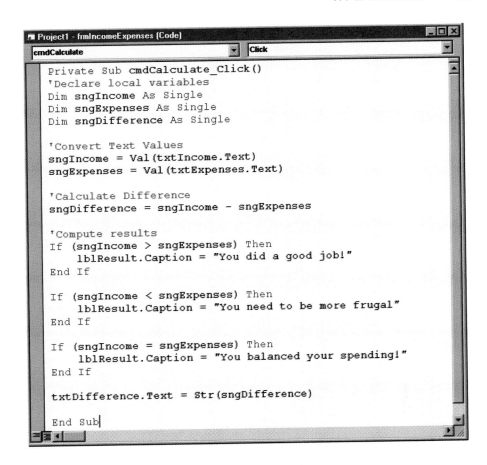

```
Private Sub cmdCalculate_Click()
'Declare local variables
Dim sngIncome As Single
Dim sngExpenses As Single
Dim sngDifference As Single

'Convert Text Values
sngIncome = Val(txtIncome.Text)
sngExpenses = Val(txtExpenses.Text)

'Calculate Difference
sngDifference = sngIncome - sngExpenses

'Compute results
If (sngIncome > sngExpenses) Then
    lblResult.Caption = "You did a good job!"
End If

If (sngIncome < sngExpenses) Then
    lblResult.Caption = "You need to be more frugal"
End If

If (sngIncome = sngExpenses) Then
    lblResult.Caption = "You balanced your spending!"
End If

txtDifference.Text = Str(sngDifference)

End Sub
```

The code is straightforward. First you declare the local variables that you will need. Then you initialize them to the values from the text boxes and a simple calculation.

The values in the local variables are evaluated using three conditional statements. Each is used to check a specific condition.

The first condition checks whether the income entered is a larger number than the expenses entered. If so, the label `lblResult` is set to the value `"You did a good job!"`

Whether the first condition is evaluated to `True` or `False`, the second condition is now checked. It checks to see if the income entered is a smaller number than the expenses entered. If so, the label `lblResult` is set to the value `"You need to be more frugal."`

Regardless of the results of the first two `If` statements, the third condition is checked. It checks to see if the income entered is equal to the expenses entered. If so, the label `lblResult` is set to the value `"You balanced your spending!"`

Finally, the `sngDifference` is converted to a `String` and copied to the `txtDifference` text box.

The code could also have been written by comparing the difference between the difference of the income and expenses to 0. This can be seen in the following code. It illustrates the fact that there are many different ways to solve the same problem.

Figure 4.8
Alternative Code for
Command Button

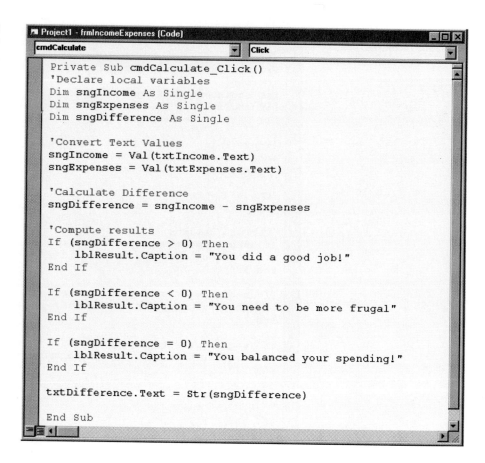

```vb
Private Sub cmdCalculate_Click()
'Declare local variables
Dim sngIncome As Single
Dim sngExpenses As Single
Dim sngDifference As Single

'Convert Text Values
sngIncome = Val(txtIncome.Text)
sngExpenses = Val(txtExpenses.Text)

'Calculate Difference
sngDifference = sngIncome - sngExpenses

'Compute results
If (sngDifference > 0) Then
    lblResult.Caption = "You did a good job!"
End If

If (sngDifference < 0) Then
    lblResult.Caption = "You need to be more frugal"
End If

If (sngDifference = 0) Then
    lblResult.Caption = "You balanced your spending!"
End If

txtDifference.Text = Str(sngDifference)

End Sub
```

Example: Voting Booth Application

With all the commotion surrounding the 2000 presidential election, you decided to develop a better voting machine. Throughout the next two chapters you will develop a number of voting booth applications. You will see how, as you learn more commands and controls in the Visual Basic language, you will be able to improve the accuracy of the voting machine. Maybe you'll be able to sell it to Florida.

Your first application will allow the voter to enter the name of the person he or she wishes to vote for and then add one to that person's counter. You will have one counter for Bush, Gore, and Nader. You will create a text box that will accept the name of the person to vote for and a command button to process the actual vote. Additionally, you will add a results command button that will display the final results of the election. Just think, no hand counts!

See the following figure as to what your application should look like:

Figure 4.9
Sketch of Application

The Coach Voting Booth

Enter the name of the candidate you wish to cast your vote for

Vote	Results

To develop this application, start with a blank form and perform the following steps.

Add Identification for Project and Form

Step 1: Set the project's Name property to TextBoxBasedVotingBooth.

Step 2: Set the Name property of the form to frmVoting.

Step 3: Set the Caption property of the form to TextBox Based Voting Booth.

Add Variable Declarations and Initialization

Step 1: Insert the following code to the General Declarations section of the form.

Figure 4.10
Declarations of Variables for Application

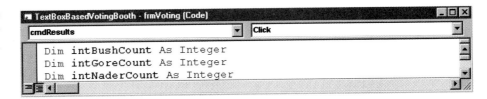

Step 2: Add the following code to the form's Load event so that the variables are initialized.

Figure 4.11
Initialization of Variables

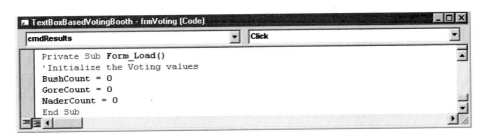

TIP

While it is not necessary to initialize variables to 0, it is a good practice to observe.

Add Title Label

Step 1: Place a label control across the top of the form.

Step 2: Set the Name property to lblTitle.

Step 3: Set the Caption property to The Coach Voting Booth.

Step 4: Set the Font property to a Size of 18 and a Style of Bold.

Step 5: Set the Alignment property to Center.

Figure 4.12
Form with Initial Label on It

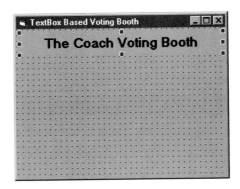

Add Instructions Label

Step 1: Place a label control below the previous one.

Step 2: Set the `Name` property to `lblDirections`.

Step 3: Set the `Caption` property to `"Enter the name of the candidate you wish to cast your vote for"`.

Figure 4.13
Form with Instructions on It

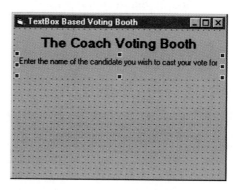

Add Results Label

Step 1: Place a label control at the bottom of the form. Make sure it is large enough to display all election results.

Step 2: Set the `Name` property to `lblResults`.

Step 3: Clear the `Caption` property.

Figure 4.14
Form with Results Label
Added to It

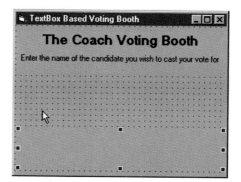

Add Voting Text Box

Step 1: Place a text box control below the directions label.

Step 2: Set the `Name` property to `txtVote`.

Step 3: Clear out the default value from the `Text` property.

Figure 4.15
Form with Text Box
Added to It

Add Vote Button

Step 1: Place a command button control in the left side of the form, below the text box.

Step 2: Set the Name property to cmdVote.

Step 3: Set the Caption property to Vote.

Step 4: Double-click on the command button.

Step 5: Attach the code to process the vote. It must add one to the appropriate variable that stores the number of votes for each person.

Figure 4.16
Form with the cmdVote
Command Button Added

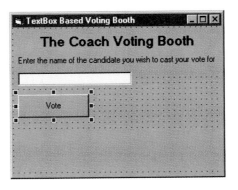

Figure 4.17
Code for the cmdVote
Command Button

```
Private Sub cmdVote_Click()
If (txtVote.Text = "Bush") Then
    intBushCount = intBushCount + 1
End If
If (txtVote.Text = "Gore") Then
    intGoreCount = intGoreCount + 1
End If
If (txtVote.Text = "Nader") Then
    intNaderCount = intNaderCount + 1
End If

'Erase the vote
txtVote.Text = ""
End Sub
```

The code in the cmdVote command button checks the value entered in the txtVote text box against the three valid choices for a vote. If it finds one of the valid choices, it adds one to the appropriate total variable. Then it clears the txtVote text box so that the next voter does not know for whom the previous vote was cast.

Add Results Button

Step 1: Place a command button control to the right of the other command button.

Step 2: Set the Name property to cmdResults.

Step 3: Set the Caption property to Results.

Step 4: Double-click on the command button.

Step 5: Attach the code to display the results of the election in the label control lblResults.

Figure 4.18
Form with the cmdResults
Command Button Added

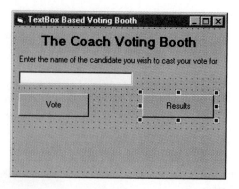

Figure 4.19
Code for the cmdResults
Command Button

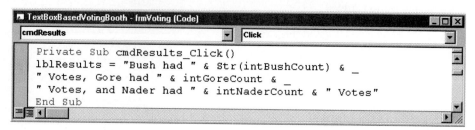

The code for the **cmdResults** command button formats the results of the election using the & operator. It is then set to the label **lblResults** for display.

TIP

When a line of code is too long to fit on a single line, you can place an underscore character at the end of the line and continue your code on the next line. Be aware that the underscore should have a space in front of it.

Visual Basic .NET Alert

While in Visual Basic 6.0 you can use a continuation with a comment, this will not be supported in Visual Basic .NET and should be avoided.

What's Wrong With Our Application?   The voting system you have developed is problematic for a number of reasons. First, it allows only three options to vote for. No way exists to enter choices other than the three. Second, if the name is entered in any variation of a proper spelling of the names other than the one in the **If** statement, then it will be ignored. Finally, the program is inefficient because if the vote is for Bush, it still checks the other options. You will develop future versions of the Voting Booth application that deal with each of these issues.

4.2 **Else and ElseIf Statements**

The previous examples were chosen because they did not require something to be performed when the condition in the `If` statement evaluated to `False`. One could get around this by skillfully crafting additional `If` statements that have the opposite condition listed. However, that would not only add unneeded complexity, but it would also slow the execution of the code.

In the real world, situations are much more complex than just checking if a condition is true and then responding with the appropriate action. For instance, if you are driving a car and you approach a light, if it is red, you stop. If it is yellow, you prepare to stop; otherwise you go.

Graphically it would look as follows:

Figure 4.20
`Else/ElseIf` Flow Chart

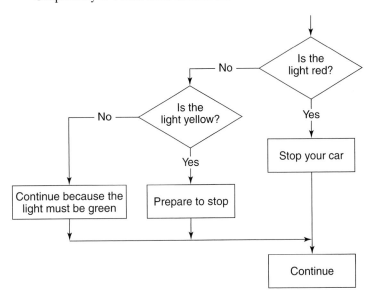

This type of situation occurs quite frequently in programming. You already saw in the Election Booth application that the use of repetitive `If` statements can be inefficient. Therefore, Visual Basic provides the **Else** and **ElseIf** keywords to handle these cases.

When an `If` statement's expression evaluates to `False`, the next `ElseIf` condition is evaluated. If is it evaluates to `True`, the statement(s) directly after it are executed. Otherwise, any additional `ElseIf` statements are evaluated in the same fashion. After all `ElseIf` statements are evaluated, if they all evaluate to `False` and an `Else` statement is included, the statement(s) directly following the `Else` keyword will be executed.

```
If (Condition) Then
     Do Something
ElseIf (Condition 2) Then
     Do Something Else
ElseIf (Condition 3) Then
     Do Something Else
...
Else
     Do Something Else
End If
```

Simple Examples   The code assumes that a command button, `cmdIfElse`, has been created to place the code and two text boxes, `txtInput` and `txtOutput` (both with their `Text` property empty), were created to hold the input and output.

Example: Improved Check for Yes Entered By User

The following code will compare the input by the user to the String "Yes". If the user enters "Yes", the code will set the txtOutput to a String indicating so; otherwise another String will be assigned to the text box.

See the following code:

```
Private Sub cmdIfElse_Click()
Dim intUserValue As Integer

intUserValue = Val(txtInput.Text)

If (txtInput.Text = "Yes") Then
    txtOutput.Text = "The user answered the question with a Yes"
Else
    txtOutput.Text "The user did not answer the question with a Yes"
End If
End Sub
```

When the program is executed and the command button is clicked, the If statement is evaluated. If the user enters "Yes", the If statement evaluates the expression by comparing "Yes" to "Yes", the conditional expression will evaluate to True. All the statements until the Else are executed. Therefore, the text "The user answered the question with a Yes" is placed in the text box. Since the conditional expression in the If statement evaluated to True, none of the statements after the Else statement are executed.

If the user does not enter "Yes", then the conditional expression will evaluate to False. All the statements until the Else are *not* executed. Instead the statements after the Else statement and before the End If statement are executed. Therefore, the text "The user did not answer the question with a Yes" is placed in the text box.

Example: Calculate if a Discount Will Be Applied

The following code will compute whether a discount should be applied to a purchase. If the purchase is more than $100, the code will place "DISCOUNT" in txtOutput. Otherwise, the code will place "FULL PRICE" in the text box.

See the following code:

```
Private Sub cmdIfElse_Click()
Dim curPurchasePrice As Currency

curPurchasePrice = Val(txtInput.Text)

If (curPurchasePrice > 100) Then
    txtOutput.Text = "DISCOUNT"
Else
    txtOutput.Text "FULL PRICE"
End If
End Sub
```

What do you think would be contained in txtOutput:

1 If the user enters 199.95 in the txtInput text box?
2 If the user enters 99.95 in the txtInput text box?

Example with 199.95 Entered in txtInput   When the program is executed and the command button is clicked, the `If` statement is evaluated. If the user enters any value greater than 100, the `If` statement evaluates the expression by comparing the value entered to 100, and the conditional expression will evaluate to `True`. Therefore, the statements until the `Else` would be executed. Since the user entered 199.95, the condition evaluates to `True` and the text `"DISCOUNT"` is placed in the text box. Additionally, none of the statements after the `Else` statement are executed.

Example with 99.95 Entered in txtInput   If the user enters a value less than or equal to 100, then the conditional expression will evaluate to `False`. Therefore, all the statements until the `Else` are *not* executed. Instead the statements after the `Else` statement and before the `End If` statement are executed. Since the user entered 99.95, the text `"FULL PRICE"` is placed in the text box.

DRILL 4.6

Using the same application, but changing the code in the command button as follows, what do you think the output would be if the value entered by the user is 0, 1, and then 2, respectively?

```
Private Sub cmdIfElse_Click()
Dim intDrillValue As Integer

intDrillValue = Val(txtInput.Text)

If (intDrillValue <= 1) Then
    txtOutput.Text = "This will output, because intDrillValue <= 1"
Else
    txtOutput.Text = "Instead this outputs, because intDrillValue > 1"
End If
txtOutput.Text = txtOutput.Text & " and this is here as well"
End Sub
```

DRILL 4.7

Using the same application, but changing the code in the command button as follows, what do you think the output would be if the value entered by the user is 0, 1, and then 2, respectively?

```
Private Sub cmdIfElse_Click()
Dim intDrillValue As Integer

intDrillValue = Val(txtInput.Text)

If (intDrillValue < 1) Then
    txtOutput.Text = "This will output, because intDrillValue < 1"
Else
    txtOutput.Text = "Instead this outputs, because intDrillValue >= 1"
End If
    txtOutput.Text = txtOutput.Text & " and this is here as well"
End Sub
```

Example: Calculate Varying Discount

The code assumes that a command button, cmdIfElseIfElse, has been created to place the code and two text boxes, txtInput and txtOutput (both with their Text property empty), were created to hold the input and output.

The code will compute how much of a discount should be applied to a purchase. If the purchase is more than $100, the discount should be 5%. However, if the purchase price is more than $500, the discount should be 10%. The code should place the amount of the discount in the txtOutput text box. If no discount is applied, then place the String "NO DISCOUNT" in the text box. The code follows:

```
Private Sub cmdIfElseIfElse_Click()
Dim curPurchasePrice As Currency

curPurchasePrice = Val(txtInput.Text)

If (curPurchasePrice > 500) Then
    txtOutput.Text = Str(curPurchasePrice*.10)
ElseIf (curPurchasePrice > 100) Then
    txtOutput.Text = Str(curPurchasePrice*.05)
Else
    txtOutput.Text = "NO DISCOUNT"
End If
End Sub
```

What do you think would be contained in txtOutput:

1 If the user enters 600.00 in the txtInput text box?
2 If the user enters 250.00 in the txtInput text box?
3 If the user enters 50.00 in the txtInput text box?

Example with 600.00 Entered by the User   When the program is executed and the command button is clicked, the If statement is evaluated. If the user enters a 600.00, then the If statement evaluates the expression by comparing the value entered to 500. Therefore, the conditional expression will evaluate to True. This causes all the statements until the ElseIf to be executed. Therefore, the purchase price is multiplied by .10 and the result is converted to a String. So, the value "60" is placed in the text box. Since the conditional expression in the If statement evaluated to True, none of the statements after the ElseIf or Else statements and before the End If are executed.

Example with 250.00 Entered by the User   If the user enters a value that is less than or equal to 500, the initial conditional expression will evaluate to False. Therefore, the second condition will be evaluated in the ElseIf statement. The ElseIf condition compares 250.00 to 100, and the conditional expression evaluates to True. This causes all the statements until the Else to be executed. Therefore, the purchase price is multiplied by .05 and the result is converted to a String. So, the value "12.5" is placed in the text box. Since the conditional expression in the If statement evaluated to True, none of the statements after the ElseIf or Else statements and before the End If are executed.

Example with 50.00 Entered by the User   Finally, if the user enters a value less than or equal to 100, neither the If or ElseIf conditional expressions evaluate to True. Therefore, the statements after the Else statement and before the End If statement are executed.

So, the text "NO DISCOUNT" is placed in the text box.

DRILL 4.8

Assume that the code for the previous example was instead coded as follows:

```
Private Sub cmdIfElseIfElse_Click()
Dim curPurchasePrice As Currency

curPurchasePrice = Val(txtInput.Text)

If (curPurchasePrice > 100) Then
    txtOutput.Text = Str(curPurchasePrice*.05)
ElseIf (curPurchasePrice > 500) Then
    txtOutput.Text = Str(curPurchasePrice*.10)
Else
    txtOutput.Text = "NO DISCOUNT"
End If
End Sub
```

What do you think would be contained in txtOutput:

1 If the user enters 600.00 in the txtInput text box?
2 If the user enters 250.00 in the txtInput text box?
3 If the user enters 50.00 in the txtInput text box?

DRILL 4.9

The code assumes that a command button, cmdIfElseIfElse, has been created to place the code and two text boxes, txtInput and txtOutput (both with their Text property empty), were created to hold the input and output.

```
Private Sub cmdIfElseIfElse_Click()
Dim intDrillValue As Integer

intDrillValue = Val(txtInput.Text)

If (intDrillValue > 0) Then
    txtOutput.Text = "The number is positive"
ElseIf (intDrillValue < 0) Then
    txtOutput.Text = "The number is negative"
Else
    txtOutput.Text = "I got a big zero"
End If

End Sub
```

What do you think would be contained in txtOutput:

1 If the user enters –1 in the txtInput text box?
2 If the user enters 0 in the txtInput text box?
3 If the user enters 1 in the txtInput text box?

Letter Grade Program   Let's write a program that will display a letter grade based on a number grade entered. The program should assign an A if the grade is greater than or equal to 90, assign a B if the grade is between 80 and 89, assign a C if the grade is between 70 and 79, or assign a D if the grade is between 60 and 69. Otherwise the program assigns an F.

The application should look as follows:

Figure 4.21
Sketch of Application

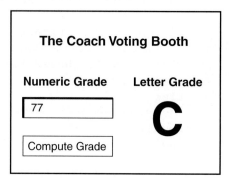

The steps to create it are as follows:

Add Identification for Project and Form

Step 1: Set the project's `Name` property to `Grader`.
Step 2: Set the `Name` property of the form to `frmGrader`.
Step 3: Set the `Caption` property of the form to `Grade Giver`.

Add Title Label

Step 1: Place a label control across the top of the form.
Step 2: Set the `Name` property to `lblTitle`.
Step 3: Set the `Caption` property to `The Coach Grade Giver`.
Step 4: Set the `Font` property to a Size of 18 and a Style of Bold.
Step 5: Set the `Alignment` property to `Center`.

Figure 4.22
Form with Title Label
Added to It

Add Numeric Grade Label

Step 1: Place a label control near the left side of the form.
Step 2: Set the `Name` property to `lblNumericGrade`.
Step 3: Set the `Caption` property to `Numeric Grade`.
Step 4: Set the `Font` property to a Size of 14 and a Style of Bold.

Figure 4.23
Form with Numeric Grade
Label Added to It

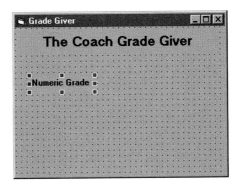

Add Voting Text Box

Step 1: Place a text box control below the label.
Step 2: Set the Name property to txtGrade.
Step 3: Clear out the default value from the Text property.

Figure 4.24
Form with txtGrade Text
Box Added to It

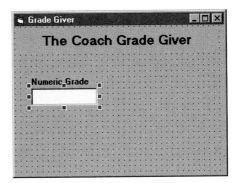

Add Letter Grade Label

Step 1: Place a label control near the right side of the form.
Step 2: Set the Name property to lblLetterGradeTitle.
Step 3: Set the Caption property to Letter Grade.
Step 4: Set the Font property to a Size of 14 and a Style of Bold.

Figure 4.25
Form with Letter Grade
Label Added to It

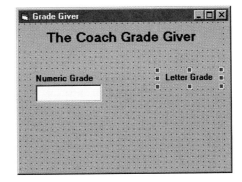

Add lblGrade Label

Step 1: Place a label control near the right side of the form.
Step 2: Set the Name property to lblGrade.
Step 3: Clear the Caption property.
Step 4: Set the Font property to a Size of 48 and a Style of Bold.
Step 5: Set the Alignment property to Center.

Figure 4.26
Form with the `lblGrade`
Label Added

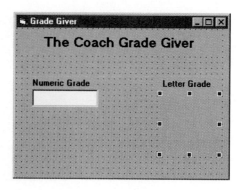

Add Compute Grade Button

Step 1: Place a command button control in the bottom left side of the form.

Step 2: Set the `Caption` property to `Compute Grade`.

Step 3: Set the `Name` property to `cmdCompute`.

Step 4: Double-click on the command button.

Step 5: Attach the code to display the results of the grade calculation in the label control `lblGrade`.

Figure 4.27
Form with `cmdCompute`
Command Button
added to It

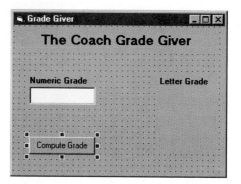

Figure 4.28
Code for `cmdCompute`
Command Button

```
Private Sub CmdCompute_Click()
Dim intGrade As Integer ' Declare temporary variable

intGrade = Val(txtGrade.Text) 'Convert user input to an Integer

'Compute Grade
If (intGrade >= 90) Then
    lblGrade.Caption = "A"
ElseIf (intGrade >= 80) Then
    lblGrade.Caption = "B"
ElseIf (intGrade >= 70) Then
    lblGrade.Caption = "C"
ElseIf (intGrade >= 60) Then
    lblGrade.Caption = "D"
Else
    lblGrade.Caption = "F"
End If

End Sub
```

Note that in this example, without the `ElseIf` it would be difficult, given what you know so far, to construct a simple `If` statement program that printed the desired letter grade for a numerical grade.

The code in the command button is simple. It converts the user's input to an `Integer`. The converted grade is then compared to 90. Any grade greater than or equal to 90 causes the letter A to be assigned to the label control `lblGrade`. The rest of the conditions are not checked. If the grade is not greater than or equal to 90, it must be less than 90. Therefore, when you have a grade in the 80s, the first `ElseIf` statement is enough to check for a B. Similarly, you check for a C and D. Finally, if the grade is not greater than or equal to a 60, you output an F.

Example: Improved Voting Booth

Earlier we indicated that there were a few problems with the existing voting machine. Two of them we will address with an improved Voting Booth application. Your new application will take advantage of `ElseIf` and `Else` statements to total the votes more efficiently as well as keep a total of the improper votes. Remember the 10,000, supposed undervotes in Florida? Well now you can track them. Aside from curiosity's sake, there is an important reason to track them. A good voting machine should prevent mistakes from ever being entered. Therefore, one way to judge the relative worth of a voting booth would be to calculate the number of errors that are produced when using it.

The application will look relatively the same. The only visible difference will be the addition of the display of the number of improper votes being cast. This can be seen in the following figure:

Figure 4.29
Voting Booth Application
with Results

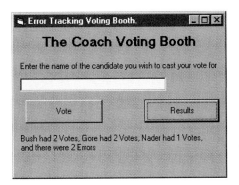

TIP

You could choose to use a message box to display the results. This will be an assignment at the end of the chapter.

Add Identification for Project and Form

Step 1: Set the project's `Name` property to `ErrorTrackingVotingBooth`.
Step 2: Set the `Name` property of the form to `frmVoting`.
Step 3: Set the `Caption` property of the form to `Error Tracking Voting Booth`.

Modify the Application's Code

You must modify the four code snippets associated with this application. The new code must first declare an additional variable to hold the number of errors encountered.

Then you must make sure that you initialize that variable to 0 as you did with the other variables. This is seen in the following figures:

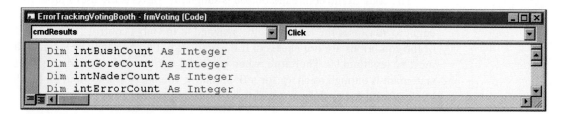

```
ErrorTrackingVotingBooth - frmVoting (Code)
cmdResults                               Click

    Dim intBushCount As Integer
    Dim intGoreCount As Integer
    Dim intNaderCount As Integer
    Dim intErrorCount As Integer
```

Figure 4.30   Variable Declaration for New Voting Application

```
ErrorTrackingVotingBooth - frmVoting (Code)
Form                                     Load

    Private Sub Form_Load()
    'Initialize the Voting values
    intBushCount = 0
    intGoreCount = 0
    intNaderCount = 0
    intErrorCount = 0
    End Sub
```

Figure 4.31   Initialize the Variables to 0

Next, you need to modify the command button `cmdVote` so that it will use `ElseIf` and `Else` statements to process the vote efficiently and so that it now records the number of errors by using the `Else` statement.

```
ErrorTrackingVotingBooth - frmVoting (Code)
Form                                     Load

    Private Sub cmdVote_Click()
    If (txtVote.Text = "Bush") Then
       intBushCount = intBushCount + 1
    ElseIf (txtVote.Text = "Gore") Then
       intGoreCount = intGoreCount + 1
    ElseIf (txtVote.Text = "Nader") Then
       intNaderCount = intNaderCount + 1
    Else
       intErrorCount = intErrorCount + 1
    End If

    'Erase the vote
    txtVote.Text = ""
    End Sub
```

Figure 4.32   Code for the `CmdVote` Command Button

Finally, you need to modify the command button `cmdResults` so that it will display the additional information. It is shown in the following figure:

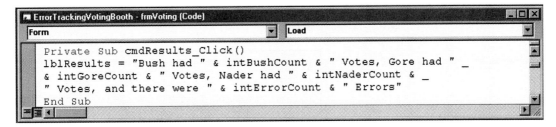

Figure 4.33   Code for `cmdResults` Command Button

4.3   Compound Conditional Statements

Sometimes comparisons are not as simple as a single comparison. For instance, what happens if, while driving your car, you go through a red light? The answer depends. If you go through the light and it is red and another car is in the intersection, an accident occurs. If you go through the light and it is red and a policeman is there, you will get a ticket. If you go through the light and no car or policeman is there, you will get through the light safely. These more complex conditions are known as **Compound Conditions**.

Visual Basic gives you additional expression operators to help you map a problem or algorithm to a program. It is not uncommon to require Boolean logic operators like And, Or, and Not to assist in representing a condition properly.

And is used to represent the logical anding of two conditions. If you are unfamiliar with Boolean logic, here is a simple truth table of all the possible conditions:

```
True And True = True
True And False = False
False And True = False
False And False = False
```

Or is used to represent the logical or. Here is a truth table of all of the possibilities:

```
True Or True = True
True Or False = True
False Or True = True
False Or False = False
```

In addition, Visual Basic provides the **Not** operator to negate the value of an expression. Here is a truth table of all the possibilities:

```
Not True = False
Not False = True
```

Here are some sample expressions that evaluate to `True`:

(1 = 1) And (2 = 2)
(2 >= 1) Or (1 <> 1)
(2 >= 2) And (1 < 3)
(1 <= 2) Or (2 > 1)
(1 < 2) And (1 <> 2)
("CAT" = "CAT") And (1 < 2)
("a" <> "c") Or ("b" <> "c")
Not ("A" = "a")

Here are some sample expressions that evaluate to `False`:

(1 = 2) Or (2 = 1)
(2 <= 1) Or (1 > 2)
(2 < 2) And (1 = 1)
(3 > 4) And (3 < 5)
(1 >= 2) Or (2 < 1)
Not (1 = 1)
("a" = "A") Or ("b" = "B")

DRILL 4.10

Indicate whether each expression evaluates to `True` or `False`.

```
1 Not (5 >= 4)
2 (-3 < -4) Or (1 = 1)
3 ("BOB" = "bob") And (2 >= 2)
4 (2 < 1) Or (5 <> 4)
5 (1 < 2) Or (4 >= 4)
6 Not (4 <= 4) And (1 <= 1)
```

Simple Examples   The code assumes that a command button, `cmdCompoundIf`, has been created to contain the code. Additionally, three text boxes, `txtRetailPrice`, `txtSalePrice`, and `txtOutput` (all with their `Text` property empty) have been created to hold the input and output of the user.

Example: And Operator

You can use compound conditional expressions in a program the same way you did with the previous conditional statements. Observe the following code snippet that shows the use of a compound conditional expression.

```
Private Sub cmdCompoundIf_Click()
Dim curRetailPrice As Currency
Dim curSalePrice As Currency
```

(continues)

(continued)

```
curRetailPrice = Val(txtRetailPrice.Text)
curSalePrice = Val(txtSalePrice.Text)

If ((curRetailPrice = curSalePrice) And (curRetailPrice > 100)) Then
    txtOutput.Text = "This product is not on sale and expensive"
Else
    txtOutput.Text = "This product may not be too expensive and may be on sale"
End If
End Sub
```

What do you think would be contained in `txtOutput`:

1 If the user enters 50.25 for the retail price and 50.25 for the sales price?
2 If the user enters 125.13 for the retail price and 125.13 for the sales price?
3 If the user enters 99.90 for the retail price and 125.13 for the sales price?
4 If the user enters 99.90 for the retail price and 75.00 for the sales price?

Example with a Retail Price of 50.25 and a Sales Price of 50.25   When the application is executed and the command button is clicked, the `If` statement is evaluated. When the user enters 50.25 and 50.25 for the retail and sales prices, the `If` statement evaluates the expression by comparing the retail price to the sales price. Since both are equal to 50.25, that part of the expression evaluates to `True`. The second condition is then checked. The retail price is compared to 100. Since the retail price is not greater than 100, the comparison evaluates to `False`. Because the two subconditions are combined with an `And` operator, both must evaluate to `True` for the entire conditional expression to evaluate to `True`. Therefore, the conditional expression evaluates to `False` and the code associated with the `Else` statement is executed. The text `"This product may not be too expensive and may be on sale"` is assigned to the output text box.

Example with a Retail Price of 125.13 and a Sales Price of 125.13   When the application is executed and the command button is clicked, the `If` statement is evaluated. When the user enters 125.13 and 125.13 for the retail and sales prices, the `If` statement evaluates the expression by comparing the retail price to the sales price. Since both are equal to 125.13, that part of the expression evaluates to `True`. The second condition is then checked. The retail price is compared to 100. This time the retail price is greater than 100, so the comparison evaluates to `True`. Because the two subconditions are combined with an `And` operator, both must evaluate to `True` for the entire conditional expression to evaluate to `True`. Therefore, the conditional expression evaluates to `True` and the code associated with the `If` statement is executed. The text `"This product is not on sale and expensive"` is assigned to the output text box.

Example with a Retail Price of 99.90 and a Sales Price of 125.13   When the application is executed and the command button is clicked, the `If` statement is evaluated. When the user enters 99.90 and 125.13 for the retail and sales prices, the `If` statement evaluates the expression by comparing the retail price to the sales price. This time both are not equal, so the first subexpression evaluates to `False`. The second condition is then checked. The retail price is compared to 100. The retail price is greater than 100, so the comparison evaluates to `True`. Whether one or both subexpressions evaluated to `False` is irrelevant. As long as one of them evaluates to `False`, the entire expression will evaluate to `False`. Therefore, the conditional expression evaluates to `False` and the code associated with the `If` statement is executed. The text `"This product may not be too expensive and may be on sale"` is assigned to the output text box.

Example with a Retail Price of 99.90 and a Sales Price of 75.00   When the application is executed and the command button is clicked, the `If` statement is evaluated. When the user enters 99.90 and 75.00 for the retail and sales prices, the `If` statement evaluates the expression by comparing the retail price to the sales price. This time both are not equal, so the first subexpression evaluates to `False`. The second condition is then checked. The retail price is compared to 100. The retail price is not greater than 100, so the comparison evaluates to `False`. Therefore, the conditional expression evaluates to `False` and the code associated with the `If` statement is executed. The text `"This product may not be too expensive and may be on sale"` is assigned to the output text box.

Example: Or Operator

Assume the following code for the `cmdCompoundIf` exists in the same application as the previous example. Now however, you are demonstrating the use of an `Or` operator.

```
Private Sub cmdCompoundIf_Click()
Dim curRetailPrice As Currency
Dim curSalePrice As Currency

curRetailPrice = Val(txtRetailPrice.Text)
curSalePrice = Val(txtSalePrice.Text)

If ((curRetailPrice = curSalePrice) Or (curRetailPrice > 100)) Then
    txtOutput.Text = "This product is either on sale or very expensive"
Else
    txtOutput.Text = "This product is either not on sale or not expensive"
End If
End Sub
```

What do you think would be contained in `txtOutput`:

1 If the user enters 50.25 for the retail price and 50.25 for the sales price?
3 If the user enters 125.13 for the retail price and 125.13 for the sales price?
4 If the user enters 99.90 for the retail price and 125.13 for the sales price?
5 If the user enters 99.90 for the retail price and 75.00 for the sales price?

Example with a Retail Price of 50.25 and a Sales Price of 50.25   When the application is executed and the command button is clicked, the `If` statement is evaluated. When the user enters 50.25 and 50.25 for the retail and sales prices, the `If` statement evaluates the expression by comparing the retail price to the sales price. Since both are equal to 50.25, that part of the expression evaluates to `True`. The second condition is then checked. The retail price is compared to 100. Since the retail price is not greater than 100, the comparison evaluates to `False`. Because the two subconditions are combined with an `Or` operator, only one of the subconditions must evaluate to `True` for the entire conditional expression to evaluate to `True`. Therefore, the conditional expression evaluates to `True` and the code associated with the `If` statement is executed. Therefore, the text "`This product is either on sale or very expensive`" is assigned to the output text box.

Example with a Retail Price of 125.13 and a Sales Price of 125.13   When the application is executed and the command button is clicked, the If statement is evaluated. When the user enters 125.13 and 125.13 for the retail and sales prices, the If statement evaluates the expression by comparing the retail price to the sales price. Since both are equal to 125.13, that part of the expression evaluates to True. The second condition is then checked. The retail price is compared to 100. This time the retail price is greater than 100, so the comparison evaluates to True. Therefore, the conditional expression evaluates to True and the code associated with the If statement is executed. Therefore, the text "This product is either on sale or very expensive" is assigned to the output text box.

Example with a Retail Price of 99.90 and a Sales Price of 125.13   When the application is executed and the command button is clicked, the If statement is evaluated. When the user enters 99.90 and 125.13 for the retail and sales prices, the If statement evaluates the expression by comparing the retail price to the sales price. This time both are not equal, so the first subexpression evaluates to False. The second condition is then checked. The retail price is compared to 100. The retail price is less than 100, so the comparison evaluates to False. Therefore, the conditional expression evaluates to False and the code associated with the If statement is executed. Therefore, the text "This product is either not on sale or not expensive" is assigned to the output text box.

Example with a Retail Price of 99.90 and a Sales Price of 75.00   When the application is executed and the command button is clicked, the If statement is evaluated. When the user enters 99.90 and 75.00 for the retail and sales prices, the If statement evaluates the expression by comparing the retail price to the sales price. This time both are not equal, so the first subexpression evaluates to False. The second condition is then checked. The retail price is compared to 100. The retail price is not greater than 100, so the comparison evaluates to False. Therefore, the conditional expression evaluates to False and the code associated with the If statement is executed. Therefore, the text "This product is either not on sale or not expensive" is assigned to the output text box.

Example: Not Operator

Assume the following code for the cmdCompoundIf exists in the same application as the previous example. Now, however, you are demonstrating the use of the Not operator.

```
Private Sub cmdCompoundIf_Click()
Dim curRetailPrice As Currency
Dim curSalePrice As Currency

curRetailPrice = Val(txtRetailPrice.Text)
curSalePrice = Val(txtSalePrice.Text)

If (Not(curRetailPrice >= curSalePrice)) Then
    txtOutput.Text = "The Sales Price is greater than the Retail Price"
Else
    txtOutput.Text = "The Sales Price is less than or equal to the Retail Price"
End If
End Sub
```

What do you think would be contained in `txtOutput`:

1 If the user enters 50.25 for the retail price and 50.25 for the sales price?
2 If the user enters 49.95 for the retail price and 125.13 for the sales price?

Example with a Retail Price of 50.25 and a Sales Price of 50.25   When the application is executed and the command button is clicked, the `If` statement is evaluated. When the user enters 50.25 and 50.25 for the retail and sales prices, the `If` statement evaluates the expression by comparing the retail price to the sales price. This time the retail price is greater than or equal to the sales price, so the inner subexpression evaluates to `True`. Then the `Not` operator is applied to this result. When a `Not` operator is applied to `True`, the result is `False`. Therefore, the conditional expression evaluates to `False` and the code associated with the `Else` statement is executed. So, the text `"The Sales Price is less than or equal to the Retail Price"` is assigned to the output text box.

Example with a Retail Price of 49.95 and a Sales Price of 125.15   When the application is executed and the command button is clicked, the `If` statement is evaluated. When the user enters 49.95 and 125.15 for the retail and sales prices, the `If` statement evaluates the expression by comparing the retail price to the sales price. This time the retail price is not greater than or equal to the sales price, so the inner subexpression evaluates to `False`. Then the `Not` operator is applied to this result. When a `Not` operator is applied to `False`, the result is `True`. Therefore, the conditional expression evaluates to `True` and the code associated with the `If` statement is executed. So, the text `"The Sales Price is greater than the Retail Price"` is assigned to the output text box.

DRILL 4.11

Use the same application as the previous drills, but change the code in the command button as follows.

```
Private Sub cmdCompoundIf_Click()
Dim curRetailPrice As Currency
Dim curSalePrice As Currency

curRetailPrice = Val(txtRetailPrice.Text)
curSalePrice = Val(txtSalePrice.Text)

If ((curRetailPrice >= curSalePrice) And (Not(curSalesPrice > 75.00))) Then
    txtOutput.Text = "This crazy drill outputs True"
Else
    txtOutput.Text = "This crazy drill outputs False"
End If
End Sub
```

What do you think would be contained in `txtOutput`:

1 If the user enters 99.95 for the retail price and 50.25 for the sales price?
2 If the user enters 199.95 for the retail price and 99.95 for the sales price?

Improved Voting Booth Application   Your previous Voting Booth application allowed for the counting of votes for three candidates and a count of the number of incorrect votes. If this system were used in the real world, you would have a great number of incorrect votes that were really meant to be a vote for one of the three candidates.

Since you checked only the spelling for each name, what do you think would happen if you type `Al Gore` instead of `Gore`? The answer is that the vote would be counted as an incorrect vote. There are many ways to solve this problem; one is to use compound conditional statements to check for additional spellings.

Observe the following modifications to the `cmdVote` command button that adds additional spellings for each candidate:

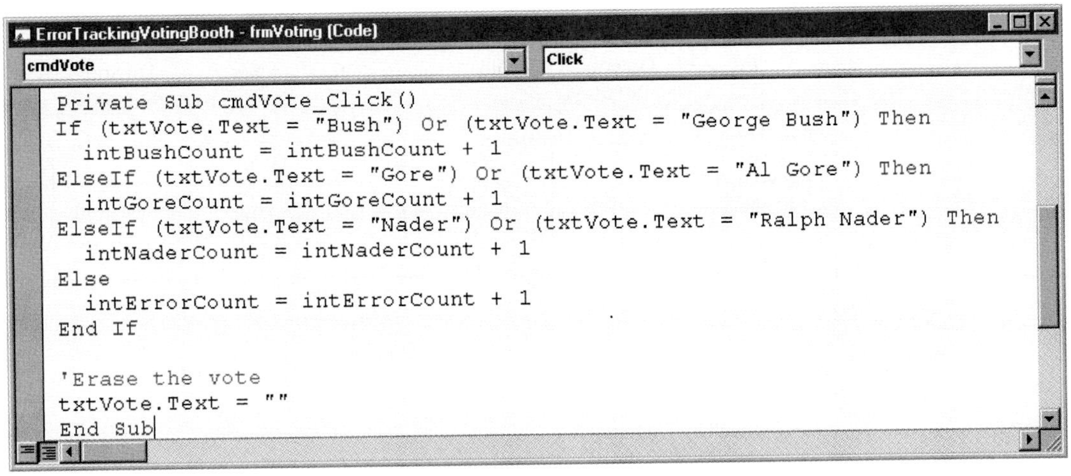

```
ErrorTrackingVotingBooth - frmVoting (Code)
cmdVote                                    Click

Private Sub cmdVote_Click()
If (txtVote.Text = "Bush") Or (txtVote.Text = "George Bush") Then
    intBushCount = intBushCount + 1
ElseIf (txtVote.Text = "Gore") Or (txtVote.Text = "Al Gore") Then
    intGoreCount = intGoreCount + 1
ElseIf (txtVote.Text = "Nader") Or (txtVote.Text = "Ralph Nader") Then
    intNaderCount = intNaderCount + 1
Else
    intErrorCount = intErrorCount + 1
End If

'Erase the vote
txtVote.Text = ""
End Sub
```

Figure 4.34   Code for `cmdVote` Command Button

Visual Basic .NET Alert

It is a very bad programming practice to write code that may have side effects within a conditional statement. Observe the following code:

```
If ((intValue1 > intValue2) Or "or _"(intValue1 > DoubleValue(intValue2)) Then
```

Imagine if `DoubleValue` multiplied its argument by 2 and stored the result back in the argument. In Visual Basic 6.0, the function would be called regardless of whether the subcondition evaluates to `True` or not. However, VB .NET uses short circuit evaluation to determine the results of conditional statements. In short circuit evaluation, once the truthfulness of a condition can be established, the remainder of the condition is not evaluated. In this case, if the expression was evaluated using the short circuit method and `intValue1 > intValue2`, then the `DoubleValue` function will never be called. Avoid situations like this!

4.4   Nested Conditional Statements

Compound conditional statements are useful for mapping real-world situations to the computer. However, if a part of the condition needs to be repeated more than once, it would be inefficient to repeat the check of that condition each time. Imagine you want to reward employees for hard work by giving them tickets to an event. Let's say you have tickets to a basketball game, football game, the philharmonic, or the opera. You could start by asking if they would like to go to the basketball game, and then ask about the football game, and then the philharmonic, and then finally the opera. If you added more choices like baseball or hockey, wouldn't it be easier if you first asked if the person was a sports fan? If not, then you could ask them about the philharmonic or opera right away.

Nesting conditional statements can do this. A graphical representation follows:

Figure 4.35
Nested Conditional Statements

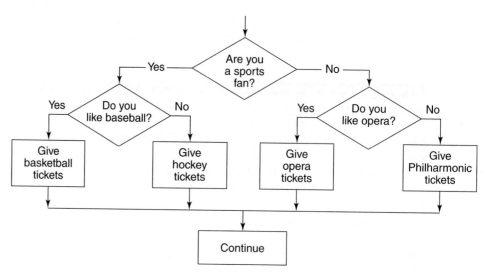

Visual Basic provides the ability to nest conditional statements. It is simply a matter of placing one conditional statement inside another. This shouldn't add too much confusion; it simply requires treating the inner `If` statement as an individual `If` statement to be evaluated as would any other statement.

Example: Select Tickets

The following code will loosely implement the flowchart in Figure 4.35. While it will not ask the questions depicted, it will process the answers to the two questions as if they were asked as portrayed in the flowchart.

The code assumes that a command button `cmdCompoundConditional` has been created to place the code and a three text boxes, `txtQuestion1`, `txtQuestion2`, and `txtOutput` (both with their `Text` property empty), were created to hold the input and output.

See the following code as an example:

```
Private Sub cmdCompoundConditional_Click()
If (txtQuestion1.Text = "Yes") Then
    If (txtQuestion2.Text = "Yes")
        txtOutput.Text = "Basketball"
    Else
        txtOutput.Text = "Hockey"
    End If
Else
    If (txtQuestion2.Text = "Yes") Then
        txtOutput.Text = "Opera"
    Else
        txtOutput.Text = "Philharmonic"
    End If
End If
End Sub
```

What do you think would be contained in `txtOutput`:

1   If the user enters `"Yes"` in `txtQuestion1` and `"Yes"` in `txtQuestion2`?
2   If the user enters `"Yes"` in `txtQuestion1` and `"No"` in `txtQuestion2`?
3   If the user enters `"No"` in `txtQuestion1` and `"Yes"` in `txtQuestion2`?
4   If the user enters `"No"` in `txtQuestion1` and `"No"` in `txtQuestion2`?

1) User Enters "Yes" and "Yes"   When the program is executed and the command button is clicked, the outer `If` statement is evaluated. Since `"Yes"` is equal to `"Yes"`, the conditional expression evaluates to `True` and therefore all the statements until the `Else` are executed.

In this case that means the 1st inner `If` statement is evaluated. Since the user entered `"Yes"` for the second question as well, the condition evaluates to `True`; therefore the text `"Basketball"` is placed in the text box. Since the conditional expression in the inner `If` statement evaluated to `True`, none of the statements after the inner `Else` statement are executed. Since you previously determined that the outer `If` statement evaluated to `True`, the outer `Else` statement is skipped as well.

2) User Enters "Yes" and "No"   When the program is executed and the command button is clicked, the outer `If` statement is evaluated. Since `"Yes"` is equal to `"Yes"`, the conditional expression evaluates to `True` and therefore all the statements until the `Else` are executed.

In this case that means the 1st inner `If` statement is evaluated. Since the user entered `"No"` for the second question, the condition evaluates to `False`; therefore the text `"Hockey"` is placed in the text box.

3) User Enters "No" and "Yes"   When the program is executed and the command button is clicked, the outer `If` statement is evaluated. Since `"No"` is not equal to `"Yes"`, the conditional expression evaluates to `False` and therefore all the statements after the `Else` are executed.

In this case that means the 2nd inner `If` statement is evaluated. Since the user entered `"Yes"` for the second question, the condition evaluates to `True`; therefore the text `"Opera"` is placed in the text box. Since the conditional expression in the inner `If` statement evaluated to `True`, none of the statements after the inner `Else` statement are executed.

4) User Enters "No" and "No"   When the program is executed and the command button is clicked, the outer `If` statement is evaluated. Since `"No"` is not equal to `"Yes"`, the conditional expression evaluates to `False` and therefore all the statements after the `Else` are executed.

In this case that means the 2nd inner `If` statement is evaluated. Since the user entered `"NO"` for the second question, the condition evaluates to `False`; therefore the text `"Philharmonic"` is placed in the text box.

WARNING

For every `If` statement, you must have an `End  If` statement. By indenting properly, it is easier to keep track of your nesting level.

DRILL 4.12

Assume that a command button `cmdCompoundConditional` has been created to place the code and two text boxes, `txtInput`, and `txtOutput` (both with their `Text` property empty), were created to hold the input and output.

Also, assume the following code:

```
Private Sub cmdCompoundConditional_Click()
Dim DrillValue As Integer
DrillValue = Val(txtInput.Text)
If (DrillValue = 1) Then
    If (DrillValue <= 1) Then
        txtOutput = "This will output, from the 1st Inner If"
    Else
        txtOutput = "This will output, from the 1st Inner Else"
    End If
Else
    If (DrillValue < 1) Then
        txtOutput = "This will output, from the 2nd Inner If"
    Else
        txtOutput = "This will output, from the 2nd Inner Else"
    End If
End If
End Sub
```

What do you think would be contained in `txtOutput`:

1 If the user enters 0 in `txtInput`?
2 If the user enters 1 in `txtInput`?
3 If the user enters 2 in `txtInput`?

Example: Improved Voting Booth Application

Imagine if instead of writing a Voting Booth application for a single presidential race, you needed to develop a Voting Booth application that could be used for additional races as well. For instance, let's change your current application to count votes for the Presidential and Vice Presidential elections. For simplicity's sake, you will limit the candidates to George Bush and Al Gore for the presidency and Dick Cheney and Joe Lieberman for the vice presidency.

You would still need a variable for each candidate to track the number of valid votes that they receive. You will also keep a single variable to track all of the improperly cast votes. These can be seen in the following code that needs to be declared in the General Declarations section of the form.

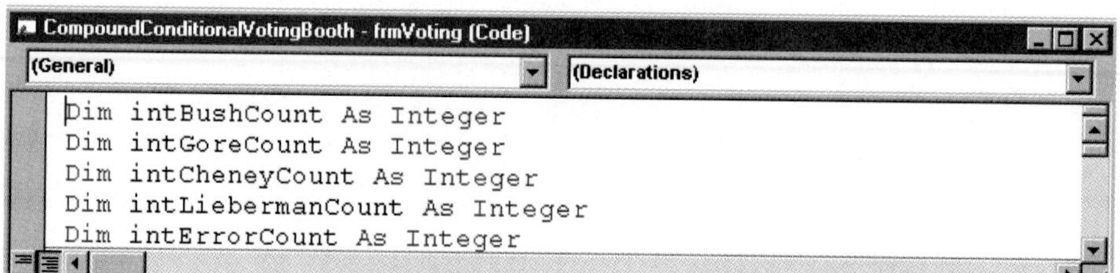

Figure 4.36
General Declarations Code

```
CompoundConditionalVotingBooth - frmVoting (Code)
(General)                              (Declarations)
    Dim intBushCount As Integer
    Dim intGoreCount As Integer
    Dim intCheneyCount As Integer
    Dim intLiebermanCount As Integer
    Dim intErrorCount As Integer
```

You would need to change the code for the `cmdResults` command button so that it outputs all of the results of the election. This can be seen in the following code:

Figure 4.37
`CmdResults`' Click Event
Code

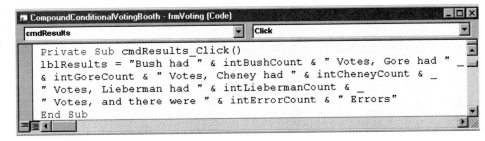

```
Private Sub cmdResults_Click()
lblResults = "Bush had " & intBushCount & " Votes, Gore had " _
& intGoreCount & " Votes, Cheney had " & intCheneyCount & _
" Votes, Lieberman had " & intLiebermanCount & _
" Votes, and there were " & intErrorCount & " Errors"
End Sub
```

The main reason for the selection of this example is to demonstrate the power of a nested conditional statement. If you didn't nest the conditional statements, your code would execute slower. Each time you check a candidate with the non-nested example, you have to recheck the condition to indicate whether this vote is for a president or vice president. While this example will not produce a noticeable difference in the speed at which it executes, when the comparisons get either more complex or numerous, this sort of inefficiency can become a real issue. Therefore, when a condition is repeatedly checked, consider using the nested form.

```
Private Sub cmdVote_Click()
If (txtRace.Text = "Pres") Then

    If (txtVote.Text = "Bush") Or (txtVote.Text = "George Bush") Then
        intBushCount = intBushCount + 1
    ElseIf (txtVote.Text = "Gore") Or (txtVote.Text = "Al Gore") Then
        intGoreCount = intGoreCount + 1
    Else
        intErrorCount = intErrorCount + 1
    End If

ElseIf (txtRace.Text = "Vice") Then

    If (txtVote.Text = "Cheney") Or (txtVote.Text = "Dick Cheney") Then
        intCheneyCount = intCheneyCount + 1
    ElseIf (txtVote.Text = "Lieberman") Or _
            (txtVote.Text = "Joe Lieberman") Then
        intLiebermanCount = intLiebermanCount + 1
    Else
        intErrorCount = intErrorCount + 1
    End If
Else
    intErrorCount = intErrorCount + 1
End If

'Erase the vote
txtVote.Text = ""
txtRace.Text = ""
End Sub
```

Figure 4.38 CmdVote's Click Event Code—Correct Code

```
CompoundConditionalVotingBooth - frmVoting (Code)                    _ □ ×
cmdVote                              ▼  Click                        ▼
    Private Sub cmdVote_Click()
    If ((txtRace.Text = "Pres") And _
        ((txtVote.Text = "Bush") Or (txtVote.Text = "George Bush"))) Then
            intBushCount = intBushCount + 1
    ElseIf ((txtRace.Text = "Pres") And _
        ((txtVote.Text = "Gore") Or (txtVote.Text = "Al Gore"))) Then
            intGoreCount = intGoreCount + 1
    ElseIf ((txtRace.Text = "Vice") And _
        ((txtVote.Text = "Cheney") Or (txtVote.Text = "Dick Cheney"))) Then
            intCheneyCount = intCheneyCount + 1
    ElseIf ((txtRace.Text = "Vice") And ((txtVote.Text = "Lieberman") _
        Or (txtVote.Text = "Joe Lieberman"))) Then
            intLiebermanCount = intLiebermanCount + 1
    Else
        intErrorCount = intErrorCount + 1
    End If

    'Erase the vote
    txtVote.Text = ""
    txtRace.Text = ""

    End Sub
```

Figure 4.39   CmdVote's Click Event Code—Incorrect Code

Figure 4.40
Form_Load Code

```
CompoundConditionalVotingBooth - frmVoting (Code)                    _ □ ×
Form                                 ▼  Load                         ▼
    Private Sub Form_Load()
    'Initialize the Voting values
    intBushCount = 0
    intGoreCount = 0
    intCheneyCount = 0
    intLiebermanCount = 0
    intErrorCount = 0
    End Sub
```

4.5   Select Case Statements

As your applications become more complex, you may have many conditions to check. Using multiple If, ElseIf, Else's can become burdensome as well as look quite busy on the page. Visual Basic gives you a better way to handle multiple options, the **Select Case** statement.

A Select Case statement gives the programmer the capability to shortcut the process of describing under what conditions certain code should be executed. The programmer must indicate an expression that the decision will be based upon. Then the programmer indicates a series of cases with code associated with each. If the case matches the expression, the code is executed. If no cases match the expression, the statements associated with the **Case Else** would be executed.

```
Select Case Expression
    Case  Possible Value or Range of Values
        Statement(s)
    Case  Another Possible Value or Range of Values
        Statement(s)
```

(continues)

(continued)

```
        .
        .
        .

     Case Else
          Statement(s)
End Select
```

The expression in a `Select Case` statement may be:

♦ A numeric variable.
♦ A string variable.
♦ A simple expression composed of operators and variables.

The possible values in a `Case` statement may be:

♦ A numeric constant.
♦ A string constant.
♦ A numeric variable.
♦ A string variable.
♦ A range of values.
♦ A combination of the above.

Simple Examples The code assumes that a command button, `cmdSelectCase`, has been created to contain the code. Additionally, the text boxes `txtInput` and `txtOutput` (with its `Text` property empty) have been created to hold the input and output of the user.

Example: Ordering Roses

You can use a `Select Case` statement in a program the same way you did with the conditional statements introduced earlier. Observe the following code snippet that shows the use of a `Select Case` statement.

```
Private Sub cmdSelectCase_Click()
Dim intExampleValue As Integer

intExampleValue = Val(txtInput.Text)

Select Case intExampleValue
    Case 12
        txtOutput.Text = "Your order of a dozen roses has been placed"
    Case 24
        txtOutput.Text = "Your order of two dozen roses has been placed"
    Case Else
        txtOutput.Text = "You must order either one or two dozen roses"
End Select
End Sub
```

What do you think would be contained in txtOutput:

1 If the user enters 12 in the text box txtPlayer?
2 If the user enters 24 in the text box txtPlayer?
3 If the user enters 0 in the text box txtPlayer?

Example with the Number of Roses Equal to 12   When the program is executed and the command button is clicked, the `Case` statement is evaluated. Since `intExampleValue` is equal to 12, the first case statement evaluates to `True`. Therefore, the value `"Your order of a dozen roses has been placed"` is assigned to the `txtOutput` text box. Once a `Case` statement is found to evaluate to `True`, the rest are ignored.

Example with the Number of Roses Equal to 24   If you changed the value of `intExampleValue` to 24, the first case would evaluate to `False`. This would cause the next `Case` statement to be evaluated. Since `intExampleValue` equals 24, this would cause the second `Case` statement to evaluate to `True`. Therefore, the value `"Your order of two dozen roses has been placed"` is assigned to the `txtOutput` text box. Again, since a `Case` statement evaluated to `True`, the rest are ignored.

Example with the Number of Roses Equal to 0   Finally, if you changed the value of `intExampleValue` to 0, then not only would the first case evaluate to `False`, but so would the second. This would cause the `Case Else` statement to be evaluated. Therefore, the `"You must order one or two dozen roses"` is assigned to the `txtOutput` text box.

Example: Player Message

`Select Case` statements can also be used with `Strings`. Observe the following code snippet that shows the use of `Strings` and assumes a text box `txtPlayer` has been created.

```
Private Sub cmdSelectCase_Click()

Select Case txtPlayer.Text
    Case "Allen Iverson"
        txtOutput.Text = "Iverson Rules the NBA"
    Case "Theo Ratliff"
        txtOutput.Text = "Ratliff is the ultimate shot blocker"
    Case Else
        txtOutput.Text = "Try again"
End Select
End Sub
```

What do you think would be contained in `txtOutput`:

1 If the user enters `"Allen Iverson"` in the text box `txtPlayer`?
2 If the user enters `"Theo Ratliff"` in the text box `txtPlayer`?
3 If the user enters `"Michael Jordan"` in the text box `txtPlayer`?

Example with "Allen Iverson" Entered in txtPlayer   When the application is executed and the command button is clicked, the `Case` statement is evaluated. Since `txtPlayer.Text` is equal to `"Allen Iverson"`, the first `Case` statement evaluates to `True`. Therefore, the value `"Iverson Rules the NBA"` is assigned to the `txtOutput` text box. Once a `Case` statement is found to evaluate to `True`, the rest are ignored.

Example with "Theo Ratliff" Entered in txtPlayer   If you changed the value of `txtPlayer.Text` to `"Theo Ratliff"`, then the first `Case` would evaluate to `False`. This would cause the next `Case` statement to be evaluated. Since `txtPlayer.Text` equals `"Theo Ratliff"`, this would cause the second `Case` statement to evaluate to `True`. Therefore, the value `"Ratliff is the ultimate` shot blocker" is assigned to the `txtOutput` text box. Again, since a `Case` statement evaluated to `True`, the rest are ignored.

Example with "Michael Jordan" Entered in txtPlayer   Finally, if you changed the value of `txtPlayer.Text` to `"Michael Jordan"`, then not only would the first case evaluate to `False`, but so would the second. This would cause the `Case Else` statement to be evaluated. Therefore, the value `"Try again"` is assigned to the `txtOutput` text box.

Multiple Strings with a Case Statement   One great feature of a `Select Case` statement is the capability to indicate a `Case` as a series of `Strings` to compare against. If you wish the same code to execute for more than one `String`, simply list them one after another separated by commas. This can be seen in the following code that illustrates the syntax of testing the value in `VariableToTestAgainst` against the `Strings` listed in the `Cases` that follow:

```
Select Case VariableToTestAgainst
    Case "FirstString", "SecondString", "ThirdString"
        txtOutput = "1st Output"
    Case "FourthString", "FifthString", "SixthString"
        txtOutput = "2nd Output"
    .
    .
    .
    Case Else
        txtOutput = "String Not Found"
End Select
```

Example: Sport Determiner

Here is a simple example demonstrating how you can check for which sport an athlete plays. It takes advantage of the use of multiple `Strings` in a `Select Case` statement to simplify the code and assumes a text box `txtAthlete` has been created:

```
Private Sub cmdSelectCase_Click()

Select Case txtAthlete.Text
    Case "Serena Williams", "Martina Hingis", "Anna Kournikova"
        txtOutput.Text = "Tennis"
    Case "Sheryl Swoopes", "Katie Smith", "Brandy Reed"
        txtOutput.Text = "Basketball"
    Case "Marion Jones", "Michelle Kwan"
        txtOutput.Text = "Olympics"
    Case Else
        txtOutput.Text = "Some Other Event"
End Select
End Sub
```

What do you think would be contained in `txtOutput`:

1 If the user enters `"Serena Williams"` in the text box `txtAthlete`?
2 If the user enters `"Katie Smith"` in the text box `txtAthlete`?
3 If the user enters `"Michael Jordan"` in the text box `txtAthlete`?

Example with "Serena Williams" Entered in txtAthlete   When the program is executed and the command button is clicked, the `Case` statement is evaluated. Since txtAthlete's Text property contains "Serena Williams", the first Case statement evaluates to True, since "Serena Williams" is one of the Strings listed. Therefore, "Tennis" is copied to txtOutput. Since a Case statement evaluated to True, the rest are ignored.

Example with "Katie Smith" Entered in txtAthlete   If you changed the value of txtAthlete to "Katie Smith", the first Case statement would evaluate to False and the second Case statement will evaluate to True. Therefore, "Basketball" is copied to txtOutput.

Example with "Michael Jordan" entered in txtAthlete   If you changed the value of txtAthlete to "Michael Jordan", the first three Case statements would evaluate to False. Therefore, the Case Else is executed and "Some Other Event" is copied to txtOutput.

Example: Basketball Score Evaluation

Select Case statements can also be used with multiple values in each Case statement. Observe the following code snippet that shows the use of a compound conditional expression and assumes a text box txtPoints has been created:

```
Private Sub cmdSelectCase_Click()
Dim intTotalPoints As Integer

intTotalPoints = Val(txtPoints.Text)
Select Case intTotalPoints
    Case 0 To 10
        txtOutput.Text = "Quite a bad night for Iverson"
    Case 11 To 20
        txtOutput.Text = "Allen should be able to do better"
    Case 21 To 30
        txtOutput.Text = "Not too shabby"
    Case Is > 30
        txtOutput.Text = "He shoots, He scores!"
    Case Else
        txtOutput.Text = "Error in Input"
End Select
End Sub
```

TIP

Expressions may take the form of Case Is Condition as in Case Is > 30. Expressions may also take the form of a range of values as in Case LowerBound to UpperBound. This is shown in your example as Case 11 to 20.

What do you think would be contained in txtOutput:

1 If the user enters 0 in the text box txtPoints?
2 If the user enters 15 in the text box txtPoints?
3 If the user enters 30 in the text box txtPoints?
4 If the user enters 50 in the text box txtPoints?
5 If the user enters –5 in the text box txtPoints?

Example with 0 Entered in txtPoints   When the application is executed and the command button is clicked, the `Case` statement is evaluated. Since `intExampleValue` is equal to 0, the first `Case` statement evaluates to `True`. Therefore, the value `"Quite a bad night for Iverson"` is assigned to the `txtOutput` text box. Since a `Case` statement evaluated to `True`, the rest are ignored.

Example with 15 Entered in txtPoints   When the application is executed and the command button is clicked, the `Case` statement is evaluated. Since `intExampleValue` equals 15 and 15 is not in the range of 0 to 10, the first `Case` statement evaluates to `False`. Therefore, the second `Case` statement is evaluated. Since 15 is within the range 11 to 20, the `Case` statement evaluates to `True`. Therefore, the `"Allen should be able to do better"` is assigned to the `txtOutput` text box. Since a `Case` statement evaluated to `True`, the rest are ignored.

Example with 30 Entered in txtPoints   When the application is executed and the command button is clicked, the `Case` statement is evaluated. Since `intExampleValue` equals 30 and 30 is not in the range of 0 to 10 or 11 to 20, the first two `Case` statements evaluate to `False`. However, when the third `Case` statement is evaluated, it evaluates to `True` since 30 is greater than 20 and less than or equal to 30. Therefore, `"Not too shabby"` is assigned to the `txtOutput` text box. Since a `Case` statement evaluated to `True`, the rest are ignored.

Example with 50 Entered in txtPoints   When the application is executed and the command button is clicked, the `Case` statement is evaluated. Since `intExampleValue` equals 50 and 50 is not in the range of 0 to 10, or 11 to 20, or 21 to 30, the first three `Case` statements evaluate to `False`. Therefore, the fourth `Case` statement is evaluated. Since 50 is greater than 30, the fourth `Case` statement evaluates to `True`. Therefore, `"He shoots, he scores!"` is assigned to the `txtOutput` text box. Since a `Case` statement evaluated to `True`, the rest are ignored.

Example with –5 entered in txtPoints   When the application is executed and the command button is clicked, the `Case` statement is evaluated. Since `intExampleValue` equals –5 and –5 is not in the range of 0 to 10, or 11 to 20, or 21 to 30, or > 30, the first four `Case` statements evaluate to `False`. Therefore, the fifth `Case Else` statement executes and "Error in Input" is assigned to the `txtOutput` text box. Since a `Case` statement evaluated to `True`, the rest are ignored.

You could have written this example without using a `Case Else`. Instead, you could have added one more case that would check to see if `TotalPoints` was less than 0.

WARNING

When you list a range of numbers for a `Case` statement, you must list the smaller number first.

DRILL 4.13

The following code assumes that a command button, cmdSelectCase, has been created to contain the code. Additionally, the text boxes txtInput and txtOutput (with its Text property empty) have been created to hold the input and output of the user.

```
Private Sub cmdSelectCase_Click()
Dim DrillValue As Integer

DrillValue = Val(txtInput.Text)

Select Case DrillValue
    Case Is < 0
        txtOutput = "Error in Input"
    Case 0 To 20
        txtOutput = "2nd Case Statement"
    Case 21 To 30
        txtOutput = "3rd Case Statement"
    Case 31 To 50
        txtOutput = "4th Case Statement"
    Case Is > 50
        txtOutput = "5th Case Statement"
    Case Else
        txtOutput = "Can I get here?"
End Select
End Sub
```

What do you think would be contained in txtOutput:

1 If the user enters 0 in txtInput?
2 If the user enters 100 in txtInput?
3 If the user enters –50 in txtInput?
4 Is there any value the user can enter that will allow the Case Else statement to execute?

Improved Compute Grade Application   Your Compute Grade application from Section 4.2 determined a letter grade for a class given a numerical grade as input. Let's rewrite that example using a Select Case statement instead of If, ElseIf, and Else statements, but to the user of the application it appears that nothing has changed.

The only code that must change is in the cmdCompute_Click() subroutine. You can take advantage of the fact that you can list multiple String values to check against for a single case on a single line to greatly simplify the code. See the following code:

Figure 4.41
Improved `cmdCompute`
`Click` Event Code

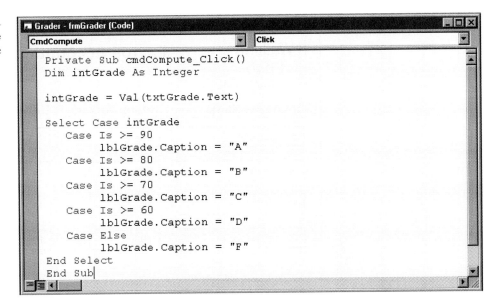

```
Grader - frmGrader (Code)
CmdCompute                                    Click
    Private Sub cmdCompute_Click()
    Dim intGrade As Integer

    intGrade = Val(txtGrade.Text)

    Select Case intGrade
        Case Is >= 90
            lblGrade.Caption = "A"
        Case Is >= 80
            lblGrade.Caption = "B"
        Case Is >= 70
            lblGrade.Caption = "C"
        Case Is >= 60
            lblGrade.Caption = "D"
        Case Else
            lblGrade.Caption = "F"
    End Select
    End Sub
```

TIP

You may be wondering why you have an `If/ElseIf/Else` construct if the `Select Case` is better. While a `Select Case` can replace the `If/ElseIf/Else` structure in many cases, it cannot in all cases. Observe that the `Select Case` structure evaluates an expression once at the top of the structure. If your `If/ElseIf/Else` structure evaluates the same expression each time, it can be replaced by a `Select Case`. However, if a different expression is evaluated in each `ElseIf` statement, it cannot be replaced. Both are useful and have their place.

◆ 4.6   Case Study

Problem Description   This chapter's case study will be a continuation of last chapter's case study to compute the payroll of four workers for a company. In this application you wish to add the functionality to compute the pay of each worker at two different pay rates. In this case, you will have a rate of $25.00/hour for workers who are in the Sales department and a rate of $15.00/hour for workers who are in the Processing department.

You will need a set of text box controls that allow the user to indicate a Department for each Employee. The following figure will demonstrate what the input to your application may look like:

After the `cmdCalculate` command button is clicked, the following would be sample output for the input shown in the previous figure:

Problem Discussion   The solution to the problem does not change much from the previous chapter's case study. The main difference is that you need to check which pay rate to use in the calculation of the weekly pay.

Problem Solution   Again, most of the controls for your application were placed on the form in the previous chapter. You need only add the controls for the Department label and text boxes. What you call the label control is unimportant. However, you should call the Department text boxes `txtDept1`, `txtDept2`, `txtDept3`, and `txtDept4`.

Although it is not required, the use of constants in this solution is desirable. You should code a constant to indicate the pay rates for the Sales and Processing departments. The constant for the Sales department and Processing department will be called `intSalesPayRate` and `intProcessingPayRate`, respectively. This way you can change either pay rate once and have it affect the entire application.

Set the Constant

Step 1: Right-click on the mouse and click on View Code.
Step 2: Type "`Const intSalesPayRate As Integer = 25`".
Step 3: Type "`Const intProcessingPayRate As Integer = 15`".

Your code should look as follows.

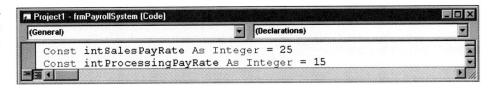

Figure 4.44
General Declarations
Section

The command button's code must set each `WeeklyPay`'s value to the number of hours worked times the pay rate associated with each employee's department. This is accomplished with an `If/ElseIf` statement. To improve the realiability of the application, you will use a compound conditional and check for two capitalizations of the department name. Once the value is calculated, it is copied to the text box control for display and added to the variable `tmpTotalPay`. When the four people's pay is calculated, the final total is copied to the text box control for display. The code follows:

```
Private Sub CmdCalculate_Click()

'Temporary Variables to Store Calculations
Dim curTotalPay As Currency
Dim curWeeklyPay As Currency

'First Week's Calculations
If (txtDept1.Text = "Sales") Then
    curWeeklyPay = Val(txtHours1.Text) * intSalesPayRate
ElseIf (txtDept1.Text = "Processing") Then
    curWeeklyPay = Val(txtHours1.Text) * intProcessingPayRate
End If
txtWeeklyPay1.Text = Str(curWeeklyPay)
curTotalPay = curWeeklyPay

'Second Week's Calculations
If (txtDept2.Text = "Sales") Then
    curWeeklyPay = Val(txtHours2.Text) * intSalesPayRate
ElseIf (txtDept2.Text = "Processing") Then
    curWeeklyPay = Val(txtHours2.Text) * intProcessingPayRate
End If
txtWeeklyPay2.Text = Str(curWeeklyPay)
curTotalPay = curTotalPay + curWeeklyPay

'Third Week's Calculations
If (txtDept3.Text = "Sales") Then
    curWeeklyPay = Val(txtHours3.Text) * intSalesPayRate
```

(continues)

(continued)

```
ElseIf (txtDept3.Text = "Processing") Then
    curWeeklyPay = Val(txtHours3.Text) * intProcessingPayRate
End If
txtWeeklyPay3.Text = Str(curWeeklyPay)
curTotalPay = curTotalPay + curWeeklyPay


'Fourth Week's Calculations
If (txtDept4.Text = "Sales") Then
    curWeeklyPay = Val(txtHours4.Text) * intSalesPayRate
ElseIf (txtDept4.Text = "Processing") Then
    curWeeklyPay = Val(txtHours4.Text) * intProcessingPayRate
End If
txtWeeklyPay4.Text = Str(curWeeklyPay)
curTotalPay = curTotalPay + curWeeklyPay


'Copy Total Pay to TextBox
txtTotalPay.Text = Str(curTotalPay)
End Sub
```

Figure 4.45
Final Application

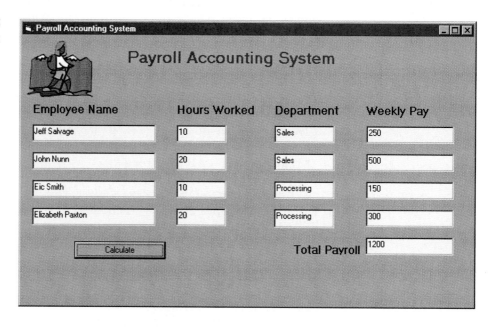

CORNER

In this chapter you have learned how to code decisions into the applications you create. With a slight modification to the `MsgBox` command you can ask the user a question and get an answer without having to create new forms.

If you want to ask a simple Yes/No question, you can ask it using the `MsgBox` command. The following code will ask the question "`Do you think the Sixers will win it all?`" and store the result in the variable `intAnswer`.

```
intAnswer = MsgBox("Do you think the Sixers will win it all?", vbYesNo)
```

The message box would look as follows:

Figure 4.46
Message Box

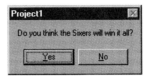

You added another value to the `MsgBox` line. You added a parameter, `vbYesNo`, which tells the `MsgBox` command to display a Yes/No style message box. This is just one of many types of message boxes that can be used. By changing the parameter, other message boxes can be selected.

By using the following constants you can create dialog boxes with the following buttons:

vbYesNo	Yes/No
vbYesNoCancel	Yes/No/Cancel
vbOKCancel	OK/Cancel
vbRetryCancel	Retry/Cancel

By using the following constants, you can check to see what the user's response was:

vbYes	Yes
vbNo	No
vbCancel	Cancel
vbOK	OK
vbRetry	Retry

You may have noticed that the title of the project is the title displayed in the message box. This does not have to be the case. If you add a title to the `MsgBox` line, an additional value of a `String` containing the title you want to display, it will appear at the top of the dialog box. The following code demonstrates adding the title "`Question`" to your dialog box example:

```
intAnswer = MsgBox("Do you think the Sixers will win it all?", _
            vbYesNo, "Question")
```

Figure 4.47
Question Message Box

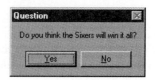

Key Words and Key Terms

<

An operator performing the less-than comparison.

>

An operator performing the greater-than comparison.

<=

An operator performing the less-than or equal-to comparison.

>=

An operator performing the greater-than or equal-to comparison.

=

An operator performing the equal-to comparison.

<>

An operator performing the not-equal-to comparison.

And

An operator used to perform the logical anding of two conditions.

Boolean

A variable datatype that allows the storage of a Boolean value.

Case

A keyword that indicates the individual cases of a Select Case statement.

Compound Conditional Expression

An expression that involves more than one subexpression.

Else

A keyword that indicates what statement(s) should be executed when an If statement evaluates to False.

Else If

A keyword that indicates another condition to check and statement(s) that should be executed when the If condition evaluates to False, but the ElseIf condition evaluates to True.

End If

A keyword that indicates the end of an If statement.

End Select

A keyword that indicates the end of a Select Case statement.

False

A keyword that indicates that an expression did not evaluate to True.

If

A keyword that indicates what statement(s) should be executed when the expression following it evaluates to True.

Nested Conditional

A conditional statement that is written inside of another conditional statement.

Not

An operator used to negate a value or expression.

Or

An operator used to perform the logical oring of two conditions.

Select Case

A keyword that indicates the beginning of a `Select Case` statement.

True

A keyword that indicates that an expression evaluated to `True`.

Answers to Chapter's Drills

Drill 4.1

1. `(5 >= 4)` evaluates to `True`. When the operator `>=` is used the expression evaluates to `True` if the value to the left is greater than the value to the right (in this case it is) or if the value to the left is equal to the value to the right (in this case it is not). Since only one of these cases must be true for the expression to be evaluated to `True`, the expression is evaluated to `True`.

2. `(-3 < -4)` evaluates to `False`. When the operator `<` is used the expression evaluates to `True` if the value to the left is less than the value to the right. Although the number 3 is less than the number 4, the value –3 is not less than the number –4.

3. `(5 = 4)` evaluates to `False`. When the operator `=` is used the expression evaluates to `True` if the value to the left is exactly the same as the value to the right. Since 5 is the value on the left and 4 is the value on the right, the values are not the same.

4. `(5 <> 4)` evaluates to `True`. When the operator `<>` is used the expression evaluates to `True` if the value to the left of the operator is not the same as the value to the right of the operator. Since 5 is not the same as 4, the expression evaluates to `True`.

5. `(4 >= 4)` evaluates to `True`. When the operator `>=` is used the expression evaluates to `True` if the value to the left is greater than the value to the right (in this case it is not) or the value to the left is the same as the value to the right (in this case it is). Since only one of these cases must evaluate to `True` for the expression to be evaluated to `True`, the expression is evaluated to `True`.

6. `(4 <= 4)` evaluates to `True`. When the operator `<=` is used the expression evaluates to `True` if the value to the left is less than the value to the right (in this case it is not) or the value to the left is the same as the value to the right (in this case it is). Since only one of these cases must evaluate to `True` for the expression to be evaluated to `True`, the expression is evaluated to `True`.

Drill 4.2

With 1 or 2 Entered in txtInput

If the user enters either 1 or 2 in the `txtInput` text box, the output would be as follows:

```
and the second statement prints
```

When the value stored in `txtInput` is equal to 1 or 2, the `If` statement evaluates to `False` since neither value is greater than 2. Therefore, the first assignment to the `txtOutput` text box is not performed. However, since the second statement has nothing to do with the `If` statement, it is executed.

With 3 Entered in txtInput

If the user enters 3 in the `txtInput` text box, the output would be as follows:

```
The first statement prints and the second statement prints
```

When the value stored in `txtInput` equals 3, then the `If` statement evaluates to `True` since 3 is greater than 2. Therefore, the first assignment to the `txtOutput` text box is performed. Since the second statement has nothing to do with the `If` statement, it is executed.

Drill 4.3
With 1 Entered in txtInput

If the user enters 1 in the `txtInput` text box, the output would be as follows:

```
The first statement prints and the second statement prints
```

When the value stored in `txtInput` equals 1, the `If` statement evaluates to `True` since 1 is less than 2. Therefore, the first assignment to the `txtOutput` text box is performed. Since the second statement has nothing to do with the `If` statement, it is executed as well.

With 2 or 3 Entered in txtInput

If the user enters either 2 or 3 in the `txtInput` text box, the output would be as follows:

```
and the second statement prints
```

When the value stored in `txtInput` is equal to 2 or 3, then the `If` statement evaluates to `False` since neither value is less than 2. Therefore, the first assignment to the `txtOutput` text box is not performed. However, since the second statement has nothing to do with the `If` statement, it is executed.

Drill 4.4
With 1 Entered in txtInput

If the user enters 1 in the `txtInput` text box, the output would be as follows:

```
and the second statement prints
```

When the value stored in `txtInput` is equal to 1, the `If` statement evaluates to `False` since 1 is not greater than or equal to 2. Therefore, the first assignment to the `txtOutput` text box is not performed. However, since the second statement has nothing to do with the `If` statement, it is executed.

With 2 or 3 Entered in txtInput

If the user enters either 2 or 3 in the `txtInput` text box, the output would be as follows:

```
The first statement prints and the second statement prints
```

When the value stored in `txtInput` equals 2 or 3, then the `If` statement evaluates to `True` since 2 and 3 are both greater than or equal to 2. Therefore, the first assignment to the `txtOutput` text box is performed. Since the second statement has nothing to do with the `If` statement, it is executed as well.

Drill 4.5
With 1 or 2 is Entered in txtInput

If the user enters either 1 or 2 in the `txtInput` text box, the output would be as follows:

```
The first statement prints and the second statement prints
```

When the value stored in `txtInput` equals 1 or 2, the `If` statement evaluates to `True` since 1 and 2 are both less than or equal to 2. Therefore, the first assignment to the `txtOutput` text box is performed. Since the second statement has nothing to do with the `If` statement, it is executed as well.

With 3 Entered in txtInput

If the user enters 3 in the `txtInput` text box, the output would be as follows:

```
and the second statement prints
```

When the value stored in `txtInput` is equal to 3, the `If` statement evaluates to `False` since 3 is not less than or equal to 2. Therefore, the first assignment to the `txtOutput` text box is not performed. However, since the second statement has nothing to do with the `If` statement, it is executed.

Drill 4.6

The output when `intDrillValue = 0` is:

```
This will output, because intDrillValue <= 1 and this is here as well
```

When `intDrillValue` is set to 0, the expression (`intDrillValue <= 1`) evaluates to `True`. The code associated with the `If` statement is executed and `"This will output, because intDrillValue <= 1"` is assigned to `txtOutput`. The code associated with the `Else` statement is therefore not executed. However, the last statement is executed because it is not in the `If` statement and therefore executes every time. So `"and this is here as well"` is concatenated to `txtOutput`.

The output when `intDrillValue = 1` is:

```
This will output, because intDrillValue <= 1 and this is here as well
```

When `intDrillValue` is set to 1, the expression (`intDrillValue <= 1`) evaluates to `True`. The code associated with the `If` statement is executed and `"This will output, because intDrillValue <= 1"` is assigned to `txtOutput`. The code associated with the `Else` statement is therefore not executed. However, the last statement is executed because it is not in the `If` statement and therefore executes all the time. So `"and this is here as well"` is concatenated to `txtOutput`.

The output when `intDrillValue = 2` is:

```
Instead this outputs, because intDrillValue > 1 and this is here as well
```

When `intDrillValue` is set to 1, the expression (`intDrillValue <= 1`) evaluates to `False`. Therefore, the code associated with the `If` statement is not executed. Instead, the code associated with the `Else` statement is. So, `"Instead this outputs, because intDrillValue > 1"` is assigned to `txtOutput`. Finally, the last statement is executed because it is not in the `If` statement and therefore executes every time. So `"and this is here as well"` is concatenated to `txtOutput`.

Drill 4.7

The output when `intDrillValue = 0` is:

```
This will output, because intDrillValue < 1 and this is here as well
```

When `intDrillValue` is set to 0, the expression (`intDrillValue < 1`) evaluates to `True`. The code associated with the `If` statement is executed and `"This will output, because intDrillValue < 1"` is assigned to `txtOutput`. The code associated with the `Else` statement is therefore not executed. However, the last statement is executed because it is not in the `If` statement and therefore executes every time. So `"and this is here as well"` is concatenated to `txtOutput`.

The output when `intDrillValue = 1` is:

```
Instead this outputs, because intDrillValue >= 1 and this is here as well
```

When `intDrillValue` is set to 1, the expression (`intDrillValue < 1`) evaluates to `False`. Therefore, the code associated with the `If` statement is not executed. Instead, the code associated with the `Else` statement is. So, `"Instead this outputs, because intDrillValue >= 1"` is assigned to `txtOutput`. Finally, the last statement is executed because it is not in the `If` statement and therefore executes every time. So `"and this is here as well"` is concatenated to `txtOutput`.

The output when `intDrillValue = 2` is:

```
Instead this outputs, because intDrillValue >= 1 and this is here as well
```

When `intDrillValue` is set to 1, the expression (`intDrillValue < 1`) evaluates to `False`. Therefore, the code associated with the `If` statement is not executed. Instead, the code associated with the `Else` statement is. So, `"Instead this outputs, because intDrillValue >= 1"` is assigned to `txtOutput`. Finally, the last statement is executed because it is not in the `If` statement and therefore executes every time. So `"and this is here as well"` is concatenated to `txtOutput`.

Drill 4.8

1) With 600.00 Entered by the User

When the program is executed and the command button is clicked, the `If` statement is evaluated. If the user enters `600.00`, the `If` statement evaluates the expression by comparing the value entered to 100. Therefore, the conditional expression will evaluate to `True`. This causes all the statements until the `ElseIf` to be executed. Therefore, the purchase price is multiplied by .05 and the result is converted to a `String`. So, the value `"30"` is placed in the text box. Since the conditional expression in the `If` statement evaluated to `True`, none of the statements after the `ElseIf` or `Else` statements and before the `End If` are executed. Note this is not what you wanted to have happen! Because you evaluated the condition comparing the value to 100 first, it will evaluate to `True` when you really want the expression `> 500` to evaluate to `True`. The order you evaluate your conditions can make a difference.

2) With 250.00 Entered by the User

When the program is executed and the command button is clicked, the `If` statement is evaluated. If the user enters `250.00`, the `If` statement evaluates the expression by comparing the value entered to 100. Therefore, the conditional expression will evaluate to `True`. This causes all the statements until the `ElseIf` to be executed. Therefore, the purchase price is multiplied by .05 and the result is converted to a `String`. So, the value `"12.5"` is placed in the text box. Since the conditional expression in the `If` statement evaluated to `True`, none of the statements after the `ElseIf` or `Else` statements and before the `End If` are executed.

3) With 50.00 Entered by the User

Finally, if the user enters a value less than or equal to 100, neither the `If` or `ElseIf` conditional expressions evaluate to `True`. Therefore, the statements after the `Else` statement and before the `End If` statement are executed. So, the text `"NO DISCOUNT"` is placed in the text box.

Drill 4.9

1) With –1 Entered by the User

When the application is executed and the command button is clicked, the `If` statement is evaluated. If the user enters a `–1`, `If` statement evaluates the expression by comparing the value entered to see if it is greater than 0. Since `–1` is not greater than 0, the conditional expression will evaluate to `False`. Therefore, the second condition will be evaluated in the `ElseIf` statement. The `ElseIf` condition compares –1 to see if it is less than 0. This time the conditional expression evaluates to `True`. This causes all the statements until the `Else` to be executed. So, `"The number is negative"` is copied to `txtOutput`.

2) With 0 Entered by the User

When the application is executed and the command button is clicked, the `If` statement is evaluated. If the user enters a 0, the `If` statement evaluates the expression by comparing the value entered to see if it is greater than 0. Since 0 is not greater than 0, the conditional expression will evaluate to `False`. Therefore, the second condition will be evaluated in the `ElseIf` statement. The `ElseIf` condition compares 0 to see if it is less than 0. Again, the conditional expression evaluates to `False`. Therefore, the `Else` statement is executed copying `"I got a big zero"` to `txtOutput`.

3) With 1 Entered by the User

When the application is executed and the command button is clicked, the `If` statement is evaluated. If the user enters a 1, the `If` statement evaluates the expression by comparing the value entered to see if it is greater than 0. Since 1 is greater than 0, the conditional expression will evaluate to `True` copying `"The number is positive"` to `txtOutput`.

Drill 4.10

Indicate whether each expression evaluates to `True` or `False`.

1. `Not (5 >= 4)` evaluates to `False`. The subexpression `(5 >= 4)` evaluates to `True`; however the `Not` operator inverts the `True` to `False`. Therefore the entire expression evaluates to `False`.

2. `(-3 < -4) Or (1 = 1)` evaluates to `True`. The subexpression `(-3 < -4)` evaluates to `False`; however, the other subexpression `(1 = 1)` evaluates to `True`. Since the two subexpressions are joined with an `Or` operator, only one of the subexpressions must evaluate to `True` for the entire expression to evaluate to `True`. Therefore the expression evaluates to `True`.

3. `("BOB" = "bob") And (2 >= 2)` evaluates to `False`. The subexpression `("BOB" = "bob")` evaluates to `False` because even though the two strings have the same letters, they are not the same capitalization. Even though the second subexpression evaluates to `True`, it doesn't matter. When two subexpressions

are joined with an `And` operator, both subexpressions must be `True` for the entire expression to evaluate to `True`.

4. `(2 < 1) Or (5 <> 4)` evaluates to `True`. The subexpression `(2 < 1)` evaluates to `False`. However, since an `Or` operator only requires one of the subexpressions to evaluate to `True`, then if the second subexpression evaluates to `True`, the entire expression would evaluate to `True`. Since `(5 <> 4)` evaluates to `True`, the entire expression evaluates to `True`.

5. `(1 < 2) Or (4 >= 4)` evaluates to `True`. The subexpression `(1 < 2)` evaluates to `True`. Since the two subexpressions are joined with an `Or` operator, the entire expression evaluates to `True` regardless of the evaluation of the second expression.

6. `Not (4 <= 4) And (1 <= 1)` evaluates to `False`. Since the two subexpressions are joined with an `And` operator, they must both evaluate to `True`. The first subexpression `Not (4 <= 4)` actually can be thought of as an expression with two subexpressions in itself. First you have the subexpression `(4 <= 4)`, which evaluates to `True`. However, when you apply the `Not` operator, that entire first subexpression evaluates to `False`. Therefore the entire expression evaluates to `False`.

Drill 4.11

1) With a Retail Price of 99.95 and a Sales Price of 50.25

When the application is executed and the command button is clicked, the `If` statement is evaluated. When the user enters `99.95` and `50.25` for the Retail and Sales prices, the `If` statement evaluates the expression by comparing the retail price to the sales price. Since `99.95` is greater than `50.25`, that part of the expression evaluates to `True`. The second condition is then checked. The sales price is compared to `75.00`. Since the sales price is not greater than `75.00`, the comparison evaluates to `False`. However, the `Not` operator has to be applied. This negates the `False` and the second subcondition evaluates to `True`. Because the two subconditions are combined with an `And` operator, both of the subconditions must evaluate to `True` for the entire conditional expression to evaluate to `True`. Therefore, the code associated with the `If` statement is executed. The text `"This crazy drill outputs True"` is assigned to the output text box.

2) With a Retail Price of 199.95 and a Sales Price of 99.95

When the application is executed and the command button is clicked, the `If` statement is evaluated. When the user enters `199.95` and `99.95` for the Retail and Sales prices, then the `If` statement evaluates the expression by comparing the retail price to the sales price. Since `199.95` is greater than `99.95`, that part of the expression evaluates to `True`. The second condition is then checked. The sales price is compared to `75.00`. Since the sales price is greater than `75.00`, the comparison evaluates to `True`. However, the `Not` operator has to be applied. This negates the `True` and the second subcondition evaluates to `False`. Because the two subconditions are combined with an `And` operator, both of the subconditions must evaluate to `True` for the entire conditional expression to evaluate to `True`. Therefore, the code associated with the `Else` statement is executed. Therefore, the text `"This crazy drill outputs False"` is assigned to the output text box.

Drill 4.12

1) With 0 Entered

When the user enters 0, the expression (`intDrillValue = 1`) evaluates to `False`, since `intDrillValue` will contain 0. Therefore, you process the code contained in the outer `Else` statement.

The expression (`intDrillValue < 1`) evaluates to `True` so, `"This will output, from the 2nd Inner If"` is assigned to `txtOutput`.

2) With 1 Entered

When the user enters 1, the expression (`intDrillValue = 1`) evaluates to `True`, since `intDrillValue` will contain 1. Therefore, you process the code contained in the inner `If` statement.

The expression (`intDrillValue <= 1`) evaluates to `True` so `"This will output, from the 1st Inner If"` is assigned to `txtOutput`.

3) With 2 Entered

When `intDrillValue` is set to 2, the expression (`intDrillValue = 1`) evaluates to `False` since `intDrillValue` will contain 2. Therefore, you process the code contained in the outer `Else` statement.

In executing the code contained within the outer `Else` statement, you must evaluate the 2nd inner `If` statement. The expression (`intDrillValue < 1`) evaluates to `False` so, `"This will output, from the 2nd Inner Else"` is assigned to `txtOutput`.

Drill 4.13
1) With 0 Entered

When the user enters 0, the first `Case` statement evaluates to `False` and the next one is tried. Since `intDrillValue` equals 0 and 0 is in the range 0 to 20, the second `Case` statement evaluates to `True`. Therefore, the `value "2nd Case Statement"` is assigned to the `txtOutput` text box. Since a `Case` statement evaluated to `True`, the rest are ignored.

2) With 100 Entered

When the user enters 100, the first, second, third, and fourth `Case` statements all evaluate to `False` since 100 is not in the range of any of the values listed. However when the fifth `Case` statement is tried, it evaluates to `True` since `intDrillValue` equals 100 and 100 is greater than 50. Therefore, the `value "4th Case Statement"` is assigned to the `txtOutput` text box. Since a `Case` statement evaluated to `True`, the rest are ignored.

3) With –50 Entered

When the user enters –50, the first `Case` statement evaluates to `True` and the value `"Error in Input"` is assigned to the `txtOutput` text box. Since a `Case` statement evaluated to `True`, the rest are ignored.

4) Any Value Entered?

As to whether or not the `Case Else` statement could ever execute, the answer is no. If you looked at all the other case statements' ranges, you would find that every possible value for an `Integer` is covered in one of the cases. Therefore, there is no value that could be entered by the user that could cause the `Case Else` to execute.

Additional Exercises

1. True or False
   a. An `If` statement can only have one `ElseIf` and `Else` statement associated with it.
   b. It is possible to have an `ElseIf` statement without associating it with an `If` statement.
   c. It is possible to have an `If` and `ElseIf` statement without an `Else` statement being associated with it.

2. Which of the following is not an operator to link conditions in a compound conditional expression?

   a. And   b. Maybe   c. Not   d. Or

3. Describe in your own words what would happen to an expression that had the Not operator applied to it twice as in: Not (Not (Expression)).

4. What is the advantage of using a nested conditional statement instead of a compound conditional statement?

5. When using a Select Case statement, which of the following statements would be used to signify the case to execute when none of the other cases are chosen?

   a. Case Else   b. Else   c. Else Case   d. Just In Case

6. Which of the following expressions evaluate to True?

   a. (2 >= 3)
   b. (-5 > -4) Or (1 <= 3)
   c. ("BOB" <> "bob") And (3 >= 2)
   d. (1 < 1) Or (1 <> 1)
   e. (1 < 1) Or (2 <> 2)
   f. (4.3 <= 4.33) And (0 <= -1)

7. What is the value in txtOutput after the following code is executed if strExampleValue is set to:

   a. "XOX"
   b. "XXX"
   c. "OOX"

```
Private Sub CmdOutput_Click()

Dim strExampleValue As String
strExampleValue = "XOX" 'or the other values

If (strExampleValue = "XXX") Then
   txtOutput.Text = "Choice 1"
ElseIf (strExampleValue = "OOO") Then
   txtOutput.Text = "Choice 2"
ElseIf (strExampleValue = "OXO") Then
   txtOutput.Text = "Choice 3"
Else
   txtOutput.Text = "Choice 4"
End If

End Sub
```

8. What is the value in txtOutput after the following code is executed if strExampleValue is set to:

   a. "XxX"
   b. "OOO"
   c. "OXO"
   d. "xox"

```
Private Sub CmdOutput_Click()

Dim ExampleValue As String
ExampleValue = "XOX" 'or the other values

If (ExampleValue = "XXX") And (ExampleValue = "xxx") Then
   txtOutput.Text = "Choice 1"
ElseIf (ExampleValue = "OOO") And (ExampleValue = "ooo") Then
   txtOutput.Text = "Choice 2"
ElseIf (ExampleValue = "XOX") And (ExampleValue = "xox") Then
   txtOutput.Text = "Choice 3"
Else
   txtOutput.Text = "Choice 4"
End If

End Sub
```

9. What is the value in txtOutput after the following code is executed if strExampleValue is set to:

a. "XxX"
b. "OOO"
c. "OXO"
d. "xox"

```
Private Sub CmdOutput_Click()

Dim ExampleValue As String
ExampleValue = "XOX" 'or the other values

If (ExampleValue = "XXX") And (ExampleValue = "xxx") Then
   txtOutput.Text = "Choice 1"
ElseIf (ExampleValue = "OOO") And (ExampleValue = "ooo") Then
   txtOutput.Text = "Choice 2"
ElseIf (ExampleValue = "XOX") And (ExampleValue = "xox") Then
   txtOutput.Text = "Choice 3"
Else
   txtOutput.Text = "Choice 4"
End If

End Sub
```

10. What is the value in txtOutput after the following code is executed if strExampleValue is set to:

a. "XxX"
b. "OOO"
c. "OXO"
d. "xox"

```
Private Sub CmdOutput_Click()

Dim ExampleValue As String
ExampleValue = "XOX" 'or the other values

If Not (ExampleValue = "XXX") And (ExampleValue = "xxx") Then
    txtOutput.Text = "Choice 1"
ElseIf (ExampleValue = "OOO") And Not(ExampleValue = "ooo") Then
    txtOutput.Text = "Choice 2"
ElseIf (ExampleValue = "XOX") And Not(ExampleValue = "xox") Then
    txtOutput.Text = "Choice 3"
Else
    txtOutput.Text = "Choice 4"
End If

End Sub
```

11. What is the value in txtOutput after the following code is executed?

```
Private Sub CmdOutput_Click()

Dim ExampleValue As Integer
ExampleValue = 10

Select Case ExampleValue
Case Is < 100
    txtOutput.Text = "Less Than 100"
Case 10
    txtOutput.Text = "Equals 10"
Case Else
    txtOutput.Text = "Other"
End Select

End Sub
```

12. What is the value in txtOutput after the following code is executed?

```
Private Sub CmdOutput_Click()

Dim ExampleValue As String
ExampleValue = "President"

Select Case ExampleValue
Case "PRESIDENT"
    txtOutput.Text = "George Bush"
Case "VICE PRESIDENT"
    txtOutput.Text = "Dick Cheney"
Case Else
    txtOutput.Text = "Other"
End Select

End Sub
```

13. Write an application that accepts two grades and outputs the larger of the two grades. If both grades are the same, output the word "EQUAL". The grades should be entered in two text boxes and output in another text box.

14. Write an application that converts English units to metric units. The application should accept a value from the user to convert and units to convert from. Each value should be stored in its own text box. When the user clicks on the command button, it should output the converted value in a third text box.

> 1 inch = 2.54 centimeters
> 1 gallon = 3.785 liters
> 1 mile = 1.609 kilometers
> 1 pound = .4536 kilograms

Make sure that your application only accepts valid choices to convert.

15. Write an application that accepts a single digit integer and outputs the word that represents that number. Both the input and output should be in text boxes. If a number other than a single digit is entered, the program should output "Error in Input".

16. Write an application that simulates as a bank account for a single person. The application should initialize the bank account to a zero balance. The balance of the bank account should be displayed in a label control. Develop the application so that it can accept deposits and withdrawals. Deposits and withdrawals should use two text boxes, one for the amount and the other to indicate whether it's a deposit or withdrawal. It should not allow withdrawals that will lower the balance below 0. If such a withdrawal is attempted, a warning message should be displayed.

17. Add data validation to the Case Study in this chapter so that the application does not process a person's pay who has a negative value entered for hours worked.

18. Write an application that plays the game Hangman. Hangman is a game where one player picks a word and another player guesses the word by picking one letter at a time. If the letter exists in the word, the letter is displayed in its proper place. If the letter is not found in the word, the player is one step closer to losing. Each time a letter is not found, the next image in the sequence shown in Figure 4.48 is displayed. If the last figure is displayed, the player has lost the game.

In order to implement this with what you know so far, you need to set some limitations. The word to guess will need to be coded directly into the application for simplicity's sake. It should be set using constants. You also will need to limit the size of the word, let's say 10 characters. To draw the Hangman, you will need to create a series of graphic files. As each incorrect guess is made, the next graphic file is displayed. As each correct guess is made, display it in the proper place.

The graphics should look as follows:

Figure 4.48
Possible Hangman Figures

19. Write an application to simulate a vending machine. The vending machine should be preloaded with different types of candy and a quantity for each. Each candy needs a price and a code. The code would be a combination of a letter and number. For simplicity just allow the letters to be an A, B, C, D, or E.

    The vending machine must have a mechanism to accept money. You can use a text box and a command button to accept it, but then would need to validate that each value is a valid denomination of currency. A better way is to create a command button for a nickel, dime, quarter, and dollar. As each button is clicked, add the appropriate amount to the total. Also, create a Change Return command button to return the money entered to the user.

    Create a series of command buttons to allow the entry of a digit from 1–3 and a letter from A–E so that the user can select a candy to purchase. Since each purchase is signified by a combination of a letter and a number, as the command buttons are clicked, display the choice being made.

    Finally add a command button to make the purchase. It should validate that you have entered enough money to make the purchase, that you have selected a valid choice for a candy, and that candy still has a quantity greater than zero. The last step is to indicate how much money is returned as change.

CHAPTER 5
Additional Visual Basic Controls

CHAPTER
OBJECTIVES

- Introduce the frame control
- Introduce the check box control
- Introduce the option button control
- Introduce the list box control
- Introduce the combo box control

Visual Basic's strength is its capability to create user-friendly applications with a minimum of effort. This chapter will show how to add controls to your applications making them more intuitive to the user. It is important to understand the appropriate time to use each type of control. We will introduce several useful controls and then show where it is applicable to use each one.

5.1 Frame Control

A **frame** control is used to encase other controls as a single entity. Observe in the following form how two frames enclose the two sets of text boxes and labels. In this case, the containment of the controls is purely cosmetic. However, with the introduction of additional controls, you will see that you will need to group some controls together with frames in order for them to behave in the manner you desire.

Figure 5.1
The Coach Realty
Application

Add a Frame to a Form

Step 1: Click on the frame icon in the Control toolbox.
Step 2: Hold the left mouse button down and draw the frame on the form in the
desired location.
Step 3: Release the mouse button.
Step 4: The frame appears.
Step 5: Change the `Caption` property to whatever title you desire for your frame.

Figure 5.2
Selecting the Frame Control

Once the frame is created, you can create other controls and place them within
this frame.

TIP

Be sure to draw controls completely within the frame or they won't be contained
within it.

5.2 **Check Box Control**

A **check box** control is extremely useful when you want to toggle a value between on or off, selected or deselected. A selected check box control will be indicated as one with a check mark visible. A deselected check box control will be indicated as an empty box.

Imagine you are developing an interface for a Real Estate program. The program's purpose might be to gather information as to the characteristics that a home-buyer desires in a house. The following figure demonstrates the use of check box controls in a form:

Figure 5.3
Realty Application Using
Check Boxes

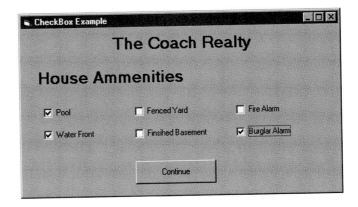

Notice how each check box has a caption displayed next to it. While one can remove the caption by blanking the `Caption` property, it is proper design to include a caption next to the check box indicating its purpose. Here you have six check boxes. The three with the captions `Pool`, `Water Front`, and `Burglar Alarm` are selected. The three with the captions `Fenced Yard`, `Finished Basement`, and `Fire Alarm` are not selected.

Add a Check Box to a Form

Step 1: Click on the check box icon in the toolbar.
Step 2: Hold the left mouse button down and draw the check box on the form in the desired location.
Step 3: Release the mouse button.
Step 4: The check box appears.

Figure 5.4
Selecting the Check Box
Control

WARNING

If you do not draw a large enough check box control, it will look like the check box on the form below. While your application can run this way, it is poor design. Check boxes should always have a label next to them.

Figure 5.5
Drawing a Small Check Box on a Form

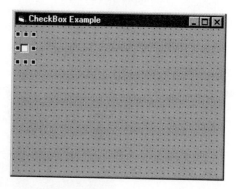

By extending the check box control, you can see that a caption is visible next to it. While you can change the default text in the `Caption` property, you must make sure that you draw the control large enough to hold whatever `Caption` you place next to the check box.

Figure 5.6
Drawing the Correct Size Check Box on a Form

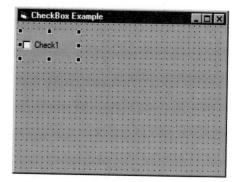

Improved Voting Booth Application   The applicability of check box controls to your Voting Booth application should be obvious. Instead of having to worry about the spelling of the candidates' names, you can redesign the interface so that it uses check box controls instead of text box controls to gather the votes. See the newly designed Voting Booth application.

Figure 5.7
Sketch of the Newly Designed Voting Booth Application

The Coach Voting Booth

President

☐ George Bush
☑ Al Gore
☐ Ralph Nader
☐ Pat Buchannan

Vice President

☐ Dick Cheney
☑ Joe Lieberman

| Vote | | Results |

Previously you had to enter a vote for each race one at a time. Now you can easily select the candidates you want from both races and not have to worry about data entry problems. You can also change the way you indicate the winner of the elections. All too often programmers will continue to do things the same way they have done things in the past. When new interface options are available, you should rethink the way you develop your application. In this case, instead of showing the results in a label, you will indicate the number of votes for each candidate next to their respective check box. This can be seen in the following figure:

Figure 5.8
Voting Booth Application
with Check Boxes

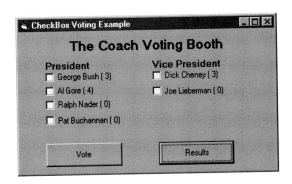

The following are the steps required developing your new application:

You need to declare an `Integer` variable for each candidate to store the number of votes they receive. The code follows:

```
Dim intBushCount As Integer
Dim intGoreCount As Integer
Dim intNaderCount As Integer
Dim intBuchannanCount As Integer
Dim intCheneyCount As Integer
Dim intLiebermanCount As Integer
```

When the `cmdResults` command button is clicked, you will append the number of votes each candidate received to the `Caption` property of the check box. You will also add a set of parentheses around the number of votes to improve readability. Since the count is stored in an `Integer` variable, you will use the `&` operator to perform the concatenation.

```
Private Sub cmdResults_Click()

chkBush.Caption = chkBush.Caption & " (" & Str(intBushCount) & ")"
chkGore.Caption = chkGore.Caption & " (" & Str(intGoreCount) & ")"
chkNader.Caption = chkNader.Caption & " (" & Str(intNaderCount) & ")"
chkBuchannan.Caption = chkBuchannan.Caption & " (" & _
    Str(intBuchannanCount) & ")"
chkCheney.Caption = chkCheney.Caption & " (" & Str(intCheneyCount) & ")"
chkLieberman.Caption = chkLieberman.Caption & " (" & _
    Str(intLiebermanCount) & ")"

End Sub
```

When the voter clicks on the cmdVote command button, you must account for his or her vote and clear the check box control. As we mentioned earlier, a selected check box will have a value of 1. Therefore, inspect each check box for a 1, increment the appropriate variable, and reset the check box value to 0. This can be seen in the following code:

```
Private Sub cmdVote_Click()
If (chkBush.Value = 1) Then
   intBushCount = intBushCount + 1
   chkBush.Value = 0 'Erase Vote
End If

If (chkGore.Value = 1) Then
   intGoreCount = intGoreCount + 1
   chkGore.Value = 0 'Erase Vote
End If

If (chkNader.Value = 1) Then
   NaderCount = NaderCount + 1
   chkNader.Value = 0 'Erase Vote
End If

If (chkBuchannan.Value = 1) Then
   BuchannanCount = BuchannanCount + 1
   chkBuchannan.Value = 0 'Erase Vote
End If

If (chkCheney.Value = 1) Then
   intCheneyCount = intCheneyCount + 1
   chkCheney.Value = 0 'Erase Vote
End If

If (chkLieberman.Value = 1) Then
   intLiebermanCount = intLiebermanCount + 1
   chkLieberman.Value = 0 'Erase Vote
End If

End Sub
```

As you did in the previous program, you must initialize all of the variables to 0.

```
Private Sub Form_Load()
'Initialize the Voting values
intBushCount = 0
intGoreCount = 0
intNaderCount = 0
intBuchannanCount = 0
intCheneyCount = 0
intLiebermanCount = 0
End Sub
```

If you think about your implementation, you might realize that we developed the Voting Booth application with the same basic problem that the Florida voting machines had. It allows you to vote more than once!

It is possible to add code to prevent duplicate votes from being counted, but then you are in no better shape than the Floridian machines. You could add code that warns voters that they have double-voted and make sure they change the vote before it counts. However, it is better to prevent the mistake from happening in the first place. The solution is discussed in the next section. You will use an option button control instead of a check box control.

5.3 Option Buttons

An **option button** control is extremely useful when you want to allow a user to enter a value from a list of values, but only allow one item from the list to be selected. Here is an example of an information form for a realty company. This form contains several option buttons that allow the user to enter the range of income for a person. Notice that an income of less than $30,000 is indicated. When you use an option button, only one of the options may be selected at a time.

Figure 5.9
Realty Application Using
Option Buttons

Proper Placement of an Option Button

Placing an option button on a form is somewhat more complicated than placing a check box. Initially, the procedure is similar.

Step 1: Click on the option button icon in the toolbar.
Step 2: Hold the left mouse button down and draw the option button on the form in the desired location. Make sure you leave enough space for the `Caption` property to be displayed.
Step 3: Release the mouse button. The option button appears.
Step 4: Change the `Caption` property to the value you wish the option button to represent.

Figure 5.10
Selecting the Option Button
from the Control Toolbar

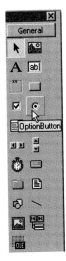

If you only want one set of option buttons on your form, this method is acceptable. However, what if you wanted a form with two sets of option buttons, as in the following form?

Figure 5.11
Multiple Sets of Option
Buttons on a Form

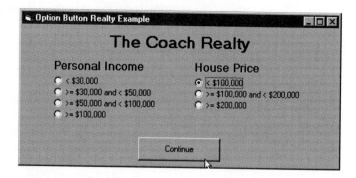

The problem is that you wish to record a value for a Personal Income and a House Price simultaneously. If you place option buttons directly on the form, you will not be able to achieve this.

Instead you must first place a frame control on the form. Then create the option button controls directly on the frame control. If you create the option button on the form and then drag it onto the frame control, it will not work. You need one frame control for each group of option buttons you desire. See the following form, which was created correctly with a frame control for Personal Income and another frame control for House Price.

Figure 5.12
Correct Multiple Sets of
Option Buttons on a Form

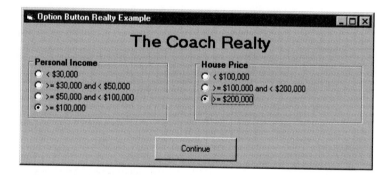

Improved Voting Booth Application   Now you can correct the problem in your Voting Booth application that allows double votes. Florida would be so jealous! Al Gore might even be president. By using a series of option buttons, you can allow only one candidate to be selected for each race. See the following figure of the newly designed Voting Booth application.

Figure 5.13
Improved Voting Booth
Application

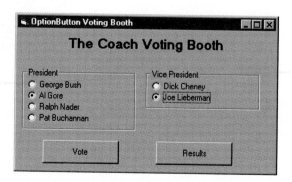

Notice that the two sets of option buttons are grouped in separate frames. If they weren't, all the option buttons on the form would be treated as one group, so you couldn't vote in both the presidential and vice presidential elections at the same time.

Notice in the following figure that you display the results of the election in the same manner that you did in the check box implementation.

Figure 5.14
Results Shown Using New
Application

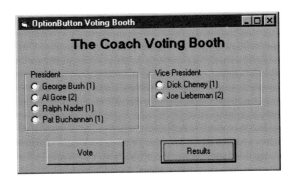

The code for the `cmdResults` command button is very similar to the code you used for check boxes instead of option buttons. When the `cmdResults` command button is clicked, you append the results of each candidate to the `Caption` associated with it.

```
Private Sub cmdResults_Click()

optBush.Caption = optBush.Caption & " (" & intBushCount & ")"
optGore.Caption = optGore.Caption & " (" & intGoreCount & ")"
optNader.Caption = optNader.Caption & " (" & intNaderCount & ")"
optBuchannan.Caption = optBuchannan.Caption & " (" & intBuchannanCount & ")"
optCheney.Caption = optCheney.Caption & " (" & intCheneyCount & ")"
optLieberman.Caption = optLieberman.Caption & " (" & intLiebermanCount & ")"

End Sub
```

The code for the `cmdVote` command button is also very similar to the code for the check box version of the Voting Booth application. This time, instead of checking to see if the value of the check box is 1, you check to see if the option button has a value of `True`. If it does, you add 1 to the appropriate candidate's counter. To reset the option button, you reset it back to `False`.

```
Private Sub cmdVote_Click()

If (optBush.Value = True) Then
   intBushCount = intBushCount + 1
   optBush.Value = False 'Erase Vote
End If

If (optGore.Value = True) Then
   intGoreCount = intGoreCount + 1
   optGore.Value = False 'Erase Vote
End If

If (optNader.Value = True) Then
   intNaderCount = intNaderCount + 1
```

(continues)

(continued)

```
   optNader.Value = False 'Erase Vote
End If

If (optBuchannan.Value = True) Then
   intBuchannanCount = intBuchannanCount + 1
   optBuchannan.Value = False 'Erase Vote
End If

If (optCheney.Value = True) Then
   intCheneyCount = intCheneyCount + 1
   optCheney.Value = False 'Erase Vote
End If

If (optLieberman.Value = True) Then
   intLiebermanCount = intLiebermanCount + 1
   optLieberman.Value = False 'Erase Vote
End If

End Sub
```

The remainder of the code for this application is the same as in the check box version.

5.4   Combo Boxes and List Boxes

Option buttons and check boxes are excellent ways of allowing a user to enter values from a list of predetermined choices. However, what happens if the number of choices to choose from is rather large? With our current methods, you would have a problem. Imagine if you had to create a form with a choice for a state. You would have to list each and every state on the form in a separate check box or option button. This would not only take a long time, but it would also produce applications that are unwieldy in size.

List boxes and combo boxes are an excellent way to solve this problem. The following figures show how your realty application would look using a set of combo boxes (Figure 5.15) and list boxes (Figure 5.16).

Figure 5.15
Realty Application with
Combo Boxes

Figure 5.16
Realty Application with List
Boxes

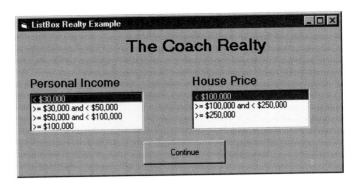

As you can see, a combo box takes up much less space than the option buttons you previously used. Fortunately, this reduction in space does not come at the cost of usability. With a combo box, the currently selected option is displayed. You can see this in the House Price combo box. However, when a combo box is clicked, all of its possible values are displayed and can be selected from. This is shown in the Personal Income combo box.

The list box is a compromise between the methods used with combo boxes and the option buttons. The developer can choose how many elements of the list are displayed at once. In Figure 5.16, all of the list items are displayed. However, we will show you how to limit this when we develop a new version of the Voting Booth application. When the number of list items is greater than the space allowed to display them, a scroll bar will appear on the right side of the list box to allow the user to display the remainder of the list.

The steps in using a combo box and list box are virtually identical.

To Add a Combo Box to a Form		To Add a List Box to a Form	
Step 1:	Click on the combo box icon in the toolbar.	Step 1:	Click on the list box icon in the toolbar.
Step 2:	Hold the left mouse button down and draw the combo box on the form in the desired location. Make sure you leave enough space for the largest value you wish to place in the combo box.	Step 2:	Hold the left mouse button down and draw the list box on the form in the desired location. Make sure you leave enough space for the largest value you wish to place in the list box.
Step 3:	Release the mouse button. The combo box appears.	Step 3:	Release the mouse button. The list box appears.
Step 4:	Click on the `List` property.	Step 4:	Click on the `List` property.
Step 5:	Click on the down arrow button in the `List` property window.	Step 5:	Click on the down arrow button in the `List` property window.
Step 6:	Enter an item to list in the combo box.	Step 6:	Enter an item to list in the list box.
Step 7:	For each additional item, press the `<CTRL>` key and the `<ENTER>` key simultaneously.	Step 7:	For each additional item, press the `<CTRL>` key and the `<ENTER>` key simultaneously.
Step 8:	Go to step 6.	Step 8:	Go to step 6.

Figure 5.17
Select Combo Box Control

Figure 5.18
Select List Box Control

Figure 5.19
Enter List Items into
a Combo Box

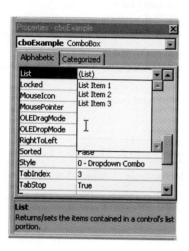

Figure 5.20
Enter List Items into
a List Box

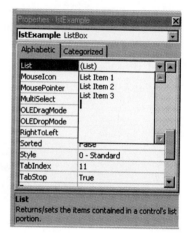

Example: Improved Voting Booth Application

With the addition of the combo box and list box controls, you can greatly increase the amount of information that you can display on a single form. Instead of just showing two races, you could show many more. Figure 5.21 demonstrates the newly created Voting Booth application that shows four races in the same space that you had two races before. In this case, you default each combo box to be blank. By clicking on the combo box, a list drops down of every person in the race. By clicking on the individual person, that person is selected from the list. In Figure 5.22, you demonstrate the application developed with list boxes. You can see that in the presidential race, only two of the candidates are displayed. The down arrow to the right of the control will allow the user to select the non-displayed candidates.

Figure 5.21
Voting Booth Application
with Combo Boxes

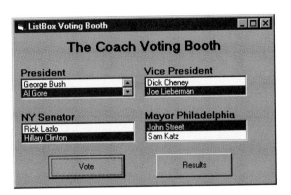

Figure 5.22
Voting Booth Application
with List Boxes

TIP

There are multiple styles to Visual Basic's combo boxes. The default style allows the user to enter values not listed in the combo box. For your voting booth, you are not going to allow unlisted values to be entered, so you set the `Style` property to `2 Dropdown List`.

To create the new Voting Booth application with combo boxes, you must add four combo boxes and labels as follows:

cboPres ComboBox

Label: President

List Item: George Bush

List Item: Al Gore

List Item: Ralph Nader

List Item: Pat Buchannan

Style: 2 Dropdown List

cboVicePres ComboBox

Label: Vice President

List Item: Dick Cheney

List Item: Joe Lieberman

Style: 2 Dropdown List

cboNYSen ComboBox

Label: NY Senator

List Item: Rick Lazlo

List Item: Hillary Clinton

Style: 2 Dropdown List

To create the new Voting Booth application with list boxes, you must add four list boxes and labels as follows:

lstPres ListBox

Label: President

List Item: George Bush

List Item: Al Gore

List Item: Ralph Nader

List Item: Pat Buchannan

lstVicePres ListBox

Label: Vice President

List Item: Dick Cheney

List Item: Joe Lieberman

lstNYSen ListBox

Label: NY Senator

List Item: Rick Lazlo

List Item: Hillary Clinton

(continues)

(continued)

cboPhilaMayor ComboBox	lstPhilaMayor ComboBox
Label: Mayor Philadelphia	Label: Mayor Philadelphia
List Item: John Street	List Item: John Street
List Item: Sam Katz	List Item: Sam Katz
Style: 2 Dropdown List	

You create both forms almost identically. See the following steps for creating both applications:

In both applications, you must modify the code of the application. The variables required for both applications are the same. You must create new counters for the additional candidates in the new races.

```
Dim intBushCount As Integer
Dim intGoreCount As Integer
Dim intNaderCount As Integer
Dim intBuchannanCount As Integer
Dim intCheneyCount As Integer
Dim intLiebermanCount As Integer
Dim intLazloCount As Integer
Dim intClintonCount As Integer
Dim intStreetCount As Integer
Dim intKatzCount As Integer
```

You also need to modify the subroutine Sub Form_Load so that the new variables are initialized to 0. This code would also be identical between the two applications. The code follows:

```
Private Sub Form_Load()
'Initialize the Voting values
intBushCount = 0
intGoreCount = 0
intNaderCount = 0
intBuchannanCount = 0
intCheneyCount = 0
intLiebermanCount = 0
intLazloCount = 0
intClintonCount = 0
intStreetCount = 0
intKatzCount = 0
End Sub
```

You must modify the cmdVote_Click routine to handle the new races and controls. The easiest way to track the votes is to use a Select Case statement for each race. You can access the value selected in the combo box by accessing the Text property. Then, you compare that value to one spelling of the candidate's name (the one in the List property), since you know the only possible spelling.

The code is nearly identical between the combo box and list box implementations. The only real difference is in the names of the controls. The two sets of code follow.

```
'Code for the ComboBox Implementation
Private Sub cmdVote_Click()
Select Case cboPres.Text
    Case "George Bush"
        intBushCount = intBushCount + 1
    Case "Al Gore"
        intGoreCount = intGoreCount + 1
    Case "Ralph Nader"
        intNaderCount = intNaderCount + 1
    Case "Pat Buchannan"
        intBuchannanCount = intBuchannanCount + 1
End Select
cboPres.ListIndex = -1 'Reset the Combo Box to unselected

Select Case cboVicePres.Text
    Case "Dick Cheney"
        intCheneyCount = intCheneyCount + 1
    Case "Joe Lieberman"
        intLiebermanCount = intLiebermanCount + 1
End Select
cboVicePres.ListIndex = -1 'Reset the Combo Box to unselected

Select Case cboNYSen.Text
    Case "Rick Lazlo"
        intLazloCount = intLazloCount + 1
    Case "Hillary Clinton"
        intClintonCount = intClintonCount + 1
End Select
cboNYSen.ListIndex = -1 'Reset the Combo Box to unselected

Select Case cboPhilaMayor.Text
    Case "John Street"
        intStreetCount = intStreetCount + 1
    Case "Sam Katz"
        intKatzCount = intKatzCount + 1
End Select
cboPhilaMayor.ListIndex = -1 'Reset the Combo Box to unselected

End Sub

'Code for the ListBox Implementation
Private Sub cmdVote_Click()
Select Case lstPres.Text
    Case "George Bush"
        intBushCount = intBushCount + 1
    Case "Al Gore"
        intGoreCount = intGoreCount + 1
    Case "Ralph Nader"
        intNaderCount = intNaderCount + 1
    Case "Pat Buchannan"
        intBuchannanCount = intBuchannanCount + 1
```

(continues)

(continued)

```
End Select
lstPres.ListIndex = -1 'Reset the ListBox to unselected

Select Case lstVicePres.Text
  Case "Dick Cheney"
     intCheneyCount = intCheneyCount + 1
  Case "Joe Lieberman"
     intLiebermanCount = intLiebermanCount + 1
End Select
lstVicePres.ListIndex = -1 'Reset the ListBox to unselected

Select Case lstNYSen.Text
  Case "Rick Lazlo"
     intLazloCount = intLazloCount + 1
  Case "Hillary Clinton"
     intClintonCount = intClintonCount + 1
End Select
lstNYSen.ListIndex = -1 'Reset the ListBox to unselected

Select Case lstPhilaMayor.Text
  Case "John Street"
     intStreetCount = intStreetCount + 1
  Case "Sam Katz"
     intKatzCount = intKatzCount + 1
End Select
lstPhilaMayor.ListIndex = -1 'Reset the ListBox to unselected

End Sub
```

Finally, you need to change the code to display the results for all four races. For lack of a better way to display the results, append each candidate's vote count to the end of either list item.

To access each list item individually requires you to access them by an index. Each list item is assigned an index number starting at 0. To access each item in the list, you place the index within parentheses. This notation is used by arrays. It will be explained in complete detail in Chapter 8.

```
'Code for the ComboBox Implementation
Private Sub cmdResults_Click()
'President
cboPres.List(0) = cboPres.List(0) & " (" & intBushCount & ")"
cboPres.List(1) = cboPres.List(1) & " (" & intGoreCount & ")"
cboPres.List(2) = cboPres.List(2) & " (" & intNaderCount & ")"
cboPres.List(3) = cboPres.List(3) & " (" & intBuchannanCount & ")"

'Vice President
cboVicePres.List(0) = cboVicePres.List(0) & " (" & intCheneyCount & ")"
cboVicePres.List(1) = cboVicePres.List(1) & " (" & intLiebermanCount & ")"

'NY Senator
cboNYSen.List(0) = cboNYSen.List(0) & " (" & intLazloCount & ")"
cboNYSen.List(1) = cboNYSen.List(1) & " (" & intClintonCount & ")"
```

(continues)

(continued)

```
'Philadelphia Mayor
cboPhilaMayor.List(0) = cboPhilaMayor.List(0) & " (" & intStreetCount & ")"
cboPhilaMayor.List(1) = cboPhilaMayor.List(1) & " (" & intKatzCount & ")"
End Sub


'Code for the ListBox Implementation
Private Sub cmdResults_Click()
'President
lstPres.List(0) = lstPres.List(0) & " (" & intBushCount & ")"
lstPres.List(1) = lstPres.List(1) & " (" & intGoreCount & ")"
lstPres.List(2) = lstPres.List(2) & " (" & intNaderCount & ")"
lstPres.List(3) = lstPres.List(3) & " (" & intBuchannanCount & ")"

'Vice President
lstVicePres.List(0) = lstVicePres.List(0) & " (" & intCheneyCount & ")"
lstVicePres.List(1) = lstVicePres.List(1) & " (" & intLiebermanCount & ")"

'NY Senator
lstNYSen.List(0) = lstNYSen.List(0) & " (" & intLazloCount & ")"
lstNYSen.List(1) = lstNYSen.List(1) & " (" & intClintonCount & ")"

'Philadelphia Mayor
lstPhilaMayor.List(0) = lstPhilaMayor.List(0) & " (" & intStreetCount & ")"
lstPhilaMayor.List(1) = lstPhilaMayor.List(1) & " (" & intKatzCount & ")"
End Sub
```

Manually Adding List Items   While Visual Basic provides an easy interface to add list items to a combo box and list box, it is not always convenient to do so interactively. Often you will want to set the list items of a combo box or list box programmatically. Imagine if instead of the applications you write being predefined, you created an application that allowed a user to customize the form without having access to the source code of the application. While you do not know enough to create a truly useful application yet, it is worth showing how to do this now.

This can be seen in the following code that illustrates the syntax of adding an item to the combo box:

ComboBox.AddItem *Value*

By repeatedly calling AddItem you can add as many items to the list as you desire.

If instead of creating the list of presidential candidates at design time, you choose to set them programmatically, the code would be as follows:

```
cboPres.AddItem "George Bush"
cboPres.AddItem "Al Gore"
cboPres.AddItem "Ralph Nader"
cboPres.AddItem "Pat Buchannan"
```

The method is the same for list boxes:

```
ListBox.AddItem Value

lstPres.AddItem "George Bush"
lstPres.AddItem "Al Gore"
lstPres.AddItem "Ralph Nader"
lstPres.AddItem "Pat Buchannan"
```

◆ 5.5   Case Study

Problem Description   This chapter's case study will be a continuation of last chapter's case study to compute the payroll of four workers for a company. In this application you wish to utilize your new controls to improve the usability of the application. By using combo boxes, you can prevent errors from being entered in the text box controls of the previous version. The most logical place for this is in the Department fields. In this example you will preload the combo boxes for Department with four departments: Sales, Phone, Processing, and Management. Their associated pay rates are $25.00, $10.00, $15.00, and $50.00 respectively.

The following figure will demonstrate what the input to your application may look like:

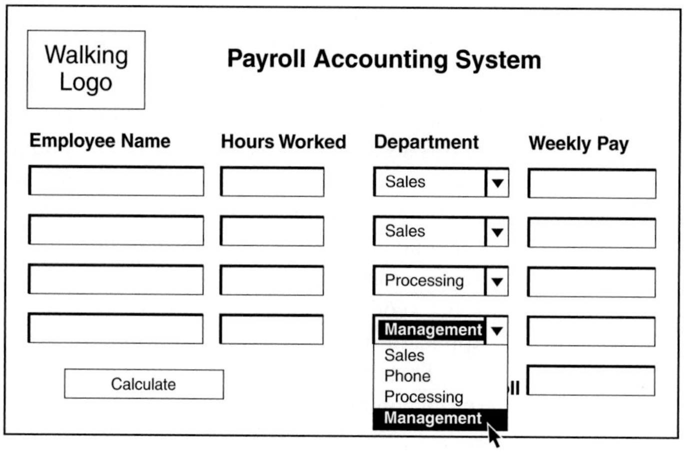

Figure 5.23
Sketch of Payroll
Application

Problem Discussion   The solution to the problem does not change much from the previous chapter's case study. The difference is mostly cosmetic and that you have added two more choices for a Department.

Problem Solution   As in the last chapter, most of the controls for your application were placed on the form in the previous chapter. You need only change the controls for the Department from text boxes to combo boxes. You will call the Department combo boxes `cboDept1`, `cboDept2`, `cboDept3`, and `cboDept4`.

You need to code two additional constants for the additional pay rates. The constant for the Phone Department and Management Department will be called `intPhonePayRate` and `intManagementPayRate`, respectively. This way you can change either pay rate once and have it affect the entire application.

Setting the Constant

Step 1: Right-click on the mouse and click on View Code.

Step 2: Scroll up to the `Declarations` area of code that contains the previous two constants.

Step 3: Type `Const intPhonePayRate = 10 As Integer`.

Step 4: Type `Const intManagementPayRate = 50 As Integer`.

Your code should look as follows:

```
Const intSalesPayRate As Integer = 25
Const intProcessingPayRate As Integer = 15
Const intManagementPayRate As Integer = 50
Const intPhonePayRate As Integer = 10
```

As before, the command button's code must set each `WeeklyPay`'s value to the number of hours worked * the pay rate associated with each employee's department. In this case, you switched from the `If/ElseIf` statement format used in Chapter 4 to `Select Case` statements.

You no longer need to check for multiple spellings of the department since the combo box will only allow valid entries to be selected. The code follows:

```
Private Sub CmdCalculate_Click()

'Temporary Variables to Store Calculations
Dim curTotalPay As Currency
Dim curWeeklyPay As Currency
'First Week's Calculations
Select Case cboDept1.Text
    Case "Sales"
        curWeeklyPay = Val(txtHours1.Text) * intSalesPayRate
    Case "Processing"
        curWeeklyPay = Val(txtHours1.Text) * intProcessingPayRate
    Case "Management"
        curWeeklyPay = Val(txtHours1.Text) * intManagementPayRate
    Case "Phone"
        curWeeklyPay = Val(txtHours1.Text) * intPhonePayRate
End Select

txtWeeklyPay1.Text = Str(curWeeklyPay)
curTotalPay = curWeeklyPay
'Second Week's Calculations
Select Case cboDept2.Text
    Case "Sales"
        curWeeklyPay = Val(txtHours2.Text) * intSalesPayRate
    Case "Processing"
        curWeeklyPay = Val(txtHours2.Text) * intProcessingPayRate
    Case "Management"
        curWeeklyPay = Val(txtHours2.Text) * intManagementPayRate
    Case "Phone"
        curWeeklyPay = Val(txtHours2.Text) * intPhonePayRate
End Select

txtWeeklyPay2.Text = Str(curWeeklyPay)
curTotalPay = curTotalPay + curWeeklyPay
```

(continues)

(continued)

```
'Third Week's Calculations
Select Case cboDept3.Text
    Case "Sales"
        curWeeklyPay = Val(txtHours3.Text) * intSalesPayRate
    Case "Processing"
        curWeeklyPay = Val(txtHours3.Text) * intProcessingPayRate
    Case "Management"
        curWeeklyPay = Val(txtHours3.Text) * intManagementPayRate
    Case "Phone"
        curWeeklyPay = Val(txtHours3.Text) * intPhonePayRate
End Select

txtWeeklyPay3.Text = Str(curWeeklyPay)
curTotalPay = curTotalPay + curWeeklyPay

'Fourth Week's Calculations
Select Case cboDept4.Text
    Case "Sales"
        curWeeklyPay = Val(txtHours4.Text) * intSalesPayRate
    Case "Processing"
        curWeeklyPay = Val(txtHours4.Text) * intProcessingPayRate
    Case "Management"
        curWeeklyPay = Val(txtHours4.Text) * intManagementPayRate
    Case "Phone"
        curWeeklyPay = Val(txtHours4.Text) * intPhonePayRate
End Select

txtWeeklyPay4.Text = curWeeklyPay
curTotalPay = curTotalPay + curWeeklyPay
'Copy Total Pay to TextBoxes
txtTotalPay.Text = Str(curTotalPay)
End Sub
```

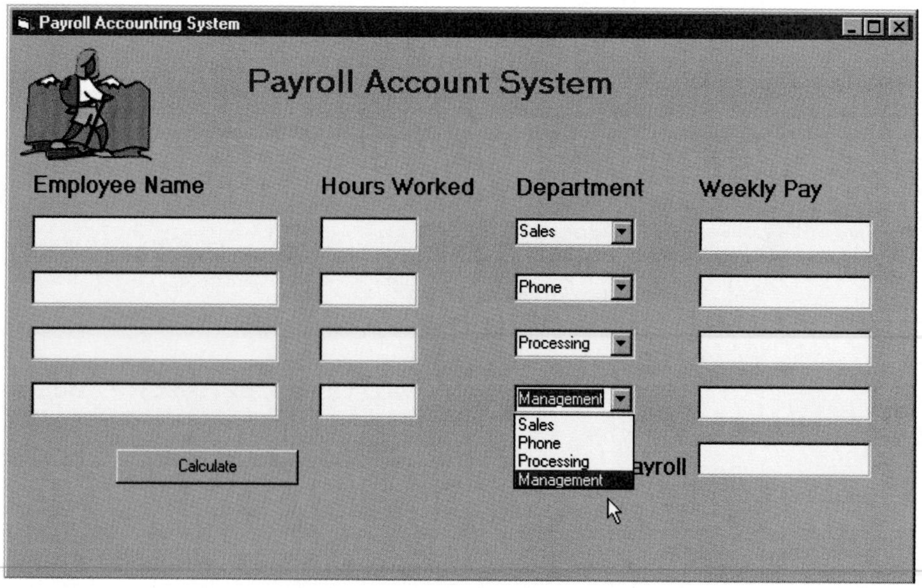

Figure 5.24
Final View of the
Application

CORNER

The Object Browser

The Object Browser is a very useful tool to understand the controls we have introduced as well as explore the other controls that come with Visual Basic. Actually, the Object Browser can be used to determine the properties, events, and other specifications of controls provided by Visual Basic as well as other objects that are provided from other applications as well as ones that you will learn to create in Chapter 12.

To use the Object Browser, click on the View menu and then select Object Browser from the pop-up menu.

The Object Browser in Figure 5.25 will appear. If you scroll down the Classes list, you will see controls like the combo box that you are already familiar with. If you click on the combo box control, you will notice its properties and events appear in the window to the right. At the bottom of the Object Browser, additional information is displayed about the specific item selected.

Figure 5.25
The Object Browser

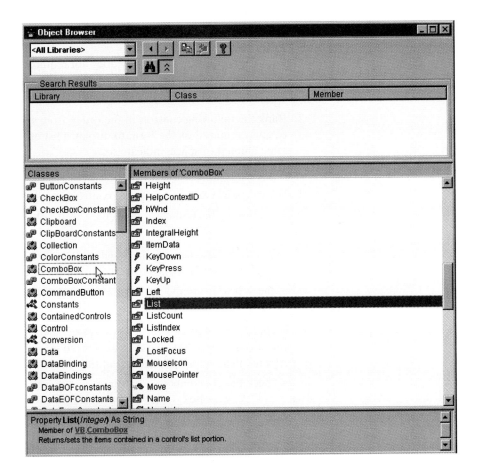

Key Words and Key Terms

Combo box

A control that allows the user to select an item from a predetermined list of choices. Only the selected item is displayed, unless the combo box is clicked.

List box

A control that allows the user to select an item from a predetermined list of choices. Some or all of the items in the list are displayed at once.

Option button

A control that allows the user to select a single item from a set of options.

Check box

A control that allows the user to select or deselect individual items.

Frame

A control that allows the user to group other controls together.

Additional Exercises

1. True or False

    a. A check box control is useful when you only want one value to be selected from a list of values.
    b. A combo box control is useful because it does not require a lot of space on the form.
    c. A check box control usually does not require a caption.
    d. You can set up different sets of option buttons by setting a property within the control to select which set it would belong to.

2. Rank the following controls in the order, from smallest to largest, of the amount of space required on the form to display a list of information. If two require the same amount of space, indicate so.

    a. check box   b. combo box   c. list box   d. option button

3. Which control can contain other controls on it?

    a. check box b. combo   c. frame   d. list box   e. option   f. text box
                       box   button

4. If you were designing a form to gather the possible majors (notice plural) a student is interested in, which control would you use to gather the information?

    a. check box b. combo   c. frame   d. list box   e. option   f. text box
                       box   button

5. If you were designing a form to gather the name of a student's favorite teacher, which control would you use to gather the information and why did you pick it? Assume there were 100 teachers at the school.

    a. check box b. combo   c. frame   d. list box   e. option   f. text box
                       box   button

6. If you were designing a form to gather the names of the car companies (notice plural) that the user liked, which control would you use to gather the information? Also, indicate why you picked it.

    a. check box b. combo   c. frame   d. list box   e. option   f. text box
                       box   button

7. Create an interface for a credit card application. The following values must be gathered: First Name, Last Name, Address, City, State, Zip, Income Level, Marital Status, and Interests. Use your creativity to develop a complete form using the appropriate controls for each data element gathered. Part of the chal-

lenge in creating a good application is deciding the appropriate values to preload into controls as predefined choices. Put some thought into the values you preload. Also add two more additional controls for information you feel appropriate for a credit card application.

8. Develop an interface for a car rental application. The application should gather the following information: Individual and Location of pickup, Pick-up Date, Drop-off Date, Car Class (Economy, Compact, Midsize, Standard, Full Size, Premium, Luxury, Convertible, Minivan), Pick-up Time (only allow exact hour times, such as 10:00 A.M. or 11:00 A.M.), Drop-off Time (only allow exact hour times, such as 10:00 A.M. or 11:00 A.M.), and Rental Car Company (Avis, Budget, Dollar, Enterprise). Use your creativity to develop a complete form using the appropriate controls for each data element gathered.

9. Modify the Voting Booth application so that voters can clear their votes before they are officially counted. This would prevent the double chad problem that voters in Florida faced when they realized they punched the wrong choice and then punched another choice.

10. Develop an interface for order fulfillment. The interface should preload the applications with choices for products and their prices. The application should allow the entry for the amount of each item desired. The application should include a command button that when clicked calculates the total cost of the order without tax, the tax of the order, and the total price. Assume the tax is 6%.

11. Rewrite the application to simulate a vending machine from Chapter 4. As before, the vending machine should be preloaded with different types of candy and a quantity for each. Each candy needs a name and price. Instead of using a code to identify the candy selection, use an option button, one associated with each candy.

    The vending machine must have a mechanism to accept money in the same manner as the previous application. You can use a text box and a command button to accept it, but then you would need to validate that each value is a valid denomination of currency. A better way is to create a command button for a nickel, dime, quarter, and dollar. As each button is clicked, add the appropriate amount to the total. Also, create a Change Return command button to return the money entered to the user.

    Finally, add a command button to make the purchase. It should validate that you have entered enough money to make the purchase. The last step is to indicate how much money is returned as change.

INTERVIEW

An Interview with Jeff Hunsaker

Jeff Hunsaker is a Microsoft Certified Solutions Developer and an Engagement Manager for Clarity Consulting, a company that focuses on custom application development using enterprise Microsoft tools. Among other projects, Jeff managed the team of consultants that upgraded Art.com's website, a unique online frame-shop, that allows its customers to select a print, then preview it on-screen in a variety of frames. He also served as webmaster and DBA while Art.com grew its staff and infrastructure.

With what challenge did Art.com present your company and was it met?

One talented gentleman developed the first version of Art.com simply using ASP and SQL Server; both hosted on the same machine. As Art.com's business rapidly expanded, they soon realized this model wouldn't support the web traffic they expected and relied on to meet revenue goals. We were charged with transforming the site into an easily maintained, scalable site. To accomplish this goal, we created a common middle tier using VB6 components, an ASP front-end, and a SQL Server backend; all using a Microsoft WLBS load-balancing solution. This way, whenever traffic increased, we could scale out by simply adding additional servers. We also developed a queued ordering system using Microsoft Message Queuing Server (MSMQ) as well as many of the feature areas available to a visitor.

Why was VB chosen for this task?

VB was chosen for its ease of implementation and its similarities to vbScript which existing Art.com staff used when developing ASP pages. Its strong facilities for retrieving and saving data also influenced the decision. Finally, using an all-Microsoft suite allowed us to avoid headaches involved with integrating products from disparate vendors.

What are some pitfalls to avoid when developing with VB?

Scalability is number one on my list. VB is an extensive development tool. There are lots of ways to accomplish an objective – unfortunately, in an enterprise environment, many alternatives are poor choices. Discovering which implementations work, perform, and scale the best will come from experience. Fortunately, developers can speed this experience using articles, presentations, and case studies available from Microsoft and many other third-party resources. Even more important is testing your scalability and performance against a real-world situation before going into production. Make sure your solution holds up against significantly more users than you expect while simulating real-world stress and using a fully loaded database. There's nothing worse than a deathly slow site because you failed to test with more than 10 concurrent users. One last pitfall: in those cases where a move to production strikes out, make sure to develop and practice a solid rollback plan beforehand.

What kinds of VB projects are you working on now?

Recently, I worked with a team that developed the Microsoft Beta Site. The site, comprised of ASP .NET, VB6, and VB .NET components, manages beta tester feedback information for Microsoft. I'm currently working on a demo site using VB .NET highlighting XML Web Services. We plan on releasing this demo in the next month.

How will VB .NET affect your work?

It's making development fun again. VB .NET and the .NET platform eliminates a lot of the tedious, repetitive, error-prone coding required to construct a solution. With .NET, I get a lot of features for free without needing to write code.

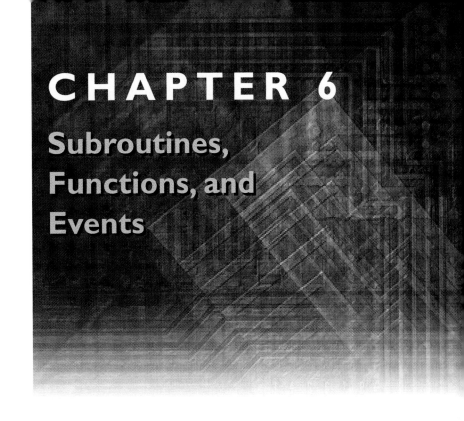

CHAPTER 6
Subroutines, Functions, and Events

As our applications grow, we have a need to break them into separate logical units. Indeed, you have already seen one way of accomplishing this.

Your applications are broken up into different controls that allow you to separate code that accomplishes one task from another. You even break up code within the control based on the actions that are performed upon the control. These actions are referred to as **events** and are one way of breaking up code into smaller, more logical units. The event you are most familiar with so far is the `Click` event. In Section 6.5 of this chapter we will introduce other events.

Another way to break up an application is by using either **functions** or **subroutines**. Functions and subroutines are used to make your programs more readable by breaking large amounts of code into smaller, more concise parts. By breaking code into functions and subroutines code can be written once and reused often, thus saving space and debugging time. They operate similarly, with one key difference. A function is used when a value is returned to the calling routine, while a subroutine is used when a desired task is needed, but no answer is returned.

6.1 What Are Subroutines and Functions?

Unlike a function that must return a value and therefore have its results assigned or passed to another routine, subroutines are called with no values being returned.

Therefore, they are invoked using the keyword **Call** just before the subroutine name, as shown in the following syntax:

```
Call SubroutineName(ArgumentList)
```

Invoking a subroutine can occur with arguments as in the following example of a call to the `SetCheckBox` subroutine that accepts a check box control as an argument:

```
Call SetCheckBox(chkCheckBox1)
```

Invoking a subroutine can also occur without arguments as in the following example of a call to the `Message` subroutine that has no arguments:

```
Call Message()
```

Invoking a Function Call

A function by definition returns a value. Therefore, a function call must be assigned to a variable of the type that the function returns as in the following syntax:

```
Variable = FunctionName(ArgumentList)
```

6.2   Built-in Functions

Before we demonstrate how to develop your functions and subroutines, we will show a few useful built-in functions Visual Basic provides.

Visual Basic provides many built-in functions to assist your coding of applications. By using built-in functions you save time in coding and debugging work that has already been provided for you.

TIP

Developers should not attempt to reinvent the wheel. Make use of built-in functions wherever possible.

The following is a description of some of the most useful built-in functions in Visual Basic.

String Functions

Function Name: `UCase`

Function Description: Returns the `String` that is passed in all uppercase letters.

Common Uses: While `UCase` can be used when the desired output is required to be in all uppercase letters, it is commonly used when you wish to validate data entered by a user against a given `String`. In your voting booth applications, you needed to check multiple capitalizations for each vote recorded. By converting the vote to uppercase, you could have only checked it once.

Syntax: `String = UCase(String)`

Examples:

Function Call	Return Value
UCase("Input String")	"INPUT STRING"
UCase("all lowercase")	"ALL LOWERCASE"
UCase("ALL UPPERCASE")	"ALL UPPERCASE"
UCase("UpPeR AnD lOwErCaSE")	"UPPER AND LOWERCASE"

Previous Way of Coding Validation

```
If (txtVote.Text = "Bush" Or txtVote.Text = "BUSH" Or _
    txtVote.Text = "bush") Then...
```

Better Way of Coding Validation

```
If (UCase(txtVote.Text) = "BUSH") Then...
```

Function Name: LCase

Function Description: Returns the String that is passed converted to all lowercase letters.

Common Uses: LCase is very similar in use to UCase. While it is more common to use UCase for data validation, LCase can be used equally as well.

Syntax: String = LCase(String)

Examples:

Function Call	Return Value
LCase("Input String")	"input string"
LCase("all lowercase")	"all lowercase"
LCase("ALL UPPERCASE")	"all uppercase"
LCase("UpPeR AnD lOwErCaSE")	"upper and lowercase"

Function Name: Trim

Function Description: Returns a String with the same content, except the leading and trailing spaces are removed.

Common Uses: Often when data is gathered additional spaces may exist before the first non-character or after the last non-blank character. It is good practice to remove these so that data may be presented cleanly.

Syntax: String = Trim(String)

Examples:

Function Call	Return Value
Trim(" InputString")	"InputString"
Trim("InputString ")	"InputString"
Trim(" InputString ")	"InputString"
Trim(" Input String ")	"Input String"

Notice that although spaces are removed from the beginning and ending of the `String`, they are not removed from the middle as in the fourth example.

The following code will initialize two `Strings`. One will contain a `String` that has had the leading and trailing spaces removed by the `Trim` function. It is displayed between two vertical bars so that it will be obvious that the spaces have been removed.

```
Dim strWithBlanks As String
Dim strBorder As String
Dim strTrimmedOutput As String
Dim strUnTrimmedOutput As String

strTest = "  Hello  " 'Two spaces before and after
strBorder = "|"

strTrimmedOutput = strBorder&Trim(strTest)&strBorder
strUnTrimmedOutput = strBorder&strTest&strBorder

MsgBox strTrimmedOutput
MsgBox strUnTrimmedOutput
```

Figure 6.1
First Output

|Hello|

Figure 6.2
Second Output

| Hello |

Function Name: `Left`

Function Description: Returns the first N characters of a `String` where N is an `Integer` passed indicating the number of characters to return. If N is greater than the number of characters in the `String`, the `String` is returned. No extra spaces are added.

Common Uses: Often you are only concerned with the first few characters of a `String`. `Left` is a great way to look at only the beginning of a `String`.

Syntax: `String = Left(String, Integer)`

Examples:

Function Call	Return Value
`Left("Beginning of String", 5)`	`"Begin"`
`Left("Beginning of String", 2)`	`"Be"`
`Left("Beginning of String", 0)`	`""`
`Left("Beginning of String", 20)`	`"Beginning of String"`

The following code shows how you might use `Left` to determine if a person's full name belongs to either a man or a women.

```
Dim strPerson1 As String
Dim strPerson2 As String
Dim strPerson3 As String
Dim strPerson4 As String

strPerson1 = "Mr. Jeff Salvage"
strPerson2 = "Ms. Charlene Nolan"
```

(continues)

(continued)

```
strPerson3 = "Mrs. Karen Charles"
strPerson4 = "Miss Lynn Bosko"

'Process Person1
If ("Mr." = Left(strPerson1, 3)) Then
  MsgBox "Person 1 is a Man"
    ElseIf ("Miss" = Left(strPerson1, 4) Or _
    "Ms." = Left(strPerson1, 3) Or _
    "Mrs." = Left(strPerson1, 4)) Then
    MsgBox "Person 1 is a Woman"
Else
    MsgBox "Is Person 1 an Alien?"
EndIf

'Process Person2
If ("Mr." = Left(strPerson2, 3)) Then
  MsgBox "Person 2 is a Man"
    ElseIf ("Miss" = Left(strPerson2, 4) Or _
    "Ms." = Left(strPerson2, 3) Or _
    "Mrs." = Left(strPerson2, 4)) Then
    MsgBox "Person 2 is a Woman"
Else
    MsgBox "Is Person 2 an Alien?"
EndIf

'Person3 and Person4 code could follow
```

Function Name: `Right`

Function Description: Returns the last N characters of a `String` where N is an `Integer` passed indicating the number of characters to return. If N is greater than the number of characters in the `String`, the `String` is returned. No extra spaces are added.

Common Uses: Often you are only concerned with the last few characters of a `String`. `Right` is a great way to look at only the end of a `String`.

Syntax: `String = Right(String, Integer)`

Examples:

Function Call	Return Value
`Right("Ending of String", 5)`	`"tring"`
`Right("Ending of String", 2)`	`"ng"`
`Right("Ending of String", 0)`	`" "`
`Right("Ending of String", 20)`	`"Ending of String"`

The following code shows how you might use `Right` to determine a person's suffix, as in Jr., Sr., or Ph.D.

```
Dim strPerson1 As String
Dim strPerson2 As String
Dim strPerson3 As String
```

(continues)

(continued)

```
strPerson1 = "Nira Herrmann, Ph.D."
strPerson2 = "John Cunningham, Sr."
strPerson3 = "Bob Bruno, Jr."

'Process Person1
If ("Ph.D." = Right(strPerson1, 5)) Then
  MsgBox "Person 1 has a doctorate degree."
ElseIf ("Sr." = Right(strPerson1, 3)) Then
  MsgBox "Person 1 has a kid with the same name"
ElseIf ("Jr." = Right(strPerson1, 3)) Then
   MsgBox "Person 1 has a father with the same name"
EndIf

'Person2 and Person3 code could follow
```

Function Name: Space

Function Description: Returns a String containing the number of spaces indicated by the argument.

Common Uses: Often you wish to add spaces to a String to set the total length of a String to an exact size. This is often used when working with fixed-width data files. We will demonstrate this in Chapter 9.

Syntax: String = Space(Integer)

Examples:

Function Call	Return Value
Space(5)	" "
Space(10)	" "
Space(0)	""
"Hello" & Space(10) & "Goodbye"	"Hello Goodbye"

Function Name: Mid

Function Description: Returns a specific number of characters from a String allowing the developer to indicate where to start and how many characters to return. The first argument is the source String. The second is an Integer indicating the starting position from which to copy. The third argument is optional and indicates the number of characters to copy. If the third argument is left out, all characters from the starting position are returned.

Common Uses: Often you wish to extract a portion of a String for use separately from the rest of the String. This is often used when working with fixed-width data files. We will demonstrate this in Chapter 9.

Syntax: Long = Mid(String, Integer (Starting Position), Optional Integer(Length))

Examples:

Function Call	Return Value
Mid("This is the String", 6, 2)	"is"
Mid("This is the String", 9, 3)	"the"
Mid("This is the String", 13, 4)	"Stri"
Mid("This is the String", 8)	" the String"

Function Name: InStr

Function Description: Returns the position the first occurrence of a substring that is searched for in the String passed.

Common Uses: InStr can be used to tell you if a String has a certain substring contained within it. It operates much like searching a document for a word.

Syntax: Long = InStr(String to be Searched, Search String)

Examples:

Function Call	Return Value
InStr("This is a very", "is")	3
InStr("ab ab ab", "ab")	1
InStr("ab ab ab", "a")	1
InStr("ab ab ab", "c")	–1

Function Name: Len

Function Description: Returns number of characters contained within a String.

Common Uses: Len is used to determine the size of a String.

Syntax: Integer = Len(String)

Examples:

Function Call	Return Value
Len("Inconceivable")	13
Len("Iocaine Powder")	14
Len("Hello, my name is Inigo Montoya. You killed my father. Prepare to die")	70
Len("")	0

DRILL 6.1

What is the output of the following code?

```
MsgBox UCase("What is the output?")
```

DRILL 6.2

What is the output of the following code?

```
MsgBox Left("What is the output?", 4)
```

DRILL 6.3

What is the output of the following code?

```
MsgBox Right("What is the output?", 4)
```

DRILL 6.4

What is the output of the following code?

```
MsgBox UCase(Left("What is the output?", 4))
```

DRILL 6.5

What is the output of the following code?

```
MsgBox Left("What is the output?", 4) & Space(5) & Trim("  ?  ")
```

Conversion Functions

Function Name: Str

Function Description: Returns a String representation of the numeric value passed to it. By default it will place a single space in front of the first numeric character.

Common Uses: Although Visual Basic will often allow you to assign a value of one type to a variable of another, it is poor programming. Future versions of Visual Basic may not allow this and then you would be required to modify your code to remain compatible. Instead, avoid future problems by manually converting numeric values to Strings before assigning them to either a variable of type String or a Text attribute in a control.

Syntax: String = Str(Numeric Value)

Examples:

```
'Proper conversion
Dim strDestination As String
Dim intSource As Integer

intSource = 1
```

(continues)

(continued)

```
strDestination = Str(intSource)


'Improper conversion
Dim strDestination As String
Dim intSource As Integer

intSource = 1

strDestination = intSource


'Run-time Error
Dim strDestination As String
Dim strSource As String

strSource = "Source"

strDestination = Str(strSource)
```

Function Name: Val

Function Description: Returns a numeric representation of the String value passed to it. Val will convert a String to a numeric until it reaches a character that is not a numeric value, a decimal point, or a white-space character. Once a non-recognizable character is read, conversion stops at that point.

Common Uses: Val is used much in the same manner as Str, except in the opposite direction.

Syntax: Numeric Value = Val(String)

Examples:

Function Call	Return Value
Val("199.11")	199.11
Val(" 199.11 ")	199.11
Val(" 1 99.1 1")	199.11
Val(" 199 ")	199
Val("$199.11")	0
Val("1,199.11")	1
Val(" ")	0
Val("123abc")	123
Val("abc123")	0

```
'Proper conversion
Dim intDestination As Integer
Dim strSource As String

strSource = "1"

intDestination = Val(strSource)
```

Function Name: CDate

Function Description: Returns a Date representation of the String value passed to it. While this sounds simple, there are multiple Date formats. CDate will consider your computer's system setting as the valid Date format.

Common Uses: CDate is used when a Date representation is needed. Often a date can be stored in a String when it is gathered from a fixed-width or comma-delimited file. If proper operations are going to be performed on the date, it is necessary to store it in its native format.

Syntax: Date = CDate(String)

Examples:

```
Private Sub cmdTestCDate_Click()
Dim strToday As String
Dim strTomorrow As String

Dim dteToday As Date
Dim dteTomorrow As Date

strToday = "September 30, 2001"
dteToday = CDate(strToday)
dteTomorrow = dteToday + 1
strTomorrow = CStr(dteTomorrow)

MsgBox strTomorrow
End Sub
```

TIP

There are many conversion functions to assist your handling of the many datatypes in Visual Basic. They all basically operate the same way; the value passed to them is converted to the type in the name of the function. Here is a list to assist you. For more information, check out the MSDN:

```
CBool(expression)
CByte(expression)
CCur(expression)
CDate(expression)
CDbl(expression)
CDec(expression)
CInt(expression)
CLng(expression)
CSng(expression)
CStr(expression)
CVar(expression)
```

DRILL 6.6

What is the output of the following code?

```
Dim sngValue1 As Single
Dim strValue2 As String

sngValue1 = 1.1
strValue2 = Str(sngValue1)
MsgBox strValue2
```

DRILL 6.7

What is the output of the following code?

```
Dim strValue As String

strValue = Str("A")
MsgBox StrValue
```

Mathematical Functions

Function Name: Int, Fix

Function Description: Returns the Integer portion of the numerical value passed to it.

Common Uses: Int or Fix are used when you wish to convert a numerical value to an Integer without regard for the decimal value. It performs a truncation of the number. Imagine if you needed to know how many complete dozens of an item you have. You could perform the calculation as follows: Int(Quanity/12).

Syntax: Integer = Int(Numerical Value)

Examples:

Function Call	Return Value
Int(199.11)	199
Int(0.1)	0
Int(1.5)	1
Int(0.99999)	0

WARNING

While Int and Fix return the same values for positive numbers, they do not necessarily return the same values for negative numbers. While Int will return the first negative number less than or equal to the number passed, Fix will return the first negative number greater than or equal to the number passed.

Function Call	Return Value
Int(-199.11)	-200
Int(-0.1)	-1
Fix(-199.11)	-199
Fix(-0.1)	0

Function Name: Round

Function Description: Returns the Integer portion of the numerical value passed to it by rounding it to the closest Integer.

Common Uses: Although Int is used more often than Round to convert a decimal value to an Integer, Round can be used when you are concerned with having the most accurate conversion possible.

Syntax: Integer = Round(Numerical Value)

Examples:

Function Call	Return Value
Round(199.11)	199
Round(0.1)	0
Round(1.5)	2
Round(0.99999)	1

Function Name: Sqr

Function Description: Returns the square root of a numerical value.

Common Uses: Used whenever the computation of a square root is required.

Syntax: Double = Sqr(Numerical Value)

Examples:

Function Call	Return Value
Sqr(4)	2
Sqr(16)	4
Sqr(26)	5.09901951359278
Sqr(2.3)	1.51657508881031

 DRILL 6.8

What is the output of the following code?

```
MsgBox Str(Int(9.9))
```

 DRILL 6.9

What is the output of the following code?

```
MsgBox Str(Round(9.9))
```

Miscellaneous Functions

Function Name: IsNumeric

Function Description: Returns True if the value passed to it evaluates to a numerical datatype; otherwise it returns False.

Common Uses: IsNumeric can be used to verify that a value can be evaluated as a number. Instead of possibly getting either inaccurate results or a run-time error, by using IsNumeric, a proactive approach to error handling can be achieved.

Syntax: Boolean = IsNumeric(Expression)

Examples:

Function Call	Return Value
IsNumeric("199.11")	True
IsNumeric(199.11)	True
IsNumeric("ABC")	False
IsNumeric("123ABC")	False
IsNumeric("1,999")	True
IsNumeric("$1,1999")	True
IsNumeric("50%")	False
IsNumeric("One)	False

Further Example:

```
If IsNumeric (txtInput.Text) Then
    intTotal = intTotal + Val(txtInput.Text)
Else
    MsgBox "Not a number", , "IsNumeric Error"
EndIf
```

Function Name: IsDate

Function Description: Returns True if the value passed to it evaluates to a valid Date; otherwise it returns False.

Common Uses: IsDate can be used when you are about to convert a value to a Date representation. Instead of possibly getting either inaccurate results or a run-time error, by using IsDate, a proactive approach to error handling can be achieved.

Syntax: Boolean = IsDate(Expression)

Examples:

Function Call	Return Value
IsDate("January 1, 2001")	True
IsDate("1/1/2001")	True
IsDate("1/1/01")	True
IsDate(#1/1/01#)	True
IsDate(1/1/01)	False
IsDate("Today")	False

Function Name: Date

Function Description: Returns the current system date.

Common Uses: Date can be used anytime the developer wishes to access the system date. While it is returned as a Variant, it can be used as a native date format or converted to a String representation.

Syntax: Variant = Date()

Examples:

```
'Code to display Yesterday's Date in a Message Box
Dim dteToday As Date
Dim dteYesterday As Date
Dim strYesterday As String

dteToday = Date()
dteYesterday = dteToday -1
strYesterday = CStr(dteYesterday)
```

Function Name: Time

Function Description: Returns the current system time.

Common Uses: Time can be used anytime the developer wishes to access the system time. While it is returned as a Variant, it can be used as a native date format or converted to a String representation. While there is no Time datatype, you can store a Time in the Date datatype.

Syntax: Variant = Time()

Examples:

```
'Code to display the current Time in a Message Box
Dim dteNow As Date

dteToday = Time()
```

Function Name: Rnd

Function Description: Returns a pseudo random decimal number that is greater than or equal to 0 and less than 1. By passing Rnd an optional numeric argument, you can further control the type of random number you generate. See the MSDN for more details.

Common Uses: Most often used for simulations, the Rnd function is used to simulate a random event. By combining the output of the Rnd function with some basic mathematics, random numbers can be generated between a given range.

Syntax: Variant = Rnd()

Examples:

Function Call	Return Value
`Int(Rnd()*3)`	Generates a random number from 0 to 2
`Int(Rnd()*3)+1`	Generates a random number from 1 to 3
`Int(Rnd()*6)+1`	Generates a random number from 1 to 6
`(Int(Rnd()*6) + 1) + (Int(Rnd()*6) + 1)`	Generates a random number from 2 to 12 similar to rolling of a pair of dice

 TIP

When you use the `Rnd` function, each time you run the application the same sequence of random numbers will be generated. By adding the keyword `Randomize` to the application before the calls to `Rnd`, new sequences of random numbers will be generated each time the application is run.

Function Name: `Format`

Function Description: Returns a `String` representation of the expression passed formatted according to instructions passed to it in the second argument. Format may be used to improve the appearance of numbers, dates, times, or string values.

Common Uses: `Format` is used any time the user needs to beautify the output of a value.

Syntax: `String = Format(Expression, String)`

Second Argument:

Standard Format	Description
`Currency`	Displays the number as a monetary value. A dollar sign preceeds the number that is formatted to two decimal places. If a number requires it, a comma is placed to the left of every three digits (except for the two for the decimal places). If the number is negative, it is enclosed in parentheses.
`Date`	There are many standard date formats. `General Date` will format a date/time as mm/dd/yyyy and hh:mm:ss if there is a time. Other formats include: `Long Date`—Displays full names in the date `Medium Date`—Displays abbreviated names in date `Short Date`—Displays as mm/dd/yy
`Fixed`	Displays the number with two decimal places and at least one digit to the left of the decimal place.
`Percent`	Displays the number as a percentage. It multiplies the number passed by 100 (with two decimal places) and places a percent sign to the right.

(continues)

(continued)

Standard	Displays a number with two decimal places. If the number requires it, a comma is placed to the left of every three digits (except for the two for the decimal places). If the number is negative, a negative sign is displayed to the left of the number.
Time	There are many standard time formats: Long Time—Displays as hh:mm:ss PM Medium Time—Displays as hh:mm PM Short Time—Display as hh:mm

Examples:

Function Call	Return Value
Format(123.1, "Currency")	$123.10
Format(#03/03/2001#, "Short Date")	3/3/01
Format(123.1, "Fixed")	123.10
Format(123.1, "Percent")	12310.00%
Format(123.1, "Standard")	123.10
Format(#10:30:01 AM#, "Time")	10:30

Custom format strings can be made by combining different predetermined format characters.

TIP

There are many more formatting options. Check out the MSDN for more specifics.

Format Character	Description
0	When a format string specifies a 0, if the expression has a digit in that position where the 0 is, the digit is displayed; otherwise a 0 is displayed.
#	When a format string specifies a #, if the expression has a digit in that position that the # is, the digit is displayed; otherwise nothing is displayed.
decimal point	Forces a decimal place to be displayed. Does not necessarily force a digit to be displayed to the right.
comma	Places a comma in the number. Usually used in the standard position, every three digits to the left of the decimal place.
@	When a format string specficies the number of digits to display, an @ can be used to display a space for the characters that would not normally be displayed by a string representaion.
!	Displays characters with a left justification when using @ to format them.
<	Displays characters as all lowercase.
>	Displays characters as all uppercase.

Examples:

Function Call	Return Value
Format(123.1, "00000.00")	00123.10
Format(0, "00000.00")	00000.00
Format(123.1, "00000")	00123
Format(123.1, "#######.##")	123.10
Format(123.1, "0###.##")	0123.10
Format(123.1, "0,###.##")	0,123.10
Format("Hello", "@@@@@@@@")	" Hello"
Format("Hello", "!@@@@@@@@")	"Hello "
Format("Hello", "<@@@@@@@@")	"hello "
Format("Hello", ">@@@@@@@@")	"HELLO "

TIP

The many options of the Format function may be overwhelming. Instead, you might try using FormatCurrency, FormatDateTime, FormatPercent, or FormatNumber. These functions have options of their own and are an easy way to format a value to a currency, date, percent, or number.

Function Call	Return Value
FormatCurrency(199.33)	$199.33
FormatDateTime(Now())	5/7/01 9:42:15 AM
FormatPercent(.55)	55.00%
FormatNumber("123.11")	123.11

DRILL 6.10

What is the range of values produced by the following code?

```
MsgBox Str(Int(Rnd()*100))
```

DRILL 6.11

What is the range of values produced by the following code?

```
MsgBox Str(Int(Rnd()*10+3))
```

DRILL 6.12

What is the String produced by the following call to Format?

```
Format(1111.1111, "Standard")
```

DRILL 6.13

What is the `String` produced by the following call to `Format`?

```
Format(1111.1111, "0000.000")
```

DRILL 6.14

What is the `String` produced by the following call to `Format`?

```
Format(#03/01/2001#, "Date")
```

6.3   Writing Functions and Subroutines

While the functions built into Visual Basic are useful, they are not all inclusive. More often than not developing your applications will require coding your own functions and subroutines.

While Visual Basic provides a graphical interface for creating functions and subroutines, we do not find it very helpful. Instead, we will demonstrate how to create functions and subroutines by coding them directly.

The syntax for a function is as follows:

```
Scope Function FunctionName(ArgumentList) As ReturnType
    BodyOfFunction
End Sub
```

Coding a Function

A function is declared with a scope of either `Private` or `Public`. Usually, functions will be written as `Private`, indicating that they are usable only in the form that they are coded. However, if you specify a `Public` scope, the function would be visible to other forms. (Currently you have not learned how to create multiple forms in a project.)

Using the `Function` keyword makes the distinction between a function and subroutine.

The `FunctionName` is used to identify this function from any others. Naming a function follows the same rules as naming a variable. You have already seen function names when you used the built-in functions like `UCase`, `IsDate`, or `Str`.

The `ArgumentList` is a list of variables that will be passed to the function. Arguments are passed to functions so that the function can perform its operation on many different values. An argument list is specified.

The `ReturnType` is the type of variable that is returned from the function.

The `BodyOfFunction` is the code that accomplishes the function's task.

Example: Max Function

Here is an example of a function that returns the maximum of two integers. It compares the first argument, `intValue1`, to the second argument, `intValue2`. If the first argument is greater than the second argument, then the first argument is set as the return value by assigning it to the name of the function, `Max`. If the first argument is not greater than the second argument, then the second argument is assigned to `Max`. You may be wondering what happens if the first argument equals the second argument. While not explicitly tested for, when the first argument equals the second argument, `Max` is set to the second argument.

```
Private Function Max(intValue1 As Integer, intValue2 As Integer) _
    As Integer
If (intValue1 > intValue2) Then
    Max = intValue1
Else
    Max = intValue2
End If
End Function
```

TIP

Students often confuse the many uses of a function name. There are actually three places where a function name can be used:

◆ Naming the function.
◆ Setting the return value.
◆ Calling the function.

The first two can be seen in the code for the `Max` function. The third can be seen in the following code for the command button `cmdFunctionExample`'s `Click` event where the `Max` function is called.

```
Private Sub cmdFunctionExample_Click()
Dim Maximum As Integer
Maximum = Max(1, 2)
MsgBox "The Maximum value is " & Str(Maximum)
End Sub
```

Example: PayRate Function

Here is an example of a function that returns the pay rate of a department. This is the same calculation you have performed in your case study. However, now you can use the function `PayRate` to simplify your payroll calculation. The function accepts the department as a `String` argument and returns the pay rate associated with the department. Note that the function assumes a valid department; otherwise it will return 0.

```
Private Function PayRate(strDepartment As String) As Currency
Select Case strDepartment
    Case "Sales"
        PayRate = intSalesPayRate
    Case "Processing"
        PayRate = intProcessingPayRate
    Case "Management"
        PayRate = intManagementPayRate
    Case "Phone"
        PayRate = intPhonePayRate
```

(continues)

```
(continued)

    Case Else
        PayRate = 0
End Select
End Function
```

Coding a Subroutine

Coding a subroutine does not vary much from coding a function. The only difference is that a subroutine cannot return a value.

The syntax for a subroutine is as follows:

```
Scope Sub SubroutineName(ArgumentList)
    Body of Subroutine
End Sub
```

Example: ThankYouMessage Subroutine

The `ThankYouMessage` subroutine simply outputs a message in a message box. This particular subroutine contains no arguments. A subroutine does not require arguments; they are strictly optional. The code follows:

```
Private Sub ThankYouMessage()
    MsgBox("Thank You Pat Croche for a Great Basketball Team!")
End Sub
```

Example: ComputeGrade Subroutine

Here is a subroutine that accepts an `Integer` argument that indicates a person's average and displays a message box containing the letter grade associated with the person's average.

```
Private Sub ComputeGrade(intStudentAverage as Integer)
Select Case intStudentAverage
    Case 90 To 100
        MsgBox "A"
    Case 80 To 89
        MsgBox "B"
    Case 70 To 79
        MsgBox "C"
    Case 60 To 69
        MsgBox "D"
    Case Else
        MsgBox "F"
End Select
End Sub
```

The `ComputeGrade` subroutine could be called from a command button and passed a value contained in a text box to the subroutine. Note how the following code converts the text box value to an `Integer` before you pass it.

```
Private Sub cmdComputeGrade_Click()

Call ComputerGrade(Int(txtStudentGrade.Text))

End Sub
```

Visual Basic .NET Alert

The preferred method to calling a subroutine follows the following syntax:

```
Call SubroutineName(Argument List)
```

While there are three methods to calling a subroutine in Visual Basic 6.0, only two will be supported in Visual Basic .NET. The first is the same as shown here, but the second method works differently from Visual Basic 6.0 to .NET, so we will not even introduce it.

Example: ChangePicture Subroutine

Subroutines can be used to change the properties of a control. Observe the following subroutine, `InitializePicture`. It accepts a picture box as the first argument and a `String` containing the new picture file location and name as the second argument. The subroutine will set the `Picture` attribute to the new filename, and set the `TabStop` and `BorderStyle` attributes to 0. The code follows.

```
Private Sub InitializePicture(picControl As PictureBox, strNewPicture As String)

picControl.Picture = LoadPicture(strNewPicture)
picControl.TabStop = False
picControl.BorderStyle = 0

End Sub
```

The `InitializePicture` subroutine could be called from a command button as shown in the following code:

```
Private Sub cmdInitialize_Click()

Call InitializePicture(picPicture1, "c:\VB Coach\Chapter 6\DontTouchThis.jpg")

End Sub
```

Local Variables

Variables can be declared within the body of the function or subroutine. They are declared in the same manner you have declared variables in the past. There is no difference in scope when declaring variables within a function than within an event. Variables declared within a function are only accessible from within the function or subroutine that they are declared within.

TIP

Visual Basic provides a method to create a procedure using a graphical user interface. Once a developer is in the code window, they can select Add Procedure from the Tools menu. The following window appears:

Figure 6.3
GUI Interface for Procedure
Creation

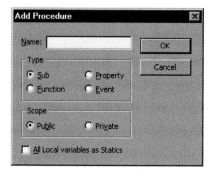

From this GUI, you can specify the name of the procedure, its scope, and what type of procedure it will be.

6.4   Pass By Reference and Pass By Value

Visual Basic's argument passing defaults to pass a reference to the argument to the subroutine or function call. However, sometimes you may wish to pass a copy of the argument. If you pass a value as a copy, any changes made to the value in the subroutine or function does not affect the original value of the argument in the calling routine.

Visual Basic defaults to passing arguments by reference because copying a large value to a function can be a waste of time. Arguments like `Integers`, `Booleans`, and `Currency` are relatively small and do not benefit from passing the argument by reference. However, passing large `String` variables and complex controls by value could waste time.

To give the developer maximum flexibility, Visual Basic allows you to specify either **pass by reference** or **pass by value**. You may be wondering why a programmer would select the pass by value option if pass by reference is usually quicker.

Sometimes a developer may not be the sole developer of the application. If another individual is writing supporting routines for your code, you may wish to ensure that the arguments being passed to routines are not affected by the code. You can ensure this by passing them by value.

Specifying an argument as pass by value is accomplished by placing the keyword `ByVal` in front of an argument as in the following declaration of a subroutine:

```
Private Sub SubroutineName(ByVal Argument1 As Type)
```

Similarly, by placing the keyword `ByRef` in front of an argument, the argument will be passed by reference. If you do not specify either, it is as if you have placed a `ByRef` keyword, since the default value is by reference.

```
Private Sub SubroutineName(ByRef Argument1 As Type)
```

TIP

You can mix the specification of by reference or by value within a single subroutine call. Observe the following subroutine declaration where the first argument is declared as pass by value and the second argument is declared as pass by reference.

```
Private Sub SubroutineName(ByVal Param1 As Type, ByRef Param2 As Type)
```

Visual Basic .NET Alert

In VB .NET all values will be passed by value by default. Therefore, if you know you are switching to VB .NET and the method of variable passing is important, always specify `ByVal` or `ByRef` for argument passing.

Before we show you a practical use for pass by reference, practice the following drills.

DRILL 6.15

What is the output of the following code when the `cmdCalculate` command button is clicked?

```
Private Sub cmdCalculate_Click()
Dim intTestValue As Integer
intTestValue = 5
MsgBox Str(SumValues(intTestValue)) & " " & Str(intTestValue)
End Sub

Private Function SumValues(intMaxNum As Integer) As Integer
Dim intSum As Integer
intSum = 0
Do While (intMaxNum > 0)
   intSum = intSum + intMaxNum
   intMaxNum = intMaxNum - 1
Loop
intSumValues = intSum
End Function
```

DRILL 6.16

What is the output of the code in Drill 6.15 when the `intMaxNum` argument is changed to pass by value by changing the function declaration as follows:

```
Private Function SumValues(ByVal intMaxNum As Integer) As Integer
```

DRILL 6.17

What is the output of the following code when the cmdCalculate command button is clicked?

```
Private Sub cmdCalculate_Click()
Dim intTestValue1 As Integer
Dim intTestValue2 As Integer

intTestValue1 = 5
intTestValue2 = 7

Call DrillRoutine(intTestValue1, intTestValue2)
MsgBox Str(intTestValue1) & " " & Str(intTestValue2)

End Sub


Private Sub DrillRoutine(ByVal intParam1 As Integer, _
                         ByRef intParam2 As Integer)
intParam1 = 10
intParam2 = 20
End Sub
```

DRILL 6.18

What is the output of the following code when the cmdCalculate command button is clicked?

```
Private Sub cmdCalculate_Click()
Dim intTestValue1 As Integer
Dim intTestValue2 As Integer

intTestValue1 = 5
intTestValue2 = 7
Call DrillRoutine(intTestValue1, intTestValue2)
MsgBox Str(intTestValue1) & " " & Str(intTestValue2)
End Sub

Private Sub DrillRoutine(ByRef intParam1 As Integer, _
                         ByRef intParam2 As Integer)
intParam1 = 10
intParam2 = 20
End Sub
```

DRILL 6.19

What is the output of the following code when the `cmdCalculate` command button is clicked?

```
Private Sub cmdCalculate_Click()
Dim intTestValue1 As Integer
Dim intTestValue2 As Integer

intTestValue1 = 5
intTestValue2 = 7

Call DrillRoutine(intTestValue1, intTestValue2)
MsgBox Str(intTestValue1) & " " & Str(intTestValue2)

End Sub

Private Sub DrillRoutine(ByVal intTestValue1 As Integer, _
                         ByVal intTestValue2 As Integer)
intTestValue1 = 10
intTestValue2 = 20
End Sub
```

DRILL 6.20

What is the output of the following code when the `cmdCalculate` command button is clicked?

```
Private Sub cmdCalculate_Click()
Dim intTestValue1 As Integer
Dim intTestValue2 As Integer

intTestValue1 = 5
intTestValue2 = 7

Call DrillRoutine(intTestValue1, intTestValue2)
MsgBox Str(intTestValue1) & " " & Str(intTestValue2)

End Sub

Private Sub DrillRoutine(intTestValue1 As Integer, _
                         intTestValue2 As Integer)
intTestValue1 = 10
intTestValue2 = 20
End Sub
```

Example: Compute Change Application Utilizing Pass By Reference

So far all the examples of functions and routines could have been written either as pass by value or pass by reference. Here's a perfect example of where you actually need pass by reference so that you can develop an elegant solution to the problem. The application may seem simple in its definition, but requires some thought to develop a solution.

You will develop an application that will accept as input a purchase price and an amount paid. The application will output the change due to the person in the highest denominations of the bills and change. Assume that you can give change in denominations of $100, $50, $20, $10, $5, $1, 25 cents, 10 cents, 5 cents, and 1 cent.

Observe the behavior of the application if the purchase price is $511.13 and the amount paid is $1000.00. The output, in a text box, shows the denominations required to give a total of $488.87 in change. The application looks as follows:

Figure 6.4
Make Change Application

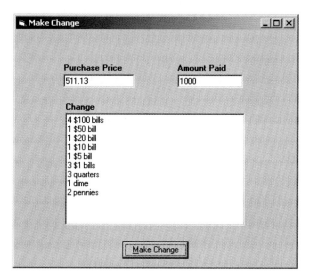

What strategy should you employ to solve this problem? You need to figure out how many of the largest of each denomination you can return. Look at the following code and then the explanation for a clear, concise solution to your problem.

You are going to break your problem into sections. The first is simple; it passes the text box controls' values to the function MakeChange, which will start the actual *work* of the application.

```
Private Sub cmdMakeChange_Click()
    Call MakeChange(Val(txtPurchasePrice.Text), _
                    Val(txtAmountPaid.Text))
End Sub
```

The MakeChange routine will be the *driver* of the application. It accepts a purchase price and the amount paid. It outputs the correct change. Instead of complicating MakeChange, you call a support function called PrintBills. PrintBills does the real work. Once you calculate the amount of change required, MakeChange calls PrintBills with each denomination that you can give as change. PrintBills then outputs the amount given for that denomination and reduces the amount of change remaining to be given by said amount.

```
Private Sub MakeChange(curPurchasePrice As Currency, _
                       curAmountPaid As Currency)

Dim curTotalChange As Currency


curTotalChange = curAmountPaid - curPurchasePrice
Call PrintBills(curTotalChange, 100)
Call PrintBills(curTotalChange, 50)
Call PrintBills(curTotalChange, 20)
Call PrintBills(curTotalChange, 10)
Call PrintBills(curTotalChange, 5)
Call PrintBills(curTotalChange, 1)
Call PrintBills(curTotalChange, 0.25)
Call PrintBills(curTotalChange, 0.1)
Call PrintBills(curTotalChange, 0.05)
Call PrintBills(curTotalChange, 0.01)
End Sub
```

PrintBills calculates the largest number of the current denomination by converting the result of the division to an Integer. Since the calculation returns an Integer value, it can be used directly as the amount of that denomination. Then the rest of the function simply selects the proper wording for that denomination.

```
Private Sub PrintBills(curTChange As Currency, _
                       curDenomination As Currency)


Dim intNumBills As Integer

intNumBills = Int(curTChange / curDenomination)
curTChange = curTChange - curDenomination * curNumBills

If (intNumBills > 0) Then
  If (curDenomination >= 1) Then
    txtChange.Text = txtChange.Text & intNumBills & _
              " $" & curDenomination & " bill"
  Else
    If (curDenomination = 0.25) Then
      txtChange.Text = txtChange.Text & intNumBills & " quarter"
    ElseIf (curDenomination = 0.1) Then
      txtChange.Text = txtChange.Text & intNumBills & " dime"
    ElseIf (curDenomination = 0.05) Then
      txtChange.Text = txtChange.Text & intNumBills & "nickle"
    ElseIf ((curDenomination = 0.01) And (intNumBills = 1)) Then
      txtChange.Text = txtChange.Text & intNumBills & " penny"
    Else
      txtChange.Text = txtChange.Text & intNumBills & " pennies      "
    End If
  End If

  If (intNumBills > 1) Then
    txtChange.Text = txtChange.Text & "s"
  End If
```

(continues)

(continued)

```
  txtChange.Text = txtChange.Text & "    "
End If
End Sub
```

The use of pass by reference may not be readily apparent in the elegance of the solution. Since `TotalChange` is passed from `MakeChange` to `PrintBills` by reference (the default), the changes made to `curTChange` in `PrintBills` are remembered in `TotalChange` when the application returns to the `MakeChange` subroutine. If `TotalChange` was passed by value, this application will not work.

TIP

An important point that beginner programmers often miss is that variables are passed by position, not by name. Notice the arguments for `MakeChange` are `curTChange` and `curDenomination`. This means that the first argument will always be the current change and the second argument will always be the current denomination regardless of the variable name used to pass it.

In your example you use `curTotalChange` as the variable to pass for `curTChange` and you use a series of constants to pass for `curDenomiation`.

6.5 Important Events

Visual Basic's strength lies in the inherent ease of creating interactive applications. An interactive application must have the capability to respond to the user's actions in a robust manner. You have already seen a few ways that Visual Basic accomplishes this. Although we haven't stressed it until now, Visual Basic responds to a user's actions by processing **events**. Visual Basic has many predefined events that allow the programmer to attach code to be executed when an event occurs.

In your very first application, you coded an event and didn't event know it. When you wanted to add functionality to your `Lady Or The Tiger` application, you attached it to the command button's `Click` event. A `Click` event occurs when the user clicks on the control. The code associated with the event is executed.

Click Event

To create code for a `Click` event, double-click on the control that you wish to create a `Click` event for while you are in the design mode. You will be presented with the following syntax, less the comment, that you can add your code to. In your first application you added code to change the application so that it displayed the tiger or lady instead of the door. You can use this event for many purposes. The possibilities are limitless.

```
Private Sub ControlName_Click()
    Event Code Goes Here
End Sub
```

Form_Load Event

Another event that you are already familiar with is the `Form_Load` event. You have used it to initialize values for the form before it loads. To set code for the `Form_Load` event, select the form from the object list box.

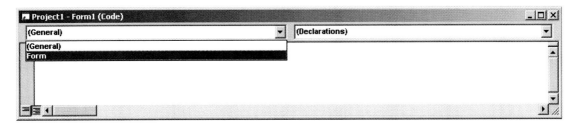

Figure 6.5
Selecting `Form` Events

By default, the event that is active is the `Form_Load` event. The following code is presented and you can add your event code within the event to handle your initialization.

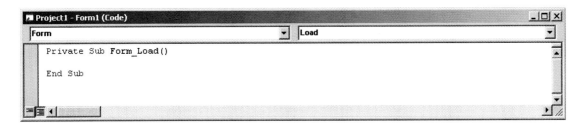

Figure 6.6
`Form_Load` Event

LostFocus Event and SetFocus Method

Data validation is a key concept in robust applications. One could wait until all the data has been entered to check to see if the data entered is correct, or one can attach a `LostFocus` event to the controls for which you wish data validation to occur. `LostFocus` is an event that is triggered when a control loses the current focus of the application.

Observe the following example of checking the `txtDepartment` text box to see if the value entered is `Management`, `Sales`, `Processing`, or `Phone`.

First, you must select the `txtDepartment` text box from the object list box, shown in the following figure:

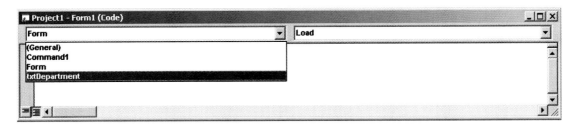

Figure 6.7
Selecting `txtDepartment` Control

Then, because `LostFocus` is not the default event, you must select the event `LostFocus` from the procedure list box, shown in the following figure:

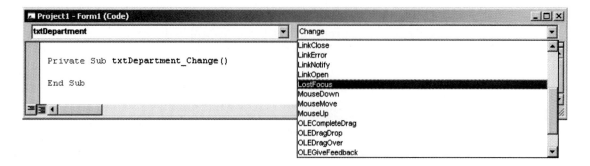

Figure 6.8

Selecting LostFocus Event

Now you can add the validation code to the LostFocus event. You need to check if the department entered is not equal to one of the valid ones. If it is not, then a message is displayed warning the user that the value entered was not valid.

```
Private Sub txtDepartment_LostFocus()
If (UCASE(txtDepartment.Text) <> "MANAGEMENT") And _
    (UCASE(txtDepartment.Text) <> "SALES") And _
    (UCASE(txtDepartment.Text) <> "PROCESSING") And _
    (UCASE(txtDepartment.Text) <> "PHONE") Then
    MsgBox "Invalid Department Entered"
End If
End Sub
```

So the big question is whether or not displaying a message stating that the user has entered invalid data is enough. In most cases, it is not. Fortunately, you have the capability to force the user to enter a valid value or not allow the user's focus to leave the current control.

Using the SetFocus method, you can shift the focus of the application back to the control that has the invalid data. Observe the rewritten LostFocus code for txtDepartment. This code returns the focus of the application to txtDepartment when an invalid department is entered.

```
Private Sub txtDepartment_LostFocus()
If (UCASE(txtDepartment.Text) <> "MANAGEMENT") And _
    (UCASE(txtDepartment.Text) <> "SALES") And _
    (UCASE(txtDepartment.Text) <> "PROCESSING") And _
    (UCASE(txtDepartment.Text) <> "PHONE") Then
    MsgBox "Invalid Department Entered"
    txtDepartment.SetFocus
End If
End Sub
```

KeyPress Event

Although performing data validation upon a control losing focus is an improvement over checking validation later in the application or not at all, sometimes there is a better way.

Why allow the user to enter values that are obviously incorrect? In some cases it is not easy to check if a value is valid until it is completely entered; what about the case where users should only enter a number, but they enter non-numeric characters? Clearly, as soon as they enter a non-numeric character, you should stop them.

This can be accomplished with the KeyPress event. The KeyPress event is triggered when a key is pressed that is not one of the non-printable characters. Keys like

<A>, <B>, <C>, <1>, <2>, and so on are all considered printable. Keys like <F1>, <F2>, and <F3> are non-printable.

When the KeyPress event is triggered, the ASCII (American Standard Code for Information Interchange) value of the character entered is passed to the event.

TIP

An ASCII value is a standard series of numeric codes for letters, numbers, and special characters. See Appendix A for a complete list of codes and their corresponding characters.

By using the built-in function IsNumeric, you can check to see if the value entered is a numeric value. If not, you can set it to 0, thus nullifying the last character entered. The code follows:

```
Private Sub txtDepartment_KeyPress(KeyAscii As Integer)
'Only allow Numbers to be entered
If Not IsNumeric(Chr(KeyAscii)) Then
   KeyAscii = 0
End If
End Sub
```

There is one problem with the previous code, can you guess what it is? There are two keys that you want to allow to be processed that are not numeric. The <BACKSPACE> and <DELETE> keys should be exempt from being ignored by your event code, so that the user can undo mistakes.

You can check for these keys by using the built-in Visual Basic constants vbKeyBack and vbKeyDelete for the <BACKSPACE> and <DELETE> keys, respectively. The code follows:

```
Private Sub txtDepartment_KeyPress(KeyAscii As Integer)
'Only allow Numbers to be entered
If Not IsNumeric(Chr(KeyAscii)) And KeyAscii <> vbKeyBack _
   And KeyAscii <> vbKeyDelete Then
   KeyAscii = 0
End If
End Sub
```

GotFocus Event

Another useful event, often used in conjunction with the LostFocus event, is the GotFocus event. In contrast to the LostFocus event, GotFocus is triggered when the control gains the focus of the application.

You may use the GotFocus event when you want to perform an action before the user can operate the control. In the following example you will set the background color of the text box txtDepartment to the color cyan so that it is obvious what control has focus. You will set the attribute BackColor to the Visual Basic constant for the color cyan vbCyan.

```
Private Sub txtDepartment_GotFocus()
txtDepartment.BackColor = vbCyan
End Sub
```

Of course, if you set the background color to cyan, you should set it back when the control uses focus. Therefore, you use the `LostFocus` event to set it back to white.

```
Private Sub txtDepartment_LostFocus()
txtDepartment.BackColor = vbWhite
End Sub
```

MouseMove, MouseDown, and MouseUp Events

Another set of events allows you to control events related to the user's mouse actions. You can set code to execute when the mouse moves over a control with the `MouseMove` event. Observe the following application that displays the picture `Dragon.jpg`.

Figure 6.9
Application without Mouse Events Triggering

By using the code, you can set the application to change the image when the user moves the mouse over it.

```
Private Sub Picture1_MouseMove(Button As Integer, _
                     Shift As Integer, X As Single, Y As Single)
picPicture1.Picture = LoadPicture("c:\VB Coach\Chapter 6\DontTouchThis.jpg")
End Sub
```

When the event triggers, the code within is executed to load a new picture to the control.

Figure 6.10
Application after MouseMove Event has Occurred

By using the `MouseDown` event, you can also set an event to occur when the left mouse button is held down. Observe the following code, which changes the picture displayed when the user holds the mouse down:

```
Private Sub Picture1_MouseDown(Button As Integer, _
                    Shift As Integer, X As Single, Y As Single)
picPicture1.Picture = LoadPicture("c:\VB Coach\Chapter 6\Ouch.jpg")
End Sub
```

Figure 6.11
Application after
`MouseDown` Event has
Occurred

Finally, you can trigger an event when the user releases the mouse button with the `MouseUp` event. In this case you reset the picture displayed to `DontTouchThis.jpg`.

```
Private Sub Picture1_MouseUp(Button As Integer, _
                    Shift As Integer, X As Single, Y As Single)
picPicture1.Picture = LoadPicture("c:\VB Coach\Chapter 6\DontTouchThis.jpg")
End Sub
```

◆ 6.6 Case Study

Problem Description   You wish to modify the case study from Chapter 5 so that instead of displaying a Weekly Pay, you display a Gross Pay, Tax, and Net Pay for each employee. Additionally, you wish to display a total Gross Pay, Tax, and Net Pay for all the Employees. For simplicity sake, you will compute the tax at a single rate of 28%.
    The completed application should look as follows:

Figure 6.12
Sketch of Application

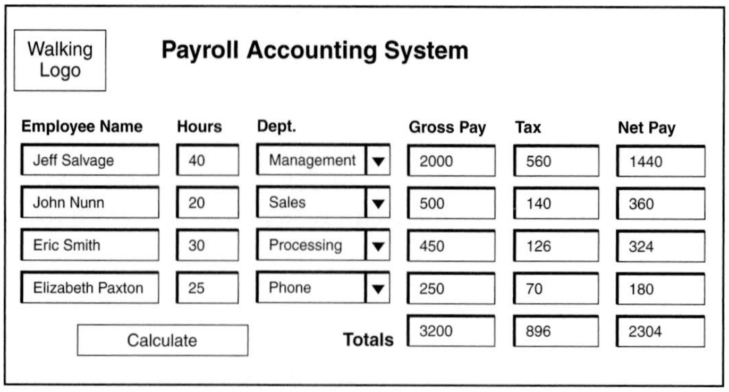

Problem Discussion   With the additional knowledge of subroutines, you can add this functionality and actually shrink the size of your code. Since the calculations required are the same for each employee, you can write one routine that accepts the text boxes and combo box for each employee as arguments. You do not need to pass the employee name text box to the subroutine since it is not used in the calculations.

Problem Solution   You need to remove the text boxes from Chapter 5's solution for Weekly Pay and add text boxes for Gross Pay, Tax, and Net Pay. You need one for each of the four employees. You also need variables to store the Total Gross Pay, Total Tax, and Total Net Pay. You can place these in the Common Declarations section of code along with the constants. This code follows:

```
Const intSalesPayRate = 25
Const intProcessingPayRate = 15
Const intManagementPayRate = 50
Const intPhonePayRate = 10
Const sngTaxRate = 0.28

'Temporary Variables to Store Calculations
Dim curTmpTotalGross As Currency
Dim curTmpTotalTax As Currency
Dim curTmpTotalNet As Currency
```

Next you must add a subroutine to compute the Gross Pay, Tax, and Net Pay for a single employee. You need to pass it the number of hours worked and department so that you can compute the necessary values. Additionally, you need to pass it the three text boxes where you will store the results. Once you have the necessary arguments, the code is similar to the previous chapter's solution. You need a `Select Case` statement in order to determine the proper pay rate. After that it's a few straightforward calculations and you are done.

```
Private Sub ComputePay(txtHours As TextBox, cmoDept As ComboBox, _
                txtGross As TextBox, txtTax As TextBox, _
                txtNet As TextBox)


Select Case cmoDept
   Case "Sales"
```

(continues)

(continued)

```
        cmoGross.Text = Str(Val(txtHours.Text) * intSalesPayRate))
    Case "Processing"
        cmoGross.Text = Str(Val(txtHours.Text) * intProcessingPayRate))
    Case "Management"
        cmoGross.Text = Str(Val(txtHours.Text) * intManagementPayRate))
    Case "Phone"
        cmoGross.Text = Str(Val(txtHours.Text) * intPhonePayRate))
End Select

txtTax.Text = Str(Val(cmoGross.Text) * Val(txtTaxRate.Text))
txtNet.Text = Str(Val(txtGross.Text) - Val(txtTax.Text))

tmpTotalGross = tmpTotalGross + Val(txtGross.Text)
tmpTotalTax = tmpTotalTax + Val(txtTax.Text)
tmpTotalNet = tmpTotalNet + Val(txtNet.Text)

End Sub
```

With the addition of the `ComputePay` subroutine, your `CmdCalculate_Click` event becomes almost trivial. You pass the proper arguments for each of the four employees and then you copy the totals to their respective text boxes.

```
Private Sub CmdCalculate_Click()

'First Week's Calculations
ComputePay txtHours1, cmoDept1, txtGross1, txtTax1, txtNet1
ComputePay txtHours2, cmoDept2, txtGross2, txtTax2, txtNet2
ComputePay txtHours3, cmoDept3, txtGross3, txtTax3, txtNet3
ComputePay txtHours4, cmoDept4, txtGross4, txtTax4, txtNet4


'Copy the Totals to their TextBoxes
txtTotalGross.Text = tmpTotalGross
txtTotalTax.Text = tmpTotalTax
txtTotalNet.Text = tmpTotalNet
End Sub
```

Figure 6.13
Final Application

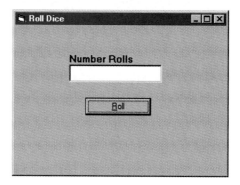

Payroll Account System

Employee Name	Hours	Dept.	Gross Pay	Tax	Net Pay
Jeff Salvage	40	Management	2000	560	1440
John Nunn	20	Sales	500	140	360
Eric Smith	30	Processing	450	126	324
Elizabeth Paxton	25	Phone	250	70	180
	Calculate	Totals	3200	896	2304

CORNER

COACH'S

With the capability of writing your own subroutines and functions comes a new option when using a Debugger.

When you step through your application you have a choice of whether you wish to step through every line of code, or skip over code like function calls.

Observe the following simple application. It contains a text box to allow the entry of the number of times a die should be rolled. A command button is included to roll a die the number of times entered in the text box.

Figure 6.14
Roll Dice Application

Number Rolls

Roll

Observe the following code that calls the `RollDice` function with the number of times to roll the die. `RollDice` returns the total value of all the dice rolled.

```
Private Sub cmdRoll_Click()
Dim intTotal As Integer

intTotal = RollDice(Val(txtNumberRolls.Text))

MsgBox Str(intTotal)

End Sub
```

(continues)

(continued)

```
Private Function RollDice(intNbrRolls As Integer)
Dim intNbrRollsCompleted As Integer
Dim intTotal As Integer

intTotal = 0

For intNbrRollsCompleted = 1 To intNbrRolls
    intTotal = intTotal + Rnd() * 6 + 1
Next intNbrRollsCompleted

RollDice = intTotal
End Function
```

While you could step through this example by pressing the <F8> key or selecting Step Into from the Debug menu, you can skip the tracing of the function call by either pressing the <SHIFT> and <F8> keys simultaneously or selecting Step Over from the Debug menu.

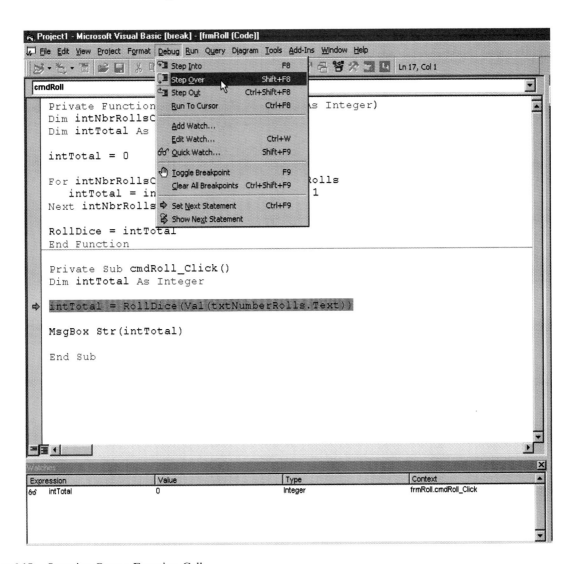

Figure 6.15   Stepping Over a Function Call

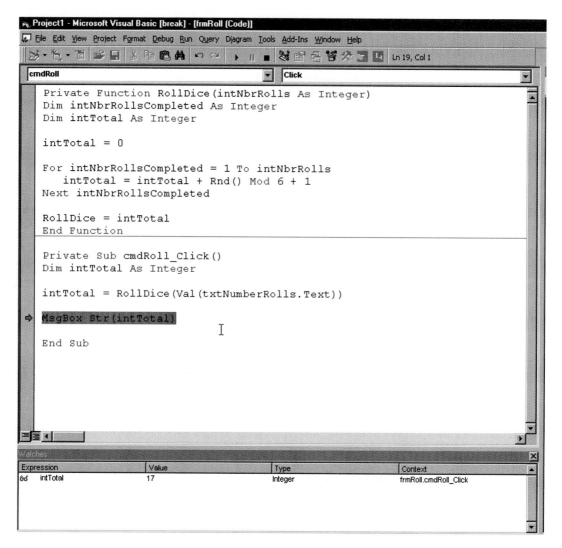

Figure 6.16   After Stepping Over a Function Call

Key Words and Key Terms

Event

A routine that is called when a specific action occurs.

Function

A routine that is called that will return a value to the calling routine

Local variable

A variable that is declared to have a scope of the function that it is declared within.

Pass by reference

When a parameter is passed so that changes to the parameter from within the routine are remembered outside of the routine.

Pass by value

When a parameter is passed so that changes to the parameter from within the routine are not remembered outside the routine.

Subroutine

A routine that is called that will not return a value to the calling routine.

Answers to Chapter's Drills

Drill 6.1
The output of the code is as follows:

```
WHAT IS THE OUTPUT?
```

The code calls the UCase function with the argument, "What is the output?", which converts all the characters to uppercase. The question mark remains unaffected.

Drill 6.2
The output of the code is as follows:

```
What
```

The code calls the Left function with two arguments. The first, "What is the output?", is a String. The second, 4, indicates how many characters from the left of the String should be returned.

Drill 6.3
The output of the code is as follows:

```
put?
```

The code calls the Right function with two arguments. The first, "What is the output?", is a String. The second, 4, indicates how many characters from the right of the String should be returned. Note that the question mark is one of those four characters.

Drill 6.4
The output of the code is as follows:

```
WHAT
```

The code calls both the Left and the UCase functions. The Left function is called with two arguments. The first, "What is the output?", is a String. The second, 4, indicates how many characters from the left of the String should be returned. Therefore, the Left function returns "What", which is passed to the UCase function as its argument. UCase then converts its argument to uppercase, giving you the output "WHAT".

Drill 6.5
The output of the code is as follows:

```
What    ?
```

The output of the code is actually the combination of three function calls: Left, Space, and Trim. First, Left, is called with the arguments "What is the output?" and 4 and returns "What". The return value "What" is appended with the return values of the other two functions. Space is called with 5, so it returns a String of 5 spaces, "   ". Trim is passed the String " ? " and returns the String with the spaces to the left and right removed. Therefore, Trim returns a String with the single character "?" returned. When all three return values are appended, the value "What   ?" is passed to MsgBox and output.

Drill 6.6

The output of the code is as follows:

```
1.1
```

The code starts by assigning the value `1.1` to the variable `sngValue1`. `Value1` is of the type `Single`, therefore when you wish to assign it to the variable `strValue2`, you use the `Str` function to convert the value stored in the variable `sngValue1` in the variable `strValue2`. Finally, the value is output in a message box.

Drill 6.7

The output of the code is as follows:

```
Run-time error '13':
Type mismatch
```

The code does not produce output; instead it produces a run-time error. The `Str` function is expecting a numeric value for its argument.

Drill 6.8

The output of the code is as follows:

```
9
```

The output of the code is produced by first calculating the result of the call to the function `Int`, which returns the `Integer` portion of the number passed to it. In this case it is `9`. Then the `Str` function is called to convert the result to a `String` so that it may be displayed in a message box.

Drill 6.9

The output of the code is as follows:

```
10
```

The output of the code is produced by first calculating the result of the call to the function `Round`, which returns the argument rounded to the nearest `Integer`. In this case it is `10`. Then the `Str` function is called to convert the result to a `String` so that it may be displayed in a message box.

Drill 6.10

`Rnd` generates a greater than or equal to 0 and less than 1. When multiplied by 100, it will generate a value greater than or equal to 0 and less than 100. This value is then converted to an `Integer` and then output. Therefore the range of values are `Integers` from 0 to 99.

Drill 6.11

`Rnd` generates a greater than or equal to 0 and less than 1. When multiplied by 10, it will generate a value greater than or equal to 0 and less than 10. By adding 3 to this generated value, the number generated is greater than or equal to 3 and less than 13. This value is then converted to an `Integer` and then output. Therefore the range of values are `Integers` from 3 to 12.

Drill 6.12

`Format` coverts the input value of 1111.1111 to a representation that includes standard comma placement and two decimal places of accuracy. Therefore the value would be 1,111.11

Drill 6.13

`Format` coverts the input value of 1111.1111 to a representation that does not include commas and has three decimal places of accuracy. Therefore the value would be 1111.111

Drill 6.14

This was a trick question. You will not get expected results, because `Date` is not a standard format.

Drill 6.15

The output of the code is as follows:

```
15 0
```

The code passes the value `intTestValue`, by reference, to the function `intSumValues`. `intSumValues` returns an `Integer` that is the sum of all the values between the value passed and 1. However, since the value passed is done so by reference, when `intMaxValue` is changed in the `Do While` loop, the original value for `intTestValue` is also changed. Therefore, when the sum of the values is returned (5+4+3+2+1 or 15), it is output along with the last value of `intMaxValue`, 0.

Drill 6.16

The output of the code is as follows:

```
15 5
```

The code passes the value `intTestValue`, by value, to the function `intSumValues`. `intSumValues` returns an `Integer` that is the sum of all the values between the value passed and 1. Since this time the value passed is done so by value, when `intMaxValue` is changed in the `Do While` loop, the original value for `intTestValue` remains the same as it was before the call to `intSumValues`.

Drill 6.17

The output of the code is as follows:

```
5 20
```

The code passes the value `intTestValue1`, by value, as well as `intTestValue2`, by reference, to the function `DrillRoutine`. Within `DrillRoutine`, the value of the first argument, `intParam1`, is set to 10. Since the first argument was passed by value, it does not affect the value of the variable `intTestValue1` in the `cmdCalculate_Click` event. Additionally, `DrillRoutine` sets the value of the second argument, `intParam2`, to 20. Since the second argument is passed by reference, it changes the value of `intTestValue2` within the `cmdCalculate_Click` event. Therefore, the values 5 and 20 are output in the message box.

Drill 6.18

The output of the code is as follows:

```
10 20
```

The code passes the values `intTestValue1` and `intTestValue2`, by refer-ence, to the function `DrillRoutine`. Within `DrillRoutine`, the value of the first argument, `intParam1`, is set to 10. Since the first argument was passed by reference, it also changes the value of the variable `intTestValue1` in the `cmdCalculate_Click` event. Additionally, `DrillRoutine` sets the value of the second argument, `intParam2`, to 20. Since the second argument is passed by refer-ence, it changes the value of `intTestValue2` within the `cmdCalculate_Click` event. Therefore, the values 10 and 20 are output in the message box.

Drill 6.19

The output of the code is as follows:

```
5 7
```

The code passes the values `intTestValue1` and `intTestValue2`, by value, to the function `DrillRoutine`. Within `DrillRoutine`, the value of the first argument, `intParam1`, is set to 10. Since the first argument was passed by value, it does not affect the value of the variable `intTestValue1` in the `cmdCalculate_Click` event. This is true even though they are named the same. Additionally, `DrillRoutine` sets the value of the second argument, `intParam2`, to 20. Since the second argument is passed by value, it also does not change the value of `intTestValue2` within the `cmdCalculate_Click` event. Therefore, the values 5 and 7 are output in the message box.

Drill 6.20

The output of the code is as follows:

```
10 20
```

Even though you did not specify whether the arguments are passed by value or passed by reference, the arguments are considered pass by reference since that is the default.

Additional Exercises

1. What is the value of the `String` produced by the following expression?

```
UCase("all lower") & LCase("####0.00")
```

2. What is the value of the `String` produced by the following expression?

```
Left("Hey what's that", 3) & Right("We have to go now!", 4)
```

3. What is the value of the `String` produced by the following expression?

```
LCase(UCase(Left("Hey what's that", 3) & Right("We have to go now!", 4)))
```

4. What is the value of the `String` produced by the following expression?

```
Trim(Space(10) & "A" & Space(10))
```

5. What is the value of the `String` produced by the following expression?

```
InStr("I really want to be on the real world", "real")
```

6. What is the value of the `String` produced by the following expression?

```
InStr("I really want to be on the real world", "REAL")
```

7. What is the value produced by the following expression?

```
Round(9.3+2.1+1.2)
```

8. What is the value produced by the following expression?

```
Int(9.3+2.1+1.2)
```

9. Will the following two sets of code produce the same results? If not, explain why.

```
Function Version1(sngValue As Single) As Single
    Version1 = Rnd(Int(sngValue))
End Function

Function Version2(sngValue As Single) As Single
    Version2 = Int(Rnd(sngValue))
End Function
```

10. Write the code required to generate a random number in the range of 1 to 10,000.
11. Write the code required to generate a random number in the range of 5 to 15.
12. What is the value produced by the following expression?

```
Format(99.123, "00.0")
```

13. What is the value produced by the following expression?

```
Format("all lowercase", "<")
```

14. What is the value produced by the following expression?

```
Format("all lowercase", ">")
```

15. Write a function called `JustTheEnds` that accepts two arguments. The first is the `String` that will be processed. The second is an `Integer` indicating the number of characters to combine from the beginning and ending of the `String` as the return value. Therefore, if `JustTheEnds` is passed `"WHAT COULD THIS BE?"`, `3`, then the function should return `"WHABE?"`

16. Write a function called `WeirdCase` that will accept a `String` and return a `String` that varies from the original `String` by its case. The first letter of the returned `String` should be uppercase, while the second character should be lowercase. The remainder of the returned `String` should alter in case accordingly. Therefore, if `WeirdCase` is called with `"ALL CAPS"`, it will return `"AlL CaPs"`.

17. Write a function called `Greater` that accepts two `Integer` arguments and returns `True` if the first argument is greater than the second argument. Otherwise it should return `False`.

18. Write a function called `Max3` that accepts three `Integer` arguments and returns the maximum value of the three arguments.

19. Write a function called `Middle` that accepts three `Integer` arguments and returns the middle value of the three arguments.

20. Write a function called `SalesTax` that accepts two arguments. The first argument, `curPurchasePrice`, should be of type `Currency`. The second argument, `sngPercentageTax`, should be of type `Single`. The function should compute and return the sales tax of the item purchased.

21. The following two sets of code can be used to compute the rolling of two dice. The first computes the roll by rolling each die separately and adding the two dice together to get the result. The second just produces a random number from 2–12 (the possible outcomes). Are both computations equally valid as a simulation of the dice rolling? Demonstrate your correctness by writing an application that computes the number of times each possible value is produced when two dice are rolled using each method. The simulation should be run for 1,000 rolls of the dice and output the results. If the results are similar, within statistical accuracy, the methods can be considered equivalent; if not, which is the better method to use?

Method 1:

```
intRoll = Int(Rnd() * 6 + 1) + Int(Rnd() * 6 + 1)
```

Method 2:

```
intRoll = Int((Rnd()*11+2))
```

22. Write a function called `RestofString` that accepts two arguments. The first is the `String` to be processed. The second is a `String` to search for within the first `String`. If the `String` is found, return a `String` containing the remainder of the `String` after the first occurrence of the search `String`. If the `String` is not found, return an empty `String`. Therefore, if `RestofString` is called with `"Hello, I must be going"` and `"I"`, the function will return `" must be going"`.

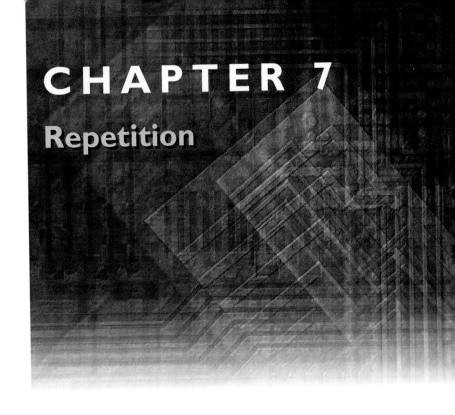

CHAPTER 7
Repetition

- Introduce the concept of executing code more than once
- Introduce the concept of `For` loops
- Introduce the concept of `Do While` loops
- Introduce the concept of `Do Until` loops
- Introduce nested loops

In Chapter 1 we discussed various algorithms. Throughout the first six chapters we have introduced many constructs to help you implement algorithms similar to the ones we discussed. However, until now, we skipped an important construct, repetition. In Chapter 1, when we developed an algorithm to brush one's teeth, we stated that we would "Move the toothbrush back and forth across your teeth" and to "Repeat until all teeth are well cleaned." The capability to repeat a step until a condition is met will now be explained.

In Visual Basic the capability to perform a statement or series of statements over and over again is accomplished in three ways: **For loops**, **While loops**, and **Do loops**.

WARNING

It is important to master conditional expression evaluation in the decision-making chapter before attempting to learn Visual Basic's looping constructs. The evaluation of conditional expressions and looping expressions are exactly the same. The conditional expression evaluation section in Chapter 4 is stated in more detail than in this chapter.

7.1 For Loops

The choice of loop construct is mainly one of style. In fact, any loop construct can be represented using any of the other loop constructs. However, usually there is a natural choice of looping construct for your problem. You usually select a `For` loop when the loop starts at a specific value, increments by a set amount, and terminates at a specific value.

While and Do loops are similar, but you typically use them when the initial condition(s) and/or terminating condition(s) are comparisons between more dynamic conditions.

The For loop is very versatile with lots of options. This does not have to be confusing. If you break the loop into separate components, understand the order in which they are executed, and evaluate them carefully, the evaluation of For loops can be simple.

The following is the syntax for the For loop:

> **TIP**
>
> The repeated nature of a loop is often referred to as *iterating*.

```
For  LoopCounter  =  InitialValue  To  TerminatingValue
     Program Statement(s)
Next  LoopCounter
```

Follow this sequence for the correct evaluation of a For loop:

1 The LoopCounter is set to value InitialValue.
2 The LoopCounter is compared to the TerminatingValue. If the LoopCounter is greater than the TerminatingValue go to Step 5. Otherwise, continue with the execution of the loop.
3 The program statement(s) contained in the body of the loop are executed.
4 The value of LoopCounter is incremented.
5 Exit the loop.

Observe the following flowchart demonstrating the behavior of the For loop:

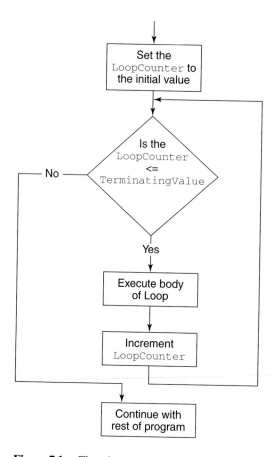

Figure 7.1 Flowchart of a For Loop

The following is an example of a `For` loop that adds up all the values between 1 and 5 and then displays the result in a message box:

```
Private Sub CmdOutput_Click()
Dim intSum As Integer
Dim intCounter As Integer
intSum = 0

For intCounter = 1 To 5
   intSum = intSum + intCounter
Next intCounter

MsgBox intSum

End Sub
```

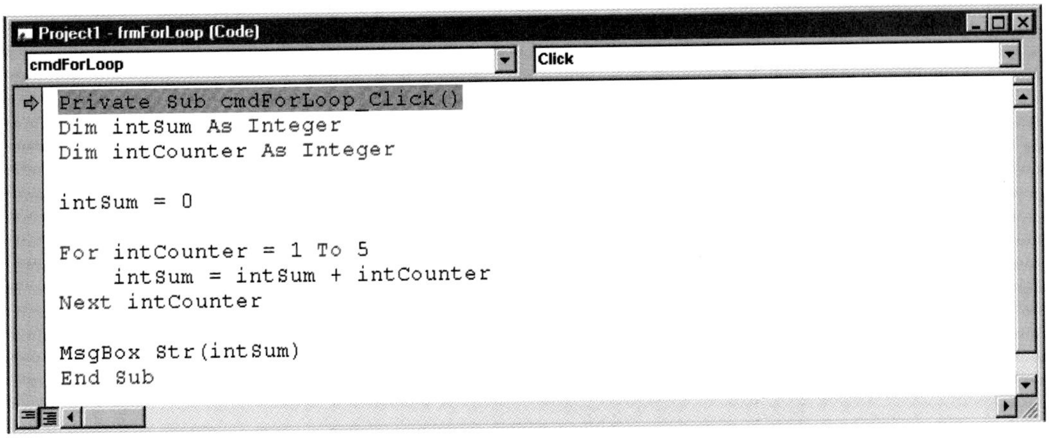

Figure 7.2   Trace of `For` Loop

To help you completely understand the execution of the `For` loop, you will trace through this example using the Debugger.

Click on the Debug menu and select Step Into. The application executes. Click on the command button and the following window will appear:

In order to trace the execution with continuous feedback, you would like the value of `intSum` and `intCounter` displayed during the entire execution of the `For` loop. You can accomplish this with the Watch Window.

The Watch Window is a special window that can be opened when the Debugger is running. It allows the programmer to list values that they wish continuously displayed while the program is being traced. Previously, if you wanted to display the contents of a variable or control, you would mouse over the reference in the code.

With this application, there are two values that are worth displaying: `intSum` and `intCounter`. To display them in a Watch Window, follow these steps:

Tracing a For Loop

Step 1: Click on the Debug menu.

Step 2: Select the Add Watch option.

Step 3: Enter the word `intSum` in the Expression text box of the Add Watch window.

Step 4: Click on the OK command button.

Step 5: The Watch Window with the `intSum` variable and its current value appear.

Step 6: Click on the Debug menu item

Step 7: Select the Add Watch option.

Step 8: Enter the word `intCounter` in the Expression text box of the Add Watch window.

Step 9: Click on the OK command button.

Step 10: The Watch Window with the `intCounter` variable and value appear.

Initially, both `intSum` and `intCounter` are equal to zero. This is shown in the following figure:

Figure 7.3

Trace of `For` Loop Showing Watch Variables

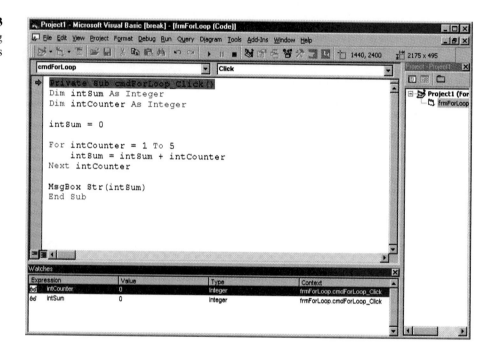

Step 1: By pressing the `<F8>` key, the application steps into the `cmdForLoop_Click()` event. Since variable declarations are not really programming lines that execute (they only allocate space), you proceed to the first programming line. This is shown in the following figure, where you are about to execute the statement highlighted in yellow:

Figure 7.4
Trace of For Loop

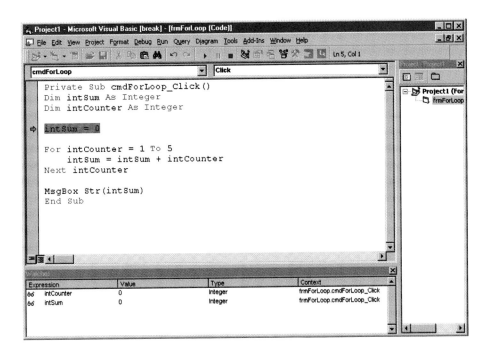

Step 2:   Although not really required, you initialize intSum to zero. Since VB initializes all numerical values to zero, no change is observed in the Watch Window
when you press the <F8> key. This is seen in the following figure:

Figure 7.5
Trace of For Loop

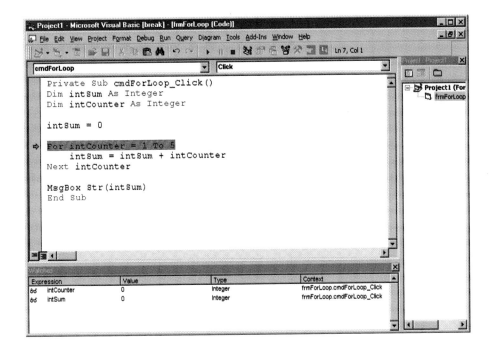

Step 3: When you press <F8> the next time, you execute the first line of the For loop. This initializes the value of the intCounter variable to 1. This is seen in the following figure, where the Watch Window displays the value of intCounter now equaling 1:

Figure 7.6
Trace of For Loop

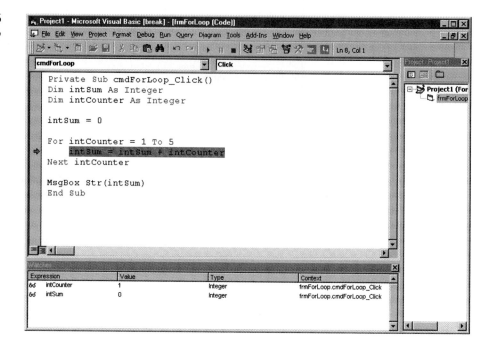

Step 4: You are now ready to execute the body of the For loop for the first time. If you press the <F8> key again, you execute the body of the loop and add intCounter to intSum. Since the intCounter is equal to 1 and the intSum is equal to 0, the result of the addition is 1. This is stored in intSum. The following figure will show both the changed value of intSum and that you are ready to execute the increment statement of the loop.

Figure 7.7
Trace of For Loop

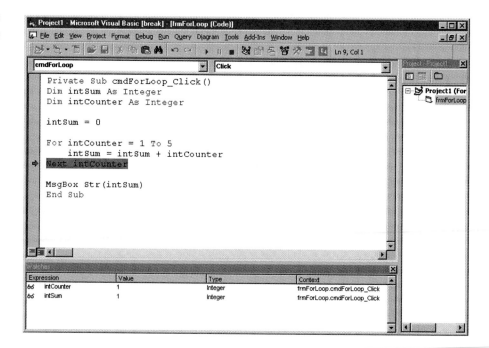

Step 5: By pressing the <F8> key again, you execute the increment statement of the
For loop. This increases the value of the intCounter variable by 1.
Therefore, intCounter now equals 2. This is seen in the following figure:

Figure 7.8
Trace of For Loop

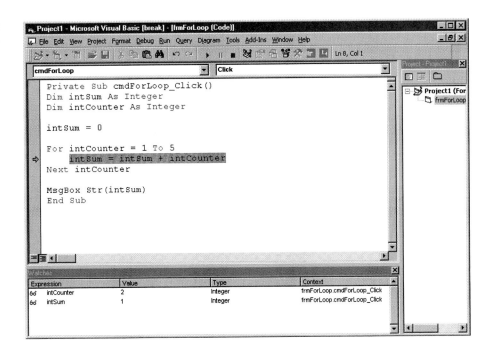

Step 6: By pressing the <F8> key again, you compare intCounter to 5. Since 2 is
less than 5, you continue by executing the body of the loop. This time, the
intCounter variable equals 2, so 2 is added to the value of the intSum variable, 1, and intSum is set to 3.

Figure 7.9
Trace of For Loop

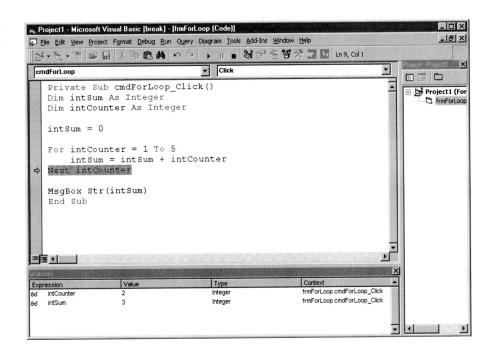

Step 7: By pressing the <F8> key again, you increment intCounter again. This increases the value of the intCounter variable by 1. Therefore, intCounter now equals 3.

Figure 7.10
Trace of For Loop

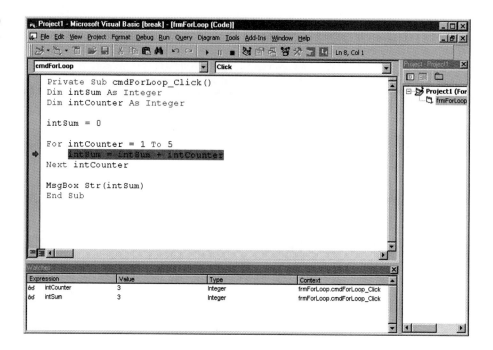

Step 8: By pressing the <F8> key again, you execute the body of the For loop once again. This time, the intCounter variable equals 3, so 3 is added to the value of the intSum variable, 3, and the intSum variable is set to 6. This is shown in the following figure:

Figure 7.11
Trace of For Loop

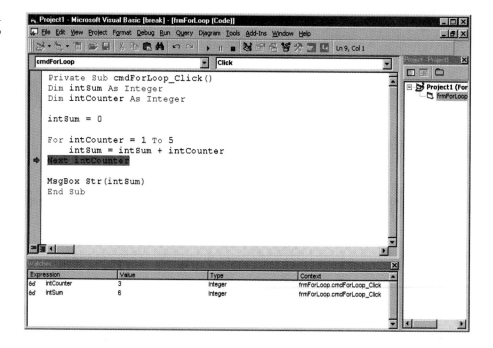

Step 9: By pressing the <F8> key again, you execute the increment statement of the For loop for the third time. This increases the value of the intCounter variable by 1. Therefore, intCounter now equals 4. The value of intSum is unaffected and still equals 6. Since the value of intCounter, 4, is less than or equal to 5, you continue executing the body of the loop. Notice that the value of intSum is not less than or equal to 5, but this is irrelevant. The value of intSum is not the value used in the check for the termination of the loop. This is seen in the following figure:

Figure 7.12
Trace of For Loop

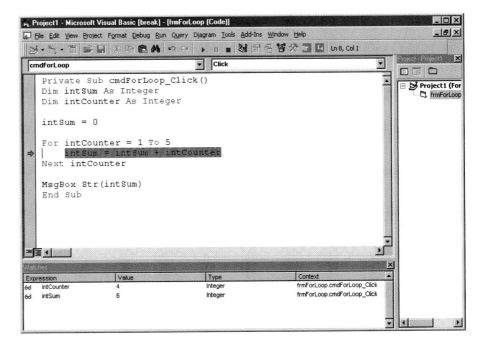

Step 10: By pressing the <F8> key again, you execute the body of the For loop another time. This time, the intCounter variable equals 4, so 4 is added to the value of the intSum variable, 6, and intSum is set to 10. This is shown in the following figure:

Figure 7.13
Trace of For Loop

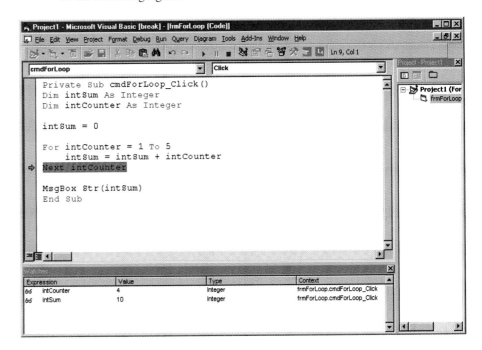

Step 11:   By pressing the <F8> key again, you execute the increment statement of the For loop for the fourth time. This increases the value of the intCounter variable by 1. Therefore, intCounter now equals 5.

Figure 7.14
Trace of For Loop

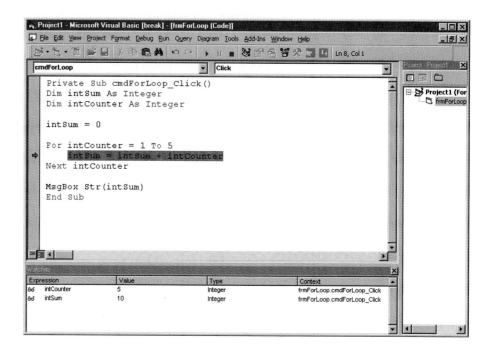

Step 12:   By pressing the <F8> key again, you compare intCounter to 5. Since 5 is less than or equal to 5, you continue executing the body of the loop. This time, 5 is added to the value of the intSum variable, 10, and intSum is set to 15.

Figure 7.15
Trace of For Loop

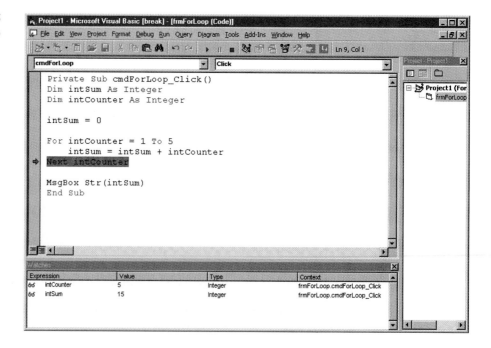

Step 13: By pressing the <F8> key again, you execute the increment statement of the For loop for the fifth time. This increases the value of the intCounter variable by 1. Therefore, intCounter now equals 6. Since the value of intCounter, 6, is *not* less than or equal to 5, you halt the execution of the loop. This is seen in the following figure:

Figure 7.16
Trace of For Loop

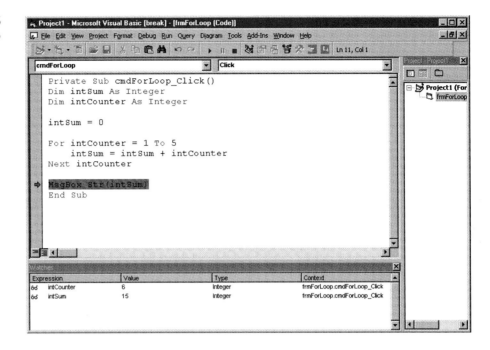

Step 14: By pressing the <F8> key again, the MsgBox command is executed and the output is as follows:

Figure 7.17
Output of For Loop

```
                                    15
```

By clicking on the OK command button, the execution of this routine is now complete.

Incrementing by Values Other than One

Often real-world situations require that you write your loops so that the increment value is something other than the default value of 1.

Visual Basic allows you to use the **Step** option of the For statement to specify an increment size other than 1. The following is the syntax for the For loop with the Step option:

```
For LoopCounter = InitialValue To TerminatingValue Step Amount
    Program Statement(s)
Next LoopCounter
```

The only difference between this and the first For loop we introduced is that by adding the Step keyword, you can indicate a value, Amount, that will be added to the loop counter on each iteration of the loop.

The following is an example of a For loop that adds up all the odd values between 1 and 5 and displays the result in a message box. By starting at 1, when you add 2 to intCounter on each iteration of the loop, you will only add odd numbers to the intSum variable. This is shown in the following code:

```
Private Sub CmdOutput_Click()
Dim intSum As Integer
Dim intCounter As Integer
intSum = 0

For intCounter = 1 To 5 Step 2
  intSum = intSum + intCounter
Next intCounter

MsgBox intSum

End Sub
```

Decrementing the Loop Counter

In addition to incrementing the loop counter, you can decrement the loop counter by simply indicating a negative value for the step size. The execution of a `For` loop with a loop counter that decrements is the same as before, but instead of adding the value indicated as the step size, it subtracts it.

See the following code that displays the numbers from 5 through 1 in the text box `txtOutput`:

> **TIP**
>
> To convert from a numeric value to a `String`, use the built-in conversion function `Str`.

```
Private Sub cmdOutput_Click()
Dim intCounter As Integer

For intCounter = 5 To 1 Step -1
  txtOutput.Text = txtOutput.Text & Str(intCounter) & " "
Next intCounter

End Sub
```

The code initializes the `intCounter` variable to 5 and loops until the `intCounter` variable is less than 1. Each iteration of the loop decrements the `intCounter` variable by 1. Within the body of the loop, the `intCounter` variable's string value is appended to the `txtOutput` text box along with a space character for clarity.

The output of the execution of the previous code produces the following values in the `txtOutput` text box:

```
9 4 3 2 1
```

Figure 7.18 Decrement Loop Example Output

For Drills 7.1 through 7.9, assume that a text box `txtOutput` and a command button `cmdOutput` have been created.

DRILL 7.1

What is the value in txtOutput's Text property after the following code has been executed?

```
Private Sub cmdOutput_Click()
Dim intCounter As Integer

For intCounter = 6 To 10
  txtOutput.Text = txtOutput.Text + Str(intCounter) + " "
Next intCounter

End Sub
```

DRILL 7.2

What is the value in txtOutput's Text property after the following code has been executed?

```
Private Sub cmdOutput_Click()
Dim intCounter As Integer

For intCounter = 1 To 10 Step 4
  txtOutput.Text = txtOutput.Text + Str(intCounter) + " "
Next intCounter

End Sub
```

DRILL 7.3

What is the value in txtOutput's Text property after the following code has been executed?

```
Private Sub cmdOutput_Click()
Dim intCounter As Integer

For intCounter = 10 To 0 Step -2
  txtOutput.Text = txtOutput.Text + Str(intCounter) + " "
Next intCounter

End Sub
```

DRILL 7.4

What is the value in txtOutput's Text property after the following code has been executed?

```
Private Sub cmdOutput_Click()
Dim intCounter As Integer
Dim intValue As Integer

intValue = 1
For intCounter = 1 To 10 Step 2
  intValue = intValue * intCounter
Next intCounter

txtOutput.Text = Str(intValue)
End Sub
```

DRILL 7.5

What is the value in txtOutput's Text property after the following code has been executed?

```
Private Sub cmdOutput_Click()
Dim intCounter As Integer

For intCounter = 1 To 10 Step -2
  txtOutput.Text = txtOutput.Text + Str(intCounter) + " "
Next intCounter

End Sub
```

DRILL 7.6

What is the value in txtOutput's Text property after the following code has been executed?

```
Private Sub cmdOutput_Click()
Dim intCounter As Integer

For intCounter = -10 To -5 Step 1
  txtOutput.Text = txtOutput.Text + Str(intCounter) + " "
Next intCounter

End Sub
```

DRILL 7.7

What is the value in txtOutput's Text property after the following code has been executed?

```
Private Sub cmdOutput_Click()
Dim intCounter As Integer

For intCounter = -10 To -5 Step 2
  txtOutput.Text = txtOutput.Text + Str(intCounter) + " "
Next intCounter

End Sub
```

DRILL 7.8

What is the value in txtOutput's Text property after the following code has been executed?

```
Private Sub cmdOutput_Click()
Dim intCounter As Integer

For intCounter = 2 To 10 Step 5
  txtOutput.Text = txtOutput.Text + Str(intCounter) + " "
Next intCounter

txtOutput.Text = txtOutput.Text + Str(intCounter)
End Sub
```

DRILL 7.9

What is the value in txtOutput's Text property after the following code has been executed?

```
Private Sub cmdOutput_Click()
Dim intCounter As Integer

For intCounter = 1 To 10 Step 1
  intCounter = intCounter + 3
  txtOutput.Text = txtOutput.Text + Str(intCounter) + " "
Next intCounter

End Sub
```

Example: Investment Application

Now that you have a strong mastery of the syntax of the For loop, let's write some applications that take advantage of them and the Visual Basic interface.

Let's create an application that allows the user to enter an initial investment amount, the percentage return on investment per year, and the number of years of the investment. The application should output in a message box the final value of the investment. See the following two figures showing the initial input form and the message box displaying the result.

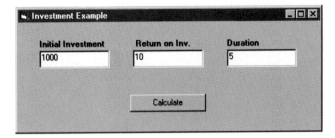

Figure 7.19   Investment Input Form

Figure 7.20   Results Message Box

Three text boxes and three labels must be added to the form. The text boxes should be called txtInitialInvestment, txtPercentageReturn, and txtDuration. In addition, a command button must be created with the following code included in its Click event:

```
Private Sub cmdCalculate_Click()
'Declare local variables
Dim curValue As Currency
Dim intLoopCounter As Integer
Dim sngPercentageReturn As Single
Dim intDuration As Integer

'Initialize variables to values stored in text boxes
curValue = CCur(txtInitialInvestment.Text)
intDuration = CInt(txtDuration.Text)
sngPercentageReturn = CSng(txtPercentageReturn)

'Process Loop
For intLoopCounter = 1 To intDuration
  curValue = curValue + (curValue * sngPercentageReturn / 100)
Next intLoopCounter

MsgBox Str(curValue)
End Sub
```

TIP

Notice that the For loop uses a variable as the upper bound of the For loop. This is a fairly common occurrence and does not present any problem.

The code computes the final investment by adding the previous year's investment to the product of the previous year's investment multiplied by the percentage return of the investment. When the loop terminates, the final value of the investment is displayed in a message box.

List Box Example

When we introduced list boxes earlier, we didn't mention an additional feature of a list box. Often, you can simplify the entry of information by allowing a user to select more than one item from the list at the same time.

Imagine you had an application that allowed a user to select three flavors of ice cream for a sundae and one topping. You could use an option button to select the topping and a list box with the capability to select more than one item for the ice cream flavors. Then you could output the type of sundae selected.

Observe the following application that displays the message box (Figure 7.21) when three flavors of ice cream are selected and then the command button `cmdOrderSundae` is clicked:

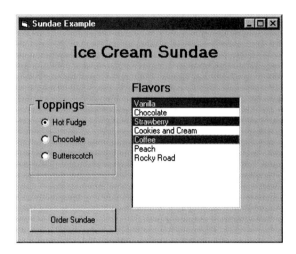

Figure 7.21   Ice Cream Sundae Interface

Figure 7.22   Ice Cream Sundae Output

The three toppings, Hot Fudge, Chocolate, and Butterscotch are represented by the option buttons `optHotFudge`, `optChocolate`, and `optButterscotch`, respectively. The flavors, Vanilla, Chocolate, Strawberry, Cookies and Cream, Coffee, Peach, and Rocky Road are represented in a list box.

By setting the `MultiSelect` property of the list box to `1-Simple`, a user can select more than one item from a list box. If he or she clicks on an item, it becomes selected. If a user clicks on the same item again, it becomes deselected. Unlike a list box with no `MultiSelect` property set, the list box will not deselect the previously selected items when another one is selected.

Determining which items of the list box are selected or deselected requires testing each item to see if it is selected. You can test any item to see if it is selected by using the following template:

```
ListBox.Selected(ItemIndex)
```

If the value evaluates to `True`, the item associated at that index `ItemIndex` has been selected.

If you wish to return the name of the item at a specific index, you can use the following template:

```
ListBox.List(ItemIndex)
```

Your application does not require checking a single item. Instead, you must check all the items to see if they have been selected. The easiest way to accomplish this is to use a `For` loop. Observe the following code for the `cmdOrderSundae` command button that will call a message box with your specific order. First it appends the type of sundae information, and then it determines the types of ice cream selected. The process is complicated a bit since you need to use the proper grammar for commas and the word "and."

```
Private Sub cmdOrderSundae_Click()
'Declare Variables
Dim intCounter As Integer
Dim strOutputString As String
Dim intSelectedCount As Integer

'Initialize Variables
intSelectedCount = 0
strOutputString = "A "

'Select Type of Sundae
If (optHotFudge.Value = True) Then
   strOutputString = strOutputString + "Hot Fudge "
End If

If (optChocolate.Value = True) Then
   strOutputString = strOutputString + "Chocolate "
End If

If (optButterscotch.Value = True) Then
   strOutputString = strOutputString + "Butterscotch "
End If

strOutputString = strOutputString + "Sundae with "

'Select Ice Cream Flavors
For intCounter = 0 To lstFlavors.ListCount - 1
   If (lstFlavors.Selected(intCounter) = True) Then
      intSelectedCount = intSelectedCount + 1

      If (intSelectedCount = 3) Then
         strOutputString = strOutputString + "and "
      End If

      strOutputString = strOutputString + lstFlavors.List(intCounter)

      If (intSelectedCount < 3) Then
         strOutputString = strOutputString + ", "
```

(continues)

(continued)

```
      End If
   End If
Next intCounter

strOutputString = strOutputString + " Ice Cream"

MsgBox strOutputString
End Sub
```

The code loops from the first index, 0, to the last index, 6. However, you do not hard code the value 6. If you choose to add more flavors, you might forget to increase the last index value. Since the list box allows you to reference the total number of items in its list programmatically, you reference that value and then subtract 1 to get the last index.

You might think you are done, but you would be wrong. Your application does not meet all the requirements specified. You were asked to write an application that allowed the selection of three ice cream flavors. Well, what happens if you select more or less than three flavors? Right now, nothing. A good programmer will validate the data entered to ensure the proper selection has been made. The following code should be added to the end of your code instead of just displaying the `strOutputString` variable automatically.

```
If (intSelectedCount = 3) Then
   MsgBox strOutputString
Else
   MsgBox "You did not select 3 flavors"
End If
```

WARNING

Visual Basic allows developers to write a For loop so that they can exit within the middle of the loop if a condition occurs. While this is valid Visual Basic coding, it should be avoided in almost every case. Usually, the need to exit within the middle of a loop indicates a poorly designed loop.

If you need to exit a For loop, all that is required is that you type `Exit For`.

Observe the following example that sets up a loop to add the numbers from 1 to 10, but drops out of the loop at 5.

```
Private Sub LoopExample()
Dim intLoopCounter As Integer
Dim intTotal As Integer

intTotal = 0

For intLoopCounter = 1 To 10
   If (intLoopCounter = 5) Then
      Exit For
   End If
   intTotal = intTotal + intLoopCounter
Next intLoopCounter
MsgBox Str(intTotal)
End Sub
```

7.2   Do Loops

Another loop construct in Visual Basic is the `Do While` loop. Often it's used when you are repeating a process that is not controlled by counting with a fixed-step amount, as in a `For` loop. Instead, you use the `Do While` construct when your loop will continue while a certain condition evaluates to `True`. There are actually a number of formats that you may use `Do` loops with; the choice is yours. Pick the one that best maps to the problem you are trying to solve.

First Do Loop Construct

The following is a template to use for the `Do` loop when you wish to test if a condition evaluates to `True`, before you execute the program statements, and to continue to execute the statement while the condition evaluates to `True`:

```
Do While (Condition)
    Program Statement(s)
Loop
```

The next four applications all accomplish the same goal, but do so using different looping constructs.

Each application displays a message box asking whether you wish to continue. If you answer `Yes`, it prompts you again until you select `No`. Once `No` has been selected, it displays the number of times `Yes` was selected.

The choice of construct is totally one of style; however, one usually is most appropriate for the problem you are trying to solve. Assume a form has been created for each application with a single command button. The command button contains the code shown.

```
'Version #1
Private Sub cmdDoLoop_Click()
'Variable Declaration
Dim intCounter As Integer
Dim intAnswer As Integer

'Variable Initialization
intCounter = 0
intAnswer = vbYes

'Do While Loop
Do While (intAnswer = vbYes)
  intAnswer = MsgBox("Continue?", vbYesNo)
  If (intAnswer = vbYes) Then
    intCounter = intCounter + 1
  End If
Loop

'Output Results
MsgBox "Number of Continues = " + Str(intCounter)
End Sub
```

Version 1 of the application declares an `Integer` to store the number of times you indicate you wish to continue. You initialize this to zero. It also declares an `Integer` to store the answer the message box receives. Because of the looping construct picked for this version, you need to initialize the `Answer` variable to `vbYes` so it will enter the body of the loop the first time.

Then the Do loop displays the first message box and waits for an answer. Once received, if the answer is Yes, it adds one to the counter. Then the loop condition is checked. If it is Yes, the loop continues. Once the loop terminates, a message box displaying the total is called.

Second Do Loop Construct

Another form of the Do loop is used when you wish the loop to execute until a given condition evaluates to True. The syntax follows:

```
Do Until (Condition)
    Program Statement(s)
Loop
```

Version 2 of the application changes the looping construct to use an Until statement. This program is virtually identical except you must change the condition to check for the case that you want the loop to terminate upon. The code follows:

```
'Version #2
Private Sub cmdDoLoop_Click()
'Variable Declaration
Dim intCounter As Integer
Dim intAnswer As Integer

'Variable Initialization
intCounter = 0

'Do Until Loop
Do Until (intAnswer = vbNo)
  intAnswer = MsgBox("Continue?", vbYesNo)
  If (intAnswer = vbYes) Then
    intCounter = intCounter + 1
  End If
Loop

'Output Results
MsgBox "Number of Continues = " + Str(intCounter)
End Sub
```

Third Do Loop Construct

Still another form of the Do loop is used when you wish to execute the program statements at least once and continue to execute the statement while the condition evaluates to True. The syntax follows:

```
Do
    Program Statement(s)
Loop While (Condition)
```

The benefit of this looping construct is that, by allowing the application to assume that the loop will execute at least once, you do not have to initialize the intAnswer variable. You'll see that it will be set to your answer before it is ever compared. The code follows:

```
'Version #3
Private Sub cmdDoLoop_Click()
'Variable Declaration
Dim intCounter As Integer
Dim intAnswer As Integer

'Variable Initialization
intCounter = 0

'Do...While Loop
Do
   intAnswer = MsgBox("Continue?", vbYesNo)
   If (intAnswer = vbYes) Then
     intCounter = intCounter + 1
   End If
Loop While (intAnswer = vbYes)

'Output Results
MsgBox "Number of Continues = " + Str(intCounter)
End Sub
```

This application is very similar to the other examples; it just contains one less step.

Fourth Do Loop Construct

The final looping construct is used when you wish to execute the program statements at least once, and continue to execute them until the given condition evaluates to `True`. The syntax follows:

```
Do
     Program Statement(s)
Loop Until (Condition)
```

You can rewrite the previous application with an `Until` statement instead of a `While` statement. This requires you changing the condition. Either program is *correct;* it's simply a matter of style:

```
'Version #4
Private Sub cmdDoLoop_Click()
'Variable Declarations
Dim intCounter As Integer
Dim intAnswer As Integer

'Variable Initialization
intCounter = 0

'Do ... Until Loop
Do
   intAnswer = MsgBox("Continue?", vbYesNo)
   If (intAnswer = vbYes) Then
     intCounter = intCounter + 1
   End If
Loop Until (intAnswer = vbNo)
```

(continues)

(continued)

```
'Output Results
MsgBox "Number of Continues = " + Str(intCounter)
End Sub
```

The only change in the application is that you changed the condition to check for a No response. When the value of intAnswer equals a No response, the loop terminates.

So which choice of looping construct did you think most fit the needs of the application for which you developed it? I would have selected either the third or fourth version, since they would not require the initialization of the Answer variable. But again, remember that this is a matter of style.

For Drills 7.10 through 7.15, assume that a text box txtOutput and a command button cmdOutput have been created.

DRILL 7.10

What is the value in txtOutput's Text property after the following code has been executed?

```
Private Sub cmdOutput_Click()
Dim intCounter As Integer

intCounter = 5
Do While (intCounter > 0)
   intCounter = intCounter - 1
   txtOutput.Text = txtOutput.Text + Str(intCounter) + " "
Loop

End Sub
```

DRILL 7.11

What is the value in txtOutput's Text property after the following code has been executed?

```
Private Sub cmdOutput_Click()
Dim intCounter As Integer
intCounter = 0

Do Until (intCounter = 10)
   intCounter = intCounter + 2
   txtOutput.Text = txtOutput.Text + Str(intCounter) + " "
Loop

End Sub
```

DRILL 7.12

What is the value in `txtOutput`'s Text property after the following code has been executed?

```
Private Sub cmdOutput_Click()
Dim intCounter As Integer

intCounter = 0
Do Until (Counter > 0)
  intCounter = intCounter - 3
  txtOutput.Text = txtOutput.Text + Str(intCounter) + " "
Loop

End Sub
```

DRILL 7.13

What is the value in `txtOutput`'s Text property after the following code has been executed?

```
Private Sub cmdOutput_Click()
Dim intCounter As Integer

intCounter = 0

Do
  intCounter = intCounter + 3
  txtOutput.Text = txtOutput.Text + Str(intCounter) + " "
Loop Until (intCounter > 5)

End Sub
```

DRILL 7.14

What is the value in `txtOutput`'s Text property after the following code has been executed?

```
Private Sub cmdOutput_Click()
Dim intCounter As Integer

intCounter = 0

Do
  intCounter = intCounter + 3
  txtOutput.Text = txtOutput.Text + Str(intCounter) + " "
Loop While (intCounter < 10)

End Sub
```

DRILL 7.15

What is the value in txtOutput's Text property after the following code has been executed?

```
Private Sub cmdOutput_Click()
Dim intCounter As Integer

intCounter = 0
Do
   intCounter = intCounter + 3
   txtOutput.Text = txtOutput.Text + Str(intCounter) + " "
Loop While (intCounter > 10)

End Sub
```

Example: Vampire Counting Application

An old story once claimed to prove the impossibility of the existence of vampires. The story alleged that a vampire needed to take a victim each night in order to survive. However, the victim became a vampire as well. That would mean each night, the number of vampires would double. With the world's population approximately six billion, how long would it take for everyone to become a vampire?

The use of a Do loop makes more sense then a For loop since you do not know the number of times the loop will execute. You will create an application that contains a command button cmdComputerDays with the following code and display the result in a message box:

```
Private Sub cmdComputeDays_Click()
Dim dblNumVampires As Double
Dim intNumDays As Integer

dblNumVampires = 1

Do While (dblNumVampires < 6000000000#)
   dblNumVampires = dblNumVampires * 2
   intNumDays = intNumDays + 1
Loop
MsgBox Str(intNumDays)
End Sub
```

TIP

Notice the # after the number representing six billion. The # was added automatically after typing 6000000000 to indicate the size of the variable.

Your code involves a few issues to point out. First, the choice of variable to hold the count of the number of vampires is not straightforward. You require a variable that can store a value in the billions. Neither an Integer nor a Long is large enough, so you must choose a Double. However, for the number of days, you can use an Integer variable type. This is because the number of days required is only 33, so you can see the world is safe from vampires.

Example: Distance Conversion Application

When competing in a race, distances are often given in either miles or kilometers. Let's write an application that will accept a total distance, the interval for which you want to display the conversion, and the units (miles or kilometers). The application should look as follows:

Figure 7.23
Distance Conversion
Application

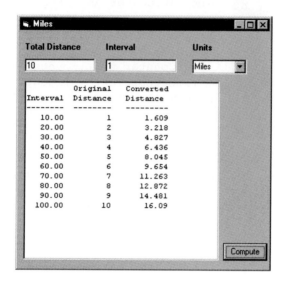

You need to create three text boxes. The first two, `txtTotalDistance` and `txtInterval`, are created as usual. The third, `txtOutput`, should have the property `MultiLine` set to `True`. Then add a combo box that contains two list values: `Miles` and `Kilometers`. Add three labels so the purpose of the text boxes and combo boxes is easily understood. Finally, add a command button with the following code:

```
Private Sub cmdCompute_Click()
'Variable Declarations
Dim dblCurrentDistance As Double
Dim dblTotalDistance As Double
Dim dblInterval As Double
Dim intIntervalNumber As Integer
Dim dblConvertValue As Double


'Constant Declarations
Const dblConvertFromKilometers As Double = 0.6215
Const dblConvertFromMiles As Double = 1.609


'Initialize Variables
dblCurrentDistance = Val(txtInterval.Text)
dblInterval = Val(txtInterval.Text)
dblTotalDistance = Val(txtTotalDistance.Text)
intIntervalNumber = 1


'Select Conversion Factor
If (cmoConvertFrom.Text = "Miles") Then
  dblConvertValue = dblConvertFromMiles
```

(continues)

(continued)

```
Else
   dblConvertValue = dblConvertFromKilometers
End If

'Display Header
txtOutput = "            Original    Converted" & vbNewLine & _
            "Interval  Distance    Distance"  & vbNewLine & _
            "_ _ _ _   _ _ _ _ _    _ _ _ _ -" & vbNewLine

'Generate Chart
Do Until (dblCurrentDistance > dblTotalDistance)
   txtOutput.Text = txtOutput.Text & Format(intIntervalNumber, "@@@@0.00") & _
   " " & Format(dblCurrentDistance, "@@@@@@@@@") & " " & _
   Format(dblCurrentDistance * dblConvertValue, "@@@@@@@@@@@") & _
   vbNewLine
   intIntervalNumber = intIntervalNumber + 1
   dblCurrentDistance = dblCurrentDistance + dblInterval
Loop
End Sub
```

7.3 Nested Loops

Just as you nested `If` statements to execute conditional statements within other conditional statements, you often **nest** loops within other loops. The execution of a nested loop is no different than the execution of loops you already have experience with.

When a loop is nested within another loop, the execution of the inner loop occurs completely for each iteration of the outer loop. Try these drills to improve your understanding of nested loops.

DRILL 7.16

What is the value in `txtOutput`'s `Text` property after the following code has been executed?

```
Private Sub cmdNested_Click()
Dim intOuterCounter As Integer
Dim intInnerCounter As Integer

For intOuterCounter = 1 To 3 Step 1
  For intInnerCounter = 1 To 3 Step 1
    txtOutput.Text = txtOutput.Text & Str(intInnerCounter) + " "
  Next intInnerCounter
Next intOuterCounter
End Sub
```

TIP

The `Next intInnerCounter` statement in the previous drill closes the innermost `For` loop. It is important when working with nested loops to indent properly so that the intent of the programmer is made clear. Otherwise, it is easy to get confused as to which `For` loop the `Next` statement belongs.

DRILL 7.17

What is the value in `txtOutput`'s `Text` property after the following code has been executed?

```
Private Sub cmdNested_Click()
Dim intOuterCounter As Integer
Dim intInnerCounter As Integer
Dim intTotal As Integer

intTotal = 0
For intOuterCounter = 1 To 5 Step 2
  For intInnerCounter = 1 To 3 Step 2
    intTotal = intTotal + intInnerCounter
  Next intInnerCounter
Next intOuterCounter

txtOutput.Text = intTotal

End Sub
```

DRILL 7.18

What is the value in `txtOutput`'s `Text` property after the following code has been executed?

```
Private Sub cmdNested_Click()
Dim intInnerCounter As Integer
Dim intOuterCounter As Integer

intOuterCounter= 0

Do
   intInnerCounter = 0
   intOuterCounter= intOuterCounter+ 3
   txtOutput.Text = txtOutput.Text + Str(intOuterCounter) + " "
   Do
     txtOutput.Text = txtOutput.Text + Str(intInnerCounter) + " "
     intInnerCounter = intInnerCounter + 2
   Loop While (intInnerCounter < 5)
Loop While (intOuterCounter < 5)

End Sub
```

DRILL 7.19

What is the value in txtOutput's Text property after the following code has been executed?

```
Private Sub cmdNested_Click()
Dim intInnerCounter As Integer
Dim intOuterCounter As Integer

intOuterCounter = 5
intInnerCounter = 0

Do
   intOuterCounter = intOuterCounter - 2
   txtOutput.Text = txtOutput.Text + Str(intOuterCounter) + " "
   Do
      txtOutput.Text = txtOutput.Text + Str(intInnerCounter) + " "
      intInnerCounter = intInnerCounter + 2
   Loop While (intInnerCounter < 5)
Loop While (intOuterCounter > 0)

End Sub
```

7.4 Setting Breakpoints with the Debugger

As you saw in the previous section, loops can execute many times. If you wish to use a Debugger to trace through a program to track down an error, it may take a very long time to find this error. This is especially true if you know that the error occurs after the inner loop of a nested loop executes. Fortunately, the Visual Basic Debugger provides a **breakpoint**.

A breakpoint allows the programmer to set the Debugger to execute until it reaches a specific line of code. Observe the following code that contains two nested For loops. To demonstrate the use of a breakpoint, you will set the code to stop each time after the inner For loop executes. You will also set watch variables on both loop counters:

```
Private Sub cmdDebug_Click()
Dim intInnerCounter As Integer
Dim intOuterCounter As Integer
Dim intSum As Long

intSum = 0

For intOuterCounter = 1 To 3
   For intInnerCounter = 1 To 100
      intSum = intSum + intInnerCounter
   Next intInnerCounter
Next intOuterCounter

txtOutput.Text = Str(intSum)

End Sub
```

In order to set the application to trace properly, you follow these steps:

Step 1: Create a form with a text box called `txtOutput`.
Step 2: Add a command button.
Step 3: Place the previous code in the command button's `Click` event.
Step 4: Press the <F8> key to start the Debugger.
Step 5: Click on the command button.
Step 6: Click on the Debug menu.
Step 7: Click on the Add Watch option.
Step 8: Enter `intOuterCounter` for the expression and click OK.
Step 9: Click on the Debug menu.
Step 10: Click on the Add Watch option.
Step 11: Enter `intSum` for the expression and click OK.
Step 12: Click on the Debug menu.
Step 13: Click on the Add Watch option.
Step 14: Enter `intInnerCounter` for the expression and click OK.
Step 15: Click to the left of the `Next intOuterCounter` statement to place a breakpoint on that line.

Your application should look as follows:

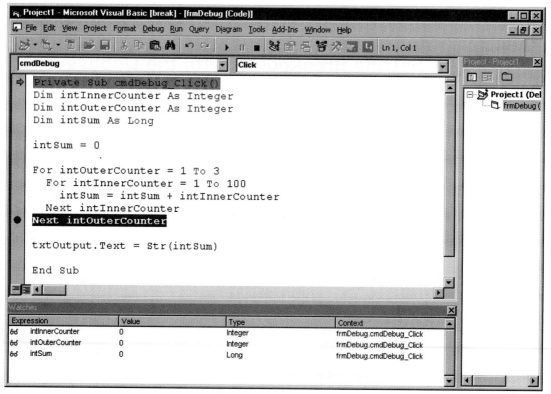

Figure 7.24 Initial Setup for Breakpoint Example

Notice that the last line of code the application will execute is a maroon color with a maroon circle in the left margin. Also notice that the `Watch` variables are both initially at 0.

You are now ready to have the application execute until it reaches the breakpoint. This will cause the application to completely execute the inner `For` loop and stop.

Step 16: Click on the continue button in the toolbar. The application will run for a short time and then your screen will look similar to the following figure:

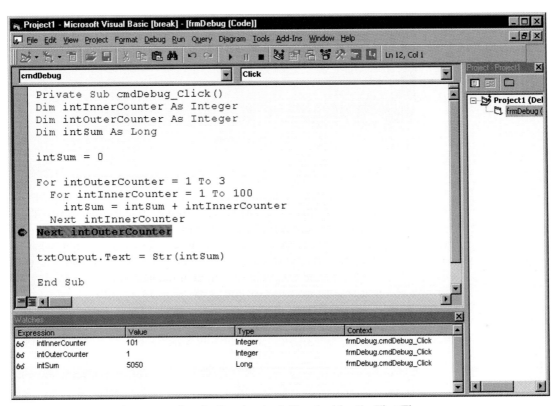

Figure 7.25   Visual Basic Environment after the Breakpoint is Reached for the First Time

Since the inner `For` loop has executed 100 times, you can see the value `intInnerCounter` is equal to 101. This make sense because when `intInnerCounter` is greater than 100, the inner loop terminates. Also notice that `intSum` is equal to 5,050, which is the value you get when all the numbers are added together from 1 to 100. Finally, notice that the `intOuterCounter` equals 1 because it has not yet been incremented.

Step 17: Click on the continue button in the toolbar again to execute the inner `For` loop a second time. The application will run for a short time and then your screen will look similar to the following figure:

Figure 7.26
Visual Basic Environment
after the Breakpoint is
Reached for the Second
Time

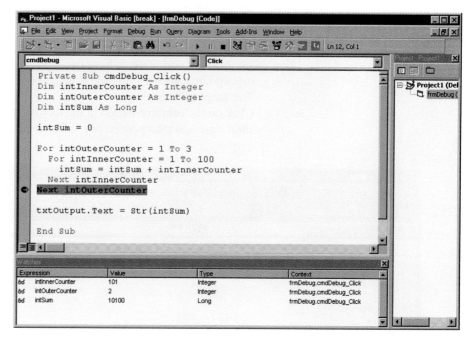

Even though the inner `For` loop has executed an additional 100 times, you can see the value `intInnerCounter` is still equal to 101. This is because `InnerCounter`'s value was reset to 1 at the beginning of the execution of the loop. Also notice that the `intSum` is now double what it was before, 10,100. This is because an additional 5,050 was added to the total during the second complete execution of the inner `For` loop. Finally, notice that the `intOuterCounter` equals 2.

Step 18:   Click on the continue button in the toolbar again to execute the inner `For` loop a third time. The application will run for a short time and then your screen will look similar to the following figure:

Figure 7.27
Visual Basic Environment
after the Breakpoint is
Reached for the Third Time

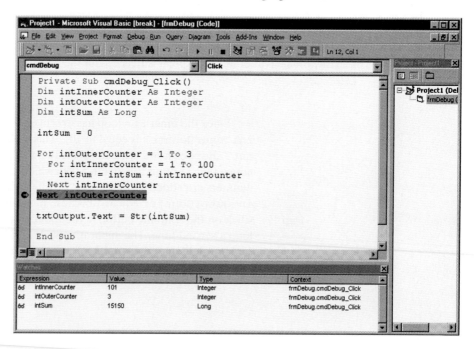

Again the inner `For` loop has executed an additional 100 times. Notice that the `intSum` is now equal to 15,150, since an additional 5,050 was added to it during the third complete execution of the inner `For` loop. Finally, notice that the `intOuterCounter` equals 3.

Step 19: Click on the continue button in the toolbar again and the program will finish its execution and display 15150 as the value in `txtOutput`.

Figure 7.28
Final Output of Breakpoint
Example

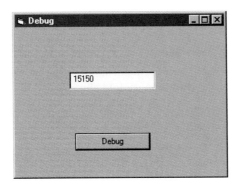

TIP

You do not have to wait until the program is running to add the watch variables. This can be done at design time as well.

7.5 Use of the MS Flex Grid Control

With the introduction of loops an additional control becomes very useful, the MS flex grid. It is not one of the default controls in your Control toolbar, so you will have to manually add it to the toolbar.

Step 1: Click on the Project menu.
Step 2: Select Components.
Step 3: The window in Figure 7.28 appears.
Step 4: Scroll down until the Microsoft flex grid control appears. Note that your window may have slightly different options.
Step 5: Click the check box associated with the Microsoft flex grid.
Step 6: Notice that the MS flex grid control now appears in the toolbar.

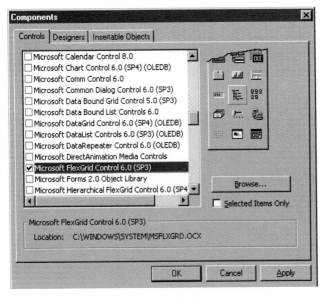

Figure 7.29 Add Component Window

Figure 7.30 MS Flex Grid Control

An MS flex grid looks similar to a spreadsheet application. It contains rows and columns. The box where a row and column intersect is known as a **cell**. A cell, which can be specified by its row and column, can be set to contain a `String` value.

Now, you can now create an application that will allow entry of sets of data and display all the sets in one control.

Example: Student Grades Application

Let's write an application that accepts a student's first name, last name, and GPA. The program should allow the addition of as many students as desired.

The application should look as follows:

Figure 7.31
Student Grades Application

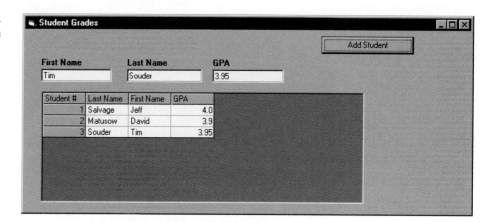

Step 1:   This form requires adding three text boxes to store each student's information: `txtFirst`, `txtLast`, and `txtGPA`. Additionally, you need to add an MS flex grid (`grdStudents`) to contain all of the students' information. Finally, a command button is required to process each student's information and place it in the MS flex grid.

In order to use an MS flex grid, you need to specify the number of rows and columns in the grid. In your example, the grid has four rows and four columns. The property for the number of rows is appropriately called `Rows`. Likewise, the number of columns is called `Cols`. Setting them is simply a matter of indicating the number of each that you wish. You may do so programmatically or from the Properties window.

In addition, you need to set the labels for the grid. The most appropriate place for this code is in the `Form_Load` event. Your labels appear gray because you used the default of an MS flex grid so that the first row and column are fixed. You can create or remove more fixed rows and columns by setting the property's `FixedRows` and `FixedColumns`. If you set them to zero, there will be no fixed rows or columns.

However, to set each individual cell of the grid, you need to indicate the specific row and column that you want to set. This is accomplished with the `Row` and `Col` properties, respectively. Complicating the matter is the fact that the first `Row` and `Col` are specified with 0, not 1.

See the following figure that displays the row and column position of each cell with the format (row, column):

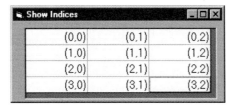

Figure 7.32
MS Flex Grid's Indices

Step 2: You should now understand enough to write the `Form_Load` code that follows:

```
Private Sub Form_Load()
grdStudents.Rows = 1
grdStudents.Cols = 4

grdStudents.Row = 0

grdStudents.Col = 0
grdStudents.Text = "Student #"

grdStudents.Col = 1
grdStudents.Text = "Last Name"

grdStudents.Col = 2
grdStudents.Text = "First Name"

grdStudents.Col = 3
grdStudents.Text = "GPA"

End Sub
```

Step 3: Each time the command button is clicked, you wish to increase the number of rows by one and copy the values in the text boxes to the newly created cells of the MS flex grid. The code in the command button is as follows:

```
Private Sub cmdAddStudent_Click()
grdStudents.Rows = grdStudents.Rows + 1

grdStudents.Row = grdStudents.Rows - 1
grdStudents.Col = 0
grdStudents.Text = grdStudents.Row
grdStudents.Col = 1
grdStudents.Text = txtLast.Text
grdStudents.Col = 2
grdStudents.Text = txtFirst.Text
grdStudents.Col = 3
grdStudents.Text = txtGPA.Text
End Sub
```

Flex Grid Example with Nested Loops

Suppose you wanted to add the functionality to the previous application so you could search the grid for a particular string. You could write a single `For` loop that compared the first name and last name columns with the `String` that you are looking for. However, suppose you increased the number of columns of data that you tracked for a student. You could add a student's major and year at school to your grid. Then, you have two choices: You could hard code the additional columns to search for within the existing `For` loop, or you could write a series of nested `For` loops that search each column and row for the `String`. The latter approach is preferable because you often add additional columns to grids as your programs grow more complex. If you write your routine in the latter manner, you can write it once and not have to modify it. Furthermore, if you write the routine as a function, you can write it once and use it anytime you need the capability to search a grid for a specific value. Your new application looks as follows:

Figure 7.33
Flex Grid Example
Application

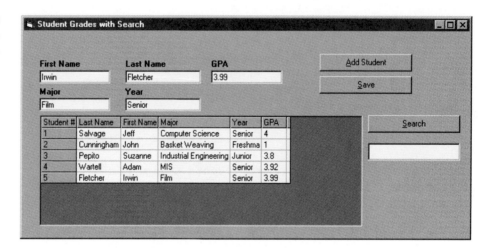

Step 1:   Add the controls shown in Figure 7.32 to the form.

Step 2:   The code for the `cmdSearch` command button is simple. You will call the `SearchGrid` function, which you will write, and pass it the grid and search string from the `txtSearch` text box. If the function returns `True`, you will output a message in a message box indicating it was found. Otherwise, you will output a message box indicating it was not found.

```
Private Sub cmdSearch_Click()
If (SearchGrid(grdStudents, txtSearch.Text)) Then
  MsgBox ("The searched value was found")
Else
  MsgBox ("The searched value was not found")
End If
End Sub
```

TIP

Code reuse is an *extremely* important programming practice to develop.

Although you could have written the search code directly into the `cmdSearch` command button, if you write this code as a function, it can be reused in other applications.

Step 3:   The function accepts as parameters an MS flex grid and a `String`. You will step through each cell in the grid and compare its contents to see if the cell contains that exact `String`. If you find the `String`, you set the function's return value to `True`. However, if you search through the entire grid and do not find it, you return `False`. The code follows:

```
Function SearchGrid(grdGrid As MSFlexGrid, strSearchString As String) As Boolean
Dim intRow As Integer
Dim intColumn As Integer

SearchGrid = False

For intRow = 0 To grdGrid.Rows - 1
  grdGrid.Row = intRow
  For intColumn = 0 To grdGrid.Cols - 1
     grdGrid.Col = intColumn
     If (grdGrid.Text = strSearchString) Then
         SearchGrid = True
     End If
  Next intColumn
Next intRow

End Function
```

◆ 7.6   Case Study

Problem Description   With the addition of the MS flex grid control and loops, you no longer need to limit the number of employees in your Payroll Accounting System. Let's improve your Payroll Accounting System so that you can enter the information about each employee one at a time.

The following figure will demonstrate what your application will look like:

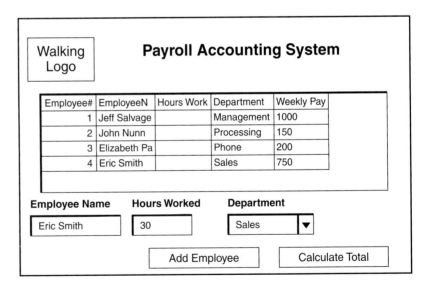

Figure 7.35   Output when Calculate Total Is Clicked

Figure 7.34   Sketch of Application

Problem Discussion   The problem can be solved by either calculating the Total Weekly Pay as each employee's data is entered, or all at once when the user has finished entering the employees' data. You have chosen the latter to reinforce the use of loops.

Problem Solution   Many parts of this application are similar to solutions in earlier chapters. You still need the constants (introduced in Chapter 3) to indicate the pay rates of each type of employee. They are declared in the following code, which should be listed in the General Declarations section:

```
Const intSalesPayRate = 25
Const intProcessingPayRate = 15
Const intManagementPayRate = 50
Const intPhonePayRate = 10
```

You need to initialize the grid so that its labels are visible when the application is executed. The code should be located in the form's Load event:

```
Private Sub Form_Load()
grdEmployees.Rows = 1
grdEmployees.Cols = 5

grdEmployees.Row = 0
grdEmployees.Col = 0
grdEmployees.Text = "Employee #"


grdEmployees.Col = 1
grdEmployees.Text = "Employee Name"

grdEmployees.Col = 2
grdEmployees.Text = "Hours Worked"

grdEmployees.Col = 3
grdEmployees.Text = "Department"

grdEmployees.Col = 4
grdEmployees.Text = "Weekly Pay"
End Sub
```

Although you do not need a series of text boxes and combo boxes as you did before, you need text boxes to enter the Employee's Name and Hours Worked, as well as a combo box for the Department. You also need a command button that will add the new Employee's information to the grid. This code follows:

```
Private Sub cmdAdd_Click()
grdEmployees.Rows = grdEmployees.Rows + 1

grdEmployees.Row = grdEmployees.Rows - 1

grdEmployees.Col = 0
grdEmployees.Text = grdEmployees.Rows - 1

grdEmployees.Col = 1
grdEmployees.Text = txtEmployee.Text

grdEmployees.Col = 2
grdEmployees.Text = txtHours.Text
```

(continues)

(continued)

```
grdEmployees.Col = 3
grdEmployees.Text = cmoDepartment.Text

grdEmployees.Col = 4
'First Week's Calculations
Select Case cmoDepartment
  Case "Sales"
    grdEmployees.Text = Str(Val(txtHours.Text) * intSalesPayRate)
  Case "Processing"
    grdEmployees.Text = Str(Val(txtHours.Text) * intProcessingPayRate)
  Case "Management"
    grdEmployees.Text = Str(Val(txtHours.Text) * intManagementPayRate)
  Case "Phone"
    grdEmployees.Text = Str(Val(txtHours.Text) * intPhonePayRate)
End Select
End Sub
```

The final code required calculates the Total Weekly Pay and displays it in a message box. The code follows:

```
Private Sub cmdTotal_Click()
Dim intCurrentRow As Integer
Dim curTotal As Currency

curTotal = 0
intCurrentRow = 1
grdEmployees.Col = 4


Do While (grdEmployees.Rows > intCurrentRow)
    grdEmployees.Row = intCurrentRow
    curTotal = curTotal + CCur(grdEmployees.Text)
    intCurrentRow = intCurrentRow + 1
Loop

MsgBox Str(curTotal)
End Sub
```

Figure 7.36
Final Application

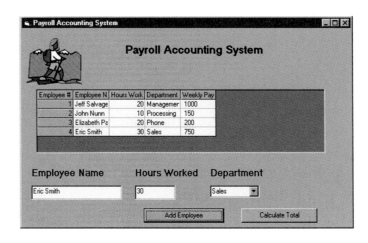

CORNER

Dynamic FlexGrid Resizing

Sometimes it is difficult to determine the exact size of a grid column before the user runs the application. If you wish, you can change the setting of the flex grid's property `AllowUserResizing` from the default `0 - flexResizeNone` to the setting `1 - flexResizeColumns`. This will allow the user to resize the width of the columns by clicking on the column line divider and pulling it in the direction they wish. By setting the property to `2 - flexResizeRows`, it will allow users to resize the height of the rows by clicking on the row line divider and pulling it in the direction they wish. Finally, if you wish to let the user modify both the column and row widths, you can set the property to `3 - flexResizeBoth`.

Keyboard Shortcuts

As your applications grow in size, controlling the flow of their execution by the `TabIndex` property (explained in Chapter 2's Coach's Corner) or the mouse can become inconvenient. Many Windows applications contain keyboard shortcuts that allow the user to use a keyboard sequence to perform actions easily.

Visual Basic allows you to attach keyboard shortcuts to command buttons with a minimum of effort. See the modified Student Search application. It looks almost the same as before. The only difference is that the first letter of each caption on the command button's has an underscore:

Figure 7.37
Keyboard Shortcut Example

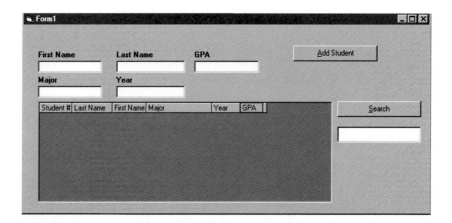

To create a keyboard shortcut, all that is required is that you place an ampersand in front of the letter of the caption that you wish to be the shortcut. Therefore, for the `cmdAddStudent` command button, the caption would be `&Add Student`, while the `cmdSearch` command button would have a caption of `&Search`.

WARNING

Do not create two shortcuts to the same letter. All shortcuts must be to a unique letter.

Pressing the <A> key while holding the <ALT> key has the same effect as clicking the command button cmdAddStudent. Similarly, pressing the <S> key while holding the <ALT> key has the same effect as clicking the command button cmdSearch.

Answers to Chapter's Drills

Drill 7.1
The output is as follows:

```
6  7  8  9  10
```

When the command button is clicked, the code executes as follows: First the intCounter variable is initialized to 6. Since 6 is less than or equal to 10, the body of the For loop executes. This appends a 6 and a space to the txtOutput text box. Then the loop counter, intCounter, is incremented by 1 to 7.

Since 7 is less than or equal to 10, the body of the For loop executes again. This time a 7 and a space are appended to txtOutput. Once again, intCounter is incremented by 1 to 8.

Since 8 is less than or equal to 10, the body of the For loop executes again. This time an 8 and a space are appended to txtOutput. Once again, intCounter is incremented by 1 to 9.

Since 9 is less than or equal to 10, the body of the For loop executes again. This time a 9 and a space are appended to txtOutput. Once again, intCounter is incremented by 1 to 10.

Since 10 is less than or equal to 10, the body of the For loop executes again. This time a 10 and a space are appended to txtOutput. Once again, intCounter is incremented by 1 to 11.

Since 11 is not less than or equal to 10, the loop terminates.

Drill 7.2
The output is as follows:

```
1  5  9
```

When the command button is clicked, the code executes as follows: First the intCounter variable is initialized to 1. Since 1 is less than or equal to 10, the body of the For loop executes. This appends a 1 and a space to the txtOutput text box. Then the loop intCounter, intCounter, is incremented by 4 to 5.

Since 5 is less than or equal to 10, the body of the For loop executes again. This time a 5 and a space are appended to txtOutput. Once again, intCounter is incremented by 4 to 9.

Since 9 is less than or equal to 10, the body of the For loop executes again. This time a 9 and a space are appended to txtOutput. Once again, intCounter is incremented by 4 to 13.

Since 13 is not less than or equal to 10, the loop terminates.

Drill 7.3
The output is as follows:

```
10  8  6  4  2  0
```

When the command button is clicked, the code executes as follows: First the intCounter variable is initialized to 10. Since 10 is greater than or equal to 0, the body of the For loop executes. This appends a 10 and a space to the txtOutput text box. Then the loop counter, intCounter, is decremented by 2 to 8.

Since 8 is greater than or equal to 0, the body of the For loop executes again. This time an 8 and a space is appended to txtOutput. Once again, intCounter is decremented by 2 to 6.

Since 6 is greater than or equal to 0, the body of the For loop executes again. This time a 6 and a space are appended to txtOutput. Once again, intCounter is decremented by 2 to 4.

Since 4 is greater than or equal to 0, the body of the For loop executes again. This time a 4 and a space are appended to txtOutput. Once again, intCounter is decremented by 2 to 2.

Since 2 is greater than or equal to 0, the body of the For loop executes again. This time a 2 and a space are appended to txtOutput. Once again, intCounter is decremented by 2 to 0.

Since 0 is greater than or equal to 0, the body of the For loop executes again. This time a 0 and a space are appended to txtOutput. Once again, intCounter is decremented by 2 to –2.

Since –2 is not greater than or equal to 0, the loop terminates.

Drill 7.4

The output is as follows:

```
945
```

When the command button is clicked, the code executes as follows: First the variable intValue is initialized to 1. Then the For loop is entered and the intCounter variable is initialized to 1. Since 1 is less than or equal to 10, the body of the For loop executes. This value intValue is multiplied by 1 and stored it back in intValue. In this case 1 is multiplied by 1, so intValue equals 1 after the body of the loop executes. Then the loop counter, intCounter, is incremented by 2 to 3.

Since 3 is less than or equal to 10, the body of the For loop executes again. This time intValue is multiplied by 3 and the result, 3, is stored in intValue. Once again, intCounter is incremented by 2 to 5.

Since 5 is less than or equal to 10, the body of the For loop executes again. This time intValue is multiplied by 5 and the result, 15, is stored in intValue. Once again, intCounter is incremented by 2 to 7.

Since 7 is less than or equal to 10, the body of the For loop executes again. This time intValue is multiplied by 7 and the result, 105, is stored in intValue. Once again, intCounter is incremented by 2 to 9.

Since 9 is less than or equal to 10, the body of the For loop executes again. This time intValue is multiplied by 9 and the result, 945, is stored in intValue. Once again, intCounter is incremented by 2 to 11.

Since 11 is not less than or equal to 10, the loop terminates.

Drill 7.5

The output is as follows:

This was a trick question! Although the For loop is coded to count from 1 to 10, you set the Step value to –2. This will cause intCounter to count down; because you cannot count down from 1 to 10, the loop never executes. Therefore, the text box is never appended to, so it displays nothing.

Drill 7.6

The output is as follows:

```
-10 -9 -8 -7 -6 -5
```

When the command button is clicked, the code executes as follows: First the For loop is entered and the `intCounter` variable is initialized to –10. Since –10 is less than or equal to –5, the body of the For loop executes. This appends a –10 and a space to the `txtOutput` text box. Then the loop counter, `intCounter`, is incremented by 1 to –9.

Since –9 is less than or equal to –5, the body of the For loop executes again. This time a –9 and a space are appended to `txtOutput`. Once again, `intCounter` is incremented by 1 to –8.

Since –8 is less than or equal to –5, the body of the For loop executes again. This time a –8 and a space are appended to `txtOutput`. Once again, `intCounter` is incremented by 1 to –7.

Since –7 is less than or equal to –5, the body of the For loop executes again. This time a –7 and a space are appended to `txtOutput`. Once again, `intCounter` is incremented by 1 to –6.

Since –6 is less than or equal to –5, the body of the For loop executes again. This time a –6 and a space are appended to `txtOutput`. Once again, `intCounter` is incremented by 1 to –5.

Since –5 is less than or equal to –5, the body of the For loop executes again. This time a –5 and a space are appended to `txtOutput`. Once again, `intCounter` is incremented by 1 to –4.

Since –4 is not less than or equal to –5, the loop terminates.

Drill 7.7

The output is as follows:

```
-10 -8 -6
```

When the command button is clicked, the code executes as follows: First the For loop is entered and the `intCounter` variable is initialized to –10. Since –10 is less than or equal to –5, the body of the For loop executes. This appends a –10 and a space to the `txtOutput` text box. Then the loop counter, `intCounter`, is incremented by 2 to –8.

Since –8 is less than or equal to –5, the body of the For loop executes again. This time a –8 and a space are appended to `txtOutput`. Once again, `intCounter` is incremented by 2 to –6.

Since –6 is less than or equal to –5, the body of the For loop executes again. This time a –6 and a space are appended to `txtOutput`. Once again, `intCounter` is incremented by 2 to –4.

Since –4 is not less than or equal to –5, the loop terminates.

Drill 7.8

The output is as follows:

```
2 7 12
```

When the command button is clicked, the code executes as follows: First the For loop is entered and the `intCounter` variable is initialized to 2. Since 2 is less than or equal to 2, the body of the For loop executes. This appends a 2 and a space to the `txtOutput` text box. Then the loop counter, `intCounter`, is incremented by 5 to 7.

Since 7 is less than or equal to 10, the body of the `For` loop executes again. This time a 7 and a space are appended to `txtOutput`. Once again, `intCounter` is incremented by 5 to 12.

Since 12 is not less than or equal to 10, the loop terminates. However, in this case your processing is not complete. The value 12 contained in the variable `intCounter` remains and is appended to `txtOutput` as the last statement of the command button's code.

Drill 7.9
The output is as follows:

```
4  8  12
```

When the command button is clicked, the code executes as follows: First the `For` loop is entered and the `intCounter` variable is initialized to 1. Since 1 is less than or equal to 10, the body of the `For` loop executes. However, this drill does something none of the others did. It modifies the value of the loop counter programmatically from within the loop. When you add 3 to `intCounter`, not only will this affect the value to be appended, but it will also affect the loop's execution. Therefore, a 4 and a space are appended to the `txtOutput` text box. Then the loop counter, `intCounter`, is incremented by 1 to 5. Remember, `intCounter` was changed to 4 in the previous statement.

Since 5 is less than or equal to 10, the body of the `For` loop executes again. Again, 3 is added to `intCounter` inside the loop. This time an 8 and a space are appended to `txtOutput`. Once again, `intCounter` is incremented by 1 to 9.

Since 9 is less than or equal to 10, the body of the `For` loop executes. Again, 3 is added to `intCounter` inside the loop. This time a 12 and a space are appended to `txtOutput`. Once again, `intCounter` is incremented by 1 to 13.

Since 13 is not less than or equal to 10, the loop terminates.

Drill 7.10
The output is as follows:

```
4  3  2  1  0
```

When the command button is clicked, the code executes as follows: First the `intCounter` variable is initialized to 5. Then the `Do` loop is entered and the `intCounter` is compared to see if it is greater than 0. Since 5 is greater than 0, the body of the `Do` loop executes. One is then subtracted from `intCounter` so that it now equals 4. Therefore, a 4 and a space are appended to the `txtOutput` text box.

The looping condition is then evaluated. Since 4 is greater than 0, the body of the `Do` loop executes again. Again, 1 is subtracted from `intCounter`, setting `intCounter` equal to 3. This time a 3 and a space are appended to `txtOutput`.

Again, the looping condition is evaluated. Since 3 is greater than 0, the body of the `Do` loop executes. Again, 1 is subtracted from `intCounter`, setting `intCounter` equal to 2. Therefore, a 2 and a space are appended to `txtOutput`.

Again, the looping condition is evaluated. Since 2 is greater than 0, the body of the `Do` loop executes. Again, 1 is subtracted from `intCounter`, setting `intCounter` equal to 1. Therefore, a 1 and a space are appended to `txtOutput`.

Again, the looping condition is then evaluated. Since 1 is greater than 0, the body of the `Do` loop executes again. Again, 1 is subtracted from `intCounter`, setting `intCounter` equal to 0. Even though 0 is not greater than 0, you continue with the execution of the body of the `Do` loop because the looping condition is not checked again until after the execution of the entire body of the loop. Therefore, a 0 and a space are appended to `txtOutput`.

Now, when 0 is compared to 0, it is no longer greater than 0, so the loop terminates.

Drill 7.11
The output is as follows:

```
2  4  6  8  10
```

When the command button is clicked, the code executes as follows: First the intCounter variable is initialized to 0. Then the Do loop is entered and the intCounter is compared to see if it equals 10. If it is, the loop terminates. Since 0 is not equal to 10, the body of the Do loop executes. 2 is then added to intCounter so that intCounter now equals 2. Therefore, a 2 and a space are appended to the txtOutput text box.

The looping condition is then evaluated. Since 2 is not equal to 10, the body of the Do loop executes again. Again, 2 is added to the intCounter, setting intCounter equal to 4. This time a 4 and a space are appended to txtOutput.

The looping condition is then evaluated. Since 4 is not equal to 10, the body of the Do loop executes again. Again, 2 is added to the intCounter, setting intCounter equal to 6. This time a 6 and a space are appended to txtOutput.

The looping condition is then evaluated. Since 6 is not equal to 10, the body of the Do loop executes again. Again, 2 is added to the intCounter, setting intCounter equal to 8. This time an 8 and a space are appended to txtOutput.

Again, the looping condition is then evaluated. Since 8 is not equal to 10, the body of the Do loop executes again. Again, 2 is added to intCounter, setting intCounter equal to –10. Even though the intCounter variable is now equal to 10, you continue with the execution of the body of the Do loop, because the looping condition is not checked again until after the execution of the entire body of the loop. Therefore, a 10 and a space are appended to txtOutput.

Now, when 10 is compared to 10, they are equal and the loop terminates.

Drill 7.12
The output is as follows:

This was a trick question! There is no output. Actually, the application will enter into an infinite loop. Since intCounter starts at 0 and has 3 subtracted from it continuously, the condition checking to see if it is greater than 0 will never evaluate to True. Since you used an Until statement instead of a While statement, the loop will execute until the expression evaluates to True, which is never.

Drill 7.13
The output is as follows:

```
3  6
```

When the command button is clicked, the code executes as follows: First the intCounter variable is initialized to 0. Then the Do loop is entered and 3 is added to intCounter, setting it equal to 3. Then a 3 and a space are appended to the txtOutput text box. Now the loop condition is checked and 3 is compared to 5.

Since 3 is not greater than 5, the body of the Do loop executes again. 3 is added to the intCounter, setting intCounter equal to 6. This time a 6 and a space are appended to txtOutput.

Again, the looping condition is then evaluated. However, since 6 is greater than 5, the loop terminates.

Drill 7.14

The output is as follows:

```
3  6  9  12
```

When the command button is clicked, the code executes as follows: First the `intCounter` variable is initialized to 0. Then the `Do` loop is entered and 3 is added to `intCounter`, setting it equal to 3. Then a 3 and a space are appended to the `txtOutput` text box. Now the loop condition is checked and 3 is compared to 10.

Since 3 is less than 10, the body of the `Do` loop executes again. 3 is added to the `intCounter`, setting `intCounter` equal to 6. This time a 6 and a space are appended to `txtOutput`.

Since 6 is less than 10, the body of the `Do` loop executes again. 3 is added to the `intCounter`, setting `intCounter` equal to 9. This time a 6 and a space are appended to `txtOutput`.

Since 9 is less than 10, the body of the `Do` loop executes again. 3 is added to the `intCounter`, setting `intCounter` equal to 12. This time a 9 and a space are appended to `txtOutput`.

Again, the looping condition is evaluated. However, since 12 is greater than 10, the loop terminates.

Drill 7.15

The output is as follows:

```
3
```

When the command button is clicked, the code executes as follows: First the `intCounter` variable is initialized to 0. Then the `Do` loop is entered and 3 is added to `intCounter`, setting it equal to 3. Then a 3 and a space are appended to the `txtOutput` text box. Now the loop condition is checked and 3 is compared to 10.

Since 3 is not greater than 10, the body of the loop terminates. Notice that although the condition never evaluated to `True`, the body of the loop executed once.

Drill 7.16

The output is as follows:

```
1  2  3  1  2  3  1  2  3
```

When the command button is clicked, the code executes as follows: First, the outer loop is entered with the `intOuterCounter` variable initialized to 1. Then the inner loop is entered with the `intInnerCounter` variable initialized to 1. You then process the inner loop in its entirety.

Since the inner loop starts at 1 and ends at 3, the value 1 2 3 is assigned to `txtOutput`. Then the `intOuterCounter` variable is incremented by 2 to 3. Since 3 is less than or equal to 5, you re-execute the inner loop.

Since no reference to `intOuterCounter` is made in the inner loop, it executes identically as before. Thus 1 2 3 is appended to `txtOutput`. Therefore, `txtOutput` now contains the `String` 1 2 3 1 2 3. Then the `intOuterCounter` variable is incremented by 2 again to 5. Since 5 is still less than or equal to 5, you re-execute the inner loop again.

As before, the execution of the inner loop appends 1 2 3 to `txtOutput`, so it contains 1 2 3 1 2 3 1 2 3 after the inner loop completes executing for the third time. When the `intOuterCounter` variable is incremented again, it sets `intOuterCounter` to 7, thus the outer loop terminates.

Drill 7.17
The output is as follows:

```
12
```

When the command button is clicked, the code executes as follows: First the `intTotal` variable is initialized to 0. Then the outer loop is entered with the `intOuterCounter` variable is initialized to 1. Next, the inner loop is entered with the `intInnerCounter` variable initialized to 1. You then process the inner loop in its entirety.

Since the inner loop starts at 1, it is added to `intTotal`. Therefore, `intTotal` equals 1. Then `intInnerCounter` is incremented by 2, so that after the first iteration of the loop, it equals 3. Since 3 is less than or equal to 3, the inner loop executes again.

This time when `intInnerCounter` is added to `intTotal`, it adds 3, so `intTotal` equals 4. When `intInnerCounter` is incremented by 2, the value of `intInnerCounter` after the second iteration of the inner loop is 5. Since 5 is not less than or equal to 3, you terminate executing the inner loop. The `intOuterCounter` variable is then incremented by 2 to 3. Since 3 is less than or equal to 5, the inner loop is executed again.

Since no reference to `intOuterCounter` is made in the inner loop, it executes identically as before. Thus 4 is added to `intTotal`. The `intOuterCounter` variable is again incremented by 2 to 5. Since 5 is less than or equal to 5, the inner loop is executed again.

Once again, 4 is added to `intTotal` during the execution of the inner loop. Finally, when `intOuterCounter` is incremented by 2 again, this time to 7, the outer loop terminates with the value of `intTotal` being 12.

Drill 7.18
The output is as follows:

```
3  0  2  4  6  0  2  4
```

When the command button is clicked, the code executes as follows: First the `intOuterCounter` variable is initialized to 0. Then the outer loop is entered with `intInnerCounter` initialized to 0 and 3 added to `intOuterCounter`. TxtOutput is then assigned the value in `OuterCounter`, 3 .

The inner loop is then entered, with the value of `intInnerCounter` appended to `TxtOutput`. Then 2 is added to `intInnerCounter`. Since `intInnerCounter` is equal to 2 and 2 is less than 5, the inner loop executes again.

This time, the value of `intInnerCounter`, 2, is appended to `TxtOutput`, so that it now equals 3 0 2. Once again 2 is added to `intInnerCounter`, and since the value of `InnerCounter`, 4, is less than 5, the inner loop executes again. Once again, 2 is added to `InnerCounter`, but now that `intInnerCounter` equals 6, it is no longer less than 5, so the inner loop terminates.

The outer loop condition is then checked. Since `intOuterCounter` still equals 3, and 3 is less than 5, the entire outer loop executes again. First, `intInnerCounter` is reset to 0. Then `intOuterCounter` has 3 added to it, equaling 6. The `intOuterCounter` is then appended to `txtOutput`, so `txtOutput` now equals 3 0 2 4 6.

The inner loop executes exactly as it did before, and therefore 0 2 4 is appended to `txtOutput`, so that `txtOutput` now equals 3 0 2 4 6 0 2 4. Finally, the value of intOuterCounter, 6, is compared to 5 and since it is not less than or equal to it, the outer loop terminates.

Drill 7.19
The output is as follows:

```
3  0  2  4  1  6  -1  8
```

When the command button is clicked, the code executes as follows: First the intOuterCounter variable is initialized to 5 and the intInnerCounter variable is initialized to 0. Then the outer loop is entered with intOuterCounter decremented by 2, so that it now equals 3. This is appended to txtOutput, so that txtOutput now equals 3.

The inner Do loop is entered and the value of intInnerCounter is appended to txtOutput, so that txtOutput now equals 3 0. Then 2 is added to intInnerCounter, so that intInnerCounter now equals 2. Since 2 is less than 5, the inner loop continues to execute.

The value of intInnerCounter is appended to txtOutput so that txtOutput now equals 3 0 2. Then 2 is added to InnerCounter so that intInnerCounter now equals 4. Since 4 is less than 5, the inner loop continues to execute.

The value of intInnerCounter is appended to txtOutput so that txtOutput now equals 3 0 2 4. Then 2 is added to intInnerCounter so that intInnerCounter now equals 6. Since 6 is not less than 5, the inner loop terminates.

The outer Do loop's condition is then checked. Since intOuterCounter equals 3, it is greater than 0 and the outer loop executes again. First, 2 is subtracted from intOuterCounter and its new value, 1, is appended to txtOutput. Thus, txtOuput now equals 3 0 2 4 1.

The inner Do loop is entered for a second time and the value of intInnerCounter, 6, is appended to txtOutput, so that txtOutput now equals 3 0 2 4 1 6. 2 is then added to intInnerCounter, so that intInnerCounter now equals 8. Since 8 is not less than 5, the inner loop terminates.

The outer Do loop's condition is then checked. Since intOuterCounter equals 1, it is greater than 0 and the outer loop executes again. First, 2 is subtracted from intOuterCounter and its new value, –1, is appended to txtOutput. Therefore, txtOutput now equals 3 0 2 4 1 6 –1.

The inner Do loop is entered for a third time and the value of intInnerCounter, 8, is appended to txtOutput, so that txtOutput now equals 3 0 2 4 1 6 8. Then 2 is added to intInnerCounter so that intInnerCounter now equals 10. Since 10 is not less than 5, the inner loop terminates.

The outer Do loop's condition is then checked. Since intOuterCounter equals –1, it is not greater than 0 and so the outer loop terminates.

Key Words and Key Terms

Breakpoint
An option in the Debugger to stop the execution of the code at a particular point.

Do Until loop
A structure that is repeated as long as a given condition has not evaluated to True.

Do While loop
A structure that is repeated as long as a given condition evaluates to True.

For loop
A structure that is repeated a fixed number of times.

Nested loop

A loop structure that has another loop structure defined within it.

Step

The amount by which the `For` loop index is incremented on each iteration of the loop.

Additional Exercises

Questions 1–5 are True/False.

1. A `Step` amount in a `For` loop must be an `Integer` value.

2. Loops may only be nested one level deep. In other words, you can nest one loop inside another, but not a loop inside a loop inside another loop.

3. Breakpoints can only be used in conjunction with loops.

4. `For` loops can `Step` in positive or negative increments.

5. An MS flex grid's indices start at 1.

6. What is the value in the text box `txtOutput` after the following code has been executed?

```
Private Sub Command1_Click()
Dim intCounter As Integer

For intCounter = 10 To 1 Step - 3
  txtOutput.Text = txtOutput.Text & Str(intCounter) & " "
Next intCounter

End Sub
```

7. What is the value in the text box `txtOutput` after the following code has been executed?

```
Private Sub Command1_Click()
Dim intCounter As Integer

For intCounter = -1 To 1 Step  2
  txtOutput.Text = txtOutput.Text & Str(intCounter) & " "
Next intCounter

End Sub
```

8. What is the value in the text box `txtOutput` after the following code has been executed?

```
Private Sub Command1_Click()
Dim intCounter As Integer

intCounter = 10
Do
   intCounter = intCounter - 2
   txtOutput.Text = txtOutput.Text & Str(intCounter) & " "
Loop Until (Counter <= 5)

End Sub
```

9. What is the value in the text box `txtOutput` after the following code has been executed?

```
Private Sub Command1_Click()
Dim intCounter As Integer

intCounter = 0
Do
   intCounter = intCounter + 2
   txtOutput.Text = txtOutput.Text & Str(intCounter) & " "
Loop While (intCounter > 5)

End Sub
```

10. What is the value in the text box `txtOutput` after the following code has been executed?

```
Private Sub Command1_Click()
Dim intCounter As Integer

intCounter = -10
Do
   intCounter = intCounter + 2
   txtOutput.Text = txtOutput.Text & Str(intCounter) & " "
Loop While (intCounter > 10)

End Sub
```

11. What is the value in the text box `txtOutput` after the following code has been executed?

```
Private Sub Command1_Click()
Dim sngCounter As Single
Dim sngTotal as Single

sngTotal = 0

For sngCounter = 0.5 To 3.5 Step 0.5
   sngTotal = sngTotal + sngCounter
Next sngCounter

txtOutput.Text = str(sngTotal)
End Sub
```

12. Write an application that counts the number of days in this year's month of February. Do not use a math trick to figure it out. Hint: Set a variable to the first day of the month and then increment it through all the days in the month.

13. A company pays its employees every Friday. Write an application that computes the number of paydays in the current month. Hint: the `Weekday` function will return `vbFriday` when the date passed to it is a Friday.

14. Chris just bought a Corvette. His payment is $790.50 a month. How many hours (round up to the nearest full hour) does it take for him to work to pay for his car each month? Because he didn't pay attention in class, his part-time job is flipping

burgers and pays \$5.50/hour. Unfortunately, he doesn't remember the divide statement, so you must solve this problem using a loop instead of a simple calculation.

15. Create an application that contains two text boxes called `txtHeight` and `txtWidth`. Additionally, create a text box called `txtOutput` that will display a rectangle in Courier font when a positive height and length are entered in their respective text boxes. The rectangle should be "drawn" with asterisks and be completely filled in. Trigger the application drawing the rectangle on a command button's `Click` event.

16. Create the same application as in Exercise 15, but draw a hollow rectangle.

17. Write an application to compute the approximate odds of rolling an exact value when two dice are rolled. Each die has a value from 1 to 6. By rolling two dice, you can generate a value from 2 to 12. The application should roll the set dice 1,000 times and determine what percentage of time the desired combination is rolled. You should validate that the value you are checking for is a valid roll. (Hint: to simulate the roll of the dice use the `rnd` function.)

18. Create a list box with 10 items in its list. Set the `MultiSelect` property to 1. Then create a command button that will unselect any items that are selected using a `For` loop.

19. Create a list box with a bunch of items in its list. Set the `MultiSelect` property to 1. Then create a command button that will select every other item in the list. Your code should work for a list box with any number of list items.

20. A person has a bank account containing \$5,000. Each year the person withdraws \$500, but gets 5% interest on the remaining amount. Write a function that returns the amount of money remaining in 10 years.

21. A person has the option to receive \$10,000 a day for a period of time, or \$1 the first day and the amount doubles each day. Write a function that computes the number of days required for the latter option to produce greater total of money for the person receiving it.

22. Change the Case Study in section 7.6 so that the user can enter the name of an employee and a message box displays that person's total pay. If the person is not found, display an appropriate message.

23. Change the Case Study in section 7.6 so that the user can enter the name of an employee and the row(s) corresponding to that employee in the grid is removed. All remaining employees after the one deleted should be moved up in the grid. Make sure that you reduce the total number of rows in the grid by the number of rows deleted. Also, if the employee is not found, display a message box indicating the employee was not found.

INTERVIEW

An Interview with Chris Dias

Chris Dias is the Group Program Manager for Visual Basic at Microsoft Corporation. Chris leads the team that manages and designs the Visual Basic product. He has worked on Visual Basic since version 3, on many areas of the product including developer support, performance, deployment, wizards, scripting, data access, data tools, as well as RAD programmability for the Server in Visual Basic .NET.

What was your first job in the computer industry like? What convinced you to stick with computers?

My first job was as a consultant in Boston. I went from company to company for a few months on small projects, working on mainframes and minis, trying to figure out what interested me and what I wanted to do. I finally ended up working at a Mutual Fund company in Boston using PCs and Visual Basic to build client server applications. Once I started working with VB, I was hooked.

What about VB hooked you?

One day, the VB 1.0 box was handed to me and I was asked to see what we could do with it. Within half an hour I had my first application—a clock straight from the help docs—and I was hooked. From there we quickly began writing client/server applications going against SQL Server.

What is it like working at Microsoft?

Microsoft is a challenging environment where you have a direct impact on millions of people. There is no other company like that—where you can come into work every day and feel as if you are making a huge difference. The people are all very smart, focused, and driven. Everyone wants one thing—to build the best product for our customers.

Please give some background on your current position.

I am the Group Program Manager for Visual Basic. The members of my team (the program managers) write the specifications, resolve issues, drive features, and are the customer advocates for the product. I've been working at Microsoft and on Visual Basic for 7+ years now.

What kinds of projects are you currently working on? What will you be doing in the future?

I am currently working on Visual Basic .NET. It is going to be the most powerful and feature-rich version of Visual Basic. It lets you easily write rich Windows and web applications, NT services, XML web services, and even simple console applications. In the future, we're going to continue to innovate, making VB the easiest, most productive development tool in the world.

What advice do you have for students entering the computer field using VB?

Have an open mind about what you don't know. The exciting challenge is figuring out the new features, tweaking an application to get in one more cool feature, and becoming an expert in the tool and platform. Challenge others' thinking about what is right and wrong. think "out of the box" meaning don't just do the same design/ui/application over and over—how can you take it to the next level? What would your customers really find useful? And finally, remember that no matter how cool the feature is, if its too hard for your users they'll never use it. Customers are #1.

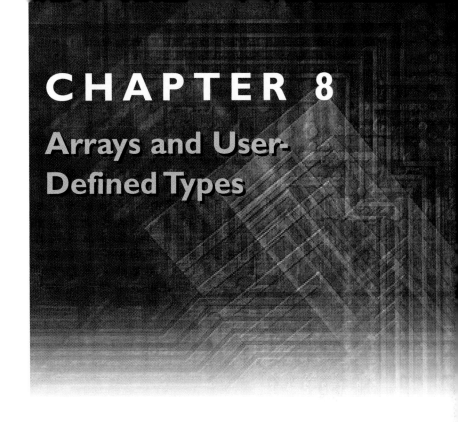

CHAPTER 8

Arrays and User-Defined Types

What would you do if you lacked the capability to use controls like the MS flex grid to store multiple values simultaneously? Controls like the MS flex grid expand on the concept of a programming construct called an **array**. An array allows you to store multiple values of a datatype in a single variable. An MS flex grid allows you to do this and provides an interface for the user to see the results graphically. Sometimes you wish to store values without showing them to the user as with an MS flex grid.

8.1 Arrays

Imagine if you wanted to develop a program that rated a TV show from 1–10, 10 being the best and 1 being the worst. The application should not only compute the average rating, but should track how many of each rating was selected.

You could write the application so that the total number of each rating was stored in a separate variable. You could create variables like `Rating1`, `Rating2`, `Rating3`, `Rating4`, `Rating5`, `Rating6`, `Rating7`, `Rating8`, `Rating9`, and `Rating10` and then increment each one every time a vote is cast corresponding to the appropriate variable. Observe the following code, which implements a rating system employing this strategy.

First, you must declare the 10 variables to store the total of each rating, as well as a variable to store the total number of votes, in the General Declarations section of the application.

```
'General Declarations
Dim intRating1 As Integer
Dim intRating2 As Integer
Dim intRating3 As Integer
Dim intRating4 As Integer
Dim intRating5 As Integer
Dim intRating6 As Integer
Dim intRating7 As Integer
Dim intRating8 As Integer
Dim intRating9 As Integer
Dim intRating10 As Integer
Dim intTotalVotes As Integer
```

Next, you need to process each vote as the voting button is clicked. You must track the total number of votes and output the result when all the votes have been cast. You can process each individual vote by using a `Select Case` statement and setting up a case up for each possible vote.

```
Private Sub cmdVoting_Click()
Select Case cboRating.Text
  Case "1"
    intRating1 = intRating1 + 1
  Case "2"
    intRating2 = intRating2 + 1
  Case "3"
    intRating3 = intRating3 + 1
  Case "4"
    intRating4 = intRating4 + 1
  Case "5"
    intRating5 = intRating5 + 1
  Case "6"
    intRating6 = intRating6 + 1
  Case "7"
    intRating7 = intRating7 + 1
  Case "8"
    intRating8 = intRating8 + 1
  Case "9"
    intRating9 = intRating9 + 1
  Case "10"
    intRating10 = intRating10 + 1
End Select

intTotalVotes = intTotalVotes + 1

If (intTotalVotes = 10) Then
  Call OutputResults
End If
End Sub
```

To simplify the processing of the results, you can move code that displays the results into another subroutine.

```
Private Sub OutputResults()
Dim strOutputString As String
    strOutputString = "1] " + Str(intRating1) + _
    ", 2] " + Str(intRating2) + ", 3]" + Str(intRating3) + _
    ", 4] " + Str(intRating4) + ", 5]" + Str(intRating5) + _
    ", 6] " + Str(intRating6) + ", 7]" + Str(intRating7) + _
    ", 8] " + Str(intRating8) + ", 9]" + Str(intRating9) + _
    ", 10] " + Str(intRating10)
  MsgBox strOutputString
End Sub
```

You might not think that was a lot of wasted code; however, if you increased the choice of ratings from 1–10 to 1–100, your application's code would grow considerably. You obviously need a better approach.

An array is the perfect solution. Arrays allow a programmer to create a single variable that can store multiple values. These values can be referenced by an index similar to the index in an MS flex grid. One major difference is that you can specify the starting and ending indices of the array.

By creating a simple form with a single combo box that contains only the value 1,2,3,4,5,6,7,8,9, and 10, and a command button to process the votes, we can improve our application. By storing each rating's votes in an array of Integers you will see that, aside from having fewer variables to deal with, you will also simplify the execution of the code.

An array is declared using the following syntax:

Dim *ArrayName*(*LowerBound* To *UpperBound*) As *VariableType*

When defining an array, its name obeys the same rules as declaring a variable.

The LowerBound of the array is the lowest index in the array, while the UpperBound is the highest index in the array. The VariableType is any valid variable.

For example, if you wished to create an array of 10 Integers to store your ratings from 1–10, you would use the following code:

```
Dim intRatings( 1 To 10) As Integer
```

 TIP

If a lower bound is not specified, then the default lower bound of the array is 0:

```
Dim intNoLowerBoundSpecified(10) As Integer
```

The previous code specifies an array, intNoLowerBoundSpecified, with indices from 0 to 9.

This would allocate an array that looks as follows:

Array intRatings										
Index	1	2	3	4	5	6	7	8	9	10
Values	0	0	0	0	0	0	0	0	0	0

To access an individual value in an array, you place the subscript of the value you wish to access inside the parentheses. Thus, if you wanted to output the value stored in the array at index 3, you could do so in a message box using the following code:

```
MessageBox Str(Ratings(3))
```

You now understand enough about arrays to rewrite our rating application. First, you see that the General Declarations section only requires that you declare the array and a single variable to store the total number of votes:

```
'General Declarations
Dim intRatings(1 To 10) As Integer
Dim intTotalVotes As Integer
```

Your processing of the vote event is so simple that you can combine the code for storing the vote and outputting the results. Since each vote corresponds to the index in the array where the total of that vote is counted, you can directly add 1 to the rating voted for by using the current vote as an index for the array. Thus, you can avoid using a `Select Case` statement. In addition, instead of having to list each variable separately when you output the results, you can use a `For` loop to step through the array and display each individual value. The code follows:

```
Private Sub cmdRating_Click()
Dim strOutputString As String
Dim intVote As Integer

intRatings(Val(cboRating.Text)) = intRatings(Val(cboRating.Text)) + 1
intTotalVotes = intTotalVotes + 1

If (intTotalVotes = 10) Then
  For intVote = 1 To 10
    strOutputString = strOutputString + Str(intVote) + "] " + _
      Str(intRatings(intVote))
  Next intVote
  MsgBox strOutputString
End If
End Sub
```

WARNING

Values that you wish to store in an array do not always map themselves directly to the indices in an array as in the previous ratings example; however, arrays can still be used.

Arrays of Other Datatypes

Arrays can be used to store values of other types of data besides `Integers`. Arrays can be created from any simple datatypes. The following code shows how you can create an array of five `Strings` and initialize them to `"Allen Iverson"`, `"Theo Ratliff"`, `"Eric Snow"`, `"George Lynch"` and `"Tyrone Hill"`.

```
Dim strSixersNames(1 To 5) As String

strSixersNames(1) = "Allen Iverson"
strSixersNames(2) = "Theo Ratliff"
strSixersNames(3) = "Eric Snow"
strSixersNames(4) = "George Lynch"
strSixersNames(5) = "Tyrone Hill"
```

If you wanted to store the salary of each player in terms of millions of dollars, you could store them in an array of `Single` variables. Therefore, if the salary is $7 million for Allen Iverson, $5.5 million for Theo Ratliff, $4 million for Eric Snow, $2.7 million for George Lynch, and $3.3 million for Tyrone Hill, you could store them in the following code:

```
Dim sngSixersSalaries(1 To 5) As Single

sngSixersSalaries(1) = 7
sngSixersSalaries(2) = 5.5
sngSixersSalaries(3) = 4
sngSixersSalaries(4) = 2.7
sngSixersSalaries(5) = 3.3
```

DRILL 8.1

If an array has five elements and a lower bound of –2, what is the upper bound of the index?

DRILL 8.2

Write the code required to declare an array of five `Strings` called `strDrillArray` with an index whose lower bound is 0 and upper bound is 4. Then initialize the array to the following values: `"First Value"`, `"Second Value"`, `"Third Value"`, `"Fourth Value"`, and `"Fifth Value"`.

DRILL 8.3

Write the code required to declare an array of 1,000 `Integers` called `intDrillArray` with an index whose lower bound is 1 and upper bound is 1,000. Then initialize the array so that each element contains the value of its index. (Hint: Use a loop.)

TIP

The variable type of all of the elements of an array must be the same variable type!

8.2 Control Arrays

While having arrays of variables like `Integers` and `Strings` is helpful, the visual nature of Visual Basic requires you to have another form of array, a **control array**. Control arrays allow you to define multiple controls on a form that can be referenced by a single name and an index to indicate which of the controls to access individually.

Control arrays basically operate the same way as the arrays you have already used.

Imagine if you wanted to create an application that allowed users to enter their nine favorite TV shows using combo boxes. You could create a combo box with all the TV shows to be selected from and then create eight more just like it. This would not only be a waste of time in creating them, but it would also make handling the data in all of them difficult as well.

Observe the following application:

Figure 8.1
TV Ranking Application

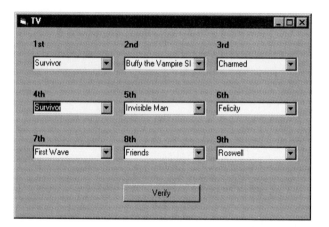

The application contains nine combo boxes where the user can select the show from a predetermined list and indicate their top nine shows. However, nothing prevents you from selecting the same show more than once. Notice that I selected "Survivor" twice. By using control arrays and adding a command button, you can attach code that will ensure users do not select the same show twice.

The simplest way to create a control array is simply to copy the control from which you wish to make an array (select the control and press <CTRL> and <C> simultaneously) and paste it back onto the form (press the <CTRL> and <V> keys simultaneously). You may have done this by accident in the past and received the following warning message:

Figure 8.2
Create a Control Array
Warning Message

If you click on the Yes button, an array will be created with the original control at index 0 and the new control at index 1. All of the properties of the original control will be copied to the new control. Additional controls can be added to the array by pasting additional copies of the control. If you click on the No button, an additional control will be added, but with a different name. Even though the control will have a different button, it will still have all the same properties as the original.

To create your application, you start by creating a single combo box, cboTVShow, and then copying it eight times. In addition, you need to add the command button, cmdVerify, that will check for a duplicate TV show selection.

If you didn't use a control array, but instead used combo boxes with different names such as cmdChoice1, cmdChoice2, cmdChoice3, and so on, you might write code as follows:

```
'Check for duplicate of first ComboBox
If (cboChoice1 = cboChoice2) Or (cboChoice1 = cboChoice3) Or _
   (cboChoice1 = cboChoice4) Or (cboChoice1 = cboChoice5) Or _
   (cboChoice1 = cboChoice6) Or (cboChoice1 = cboChoice7) Or _
   (cboChoice1 = cboChoice8) Or (cboChoice1 = cboChoice9) Then
   MsgBox "Duplicate TV Show Found"

'Check for duplicate of second ComboBox
ElseIf (cboChoice2 = cboChoice3) Or _
   (cboChoice2 = cboChoice4) Or (cboChoice2 = cboChoice5) Or _
   (cboChoice2 = cboChoice6) Or (cboChoice2 = cboChoice7) Or _
   (cboChoice2 = cboChoice8) Or (cboChoice2 = cboChoice9) Then
   MsgBox "Duplicate TV Show Found"
      .
      .
      .
```

Wow, that was a lot of code and I only wrote out two cases! The problem is that in order to check for duplicates, you must check each of the combo boxes for the values contained in each combo box. By taking advantage of using an array of combo boxes, you can use the following code to accomplish the same thing.

```
Private Sub cmdVerify_Click()
Dim intCurrentShow As Integer
Dim intShowToCheck As Integer
Dim boolDuplicateFound As Boolean

boolDuplicateFound = False

For intCurrentShow = 0 To 8
  For intShowToCheck = intCurrentShow + 1 To 8
    If (cboTVShow(intCurrentShow) = cboTVShow(intShowToCheck)) Then
      boolDuplicateFound = True
    End If
  Next intShowToCheck
Next intCurrentShow
```

(continues)

(continued)

```
If (boolDuplicateFound = True) Then
        MsgBox "Duplicate Found"
        Else
          MsgBox "Votes are Valid"
        End If
        End Sub
```

The beauty of the previous code is that if you increase the number of combo boxes, the code barely changes. The only required change is the upper bound on the For loops.

WARNING

Notice that the previous code used an index of 0 as the first index of the control array. Control arrays use 0 as the first index by default.

DRILL 8.4

Assume a control array is created from the text box txtDrillText by copying it and pasting it five times onto a form so that there now is a total of six text boxes on the form. Assume that there also exists a text box txtSearch. What is wrong with the following code that will call a message box when the text stored in txtSearch is found in one of the control arrays?

```
Dim intIndex As Integer
For intIndex = 1 To 6
   If (txtDrillText(intIndex).Text = txtSearch.Text) Then
      MsgBox "Found"
   End If
Next intIndex
```

DRILL 8.5

Assume a control array is created from the text box txtDrillText by copying it and pasting it five times onto a form so that there now exists a total of six text boxes on the form. Assume that there also exists a command button cmdAverage. Write the code required to output the average value stored in the text boxes. The values can be assumed to be Integers.

DRILL 8.6

Assume a control array is created from the text box txtDrillText by copying it and pasting it five times onto a form so that there now is a total of six text boxes on the form. Assume that there also exists a command button cmdMax. Write the code required to output the maximum value stored in the text boxes. The values can be assumed to be Integers.

8.3   Two-Dimensional Arrays

Sometimes a problem does not map itself to an array of only one dimension. As **single-dimensional arrays** simplified your handling of multiple variables, you can also simplify handling multiple arrays by using a **two-dimensional array**.

Let's revisit your rating system application. However, instead of storing the votes for one television show, let's now store the results for 10 television shows as in the following figure:

Figure 8.3
TV Ratings Application

Now you have the same dilemma that you had before you introduced arrays. With 10 TV shows you wish to track ratings for, you would need 10 sets of 10 ratings. Will you just repeat the code of your previous application for each array? No way! Visual Basic provides two-dimensional arrays, which will efficiently solve this problem.

An array is declared using the following syntax:

```
Dim ArrayName(LowerBound1 To UpperBound1, LowerBound2 To _
        UpperBound2) As VariableType
```

TIP

The lower bound of one dimension does not have to be the same as the lower bound for the other dimension. Likewise, the upper bounds of each dimension can be different.

Now, writing the application to track 10 TV shows is not significantly more complicated than tracking one TV show. First, you must create the interface to a rating for each of 10 TV shows. You can create the interface in Figure 8.3 by using a control array of combo boxes, a series of labels, and a single command button.

The only change in the General Declarations section of the application is the changing of the `Ratings` array from a single-dimensional array to a two-dimensional array. The code follows:

```
Dim intRatings(1 To 10, 1 To 10) As Integer
Dim intTotalVotes As Integer
```

General Declarations Section

The two-dimensional array of Integers can be thought of as a grid with the ratings for each TV show contained within a single row of the grid. Each column of the grid can be thought of as containing the number of votes for each rating. Therefore, the first column would contain the number of votes for a rating of 1 for all shows. This is shown in the following table:

	Rating 1	Rating 2	Rating 3	Rating 4	Rating 5	Rating 6	Rating 7	Rating 8	Rating 9	Rating 10
Show 1	(1,1)	(1,2)	(1,3)	(1,4)	(1,5)	(1,6)	(1,7)	(1,8)	(1,9)	(1,10)
Show 2	(2,1)	(2,2)	(2,3)	(2,4)	(2,5)	(2,6)	(2,7)	(2,8)	(2,9)	(2,10)
Show 3	(3,1)	(3,2)	(3,3)	(3,4)	(3,5)	(3,6)	(3,7)	(3,8)	(3,9)	(3,10)
Show 4	(4,1)	(4,2)	(4,3)	(4,4)	(4,5)	(4,6)	(4,7)	(4,8)	(4,9)	(4,10)
Show 5	(5,1)	(5,2)	(5,3)	(5,4)	(5,5)	(5,6)	(5,7)	(5,8)	(5,9)	(5,10)
Show 6	(6,1)	(6,2)	(6,3)	(6,4)	(6,5)	(6,6)	(6,7)	(6,8)	(6,9)	(6,10)
Show 7	(7,1)	(7,2)	(7,3)	(7,4)	(7,5)	(7,6)	(7,7)	(7,8)	(7,9)	(7,10)
Show 8	(8,1)	(8,2)	(8,3)	(8,4)	(8,5)	(8,6)	(8,7)	(8,8)	(8,9)	(8,10)
Show 9	(9,1)	(9,2)	(9,3)	(9,4)	(9,5)	(9,6)	(9,7)	(9,8)	(9,9)	(9,10)
Show 10	(10,1)	(10,2)	(10,3)	(10,4)	(10,5)	(10,6)	(10,7)	(10,8)	(10,9)	(10,10)

While the changes to the General Declarations section were trivial, you must rethink the code to process all 10 TV shows. First, you require a For loop to record the vote for each TV show. Then, as before, you record that a vote occurred.

If you have finished your voting, you now require a nested loop to step through all the ratings for each TV show. The code follows:

```
Private Sub cmdRating_Click()
Dim strOutputString As String
Dim intTVShow As Integer

'Process vote for each TV Show
For intTVShow = 1 To 10
   intRatings(intTVShow, cboRating(intTVShow)) = _
         intRatings(intTVShow, cboRating(intTVShow)) + 1
Next intTVShow

'Record Vote
intTotalVotes = intTotalVotes + 1

'Output Results
If (intTotalVotes = 10) Then
   For intTVShow = 1 To 10
     strOutputString = "TV Show #" + Str(intTVShow) + " "
     For intVote = 1 To 10
       strOutputString = strOutputString + Str(intVote) + "] " + _
                  Str(intRatings(intTVShow, intVote))
     Next intVote
     MsgBox strOutputString

   Next intTVShow
End If
End Sub
```

DRILL 8.7

What's wrong with the following code that declares a two-dimensional array to store the number and name of each of the players for the Sixers?

```
Dim intPlayers(1 To 5, 1 To 2) As Integer
intPlayers(1,1) = 3
intPlayers(1,2) = "Allen Iverson"
intPlayers(2,1) = 20
intPlayers(2,2) = "Eric Snow"
intPlayers(3,1) = 42
intPlayers(3,2) = "Theo Ratliff"
intPlayers(4,1) = 8
intPlayers(4,2) = "Arron McKie"
intPlayers(5,1) = 40
intPlayers(5,2) = "Tyrone Hill"
```

DRILL 8.8

What's wrong with the following code that declares a two-dimensional array of integers and initializes each value to 2?

```
Dim intDrillValues(0 To 5, 0 To 5) As Integer
Dim intRow As Integer
Dim intCol As Integer


For intRow = 5 To 1 Step -1
    For intCol = 5 To 1 Step -1
        intDrillValue[intRow][intCol] = 2
    Next intCol
Next intRow
```

DRILL 8.9

Will the following two sets of code accomplish the same result? If not, explain why not.

```
Dim intDrillValues(1 To 3, 1 To 3) As Integer
Dim intRow As Integer
Dim intCol As Integer


For intRow = 1 To 3 Step
    For intCol = 1 To 3 Step
        intDrillValue[intRow][intCol] = 2
    Next intCol
Next Row
```

and

```
Dim intDrillValues(1 To 3, 1 To 3) As Integer
Dim intRow As Integer
```

(continues)

DRILL 8.9 (continued)

```
Dim intCol As Integer

For intCol = 1 To 3 Step
   For intRow = 1 To 3 Step
        intDrillValue[intCol][ intRow] = 2
   Next intCol
Next intRow
```

DRILL 8.10

Will the following two sets of code accomplish the same result? If not, explain why not.

```
Dim intDrillValues(1 To 5, 1 To 3) As Integer
Dim intRow As Integer
Dim intCol As Integer

For intRow = 1 To 5 Step
   For intCol = 1 To 3 Step
        intDrillValue[intRow][intCol] = 2
   Next intCol
Next intRow
```

and

```
Dim intDrillValues(1 To 5, 1 To 3) As Integer
Dim intRow As Integer
Dim intCol As Integer

For intCol = 1 To 5 Step
   For intRow = 1 To 3 Step
        intDrillValue[intRow][intCol] = 2
   Next intCol
Next intRow
```

8.4   User-Defined Types

Arrays are an excellent way to group data of the same type together. However, sometimes you need to group together data of different types. Imagine if you wished to track a group of students' names, majors, number of credits taken, and GPAs. You could create four arrays to store the information, but this would prove burdensome, as the number of different items increases.

Visual Basic's **user-defined types** are a way of grouping different values together as a single entity. When data is grouped together, it is commonly referred to as a **record**. The syntax to create a user-defined type is as follows:

```
Type UserDefinedType
    Field1 As FieldType1
    Field2 As FieldType2
    Field3 As FieldType3
        .
        .
        .
    FieldN As FieldTypeN
End Type
```

To create a user-defined type for a student, use the following code:

```
Type Student
    strFirstName As String
    strLastName As String
    strMajor As String
    sngGPA As Single
    sngCredits As Single
End Type
```

Once you have created a user-defined type, you can use it to create variables just as you would any other variable type. See the following template:

```
Dim VariableName As UserDefinedType
```

To access individual fields within the user-defined type, you type the `VariableName`, a dot operator, and the `FieldName` as in the following template:

```
VariableName.FieldName
```

Observe the following code that declares a variable named `BestStudent` and initializes it to `"Jeff"`, `"Salvage"`, `"Computer Science"`, `4.0`, and `120`.

```
Dim BestStudent As Student
BestStudent.strFirstName = "Jeff"
BestStudent.strLastName = "Salvage"
BestStudent.strMajor = "Computer Science"
BestStudent.sngGPA = 4.0
BestStudent.sngCredits = 120
```

DRILL 8.11

Create a user-defined type called `Employee` with the following attributes: `strName`, `intSalary`, `strTitle`, and `strCompany` with the types `String`, `Integer`, `String`, and `String`.

You will see a more meaningful use of user-defined types in Chapter 9 when using random access files.

Putting Arrays and Control Arrays to Work For You

The following application makes excellent use of both arrays and control arrays. While the application could be written without either, the code would be immense. Remember the game you played as a child that contained fifteen small plastic squares and one blank square. Each square had a number on it. Usually, by the time you got the game, the numbers were randomly distributed, and the goal was to place them back in numerical order by moving one square at a time. You are now going to implement that game in a minimum amount of code by using arrays and control arrays. The game looks as follows:

Figure 8.4
Solved Puzzle

Figure 8.5
Unsolved Puzzle

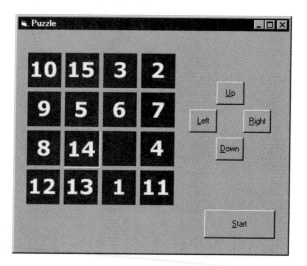

Your version of the application will allow the user to select a piece to move by clicking on the piece. The piece will be highlighted as the "14" game piece is in Figure 8.5. Then to move the piece, the user will click on one of the four directional buttons. If the move is valid, the piece will be moved. If the move is invalid, either because the space is occupied or off the board, a message box will appear with the message Invalid Move.

Implementation of the Puzzle   You need to create a series of controls on the form. The command buttons cmdUp, cmdLeft, cmdRight, cmdDown, and cmdStart are straightforward. You will also need to create 16 small graphics files to represent the game pieces. I did this in Adobe Photoshop and saved the images as .jpg files. Each .jpg file was named for the number it represents: 1.jpg, 2.jpg, 3.jpg, and so on. Finally, I named the empty square piece Blank.jpg. You may use any application you wish to create your graphics files.

When it comes to the creation of the picture box controls, the issues are a little less clear. By creating the first picture box and then creating a control array for it, you can create all 16 picture boxes with the indices shown in the following figure:

Figure 8.6
Indices of Game Board

0	1	2	3
4	5	6	7
8	9	10	11
12	13	14	15

This may not seem to be a huge advantage, but it is! By using a control array to store the pictures, you can move a picture from one location to another by referencing the index of the picture box that you want to move the picture to and from.

For example, to move a puzzle piece to the left requires checking the index one less than the position of the piece you want to move, as well as checking that you are not trying to move the leftmost piece.

Observe the implementation:

In the General Declarations section, you need to declare an array that will store the current positions of each piece as well as the currently selected piece. This is shown in the following code:

```
Dim intGamePieces(0 To 15) As Integer
Dim intCurrentPos As Integer
```

The game is played by clicking on the puzzle piece that you wish to move and then clicking on the button corresponding to the direction you wish to move the puzzle piece. Because all 16 picture boxes are defined as a control array, all of their Click events can be processed by one piece of code. Observe the Click event code for the picGamePiece that accepts an index to select which picGamePiece control you will highlight. It then calls the MoveHighlight subroutine, which removes the highlight from the previously selected puzzle piece and highlights the puzzle piece that was clicked on. Additionally, it sets the current position of the game to the index.

```
Private Sub pctGamePiece_Click(intIndex As Integer)
'Change border
Call MoveHighlight(intCurrentPos, intIndex)

'Set new current piece
intCurrentPos = intIndex
End Sub
```

The supporting routine MoveHighlight could have been included in the previous event code. However, it will be used in numerous pieces of code. Therefore, a separate subroutine was created. The subroutine uses the `BorderStyle` attribute of a picture box to highlight and unhighlight a picture box. This is shown in the following code:

```
Private Sub MoveHighlight(intCurrentPosition As Integer, _
                          intNewPosition As Integer)
'Remove border from previous current piece
picGamePiece(intCurrentPosition).BorderStyle = 0

'Set border of new current piece
picGamePiece(intNewPosition).BorderStyle = 1
End Sub
```

The code required to move up a puzzle piece is actually written in two subroutines. The main code is attached to the `cmdUp` button. It calls the second routine, `UpValid`, which returns `True` if the currently selected piece can be moved up.

If the piece can be moved up, you need to update the internal representation of the board to reflect the move. If you look at Figure 8.6 you will see that each square has an index of 4 more than the square directly below it. Therefore, to switch a piece to the square above it, you set the `intGamePieces` array to the new piece at the index of the puzzle piece minus 4. Once the internal representation has been updated, you can move the highlighting of the current piece by calling the `MoveHighlight` subroutine. Finally, you will update the picture files that are displayed in both the current and previous puzzle piece locations, as well as updating the `intCurrentPos` variable to contain the new location of the puzzle piece. If the piece cannot be moved up, a warning message is displayed to the user. This is shown in the following code:

```
Private Sub cmdUp_Click()
If (UpValid() = True) Then
    'Move internal representation of new square to piece
    intGamePieces(intCurrentPos - 4) = intGamePieces(intCurrentPos)

    'Set internal representation of old square to blank
    intGamePieces(intCurrentPos) = 0

    Call MoveHighlight(intCurrentPos, intCurrentPos - 4)
    picGamePiece(intCurrentPos).Picture = _
        LoadPicture("c:\VB Coach\Chapter 8\Blank.jpg")
    intCurrentPos = intCurrentPos - 4
    picGamePiece(intCurrentPos).Picture = LoadPicture("c:\VB Coach\Chapter 8\" + _
            Trim(Str(intGamePieces(intCurrentPos))) + ".jpg")

Else
    MsgBox "Invalid Move"
End If
End Sub
```

The `cmdUp` command button's `Click` event calls the subroutine `UpValid`. In order for a move to be valid in the upward direction, it must satisfy two conditions.

First, the position of the puzzle piece that is being moved cannot be in the top row. Therefore the index of the puzzle piece cannot be a 0, 1, 2 or 3. The second condition is that the location the piece is being moved to cannot be occupied by another puzzle piece. If either of these two conditions is true, the function returns `False`. Otherwise, it returns `True`. The code follows:

```
Private Function UpValid() As Boolean
UpValid = True

'Check that we are in the leftmost spot
If (intCurrentPos >= 0) And (intCurrentPos <= 3) Then
    UpValid = False
'Check that the space above the current one is blank
ElseIf (intGamePieces(intCurrentPos - 4) <> 0) Then
    UpValid = False
End If
End Function
```

The `cmdDown` `Click` event works very similarly to the `cmdUp` `Click` event. They operate in virtually the same manner, except that instead of subtracting 4 from the current position to obtain the index of the new position of the puzzle piece, you add 4.

```
Private Sub cmdDown_Click()
If (DownValid() = True) Then
    'Move internal representation of new square to piece
    intGamePieces(intCurrentPos + 4) = intGamePieces(intCurrentPos)
    'Set internal representation of old square to blank
    intGamePieces(intCurrentPos) = 0

    Call MoveHighlight(intCurrentPos, intCurrentPos + 4)
    picGamePiece(intCurrentPos).Picture = _
        LoadPicture("c:\VB Coach\Chapter 8\Blank.jpg")
    intCurrentPos = intCurrentPos + 4
    picGamePiece(intCurrentPos).Picture = _
        LoadPicture("c:\VB Coach\Chapter 8\" + _
        Trim(Str(intGamePieces(intCurrentPos))) + ".jpg")
Else
    MsgBox "Invalid Move"
End If
End Sub
```

The code for the `DownValid` function is similar to the code for the `UpValid` function. There are two differences. First, you now check to make sure that you are not moving the puzzle piece from the bottom row, pieces with the index 12, 13, 14, and 15. Additionally, you must add 4 instead of subtracting 4 to determine whether the new location for the puzzle piece is empty. The code follows:

```
Private Function DownValid() As Boolean
DownValid = True

'Check that we are in the leftmost spot
If (intCurrentPos >= 12) And (intCurrentPos <= 15) Then
    DownValid = False
'Check that the space above the current one is blank
ElseIf (intGamePieces(intCurrentPos + 4) <> 0) Then
    DownValid = False
End If
End Function
```

The cmdRight Click event works very similarly to the cmdUp Click event as well. They operate virtually in the same manner, except that instead of subtracting 4 from the current position to obtain the index of the new position of the puzzle piece, you add 1.

```
Private Sub cmdRight_Click()
If (RightValid() = True) Then
    'Move internal representation of new square to piece
    intGamePieces(intCurrentPos + 1) = intGamePieces(intCurrentPos)
    'Set internal representation of old square to blank
    intGamePieces(intCurrentPos) = 0

    Call MoveHighlight(intCurrentPos, intCurrentPos + 1)
    picGamePiece(intCurrentPos).Picture = _
        LoadPicture("c:\VB Coach\Chapter 8\Blank.jpg")
    intCurrentPos = intCurrentPos + 1
    picGamePiece(intCurrentPos).Picture = _
        LoadPicture("c:\VB Coach\Chapter 8\" + _
            Trim(Str(intGamePieces(intCurrentPos))) + ".jpg")
Else
    MsgBox "Invalid Move"
End If
End Sub
```

The code for the RightValid function is similar to the code for the UpValid function. Again, there are two differences. First, you now check to make sure that you are not moving the puzzle piece from the right column, pieces with the index 3, 7, 11, and 15. Unlike the previous implementations, you must check each index individually since they are not sequential. Additionally, you must add 1 instead of subtracting 4 to determine if the new location for the puzzle piece is empty or not. The code follows:

```
Private Function RightValid() As Boolean
RightValid = True

'Check that we are in the leftmost spot
If (intCurrentPos = 3) Or (intCurrentPos = 7) Or _
    (intCurrentPos = 11) Or (intCurrenPos = 15) Then
    RightValid = False
'Check that the space to the right is blank
ElseIf (intGamePieces(intCurrentPos + 1) <> 0) Then
    RightValid = False
End If
End Function
```

The final set of routines you need to write is for processing the move of a puzzle piece to the left. They are almost identical to the routines to process the move to the right. The main difference is instead of adding 1 to find the index of the new position of the puzzle piece, you subtract 1. This is shown in the following code:

```
Private Sub cmdLeft_Click()
If (LeftValid() = True) Then
    'Move internal representation of new square to piece
    intGamePieces(intCurrentPos - 1) = intGamePieces(intCurrentPos)
    'Set internal representation of old square to blank
    intGamePieces(intCurrentPos) = 0

    Call MoveHighlight(intCurrentPos, intCurrentPos - 1)
    picGamePiece(intCurrentPos).Picture = _
        LoadPicture("c:\VB Coach\Chapter 8\Blank.jpg")
    intCurrentPos = intCurrentPos - 1
    picGamePiece(intCurrentPos).Picture = _
        LoadPicture("c:\VB Coach\Chapter 8\" + _
            Trim(Str(intGamePieces(intCurrentPos))) + ".jpg")
Else
    MsgBox "Invalid Move"
End If
End Sub
```

In the `LeftValid` function you also need to check if the starting index of the piece you are moving is in the leftmost row or an index of the value 0, 4, 8, or 12. The code follows:

```
Private Function LeftValid() As Boolean
LeftValid = True

'Check that we are in the leftmost spot
If (intCurrentPos = 0) Or (intCurrentPos = 4) Or _
    (intCurrentPos = 8) Or (intCurrenPos = 12) Then
    LeftValid = False
'Check that the space to the left is blank
ElseIf (intGamePieces(intCurrentPos - 1) <> 0) Then
    LeftValid = False
End If
End Function
```

How you start the game is a matter of choice. In the simplest implementation scheme, you can just initialize each piece to be in its proper place and select the last piece as the active one. This is shown in the following code:

```
Private Sub Form_Load()
intGamePieces(0) = 1
intGamePieces(1) = 2
intGamePieces(2) = 3
intGamePieces(3) = 4
intGamePieces(4) = 5
intGamePieces(5) = 6
intGamePieces(6) = 7
```

(continues)

(continued)

```
intGamePieces(7) = 8
intGamePieces(8) = 9
intGamePieces(9) = 10
intGamePieces(10) = 11
intGamePieces(11) = 12
intGamePieces(12) = 13
intGamePieces(13) = 14
intGamePieces(14) = 15
intGamePieces(15) = 0
intCurrentPos = 14
End Sub
```

If you want to get a little fancy, you can write a function to randomize the starting positions of the puzzle pieces. This function could then be called from the `Form_Load` event as well as the `cmdStart Click` event.

The function uses a temporary array to store the numbers 1 through 15. These represent the puzzle pieces that must be randomly placed in the puzzle. You start by picking a random number from 0 to the number of pieces still to place minus 1. This allows you to select a puzzle piece from the remaining list. Each time a piece is placed, it is removed from the list. This process continues until all puzzle pieces have been placed. The code follows:

```
Private Sub Initialize()
Dim intIndex As Integer
Dim intTempGamePieces(0 To 14) As Integer
Dim intNewIndex As Integer

'Initialize the pieces in the Temp array
For intIndex = 0 To 14
  intTempGamePieces(intIndex) = intIndex + 1
Next intIndex

'Loop thru the pieces left to place
For intIndex = 14 To 0 Step -1
    'Pick a piece randomly
    intNewIndex = Int((intIndex + 1) * Rnd)

    'Copy the randomly selected piece to the Game array
    intGamePieces(intIndex) = intTempGamePieces(intNewIndex)

    'load the associated picture
    picGamePiece(intIndex).Picture = _
      LoadPicture("c:\VB Coach\Chapter 8\" + _
        Trim(Str(intTempGamePieces(intNewIndex))) + ".jpg")

    'remove the selected piece by copying an unused one over it
    intTempGamePieces(intNewIndex) = intTempGamePieces(intIndex)
Next intIndex

'Set the last spot to blank
intGamePieces(15) = 0
End Sub
```

Answers to Chapter's Drills

Drill 8.1

The upper bound would be 2. The valid indices for the array would be –2, –1, 0, 1, and 2.

Drill 8.2

```
Dim strDrillArray(0 To 4) As String
strDrillArray(0) = "First Value"
strDrillArray(1) = "Second Value"
strDrillArray(2) = "Third Value"
strDrillArray(3) = "Fourth Value"
strDrillArray(4) = "Fifth Value"
```

Drill 8.3

```
Dim intDrillArray(1 To 1000) As Integer
Dim intIndex As Integer

For intIndex = 1 To 1000
    intDrillArray(intIndex) = intIndex
Next intIndex
```

Drill 8.4

The problem is that a control array created by copying and pasting starts with a lower bound of 0, not 1. Therefore, the first text box will not be searched. Additionally, an error will occur when you refer to index 6 since it will be out of bounds of the control array.

TIP

Out of bounds is a common way to refer to an index that is not within the range of acceptable indices for an array.

Drill 8.5

```
Dim intIndex As Integer
Dim intSum As Integer

For intIndex = 0 To 5
    intSum = intSum + Val(txtDrillText(intIndex).Text)
Next intIndex
MsgBox Str(Sum/6)
```

Drill 8.6

```
Dim intIndex As Integer
Dim intMaxValue As Integer

intMaxValue = Val(txtDrillText(0).Text)

For intIndex = 1 To 5
    If (Val(txtDrillText(intIndex).Text) > intMaxValue) Then
        intMaxValue = Val(txtDrillText(intIndex).Text)
    End If
Next intIndex
MsgBox Str(intMaxValue)
```

Drill 8.7

The array is declared as an array of Integers. However, you are trying to store Strings in the second column. You cannot mix datatypes this way; you will get a run-time error.

Drill 8.8

The code fails to initialize the values in the row and columns with an index of 0. You might have thought that the Step -1 was the problem. However, although it seems odd to initialize the array in this manner, it is not incorrect. If you had written the code to step down to 0, the code would have accomplished the desired results.

Drill 8.9

The two segments of code would accomplish the same results. Although the individual cells of the two-dimensional array are loaded in different orders, the same cells will be initialized to the same values.

Drill 8.10

The two segments of code would not accomplish the same results. The first segment of code would initialize all 15 cells in the two-dimensional array to the value 2. However, the second segment of code would produce a run-time error. Because the number of elements in a row is different than the number of elements in a column, when you switch the Row and Column values in the For statement, you generate an out of bounds error when intCol = 4.

Drill 8.11

```
Type Employee
    strName As String
    strSalary As Integer
    strTitle As String
    strCompany As String
End Type
```

Key Words and Key Terms

Array

A construct that allows you to store multiple values of a datatype in a single variable.

Control array

A construct that allows you to store multiple controls with a single variable.

Record

A single entity of data relating to one unit.

Sequential file

A file format that allows consecutive access to data.

Single-dimensional array

A construct that allows you to store multiple values in a single row of data.

Two-dimensional array

A construct that contains rows and columns of the same type of data.

User-defined type

A template to combine a group of values into a single unit.

Additional Exercises

Questions 1 and 2 are True/False.

1. An array must have a lower bound of zero.

2. An array is used to set the size of a record in a random access file.

3. Write the code required to declare and initialize an array of `Strings` that contains the name of each month in the year.

4. Write a function that accepts an array of 20 `Integers` and an integer target value to search for. The function should return the number of times the target value is found.

5. Write a function that accepts an array called `curSales` of 20 `Currency` values and returns the maximum sale value in the array.

6. Write a function that accepts a two-dimensional array called `curSalesAndCost` of 20 sets of `Currency` values. The first dimension will store the sale price of the merchandise, while the second dimension will store the cost of the merchandise. The function should return the sale that has the largest profit.

7. Write a function that accepts two arrays and a `String`. The first array, `dtePurchaseDates`, should be an array of dates. The second array, `curSaleAmount`, should be an array of currency. Each array should contain 100 items. The `String`, `strMonth`, should represent the month whose total sales will be returned from the function. The function should loop through the arrays and total the sales of the month indicated and return the total.

8. Write an application that will that uses a control array to store a student's name and grade. The application should store 10 sets of student names and grades in two control arrays. The application should contain a command button that when clicked outputs the average grade, as well as the name and grade of the highest grade in the class.

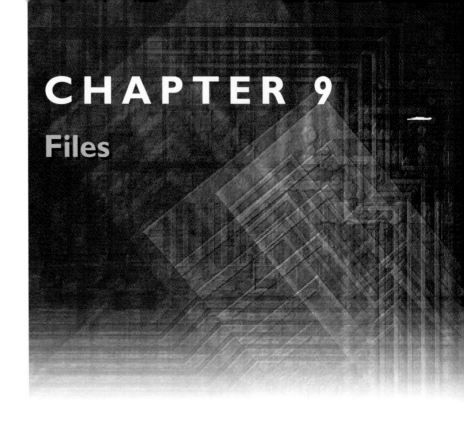

CHAPTER 9
Files

You may have noticed that in the process of developing applications, preloading data into the application was a tedious process. Indeed, if you could only create applications that stored the data you enter during the time it is executing and then lost it when you terminated the application, your applications would not be very useful.

A simple way to store data so that it is accessible the next time you wish to execute the application is to store it in a data file. We will explain two types of data files: **sequential** and **random access**. (The third type of file is a binary file; for more information see the MSDN).

9.1   Sequential Files

A sequential file allows reading or writing the file from the beginning of the file until the end of the file. Files that are read and written sequentially are plain text files commonly known as **ASCII** files. ASCII stands for American Standard Code for the Interchange of Information. You can view or edit small ASCII files using the Notepad application that comes with Windows, or you can use a word processor and then select the ASCII option when you save the file.

If you wanted to save the information in your Student Search application from Chapter 7, a sequential file of this information might look like one of the following two files:

1	Salvage	Jeff	Computer Science	Senior	4.0
2	Cunningham	John	Basket Weaving	Freshman	1.0
3	Pepito	Suzanne	Industrial Engineering	Junior	3.8
4	Wartell	Adam	MIS	Senior	3.92
5	Fletcher	Irwin	Film	Senior	3.99

Fixed-Width File

```
1, "Salvage" , "Jeff" , "Computer Science" , "Senior" , 4.0
2, "Cunningham" , "John" , "Basket Weaving" , "Freshman", 1.0
3, "Pepito", "Suzanne", "Industrial Engineering" , "Junior" , 3.8
4, "Wartell" , "Adam" , "MIS" , "Senior" , 3.92
5, "Fletcher" , "Irwin" , "Film" , "Senior" , 3.99
```

Comma-Delimited File

A **fixed-width file** contains information formatted so that each line stores each data item in a fixed location within the line. In contrast, the **comma-delimited file** stores each data item with a comma separating each item. A comma-delimited file will also place double quotes around String fields.

VB Commands to Process Input Files

Opening Files   To open a sequential file when you wish to read data from the file, use the following syntax:

```
Open FileName For Input As #Number
```

When opening an ASCII file in Visual Basic, you must provide the filename and the number of the file you are opening. The filename is the name of the file as it appears in Windows Explorer or My Computer. The file number is the identification number by which you will refer to the file. Each file you have open simultaneously must have a unique identification number between 1 and 511. To open the file StudentInfo.txt so that you may read data from it, you use the following code:

```
Open "StudentInfo.txt" For Input As #1
```

> **TIP**
>
> Instead of hard coding the file number, Visual Basic has a function FreeFile that will return the next available file number. By using this function instead of hard coding the file number, you can add flexibility as your program grows.

Reading Data   To read data from the file, you have two options. You can choose to read an entire line of data at a time and then divide the line into individual fields with the Mid function, or you can read one field at a time into individual variables. If you are using a fixed format file, it is preferable to read one line of data at a time. However, if you are reading a comma-delimited file, you will read data one field at a time.

To read an entire line of the input file at a time, you will need to declare a String variable to hold the line as you read it. By using the following command, you can read a line of the input file opened as file number 1 into the `String` `strInputLine`.

```
Line Input #1, strInputLine
```

On the other hand, if you wish to read individual fields from a comma-delimited file, you should declare a variable for each type of variable you are reading. Therefore, for your Student Search example in Chapter 7 (section 7.5), you would declare a variable for each column in the grid. Then, you can use the following code to read each variable's value from the comma-delimited input file into their respective variables.

```
Input #1, intStudentNumber, strLastName, strFirstName, strMajor, strYear, sngGPA
```

Testing for the End of File   You need to test to see if you have read all the data contained in the file. This is called an **EOF** test, where `EOF` stands for end of file. Whether you choose to read a fixed-format or comma-delimited file, the method is the same. Using the `EOF` function, you can test to see if you are at the end of the file. `EOF` accepts a file number as its parameter and returns `True` if you are at the end of the file and `False` otherwise.

Closing a File   You must always remember to close a file that you have previously opened. Use the following syntax, where `FileNumber` is the number of the file you previously opened:

```
Close #FileNumber
```

Putting It All Together with Fixed-Format Input Files   Putting it all together, observe how you would open the file `StudentsFixed.txt` in the directory `C:\VB Coach\Chapter 9` and preload the information you previously entered into the Student Search application. By adding this code to the `Form_load` event, you can start the application with all the information you saved previously loaded.

The code opens the fixed-text file and adds a row to the `grdStudents` MS flexgrid for each line in the input file. Since you read a complete line at a time, you need to divide the line into its individual fields by using the `Mid` function. Although not required, you use the `Trim` function with `Mid` so that no additional spaces are stored in the grid. This can be seen in the following code:

```
Dim strInputLine As String
Dim intStudentFile As Integer

intStudentFile = FreeFile
Open "C:\VB Coach\Chapter 9\StudentsFixed.txt" For Input As #intStudentFile

Do While Not (EOF(intStudentFile))
  Line Input #intStudentFile, strInputLine
  grdStudents.Rows = grdStudents.Rows + 1
  grdStudents.Row = grdStudents.Rows - 1

  'Student #
  grdStudents.Col = 0
  grdStudents.Text = Trim(Mid(strInputLine, 1, 5))
```

(continues)

(continued)

```
'Last Name
grdStudents.Col = 1
grdStudents.Text = Trim(Mid(strInputLine, 6, 10))

'First Name
grdStudents.Col = 2
grdStudents.Text = Trim(Mid(strInputLine, 16, 10))

'Major
grdStudents.Col = 3
grdStudents.Text = Trim(Mid(strInputLine, 25, 25))

'Year
grdStudents.Col = 4
grdStudents.Text = Trim(Mid(strInputLine, 51, 10))

'GPA
grdStudents.Col = 5
grdStudents.Text = Trim(Mid(strInputLine, 61, 5))

Loop

Close #intStudentFile
```

> **WARNING**
>
> Notice that at the end of reading the entire input file, you make sure that you close it. Never forget to close your files when you are finished with them because if you do, you may not be able to open them again without rebooting the computer. Also, leaving files open unnecessarily wastes computer resources.

Putting It All Together with Comma-Delimited Input Files If you decided to use a comma-delimited file for input instead not much would change. You declare a temporary variable for each field in the input file and use these variables to read all the values in a single line at once. Then, you set the corresponding cells of the grid to these values. This is seen in the following code that would be added to the `Form_Load` event:

```
Dim intStudentNumber As Integer
Dim intStudentFile As Integer
Dim strLastName As String
Dim strFirstName As String
Dim strMajor As String
Dim strYear As String
Dim sngGPA As Single
```

(continues)

(continued)

```
intStudentFile = FreeFile
Open "C:\VB Coach\Chapter 9\StudentsComma.txt" For Input As #intStudentFile
Do While Not (EOF(intStudentFile))
  Input # intStudentFile, intStudentNumber, strLastName, strFirstName, _
    strMajor, strYear, sngGPA
  grdStudents.Rows = grdStudents.Rows + 1
  grdStudents.Rows = grdStudents.Rows - 1

  'Student #
  grdStudents.Col = 0
  grdStudents.Text = Str(intStudentNumber)

  'Last Name
  grdStudents.Col = 1
  grdStudents.Text = strLastName

  'First Name
  grdStudents.Col = 2
  grdStudents.Text = strFirstName

  'Major
  grdStudents.Col = 3
  grdStudents.Text = strMajor

  'Year
  grdStudents.Col = 4
  grdStudents.Text = strYear

  'GPA
  grdStudents.Col = 5
  grdStudents.Text = Str(sngGPA)

Loop

Close #intStudentFile
```

TIP

By issuing the `Close` command without a file number specified, all files currently open will be closed.

VB Commands to Process Output Files

Opening Output Files   With some slight changes in syntax, you can take data from a Visual Basic application and store it in an ASCII file. Again you have choices. Besides having to decide if the file will be formatted as fixed-width or comma-delimited, you must also decide if you are going to create a new file or simply append the data to an existing file. The only difference in how you handle new output files from those you are going to append to is in the way you open the file. Observe the following two templates to open an ASCII file for output:

```
Open FileName For Output As #Number
```

WARNING

If a file already exists and it is opened for output, it will be overwritten.

```
Open FileName For Append as #Number
```

Writing Data to a File   Once the file is open, you can write data to it. If you wish to write data in a fixed-width format, you will format the information for an entire line and then write that line to the file. This means that you must append all the fields contained in one line together, with each field containing the proper padding so that the fixed-length nature of the file is maintained.

The following is what two `Strings`, `"Jeff"` and `"Salvage"`, each padded to 10 characters, would look like if they were concatenated together:

```
"Jeff      Salvage   "
```

In contrast, if the two `Strings`, `"Jeff"` and `"Salvage"`, were not padded but still concatenated, they would look as follows:

```
"JeffSalvage"
```

The following function `PadRight` will be helpful to you.

```
Function PadRight(strValue As String, intSize As Integer) As String

strValue = Trim(strValue)
PadRight = strValue + Space(intSize - Len(strValue))
End Function
```

By passing `PadRight` a `String` and the size you wish it to be, it will return that `String`, stripped of any spaces to the left and the appropriate number of spaces appended to the right. This will simplify your handling of fixed-format files.

Therefore, to build the `String` that you will output, you can use the following syntax:

```
'First data field in the line
OutputLine = PadRight(strValue1, intstrValue1Size)

'Second data field in the Line as well as any others
OutputLine = OutputLine + PadRight(strValue2, intstrValue2Size)
```

TIP

`Trim` and `Space` are two functions built into Visual Basic to make working with `Strings` easier. `Trim` will remove any additional spaces from the left or right of the `String`, while `Space` will generate as many spaces as the parameter passed to it indicates.

Closing an Output File   When you have written all the data you wish to the output file, you close the file in the same manner as with input files.

Saving Student Search Data with Fixed-Width File Format

To save the contents of the grid to the file, you can output the complete contents as either a fixed-format or as a comma-delimited format. You will show both by adding a command button cmdSave and then adding the code to the command button's Click event.

```
Private Sub cmdSave_Click()
Dim intCurrentRow As Integer
Dim strOutputLine As String
Dim intStudentFile As Integer

intStudentFile = FreeFile
Open "C:\VB Coach\Chapter 9\StudentsFixed.txt" For Output As #intStudentFile

intCurrentRow = 1

Do While (intCurrentRow < grdStudents.Rows)
  'Student #
  grdStudents.Row = intCurrentRow
  grdStudents.Col = 0
  strOutputLine = PadRight(grdStudents.Text, 5)

  'Last Name
  grdStudents.Col = 1
  strOutputLine = strOutputLine + PadRight(grdStudents.Text, 10)

  'First Name
  grdStudents.Col = 2
  strOutputLine = strOutputLine + PadRight(grdStudents.Text, 10)

  'Major
  grdStudents.Col = 3
  strOutputLine = strOutputLine + PadRight(grdStudents.Text, 25)

  'Year
  grdStudents.Col = 4
  strOutputLine = strOutputLine + PadRight(grdStudents.Text, 10)

  'GPA
  grdStudents.Col = 5
  strOutputLine = strOutputLine + PadRight(grdStudents.Text, 5)

  Print #1, OutputLine
  intCurrentRow = intCurrentRow + 1
Loop

Close #intStudentFile

End Sub
```

Example: Saving Student Search Data with Comma Delimited File Format

```
Private Sub cmdSave_Click()
Dim intCurrentRow As Integer

Dim intStudentNumber As Integer
Dim strLastName As String
Dim strFirstName As String
Dim strMajor As String
Dim strYear As String
Dim sngGPA As Single

Dim intStudentFile as Integer

intStudentFile = FreeFile
Open "C:\VB Coach\Chapter 9\StudentsComma.txt" For Output As #intStudentFile

intCurrentRow = 1

Do While (intCurrentRow < grdStudents.Rows)
  'Student #
  grdStudents.Row = intCurrentRow
  grdStudents.Col = 0
  intStudentNumber = Val(grdStudents.Text)

  'Last Name
  grdStudents.Col = 1
  strLastName = Trim(grdStudents.Text)

  'First Name
  grdStudents.Col = 2
  strFirstName = Trim(grdStudents.Text)

  'Major
  grdStudents.Col = 3
  strMajor = Trim(grdStudents.Text)

  'Year
  grdStudents.Col = 4
  strYear = Trim(grdStudents.Text)

  'GPA
  grdStudents.Col = 5
  sngGPA = Val(grdStudents.Text)

  Write #intStudentFile, intStudentNumber, strLastName, strFirstName, _
       strMajor, strYear, sngGPA
  intCurrentRow = intCurrentRow + 1
Loop

Close #intStudentFile

End Sub
```

TIP

It's always a good idea to give users feedback as to the progress of their action. Previously, you were able to determine that the action was performed because you saw the results on the form. However, when saving a file, you do not know if the action has actually occurred without physically checking for the existence of the file. In the future, we will show you how to create a progress bar, but for now, it's a good idea to include a message box indicating the completion of the save. You can add this to the end of the cmdSave command button.

DRILL 9.1

Write the code required to read in four String values from the fixed-format data file DrillFile.txt into four String variables strString1, strString2, strString3, and strString4. The maximum size of the four Strings are 10, 20, 15, and 25, respectively.

DRILL 9.2

Write the code required to write four String values to a comma-delimited data file DrillFile.txt from four String variables strString1, strString2, strString3, and strString4.

DRILL 9.3

Write the code required to write four String values to a fixed-width data file DrillFile.txt from four String variables strString1, strString2, strString3, and strString4. The maximum size of the four Strings are 10, 20, 15, and 25, respectively.

9.2 Random Access Files

While sequential files give you the capability to store data permanently, their ability to arbitrarily access different values within the file is limited by their sequential access method. **Random access files** allow you to access data in a file with much more flexibility. You can move forward and back throughout the file reading or writing records as you go. However, in order to accomplish this, you must have each record formatted to a single size.

The nature of a random access file means that you do not have to choose between opening a file for either input or output. Instead, when you open a file for random access, you can read or write data one record at a time.

To open a random access file, use the following format:

```
Open FileName For Random As #FileNumber Len = Len(RecordType)
```

Random access files do not differ from sequential files in their specification of a FileName or FileNumber. However, they do require the specification of the length of the record in the file. Although this could be hard-coded, it would be bad practice to do so. Instead, you should use the Len function to determine the actual length of the record type. This will ensure that if you change the structure of the user-defined type the record is based upon, you will not have to worry about changing the length in the open statements of the files that access it.

Random Access File Application

Let's write a simple application that not only allows you to read and write a single student's record at a time, but also allows you to update a record once it has been written to the random access file. When the application's form is loaded, it will open the file containing the data and initialize any variables needed to access the data. When the application is quit and the form closes, the application will automatically close the data file. The application would look as follows:

Figure 9.1
Random Access File
Application

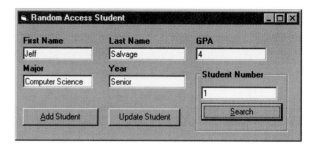

You need two declarations in the General Declarations section of the form. First, you need a variable that will store the total number of records within the file. Second, you need a variable to store the file identification number of the file you are opening. This could be hard-coded, but it is better programming practice to allow Visual Basic to pick it for you. Finally, you need a user-defined type that will provide the details for the format of your record within the file. This is shown in the following code:

```
Dim intTotalRecords As Integer
Dim intFileNumber As Integer

Private Type StudentRecord
   intStudentNumber As Integer
   strLastName As String * 10
   strFirstName As String * 10
   strMajor As String * 25
   strYear As String * 10
   sngGPA As Single
End Type
```

When the form is loaded, you need to first get the file identification number that you will refer to your data file from within the application. This will be stored in the variable `intFileNumber`. Then you must open the actual data file as a random access file. Additionally, you need to calculate the total number of records. This can be accomplished by dividing the length of the file by the length of an individual record in the file.

TIP

The length of a file can be calculated by using the `LOF` function that accepts a file number and returns the length of the file.

The Form_Load code follows:

```
Private Sub Form_Load()
Dim IndividualStudent As StudentRecord
Dim intFileNumber As Integer

intFileNumber = FreeFile

Open "C:\VB Coach\Chapter 9\StudentsRandom.txt" For Random As #intFileNumber _
    Len = Len(IndividualStudent)

intTotalRecords = LOF(intFileNumber) / Len(IndividualStudent)
End Sub
```

To ensure that the file is closed properly, you will place the code to close the file in the Form_Close event handler as shown in the following code:

```
Private Sub Form_Unload(Cancel As Integer)
Close #intFileNumber
End Sub
```

You have three actions to implement: reading an existing record, writing a new record, and updating an existing record.

To retrieve a specific record from a file, you must first declare a user-defined type, RecordType, and a variable from that type, CurrentRecord. Then you can use the following template:

```
Get #FileNumber, RecordNumber, CurrentRecord
```

To write information to a random access file, you must also declare the user-defined type and variable of that type. Once you have stored the information you wish to write in the variable, you can write it to a file using the following template:

```
Put #FileNumber, RecordNumber, CurrentRecord
```

Updating a record in a random access file is accomplished using the same code as writing a record initially. The only difference is that you must make sure that the record number is the same as the one you wish to update.

With this information, you can complete your application.

When the cmdSearch command button is clicked, you need to find the record indicated by the txtSearch text box. Once the information is gathered into the record, you can copy the contents to each corresponding text box. This is shown in the following code:

```
Private Sub cmdSearch_Click()
Dim IndividualStudent As StudentRecord

Get #intFileNumber, Val(txtSearch.Text), IndividualStudent

txtStudentNumber = Str(IndividualStudent.intStudentNumber)
txtLast.Text = IndividualStudent.strLastName
txtFirst.Text = IndividualStudent.strFirstName
txtMajor.Text = IndividualStudent.strMajor
txtYear.Text = IndividualStudent.strYear
txtGPA.Text = Str(IndividualStudent.sngGPA)
End Sub
```

Writing the individual records to the file is a matter of copying the values in the text boxes to their corresponding fields within the record, incrementing the record counter, and then placing the actual record in the file. Finally, it's a good practice to clear the form of the previously entered values. This is all shown in the following code:

```
Private Sub cmdAddStudent_Click()
Dim IndividualStudent As StudentRecord

IndividualStudent.intStudentNumber = Val(txtStudentNumber.Text)
IndividualStudent.strLastName = txtLast.Text
IndividualStudent.strFirstName = txtFirst.Text
IndividualStudent.strMajor = txtMajor.Text
IndividualStudent.strYear = txtYear.Text
IndividualStudent.sngGPA = Val(txtGPA.Text)

intTotalRecords = intTotalRecords + 1

Put #intFileNumber, intTotalRecords, IndividualStudent

txtStudentNumber = ""
txtLast.Text = ""
txtFirst.Text = ""
txtMajor.Text = ""
txtYear.Text = ""
txtGPA.Text = ""
End Sub
```

The code required to update a record does not vary much from the code to add a record. In both cases you must copy the values from the individual text boxes to a `StudentRecord` variable. The main difference is that when you write the record to the file, you write it to the record number indicated by the `txtSearch` text box instead of one more than the total number of records currently in the file. Finally, as before, you clear the text boxes of their previous values. This is shown in the following code:

TIP

The code for `cmdUpdate_Click` and `cmdAddStudent_Click` can be shared by creating a separate function that contains the repeated code.

```
Private Sub cmdUpdate_Click()
Dim IndividualStudent As StudentRecord

IndividualStudent.strLastName = txtLast.Text
IndividualStudent.strFirstName = txtFirst.Text
IndividualStudent.strMajor = txtMajor.Text
IndividualStudent.strYear = txtYear.Text
IndividualStudent.sngGPA = txtGPA.Text

Put #intFileNumber, Val(txtSearch.Text), IndividualStudent

txtLast.Text = ""
txtFirst.Text = ""
txtMajor.Text = ""
txtYear.Text = ""
txtGPA.Text = ""

End Sub
```

While random access files have their place, with the advent of database applications, their use is limited to applications that have minimum data requirements that cannot use a database due to overhead or additional cost of implementation.

 ## 9.3   Case Study

Problem Description   Until now, the payroll system that you developed needed the information to be entered every time the application was executed. Clearly, an efficient payroll system cannot operate in this manner. You need to add the capability to save data and then automatically reload it when the application starts up.

The application looks identical to Chapter 7's application because you will perform the load and save operations in the `Form_Load` and `Form_Unload` events, respectively.

Problem Discussion   The problem description doesn't indicate the type of data file for the application. Indeed, the user of the application would not know what type of data file was used simply by operating the application.

While the decision is mostly one of personal choice, using a random access file would be the least appropriate choice. If you changed the problem description so that data was saved as it was changed, a random access file format would be a good choice. However, with the stipulation that you will only save data upon exiting the application, there is no need for a random access file format.

Therefore, the choice is either to use a fixed-format file or a comma-delimited format. Personally, if size isn't an issue, I prefer the fixed-format file because when you open it in Notepad, it's easier to read. Therefore, your implementation will follow this format.

> **TIP**
>
> Comma-delimited files are often used when importing the results to programs like Microsoft Excel.

Problem Solution   The only changes to the application are in the `Form_Load` and `Form_Unload` events. The `Form_Load` code starts as it did before; however, once the MS flex grid is formatted, you must load the data in the `CaseStudy.txt` data file. You read in each line of data, divide the line into separate data values, and then copy those values to their appropriate place in the MS flex grid. The code follows:

```
Private Sub Form_Load()
Dim intPayrollFile As Integer
Dim strInputLine As String

grdEmployees.Rows = 1
grdEmployees.Cols = 5
grdEmployees.Row = 0
grdEmployees.Col = 0
grdEmployees.Text = "Employee #"
```

(continues)

(continued)

```
grdEmployees.Col = 1
grdEmployees.Text = "Employee Name"

grdEmployees.Col = 2
grdEmployees.Text = "Hours Worked"

grdEmployees.Col = 3
grdEmployees.Text = "Department"

grdEmployees.Col = 4
grdEmployees.Text = "Weekly Pay"

intPayrollFile = FreeFile
Open "C:\VB Coach\Chapter 9\CaseStudy.txt" For Input As #intPayrollFile

Do While Not (EOF(intPayrollFile))
  Line Input #intPayrollFile, strInputLine
  grdEmployees.Rows = grdEmployees.Rows + 1
  grdEmployees.Row = grdEmployees.Rows - 1

  'Employee Number
  grdEmployees.Col = 0
  grdEmployees.Text = Str(grdEmployees.Row)


  'Employee Name
  grdEmployees.Col = 1
  grdEmployees.Text = Trim(Mid(strInputLine, 1, 20))

  'Hours Worked
  grdEmployees.Col = 2
  grdEmployees.Text = Trim(Mid(strInputLine, 21, 10))

  'Department
  grdEmployees.Col = 3
  grdEmployees.Text = Trim(Mid(strInputLine, 31, 15))

  'Weekly Pay
  grdEmployees.Col = 4
  grdEmployees.Text = Trim(Mid(strInputLine, 46, 10))

Loop

Close #intPayrollFile

End Sub
```

The Form_Unload code needs to open a file for output, loop through all of the rows in the MS flex grid, format each value to its proper size, and then output the values as a single line to the data file. This is done in the following code:

```
Private Sub Form_Unload(Cancel As Integer)
Dim intCurrentRow As Integer
Dim intPayrollFile As Integer

Dim strEmployeeName As String
Dim strHoursWorked As String
Dim strDepartment As String
Dim strWeeklyPay As String

intPayrollFile = FreeFile
Open "C:\VB Coach\Chapter 9\CaseStudy.txt" For Output As #intPayrollFile

intCurrentRow = 1

Do While (intCurrentRow < grdEmployees.Rows)
   'Employee Name
   grdEmployees.Row = intCurrentRow
   grdEmployees.Col = 1
   strEmployeeName = PadRight(grdEmployees.Text, 20)

   'Hours Worked
   grdEmployees.Col = 2
   strHoursWorked = PadRight(grdEmployees.Text, 10)

   'Department
   grdEmployees.Col = 3
   strDepartment = PadRight(grdEmployees.Text, 15)

   'Weekly Pay
   grdEmployees.Col = 4
   strWeeklyPay = PadRight(grdEmployees.Text, 10)

   Print #intPayrollFile, strEmployeeName + strHoursWorked + _
       strDepartment + strWeeklyPay
   intCurrentRow = intCurrentRow + 1
Loop

Close #intPayrollFile

End Sub
```

Common Dialog Box

So far, all of the programs you have used with data files were written with the filename and its path hard coded into the application. This can be very inconvenient if the filename changes. However, you can use a built-in dialog box that will prompt the user to select a file from the hard drive. It returns a `String` containing the path and the filename that can be used in your application to open the file.

Two of the most useful common dialog boxes are the File Open and File Save As dialog boxes:

Figure 9.2
Open Dialog Box

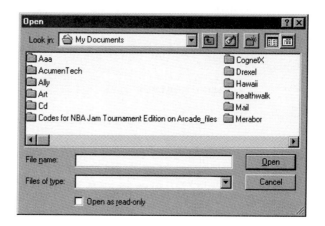

Figure 9.3
Save As Dialog Box

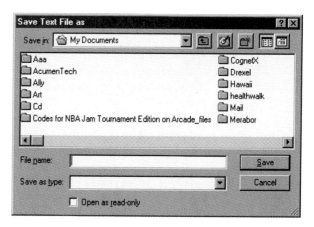

To use the common dialog control, you will need to add the control to your project.

Since a common dialog control is not one of the default controls in the toolbar, you will have to add it. Select the Components menu from the Project menu. When the Components window appears (Figure 9.4) select the check box for the Microsoft Common Dialog Control 6.0. This will add the control to the Control toolbar.

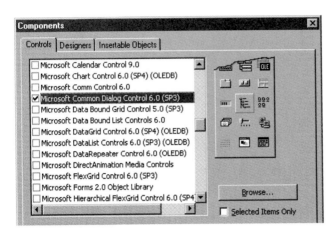

Figure 9.4   Common Dialog Control

Figure 9.5   Updated Toolbar

Although you will place a common dialog control on the form just like any other control, it will not be visible when you run your application.

Figure 9.6
Dialog Box Placed on
Control

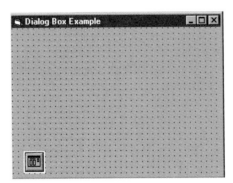

Setting Attributes for a Common Dialog Box   Once a control is placed on the form, you can specify attributes so that your dialog box behaves exactly the way you desire. While there are many attributes, here are the most important ones:

◆ **CancelError**   Developers must decide what will happen if the user does not select a file. By setting `CancelError` to `True` a run-time error will occur when a file isn't selected. If `CancelError` is set to `False`, the application will continue to execute normally.

◆ **DialogTitle**   Good application development provides users with directions to help clarify what they are trying to accomplish. Therefore, in most cases this attribute should be used to indicate what file is being opened or saved.

◆ **Filter**   Often the user wishes to limit the type of file visible in the dialog box to a specific type. By specifying the `Filter` attribute, you can limit the types of files displayed using standard filename wildcard patterns. In order to indicate a filter, you must first specify a description of the limitation as in `Text Files(*.txt)` and then the actual wildcard pattern to limit the files displayed as in `*.txt`. These two specifications must be separated by the pipe symbol (|)

Therefore, to set the filter of the dialog box `dlgExample` to show only text files, use the following code:

```
dlgExample.Filter = "Text Files(*.txt)|*.txt"
```

♦ **InitDir**   If this attribute is left unspecified the dialog box will be opened using the current directory. However, if you wish the dialog box to open in another directory, you can specify it by assigning the `InitDir` attribute to the directory path you wish to open.

Additional attributes exist so that you can open a Color, Font, Printer, and Help dialog box. Please check the MSDN for more information about these dialog boxes.

Open File Example   Observe the following code that will present the user with a dialog box to show an Open File dialog box. It will only show text files and have a title of Select a Text File. Additionally, if you do not select a file, you display a message to the user and exit the subroutine.

```
Private Sub cmdSelect_Click()
Dim strTextFileName As String ' Variable to store filename

'Set File Open dialog properties
With dlgFileOpen
    .CancelError = False
    .Filter = "Text Files(*.txt)|*.txt"
    .DialogTitle = "Select a Text File"
    .ShowOpen
End With

If (Len(dlgFileOpen.FileName) > 0) Then
    strTextFileName = dlgFileOpen.FileName   'Set variable to filename
Else
    MsgBox "No File Selected"
    Exit Sub
End If
End Sub
```

File Save Example   Observe the following code that will present the user with a dialog box to show a File Save dialog box. It will only show text files and have a title of Save Text File As. Additionally, if you do not select a file, you display a message to the user and exit the subroutine.

```
Private Sub cmdSelect_Click()
Dim strTextFileName As String ' Variable to store filename

'Set File Open dialog properties
With dlgFileSave
    .CancelError = False
    .Filter = "Text Files(*.txt)|*.txt"
    .DialogTitle = "Save Text File as"
    .ShowSave
End With
```

(continues)

(continued)

```
If (Len(dlgFileSave.FileName) > 0) Then
    strTextFileName = dlgFileSave.FileName    'Set variable to filename
Else
    MsgBox "No File Selected"
    Exit Sub
End If
End Sub
```

TIP

The keyword `With` allows you to specify attributes in a shorthand notation. Without it, you would be forced to write out the `dlgFileSave` name for each property.

Example using `With`:

```
With dlgFileSave
    .CancelError = False
    .Filter = "Text Files(*.txt)|*.txt"
End With
```

Example not using `With`:

```
dlgFileSave.CancelError = False
dlgFileSave.Filter = "Text Files(*.txt)|*.txt"
```

Answers to Chapter's Drills
Drill 9.1

```
Dim intDrillFile As Integer
Dim strString1 As String
Dim strString2 As String
Dim strString3 As String
Dim strString4 As String

intDrillFile = FreeFile
Open "C:\VB Coach\Chapter 9\DrillFile.txt" For Input As #intDrillFile


Input #intDrillFile, strString1, strString2, strString3, strString4


Close #intDrillFile
```

Drill 9.2

```
Dim intDrillFile As Integer
Dim strString1 As String
Dim strString2 As String
Dim strString3 As String
Dim strString4 As String
Dim strInputLine As String

intDrillFile = FreeFile
Open "C:\VB Coach\Chapter 9\DrillFile.txt" For Input As #intDrillFile

Line Input #intDrillFile, strInputLine

strString1 = Trim(Mid(strInputLine, 1, 10))
strString2 = Trim(Mid(strInputLine, 1, 20))
strString3 = Trim(Mid(strInputLine, 1, 15))
strString4 = Trim(Mid(strInputLine, 1, 25))

Close #intStudentFile
```

Drill 9.3

Write the code required to write four `String` values to a comma-delimited data file `DrillFile` from four `String` variables `String1`, `String2`, `String3`, and `String4`.

```
Dim intDrillFile As Integer
Dim strString1 As String
Dim strString2 As String
Dim strString3 As String
Dim strString4 As String

intDrillFile = FreeFile
Open "C:\VB Coach\Chapter 9\DrillFile.txt" For Output As #intDrillFile

strString1 = "Some Value 1"
strString2 = "Some Value 2"
strString3 = "Some Value 3"
strString4 = "Some Value 4"

Write #intDrillFile, strString1, strString2, strString3, strString4

Close #intDrillFile
```

Drill 9.4

```
Dim intDrillFile As Integer
Dim strString1 As String
Dim strString2 As String
Dim strString3 As String
Dim strString4 As String
Dim strOutputLine As String
```

(continues)

(continued)

```
intDrillFile = FreeFile
Open "C:\VB Coach\Chapter 9\DrillFile.txt" For Output As #intDrillFile

strOutputLine = Trim(PadRight(strString1, 10) + Trim(PadRight(strString2, 20) + _
            Trim(PadRight(strString3, 15) + Trim(PadRight(strString4, 25))

Print #intDrillFile, strOutputLine

Close #intDrillFile
```

Key Words and Key Terms

ASCII
A standard file format. ASCII stands for American Standard Code for the Interchange of Information.

Comma-delimited file
A file format that contains information organized so that each data item is stored with a comma separating each item.

EOF
A function that checks to see if a file is at the end.

File Save dialog box
A control that allows the developer to display a dialog box allowing the user to select a file. The control returns the filename including its complete path.

Fixed-width file
A file format that contains information organized so that each line stores each data item in a fixed location within the line.

FreeFile
A function that returns the number of the next available file.

Random access file
A file format that contains information organized in records. Each record is stored in a fixed format, so that the developer can access records easily and non-sequentially.

Additional Exercises

Questions 1–3 are True/False.

1. You can tell the difference between a file that is in a fixed-width format and a comma-delimited format by the statement that opens it.

2. A comma-delimited file can be opened for input and output simultaneously.

3. A random access file separates each field with a comma.

For the next six questions, use the following information:

Comma-Delimited File

```
Student #, Last Name, First Name, Major, Year, GPA
```

Fixed-Width Format

```
Student Number 1-5
Last Name 6-15
First Name 16-25
Major 26-50
Year 51-60
GPA 61-65
```

Random Access File Format

```
Private Type StudentRecord
    strLastName As String * 10
    strFirstName As String * 10
    strMajor As String * 25
    strYear As String * 10
    strGPA As Single
End Type
```

4. Write a program that opens a fixed-width format file and saves it to a random access file.

5. Write a program the opens a comma-delimited file and saves it to a random access file.

6. Write a program that opens a random access file and saves it to a fixed-width format file.

7. Write a program that opens a random access file and saves it to a comma-delimited file.

8. Write a program that opens a comma-delimited file and saves it to a fixed-width format file.

9. Write a program that opens a fixed-width format file and saves it as a comma-delimited file.

10. Modify the case study so the user can click on a button so that any changes made to the data are not saved automatically as in the current implementation.

INTERVIEW

An Interview with Aric Levin

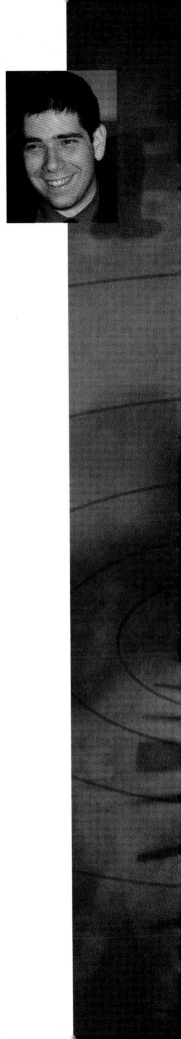

Aric Levin is the Vice President of Technology at Westside Technologies, a consulting firm that designs and implements advanced information management systems based on Microsoft Technologies. Among other projects, Aric manages the software development efforts and infrastructure needs of one of Westside Technologies' major clients, Sound Dogs, the premier sound design team for Hollywood's feature film industry. Aric started as one of the software developers who created Sounddogs.com, the host site of their vast sound effects library, with over 70,000 sound effects.

What is your educational background?

I started my computer training in high school and was trained in computers in the IDF (Israeli army), 1 year of USC after which I continued my studies in AICS. Most of my educational background was received on the job.

What was your first job in the computer industry? What did it entail?

My first job in the industry was working for a Microsoft Certified Technical Education Center. I was teaching Microsoft, Borland, and Lotus technologies through private lessons, class instruction and lecturing in seminars.

How did you use Visual Basic to create the Sound Dogs Sound Effects Library? Why was it chosen as the software to employ?

Sound Dogs sells sound effect files over the Internet using an automated system. VB was primarily chosen for the low cost of maintenance, and high connectivity value (i.e., it could easily connect with components from inside the company as well as outside). As the effect library website grew, we were able to scale it up, using more and more advanced technologies that VB let us produce. At each point, there were no other design tools that would let us produce this quality of software, with this rate of scalability at the cost we were paying our developers.

Has it been difficult or relatively easy to update the Library to new versions of VB? How will Visual Basic .NET enhance the site?

The site was continually upgraded to incorporate new VB features. When we started, we were using Visual Basic 4 with a custom CGI interface. At a later stage, we moved up to SQL server with Visual Basic 5, then Visual Basic 6 with COM+. Finally, we have moved to a fully transactional system, using stored procedures, ASP, different VB components running on different systems and several systems distributing the overall processing load.

VB .NET will allow us to extend our services to end users and sound-effect consumers with very little overhead. We will be able to offer extended services to programs that want to integrate our sound effects search and retrieval directly into their end-user applications. VB .NET's web development platform will be a welcomed enhancement to our development systems.

What are some of the strengths/weaknesses of VB and now VB .NET that you've encountered?

VB's strength is the easy maintenance and quick development, that incorporates component development to scale up applications (And reduce development cost).

VB .NET has a few weaknesses that we've seen so far. The first is that it is a non-trivial task to upgrade existing projects to VB .NET due to major language overhaul (i.e., a costly learning curve and upgrade cost for our existing codebase). In addition, the new CLR library will take a while to get a grasp on. Finally, Intermediate language regresses VB back to its P-Code (non-compiled) days.

CHAPTER 10

Introduction to Database Concepts

When computers were first invented, their capacity to store data was very limited. Their main purpose was to perform calculations faster and more accurately than a human. As the capability to store more data grew, the need for a way to store, organize, and access this data in a more systematic manner became apparent.

If data were stored on a hard drive in no apparent order, it would be just that, data. Data can be thought of as the raw values obtained from a process. However, if that data is organized into a meaningful format so that it becomes valuable in answering questions, it has become **information**.

This is a key issue as you start to explore databases. A database is a collection of tables organized so that the data makes sense. A **table** usually contains data relating to one entity. One table may contain the demographic information for a person, while another table may contain the payroll information related to that person. In relational databases, a common field would link these tables so that a person's payroll information could be easily associated with their demographic information.

Observe the following table that stores the names of six basketball players and their statistics. It contains a **field** for each piece of data being stored: Last Name, First Name, Team, Games Played, Points, Rebounds, and Assists.

Figure 10.1
PlayerStats Table

You may notice that a table looks very much like the MS flex grid you used earlier. While it contains rows (known as **records**) and columns (known as **fields**) and is similar in appearance, tables have an important difference. **Data validation** occurs when values are entered into a table. When data is entered into a table, it is checked to make sure it doesn't violate any rules set forth by the creator of the table. Different software packages, known as **database management systems (DBMS)**, allow the user to specify different types of constraints on the data being entered. Universally, all DBMS verify that the data being entered in each field matches the type of data that was specified. When this table was created, the following datatypes were associated with each field:

Field Name	Datatype	Size
Last Name	Text	15
First Name	Text	10
Team	Text	15
Games Played	Number	Integer
Points	Number	Integer
Rebounds	Number	Integer
Assists	Number	Integer

Other constraints can be placed on data, but the extent to which a programmer can specify rules to do so depends highly on the choice of DBMS used.

10.1 Displaying Data Stored in a Database

One of the single most important features of Visual Basic is the ease with which it allows the programmer to access data stored in a database. By providing controls to interface with the database, much of the complexity of database programming is removed. For simplicity's sake, you will only access one table at a time in this chapter. However, in Chapter 11 you will explore how to relate data from one table to another.

Using the Data Control

The **data** control is one of 21 default controls (Figure 10.2) that appear in the Control toolbar. Observe the following figure that shows what the control looks like in the toolbar, and Figure 10.3 that shows what the control looks like when placed on a form:

Figure 10.2
Data Control

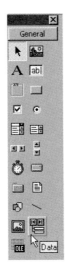

Figure 10.3
Data Control on
Form

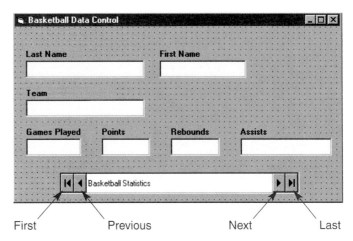

When a correctly configured data control is placed on the form, and text box controls are configured to access the data provided by the data control, information from a database can be displayed and manipulated in your form.

By placing a data control on the form and associating all the text boxes with their corresponding fields in the database, you can display the following information when the form loads:

Figure 10.4
Application Using Data
Control

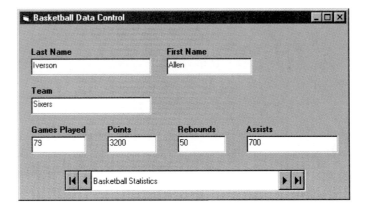

When a form loads with a data control and associated text boxes, it will display the first record in the table it is associated with. Since Allen Iverson was the first player in the table, his data is shown.

If you wish to move to the next record in the table, click on the `Next` button. All of the values contained in the text boxes are automatically are updated with the data in the next record of the table. In this case, you move to record 2, the data associated with Eric Snow. This is shown in the following figure:

Figure 10.5
Application Showing Second
Record of Table

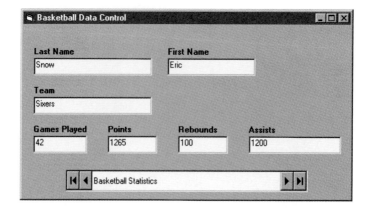

Moving one record at a time may be a little slow, especially if there is a large number of records in the table. Therefore, this control allows you to move directly to the last record in the table by clicking on the Last button. This displays the data related to Marcus Camby as shown in the following figure:

Figure 10.6
Application Showing Last
Record in Table

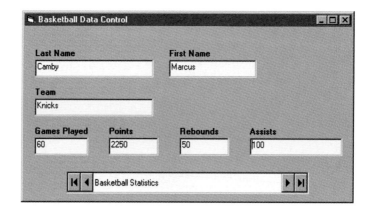

If you want to move one record back, you can use the Previous button. Moving back from the last record places you at the next to last record, belonging to Shaquille O'Neal. This is shown in the following figure:

Figure 10.7
Application Showing Next
to Last Record in Table

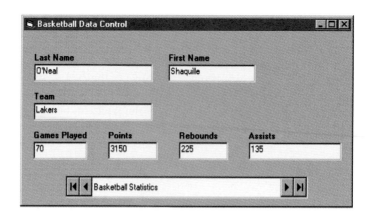

If you wish to return to the first record, you can use the First button.

DRILL I0.I

You may have noticed a pattern to the style of these buttons. Can you guess what it is?

Configuring the Controls

The first step in creating a form that accesses a database is to add a data control to the form. In order for the data control to be linked with the desired table, certain properties must be set.

Although not required, it is a good practice to change the name of the data control from its default name to a name starting with "dat" and ending in a meaningful phrase that describes the table. In your case, you will call the data control `datBasketball`.

Additionally, it is always a good practice to change the `Caption` property to display a meaningful name on the form when the data control is shown. In your case, you will change the `Caption` to `Basketball Statistics`.

Setting the Connect Property

The first step in connecting to a database is to select the type of database that you wish to connect. By clicking on the `Connect` property, a list of possible data sources is presented. You are going to select Access, but you can select from other database files types as well as other data-storing types like Excel.

Figure 10.8
Setting `Connect` Property

Setting the Database Name

The next step is to select the database name to connect to. This can be accomplished in two ways. Either you can enter the exact file path directly, or you can click on the <...> button from within the `DatabaseName's` property window and select the file from the hard drive.

Setting the RecordSource

Although your example only contains a single table, most applications will use more than one table. The file that you selected in the `DatabaseName` property selected a database, not a table. With the `RecordSource` property, you select the individual table to use for this data control. In your example, you will select the table `PlayerStats`.

Connecting Other Controls to the Database

In your example, you connected each text box to an individual field in the table. With the connection to the database already complete, the only remaining task is to connect each text box to the field you wish to associate it with. The procedure is the same for each text box.

First, you must set the `DataSource` property of the text box so that the text box knows which database it will be associated with. Although we haven't mentioned it, it's possible to have more than one data control placed on the form simultaneously. In your form, there is only one `DataSource`, `datBasketball`.

Figure 10.9
Setting `DataSource` Property

Additionally, you need to specify which field within the table is specified by the `DataSource`. This is done by specifying the `DataField` property. When the `DataSource` has already been specified, the `DataField` will be preloaded with a pull-down menu that contains all of the fields in the table. Select one field from the list to associate it with the text box control.

Figure 10.10
Setting `DataField`
Property

You must have the data control already configured before attempting to set the individual controls to access the database. Otherwise, the selections in the property field will not be preloaded as they were in your example.

Controlling the Database with Code

Visual Basic allows you to navigate the database programmatically. Because the interface provided by a data control is not necessarily the one you wish to use in all applications, you can write code and associate it with command buttons to develop the interface you desire.

For simplicity's sake, we will demonstrate how to mimic the actions of a data control by creating four command buttons: `cmdFirst`, `cmdNext`, `cmdPrevious`, and `cmdLast`.

When you created a data control on your form and associated the Access table with it by using the `RecordSource`, you created an object called a `RecordSet`. A `RecordSet` is an object that provides a way to interface with a table or results from an executed command. It will provide an interface to commands that you will require when manipulating the table in Visual Basic.

MoveFirst and MoveLast   This is identical to the operation performed when the user clicked on the First or Last button of the data control. When the programmer issues a `MoveFirst` or a `MoveLast` command to the `RecordSet`, the first record in the table is considered the current record. Any controls bound to the `RecordSet` will have their values automatically updated to the corresponding fields in this record.

To issue the `MoveFirst` command, use the following syntax:

DataControl`.RecordSet.MoveFirst`

In your basketball example, you would use the following code:

`datBasketball.RecordSet.MoveFirst`

To issue the `MoveLast` command, use the following syntax:

DataControl`.RecordSet.MoveLast`

In your basketball example, you would use the following code:

```
datBasketball.RecordSet.MoveLast
```

MoveNext and MovePrevious You might think that using the commands `MoveNext` and `MovePrevious` are as straightforward. Indeed in most ways they are; however, there is an important consideration to bear in mind.

These two commands follow the same syntax as in the following two examples to issue the `MoveNext` and `MovePrevious` commands:

```
DataControl.RecordSet.MoveNext
```

and

```
DataControl.RecordSet.MovePrevious
```

To issue them in your basketball example, you would use the following code:

```
datBasketball.RecordSet.MoveNext
```

or

```
datBasketball.RecordSet.MovePrevious
```

So where is the complication? What happens if you issue a `MovePrevious` command when the `RecordSet` is pointing to the first record in the table?

By trying to move before the first or after the last record of a table, you will get a run-time error similar to the following figure:

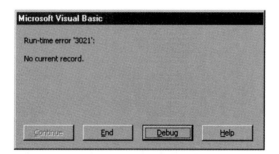

Figure 10.11
Run-Time Error for BOF
or EOF

The solution to the problem is simple enough. Visual Basic provides two functions, `BOF` and `EOF`, to check to see if you are at the beginning or end of the file. By checking after you move to the previous or next record for BOF or EOF, you can warn users that they have moved past the beginning or end of the file and move them back to the first or last record. This is shown in the following two sets of code:

```
Private Sub cmdPrev_Click()
datBasketball.RecordSet.MovePrevious

If (datBasketball.RecordSet.BOF = True) Then
  MsgBox "You are at the first record in the table"
  datBasketball.RecordSet.MoveNext
```

(continues)

(continued)

```
End If
End Sub

Private Sub cmdNext_Click()
datBasketball.RecordSet.MoveNext

If (datBasketball.RecordSet.EOF = True) Then
   MsgBox "You are at the last record in the table"
   datBasketball.RecordSet.MovePrevious
End If
End Sub
```

TIP

By using the `With` command, you can shorten the amount of code required when dealing with complex references like `datControlName.Recordset.Property`. Observe the rewritten code for `cmdNext_Click()`.

```
Private Sub cmdNext_Click()

With datBasketball.RecordSet
   .MoveNext

   If (.EOF = True) Then
       MsgBox "You are at the last record in the table"
       .MovePrevious
   End If
End With
End Sub
```

Using AbsolutePosition and RecordCount

While your solution to the problem of moving past the first or last record of a table is certainly functional, it doesn't subscribe to good application development practices. Why allow the user to make the mistake to begin with? If you know the user is at the first record, why not disable the `cmdPrevious` command button? Likewise, if the user is at the last record, you could disable the `cmdNext` command button.

By using the `RecordCount` and `AbsolutePosition` properties of a recordset, you can compare the current position within the `RecordSet` to the total number of records and recognize when you are about to move past the last record in the table. By comparing the `AbsolutePosition` to 0, you can tell if you are at the first record.

Using this information, you can rewrite your command button code to take advantage of this feature. First, you will disable the `cmdPrev` button since the `RecordSet` will be positioned at the first record and there will be no reason to move forward from the initial record. The code for the `Form_Load` event follows:

```
Private Sub Form_Load()
cmdPrev.Enabled = False
End Sub
```

The code for cmdFirst's Click event moves to the first record, but also disables the cmdPrev command button. Although you might not need to enable cmdNext's command button because it may already be enabled, it doesn't hurt to enable it again. If you checked to see if it were enabled before you actually set it, you would be wasting code and time.

```
Private Sub cmdFirst_Click()
datBasketball.RecordSet.MoveFirst
cmdPrev.Enabled = False
cmdNext.Enabled = True
End Sub
```

Similarly, the code for cmdLast's Click event follows:

```
Private Sub cmdLast_Click()
datBasketball.RecordSet.MoveLast
cmdNext.Enabled = False
cmdPrev.Enabled = True
End Sub
```

The code for the cmdPrev command button changes a bit from before. Now, you no longer have to check to see if you are at the beginning of the file because the command button will be disabled if you are at the first record.

However, you do need to check to see if moving to the previous record causes the current record to become the first record. You can do this by comparing the AbsolutePosition of the RecordSet to 0. If you are at the first record, disable the cmdPrev command button. Additionally, enable the cmdNext command button because you know that if you have moved to the previous record, you can't be at the last record. The code follows:

```
Private Sub cmdPrev_Click()
With datBasketball.RecordSet
  .MovePrevious

  If (.AbsolutePosition = 0) Then
    cmdPrev.Enabled = False
  End If
End With

cmdNext.Enabled = True

End Sub
```

The code for the cmdNext command button is similar to that of cmdPrev's command button. However, instead of comparing the AbsolutePosition to 0, you need to compare it to the total number of records in the table. This can be determined using the RecordCount property. RecordCount returns the total number of records in the table. Since AbsolutePosition returns the position within the table, starting at 0, you need to compare RecordCount to AbsolutePosition + 1 to determine if you have reached the last record in the database.

```
Private Sub cmdNext_Click()
With datBasketball.RecordSet
  .MoveNext
```

(continues)

(continued)

```
If (.RecordCount = .AbsolutePosition + 1) Then
  cmdNext.Enabled = False
End If

End With

cmdPrev.Enabled = True

End Sub
```

10.2 Adding and Editing Data in a Database

The data that you have been viewing in your table was placed there directly in the database application. Visual Basic gives you two operations that will allow you to add and update records in a table.

To add a record to a table connected to a data control, three steps must be followed:

Step 1: All of the data-bound controls must be cleared. By issuing the following statement, you can accomplish this.

> *DataControl*`.RecordSet.AddNew`

Step 2: Update all of the data-bound controls to the value you wish stored in the new record in the database. This can be accomplished either by using the data-bound control interactively, or by issuing the following statement:

DataControl`.RecordSet.Fields(`"*FieldName*"`).Value = `*NewValue*

Step 3: The new data must be saved to the database using the following statement:

> *DataControl*`.RecordSet.Update`

Complete Example of Adding a Record

The following code could be executed if you wish to add a new record to your PlayerStats table with the data: `"Jones"`, `"Jumaine"`, `"Sixers"`, 30, 500, 120, 100.

```
With datBasketball.RecordSet
   .AddNew
.Fields("Last Name").Value = "Jones"
.Fields("First Name").Value = "Jumaine"
.Fields("Team").Value = "Sixers"
.Fields("Games Played").Value = 30
.Fields("Points").Value = 500
.Fields("Rebounds").Value = 120
.Fields("Assists").Value = 100
.Update
End With
```

TIP

If you are wondering where the field names came from, refer back to the table shown in Figure 10.1.

TIP

The order in which you set the individual fields in a table does not matter.

Editing an Existing Record

The only difference between adding a new record and editing an existing record is using the .AddNew statement for adding and .Edit for editing the contents of a record. As long as the record you wish to update is your current record, you can issue an .Edit command, update the data fields you desire, and then issue the .Update command.

Problems with Modifying the Database

Just as you had potential problems with moving past the last record or before the first record of a database, problems exist if you move to another record before you save the changes made to either an existing record or a new one.

Nothing prevents the user from switching to another record using one of the navigational command buttons. If this occurs, the changes made to the current records are lost. While you could write your application to save the changes automatically, this could lead to unwanted changes being committed to the database.

The solution is to enable and disable the navigational command button, the data saving command button, as well as the text boxes. Observe a new version of your application with cmdAdd, cmdSave, cmdEdit, and cmdCancel command buttons added.

You can see the initial setup for the application in the following figure:

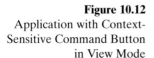

Figure 10.12
Application with Context-Sensitive Command Button in View Mode

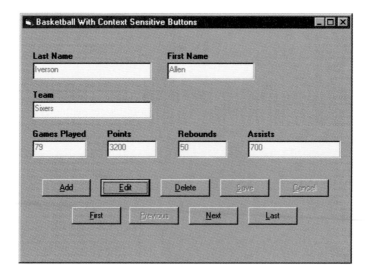

When you navigate from record to record, you should not be able to make changes to the text boxes' contents. You can see in the previous figure that all of the text boxes are disabled. Additionally, when you are navigating, there is no reason to use the `cmdSave` or `cmdCancel` command button. Therefore, they are disabled as well.

However, if you add or edit a record, all of the navigational buttons should be disabled as well as the `cmdAdd` and `cmdEdit` command buttons. The text boxes will all be enabled as well as the `cmdSave` and `cmdCancel` command buttons. This is shown in the following figure:

Figure 10.13
Application with Context-Sensitive Command Button in Edit Mode

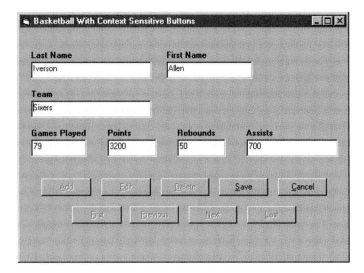

Because you will enable and disable the text boxes from multiple locations within the code, it is best to write two subroutines: `DisableTextBoxes` and `EnableTextBoxes`. These will be called from the data-saving command buttons to disable the text boxes when the user is navigating through the records in the table, and enable the text boxes when the user is about to edit or add data to the table. The code for both functions follows:

```
Private Sub DisableTextBoxes()
txtLast.Enabled = False
txtFirst.Enabled = False
txtTeam.Enabled = False
txtGamesPlayed.Enabled = False
txtPoints.Enabled = False
txtRebounds.Enabled = False
txtAssists.Enabled = False
End Sub

Private Sub EnableTextBoxes()
txtLast.Enabled = True
txtFirst.Enabled = True
txtTeam.Enabled = True
txtGamesPlayed.Enabled = True
txtPoints.Enabled = True
txtRebounds.Enabled = True
txtAssists.Enabled = True
End Sub
```

Similarly to the navigational buttons, the data-saving buttons will be enabled and disabled from multiple locations. Therefore you will create two subroutines: `SetDataSaveButtons` and `SetDataButtons`. The `SetDataSaveButtons` subroutine will enable the `cmdSave` and `cmdCancel` command buttons and also disable the `cmdAdd` and `cmdEdit` command buttons. The code follows:

```
Private Sub SetDataSaveButtons()
cmdAdd.Enabled = False
cmdEdit.Enabled = False
cmdSave.Enabled = True
cmdCancel.Enabled = True
End Sub
```

The `SetDataButtons` subroutines will enable the `cmdAdd` and `cmdEdit` command buttons while disabling the `cmdSave` and `cmdCancel` command buttons.

```
Private Sub SetDataButtons()
cmdAdd.Enabled = True
cmdEdit.Enabled = True
cmdSave.Enabled = False
cmdCancel.Enabled = False
End Sub
```

In order to disable all the navigational command buttons when you add or edit a record, you developed a subroutine `DisableNavButtons` to handle the statements required. This is shown in the following code:

```
Private Sub DisableNavButtons()
cmdFirst.Enabled = False
cmdLast.Enabled = False
cmdNext.Enabled = False
cmdPrev.Enabled = False
End Sub
```

Finally, when you cancel or save changes to a record, or when you first load the form, you are going to have to set the navigational command buttons based on the number of records in the table and the current record. This was placed into a subroutine, `SetNavButtons`, so that the code would not have to be repeated. The code follows:

```
Private Sub SetNavButtons()
With datBasketball.RecordSet

    'CmdPrev should be disabled when we are at the first record
    If (.AbsolutePosition = 0) Then
        cmdPrev.Enabled = False
    Else
        cmdPrev.Enabled = True
    End If

    'CmdNext should be disabled when we are at the last record
    If (.AbsolutePosition + 1 = .RecordCount) Then
        cmdNext.Enabled = False
    Else
```

(continues)

(continued)

```
        cmdNext.Enabled = True
    End If

    cmdFirst.Enabled = True
    cmdLast.Enabled = True
End With
End Sub
```

The four `Click` events for the navigational command buttons are straightforward.

```
Private Sub cmdFirst_Click()
datBasketball.RecordSet.MoveFirst
cmdPrev.Enabled = False
cmdNext.Enabled = True
End Sub

Private Sub cmdLast_Click()
datBasketball.RecordSet.MoveLast
cmdNext.Enabled = False
cmdPrev.Enabled = True
End Sub

Private Sub cmdNext_Click()
With datBasketball.Recordset
  .MoveNext

If (.RecordCount = .AbsolutePosition + 1) Then
   cmdNext.Enabled = False
End If

End With

cmdPrev.Enabled = True

End Sub

Private Sub cmdPrev_Click()
With datBasketball.RecordSet
  .MovePrevious

  If (.AbsolutePosition = 0) Then
     cmdPrev.Enabled = False
  End If
End With

cmdNext.Enabled = True
End Sub
```

Armed with these six subroutines, writing the four save data command button events (`Add`, `Cancel`, `Edit`, `Delete`) is greatly simplified.

When the user clicks on the `cmdAdd` command button, the application must enable all of the text boxes. This is accomplished with a call to the `EnableTextBoxes` subroutine. Then the navigational command buttons must be disabled, which is accomplished by a call to the `DisableNavButtons` subroutine. Then the application must toggle the save data command buttons so the ones that were enabled (`cmdAdd` and `cmdEdit`) are disabled and the ones that were disabled (`cmdSave` and `cmdCancel`) are enabled. This is done with a call to `SetSaveDataButtons`. Finally, the `.AddNew` command is issued to the data control's recordset. This is shown in the following code:

```
Private Sub cmdAdd_Click()
Call EnableTextBoxes
Call DisableNavButtons
Call SetDataSaveButtons

datBasketball.RecordSet.AddNew
End Sub
```

When the user clicks on the `cmdCancel` command button, the application must disable all of the text boxes. This is accomplished with a call to the `DisableTextBoxes` subroutine. Then the navigational command buttons must be enabled, which is accomplished by a call to the `SetNavButtons` subroutine. Then the application must toggle the save data command buttons so the ones that were disabled (`cmdAdd` and `cmdEdit`) are enabled and the ones that were enabled (`cmdSave` and `cmdCancel`) are disabled. This is done with a call to `SetDataButtons`. Finally, in order to cancel any pending updates, the `.CancelUpdate` command is issued to the data control's recordset. This is shown in the following code:

```
Private Sub cmdCancel_Click()
Call DisableTextBoxes
Call SetNavButtons
Call SetDataButtons
datBasketball.RecordSet.CancelUpdate
End Sub
```

When the user clicks on the `cmdEdit` command button, the application must enable all of the text boxes. This is accomplished with a call to the `EnableTextBoxes` subroutine. Then the navigational command buttons must be disabled, which is accomplished by a call to the `DisableNavButtons` subroutine. Then the application must toggle the save data command buttons so the ones that were enabled (`cmdAdd` and `cmdEdit`) are disabled and the ones that were disabled (`cmdSave` and `cmdCancel`) are enabled. This is done with a call to `SetDataSaveButtons`. Finally, the `.Edit` command is issued to the data control's recordset. This is shown in the following code:

```
Private Sub cmdEdit_Click()
Call EnableTextBoxes
Call DisableNavButtons
Call SetDataSaveButtons
datBasketball.RecordSet.Edit
End Sub
```

When the user clicks on the `cmdSave` command button, the application must disable all of the text boxes. This is accomplished with a call to the `DisableTextBoxes` subroutine. Then the navigational command buttons must be enabled, which is accomplished by a call to the SetNavButtons subroutine. Then the application must toggle the save data command buttons so the ones that were disabled (cmdAdd and cmdEdit) are enabled and the ones that were enabled (cmdSave and cmdCancel) are disabled. This is done with a call to SetDataButtons. Finally, the .Update command is issued to the data control's recordset. This is shown in the following code:

```
Private Sub cmdSave_Click()
Call DisableTextBoxes
Call SetNavButtons
Call SetDataButtons
datBasketball.RecordSet.Update
End Sub
```

10.3 Deleting Data in a Database

So far we have discussed all of the basic operations performed on records in a table except one. You still must learn how to delete a record from a database. While you may think it is as simple as issuing the .Delete command, you would be mistaken. Issues arise when you wish to delete either the last record in the table or the only record in the table.

The problem arises when you delete a record because you must move to one of the remaining records so that a valid record is displayed in the data-bound controls. However, where is a valid record? If you are on the first record of many, the answer is simple, the record after the first. This can be accessed by issuing a .MoveNext command to the data control. However, what if you are at the last record? Then the easiest way to access a valid record is to move to the record before the record you deleted. This can be accomplished with a .MovePrevious command.

The situation is further complicated if the record that you delete is the last record in the database. With no records remaining, you cannot move to a valid record! The following code shows the code required to delete a record. In the case that no records exist after the deletion, all command buttons except for cmdAdd are disabled.

```
Private Sub cmdDelete_Click()
With datBasketball.RecordSet
    'Delete Record
    .Delete

    'Attempt to Move to a Valid Record
    .MoveNext

    'If past last record
    If .EOF Then
        'Attempt to Move to a Valid Record
        .MovePrevious
        'If no records exist
        If .BOF Then
            'Disable the Navigational Controls
            Call DisableNavButtons
            'Only allow Adding a Record
            cmdAdd.Enabled = True
            cmdEdit.Enabled = False
```

(continues)

(continued)

```
            cmdDelete.Enabled = False
            cmdSave.Enabled = False
            cmdCancel.Enabled = False
        End If
    End If
End With
End Sub
```

WARNING

By adding the `cmdDelete` command button, additional changes must be made to your application. You need to add the `cmdDelete` command button to the subroutines `SetDataButtons` and `SetSaveDataButtons`. However, we will leave this as an exercise to the reader as you will code these subroutines properly in the case study later in this chapter.

10.4 Binding a Database to Combo Box Controls

The capability to link controls with a database doesn't end with a text box control. You can link a combo box so that the results of the user's selection are stored in the database. Additionally, you will find that you cannot only store the results in a database, but preload the combo box's from a table within the database.

Adding a Combo Box with a Manually Entered List

Observe the addition of a combo box to your application. You have preloaded the choices (Center, Forward, and Guard) manually using the List property that you have used in previous sections. By adding a Position field to the table PlayerStats in the database Basketball, you can bind the combo box in the same way you bound the text boxes to their associated database fields.

Figure 10.14
Application with Combo
Box Added

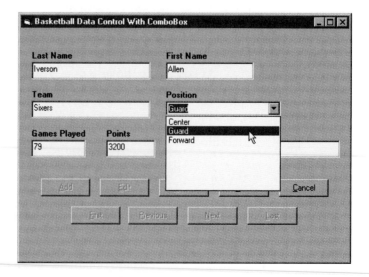

Step 1: Add a combo box named cboPosition to the form.
Step 2: Add the list choices Center, Forward, and Guard to the combo box using
        <CTRL> <ENTER> between each entry.
Step 3: Set the `DataSource` property to `datBasketball`.
Step 4: Set the `DataField` property to `Position`.

Now when you navigate through the database, the `cboPosition` combo box will reflect the values stored in the Position field of the PlayerStats table. However, other code must be changed in order to enable and disable the `cboPosition` combo box at the proper time.

The following code must be added to the `DisableTextBoxes` subroutine:

```
cboPosition.Enabled = False
```

The following code must also be added to the `EnableTextBoxes` subroutine:

```
cboPosition.Enabled = True
```

TIP

The default style of a combo box allows the user to enter values into the combo box other than those listed. When storing values in a database, this may not be desired. Fortunately, you can change the `Style` property to `2 - Dropdown List`, which will only allow selections to be made from the preloaded list.

Figure 10.15
Setting `Style` Property of
Combo Box

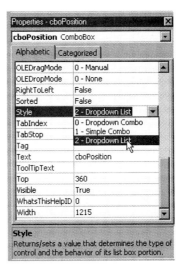

Adding a DB Combo with Database-Generated List

While it may seem convenient to add the choices to a combo box manually, in the real world, these choices may change over time. Once an application is deployed, changing manually entered combo box choices requires a change to the application. However, if you take advantage of the feature that allows these choices to be set from a database, only the values in the database would need to be changed.

This can be accomplished using a DB combo control. A DB combo is very similar to a combo box, except that it allows you to bind the choices for the `List` property to a field in a table.

Since a DB combo is not one of the default controls in the toolbar, you will have to add it. Select the Components menu from the Project menu. When the Components window appears (Figure 10.16) select the Microsoft Data Bound List Controls 6.0 check box. This will add two controls to the Control toolbar. The first, DB list, is similar to a list box, but with the capability to bind the `List` items to a database field in a table. The second, DB combo, is the one you wish to use in your current application.

Figure 10.17
Updated
Toolbar

Figure 10.16
Adding Data Bound
List Controls

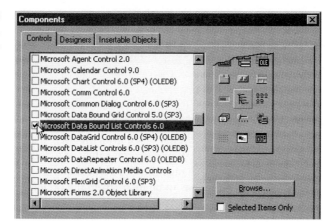

In order for a DB combo control to behave the way you wish, you must specify sources for the preloaded list of choices as well as the field in the table to bind the selection to.

First, you must specify the source of the preloaded list. This is accomplished with two properties, `RowSource` and `ListField`. `RowSource` is used to specify the data control that will fill the DB combo control with values. `ListField` is used to select the specific field in the data control indicated by `RowSource`.

Next, you must specify the location to store the data you select. This is accomplished with the two properties `DataSource` and `BoundColumn`. `DataSource` is used to specify the data control that will bind the choice to a table specified by the data control. `BoundColumn` is used to select the specific field in the data control indicated by `DataSource` to store the selected choice.

Adding DB Combo Controls to Your Form

Let's add this control to your application for the Position and Team fields in the PlayerStats table. Each DB combo control will link to a table with predetermined choices. So, you need to create a Position table with the field Position. The table will contain three records: Center, Guard, and Forward. Likewise, you will create a table called League with a field called Team. It will contain a record for every team in the league.

Once these two tables are created, you can add two DB combo controls, one linked to each field.

You will need a Data control for each table, one for the Team information and one for the Position information. The following steps will create them:

Add a Data Control for Team Information

Step 1: Add a data control to the form.

Step 2: Change the Name properties to datTeam.

Step 3: Change the DatabaseName to the actual name of the database file, in my case C:\VB Coach\Chapter 9\Basketball.mdb.

Step 4: Change the RecordSource to Team.

Add a Data Control for Position Information

Step 1: Add another data control to the form.

Step 2: Change the Name property to datPosition.

Step 3: Change the DatabaseName to the actual name of the database file, in my case C:\VB Coach\Chapter 9\Basketball.mdb.

Step 4: Change the RecordSource to Position.

Add a DB Combo Control for Team Selection

Step 1: Add a DB combo control to the form.

Step 2: Change the Name property to dbcTeam.

Step 3: Set the RowSource property to datTeam.

Step 4: Set the DataSource property to datBasketball.

Step 5: Set the BoundColumn property to Team.

Step 6: Set the DataField property to Team.

Step 7: Set the ListField property to Team.

Step 8: Set the Style to 2 - dbcDropdownList, so users will not be able to add their own teams to the list.

Step 9: Clear the Text property.

Add a DB Combo Control for Position Selection

Step 1: Add a DB combo control to the form.

Step 2: Change the Name property to dbcPosition.

Step 3: Set the RowSource property to datPosition.

Step 4: Set the DataSource property to datBasketball.

Step 5: Set the BoundColumn property to Position.

Step 6: Set the DataField property to Position.

Step 7: Set the ListField property to Position.

Step 8: Set the Style to 2 - dbcDropdownList, so user will not be able to add their own positions to the list.

Step 9: Clear the Text property.

 TIP

With the addition of command buttons to your application, there is no need to display the data controls. By setting the Visible property to False, the data controls can be hidden.

10.5 **Binding a Database to Grid Controls**

While binding database values to a control like a DB combo or text box can be useful, it is a tedious task if you wish to bind all the fields of a table to controls. Also, it only allows the values of a single record to be viewed at a time. This can be solved by using a data bound grid.

The MS flex grid that we introduced in Chapter 7 will not be sufficient to directly map data from a table to a grid. Instead, you need to use a different control.

A data grid is not one of the default controls in the toolbar, so you will have to add it. Select the Components menu from the Projects menu. When the Components window appears (Figure 10.18) select the Microsoft Data Bound Grid Control 5.0 check box. This will add a data grid control to the Control toolbar.

Figure 10.18
Adding Data Bound
Grid Controls

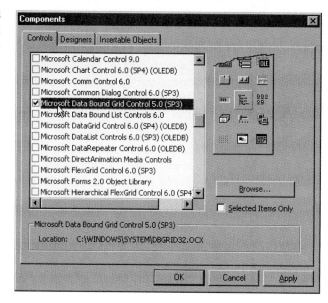

Figure 10.19
Updated
Toolbar

Using a data grid bound to a data control and minimal specifications, it is possible to create the following application that functions as a complete database application:

Figure 10.20
Application Using Data
Bound Grid Control

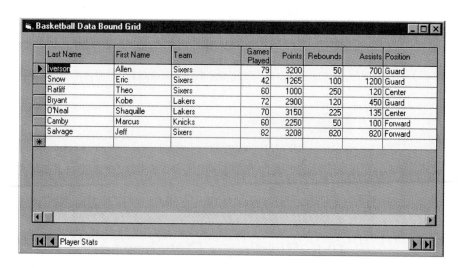

The data grid control retrieves all records in the table specified in the data control and allows the user to add, edit, or delete any records at will. If the data grid is not large enough to display the entire set of fields, a scroll bar will appear at the bottom of the grid, as it does here, to allow the user to access all of the fields in the table. If more rows exist than can be displayed at once, a vertical scroll bar will appear to the right, allowing the user to access any record.

To create this application, you must first create a data control.

Add a Data Control for the PlayerStats Information

Step 1: Add a data control to the form.
Step 2: Change the `Name` property to `datBasketball`.
Step 3: Change the `DatabaseName` to the actual name of the database file, in my case `C:\VB Coach\Chapter 10\Basketball.mdb`.
Step 4: Change the `RecordSource` to `PlayerStats`.

Specifying the Basketball data grid Control

Step 1: Add a data grid control to the form.
Step 2: Change the `Name` property to `grdBasketball`.
Step 3: Set the `DataSource` property to `datBasketball`.
Step 4: Set the `AllowAddNew` property to `True`.
Step 5: Set the `AllowAddDelete` property to `True`.

One big disadvantage of the data grid is that it does not allow you to control the input of data with controls like combo boxes, which allow only predetermined choices to be entered for a field. This is a major annoyance that can be fixed in one of two ways. First, you can buy a third-party plug-in that provides a grid with the features you desire. Since there are an endless number of companies and controls, the coverage of them is outside the scope of this text.

However, we won't leave you hanging without a solution. In Chapter 12 we will cover applications with multiple forms and solve the problem in that way.

◆ 10.6 Case Study

Problem Description   With the addition of the databases, you can now store the information about your Payroll Accounting System in a table. Since you can now store many records efficiently, you will now track work by the day instead of by the week.

The following figure will demonstrate what your application will look like:

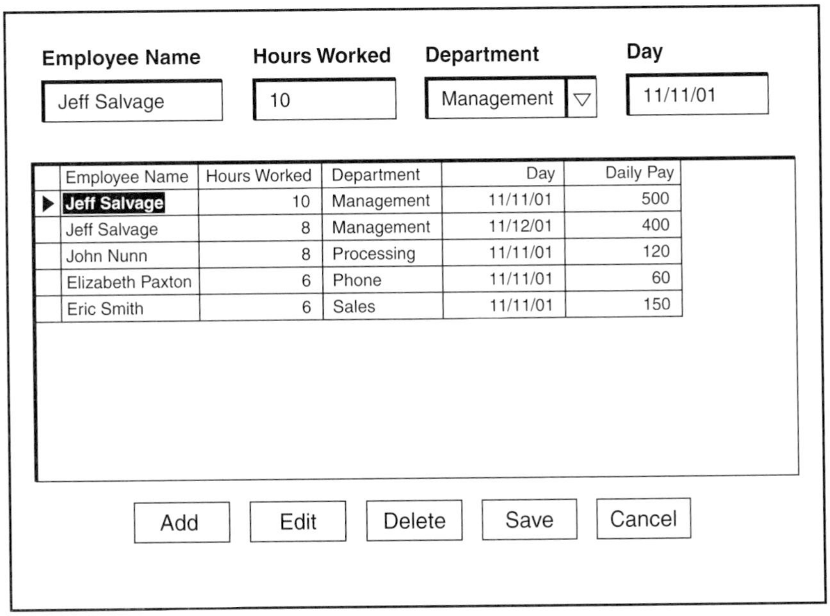

Figure 10.21
Case Study with Grid
Control and Database
Connectivity

Problem Discussion   The real-world use of a data bound grid requires some compromises. You cannot simply place a grid on a form and let the user enter, edit, and delete data at will. Data entered into a real system must be validated for correctness. The easiest way to do this is to let the grid present the data to the user and let the user select the current record in an easy manner. Then you can allow data entry of the current record into text boxes and combo boxes, where you can validate whether the information is valid.

Problem Solution   You need two data sources for your application. One will link to a table containing the Payroll information you wish to store and the other will contain the valid choices for the department.

Add a Data Control for the Payroll Information

Step 1: Add a data control to the form.
Step 2: Change the `Name` property to `datPayroll`.
Step 3: Set the `DatabaseName` property to the filename containing your database; mine is `C:\VB Coach\Chapter 10\Payroll.mdb`.
Step 4: Set the `RecordSource` property to `Payroll`.
Step 5: Set the `Visible` property to `False`.

Add a Data Control for the Department Information

Step 1: Add a data control to the form.
Step 2: Change the `Name` property to `datDepartment`.
Step 3: Set the `DatabaseName` property to the filename containing your database; mine is `C:\VB Coach\Chapter 10\Payroll.mdb`.
Step 4: Set the `RecordSource` property to `Department`.
Step 5: Set the `Visible` property to `False`.

Add a DB Grid to the Form

You need to add a DB grid to the form, link it to the Payroll database, and then disable it so that the user cannot edit directly within it.

Step 1: Add a DB grid control to the form.
Step 2: Change the `Name` property to `grdPayroll`.
Step 3: Set the `DataSource` property to `datPayroll`.
Step 4: Set the `AllowUpdate` property to `False`.

Specifying the Employee Name Text Box Control

Step 1: Add a text box control to the form.
Step 2: Change the `Name` property to `txtEmployeeName`.
Step 3: Set the `DataSource` property to `datPayroll`.
Step 4: Set the `DataField` property to `EmployeeName`.

Specifying the Hours Worked Text Box Control

Step 1: Add a text box control to the form.
Step 2: Change the `Name` property to `txtHoursWorked`.
Step 3: Set the `DataSource` property to `datPayroll`.
Step 4: Set the `DataField` property to `HoursWorked`.

Specifying the Department DB Combo Control

Step 1: Add a DB combo control to the form.
Step 2: Change the `Name` property to `dbcDepartment`.
Step 3: Set the `DataSource` property to `datPayroll`.
Step 4: Set the `DataField` property to `Department`.
Step 5: Set the `BoundField` property to `Department`.

Step 6: Set the `RowSource` property to `datDepartment`.

Step 7: Set the `ListField` property to `Department`.

Specifying the Day Text Box Control

Step 1: Add a text box control to the form.

Step 2: Change the `Name` property to `txtDay`.

Step 3: Set the `DataSource` property to `datPayroll`.

Step 4: Set the `DataField` property to `Day`.

Add Command Buttons to the Form   Five command buttons must be added to the form. Each button implements one of the following operations: Add, Edit, Delete, Save, and Cancel.

The following five subroutines should be added to the form to allow coding of the `Click` events for the command button to be simplified:

◆ The first subroutine, `SetSaveDataButtons`, disables the Add, Edit, and Delete buttons, while enabling the Save and Cancel buttons.

```
Private Sub SetSaveDataButtons()
cmdAdd.Enabled = False
cmdEdit.Enabled = False
cmdDelete.Enabled = False
cmdSave.Enabled = True
cmdCancel.Enabled = True
End Sub
```

◆ The second subroutine, `SetDataButtons`, enables the Add, Edit, and Delete buttons, while disabling the Save and Cancel buttons.

```
Private Sub SetDataButtons()
cmdAdd.Enabled = True
cmdEdit.Enabled = True
cmdDelete.Enabled = True
cmdSave.Enabled = False
cmdCancel.Enabled = False
End Sub
```

◆ The third subroutine, `DisableDataEntryBoxes`, disables all of the data entry controls for a single record.

```
Private Sub DisableDataEntryBoxes()
txtEmployeeName.Enabled = False
txtHoursWorked.Enabled = False
dbcDepartment.Enabled = False
txtDay.Enabled = False
End Sub
```

◆ The fourth subroutine, `EnableDataEntryBoxes`, enables all of the data entry controls for a single record.

```
Private Sub EnableDataEntryBoxes()
txtEmployeeName.Enabled = True
txtHoursWorked.Enabled = True
dbcDepartment.Enabled = True
txtDay.Enabled = True
End Sub
```

◆ The fifth subroutine, `SetDailyPay`, calculates the daily pay for an individual record:

```
Private Sub SetDailyPay()
With datPayroll.RecordSet
    Select Case dbcDepartment
        Case "Sales"
            .Fields("Daily Pay") = Val(txtHoursWorked.Text) * intSalesPayRate
        Case "Processing"
            .Fields("Daily Pay") = Val(txtHoursWorked.Text) * intProcessingPayRate
        Case "Management"
            .Fields("Daily Pay") = Val(txtHoursWorked.Text) * intManagementPayRate
        Case "Phone"
            .Fields("Daily Pay") = Val(txtHoursWorked.Text) * intPhonePayRate
    End Select
End With
End Sub
```

Click Event Code for Command Buttons   When the user adds a record, you must disable the DB grid control so that the user cannot switch current records while data is being entered. Additionally, you need to enable all of the controls to enter data for a single record, as well as setting the command button so that you can save or cancel the changes made by the user. Finally, you issue the `.AddNew` command.

```
Private Sub cmdAdd_Click()
grdPayroll.Enabled = False
Call EnableDataEntryBoxes
Call SetDataSaveButtons

datPayroll.RecordSet.AddNew
End Sub
```

When the user saves a record, you must enable the DB grid control so that the user can switch the current record so that other data may be processed. Additionally, you need to disable all of the controls to enter data for a single record, as well as setting the command buttons so that you can add, edit, or delete a record. Finally, you issue the `.CancelUpdate` command.

```
Private Sub cmdCancel_Click()
grdPayroll.Enabled = True
Call DisableDataEntryBoxes
Call SetDataButtons
datPayroll.RecordSet.CancelUpdate
End Sub
```

The code to delete a record is identical to the code we discussed in Section 10.4. It is listed again here for convenience:

```
Private Sub cmdDelete_Click()
With datPayroll.RecordSet
    'Delete Record
    .Delete
```

(continues)

(continued)

```
        'Attempt to Move to a Valid Record
        .MoveNext

        'If past last record
        If .EOF Then
            'Attempt to Move to a Valid Record
            .MovePrevious
            'If no records exist
            If .BOF Then
                'Only allow Adding a Record
                cmdAdd.Enabled = True
                cmdEdit.Enabled = False
                cmdDelete.Enabled = False
                cmdSave.Enabled = False
                cmdCancel.Enabled = False
            End If
        End If
    End With
End Sub
```

When the user edits a record, you must disable the DB grid control so that the user cannot switch current records when data is being updated. Additionally, you need to enable all of the controls to enter data for a single record, as well as setting the command buttons so that you can save or cancel the changes made by the user. Finally, you issue the `.Edit` command.

```
Private Sub cmdEdit_Click()
grdPayroll.Enabled = False
Call EnableDataEntryBoxes
Call SetDataSaveButtons
datPayroll.RecordSet.Edit
End Sub
```

When the user saves a record, you must enable the DB grid control so that the user can switch the current record so that other data may be processed. Additionally, you need to disable all of the controls to enter data for a single record, as well as setting the command buttons so that you can add, edit, or delete a record. Finally, you issue the `.AddUpdate` command.

```
Private Sub cmdSave_Click()
grdPayroll.Enabled = True
Call DisableDataEntryBoxes
Call SetDataButtons

Call SetDailyPay

datPayroll.RecordSet.Update
End Sub
```

The final step is to initialize the buttons and disable the data entry controls when the form initializes:

```
Private Sub Form_Initialize()
Call SetDataButtons
Call DisableDataEntryBoxes
End Sub
```

Figure 10.22
Final Application

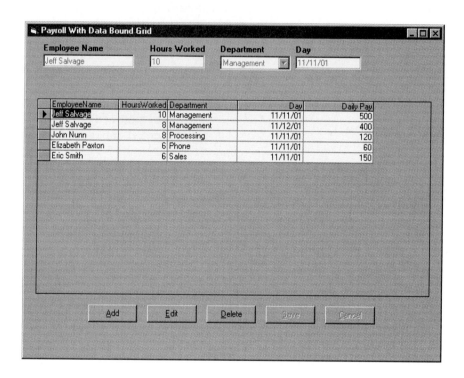

Beautifying a Data Grid Control

When you bound the data grid in Section 10.6, you used the default settings for the width of each field. This can create a problem if the type of data stored in each field varies. When one field has a maximum size that is much smaller than another, you should resize that field to only use as much space as is required.

While in design mode, if you right-click over the data grid control, a pop-up menu will appear as in the following figure:

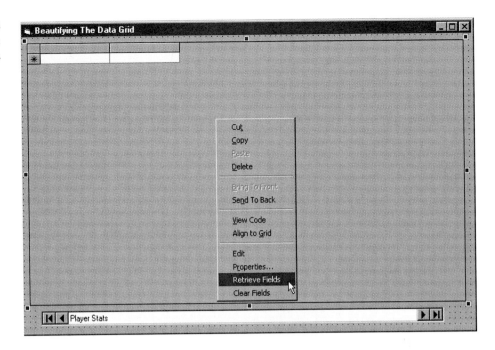

Figure 10.23
Pop-up Menu to Retrieve
Field Names

By selecting Retrieve Fields, the name of each field appears at the top of the grid, as shown in the following figure:

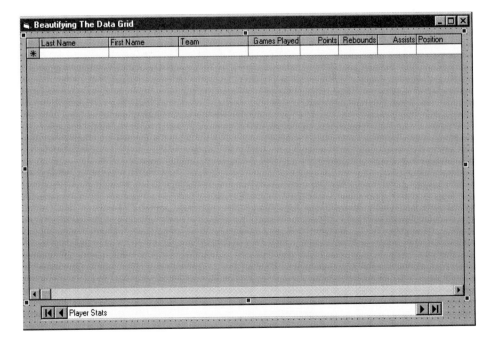

Figure 10.24
Data Bound Grid with Field
Names Retrieved

If you right-click again on the grid and select edit, you will gain the capability to resize the individual fields. By moving the mouse over the field dividers and then holding the mouse button down, you can move the divider to the left or right so that you can decrease or increase the size of the fields. This is shown in the following figure:

Figure 10.25
Editing Field Widths of a
Data Bound Grid

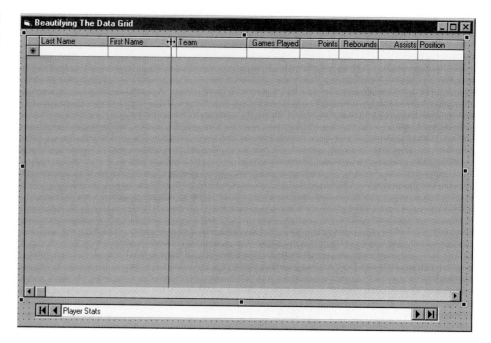

One last beautification can be accomplished by changing the `HeadLines` property to 2. This is useful because fields like Games Played do not require a wide enough column to display the entire name. By splitting the header title in two, the width of the field can be reduced while still being fully readable. The final application now looks as follows:

Figure 10.26
Updated View of Data
Bound Grid in Application

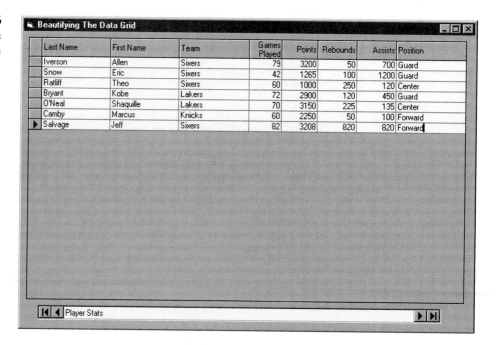

Setting Up an Access Database

While there are many different databases that Visual Basic can connect with, the most common is Microsoft Access. The following is a very brief explanation of how to create a new database with Microsoft Access.

To create a new database, start up Microsoft Access and select the new database option. You will be presented with the following window.

Figure 10.27
New Database Window

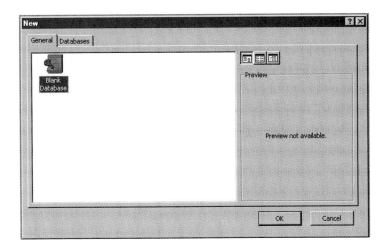

By clicking on Blank Database, you will be presented with a File New Database dialog box to select the filename and location of the new database. In the following figure you have selected the `Chapter 9` directory and have set the name to `NewDatabase`:

Figure 10.28
File New Database Dialog
Box

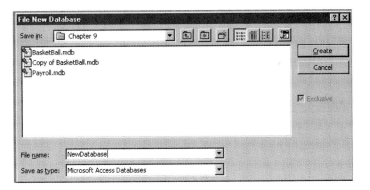

Once the name of the database has been chosen, you are presented with the Database form. It contains many options, but you will focus on the Tables tab. Currently, there are no tables in your database.

Figure 10.29
Database Form

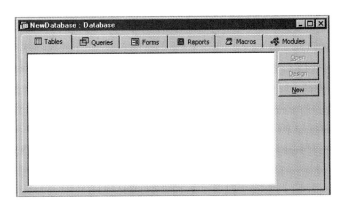

By clicking on the New button, you can add a table to the database. You have several choices for the method you may create the table; however, we will pick the Design View.

Figure 10.30
Table Creation Method

When Design View is selected, the following window appears allowing you to specify the fields for your table. You can type the Field Name in the first box of the form. (Unlike variable names, field names can contain spaces.)

Next you specify the type of data. Unlike Visual Basic, which stores textual data in a `String`, Access uses the `Text` datatype. `Text` is the default type.

Although optional, it is a good idea to fill out the Description field to add a comment to the field.

Finally, you can specify more details about the field in the General tab located at the bottom of the form. Highlighted below is the most used property, `Field Size`. Here it indicates a text size of 50, however, this is wasteful if your `Strings` won't be larger than 10. Set it to the maximum size of the `Text` field you are declaring.

Figure 10.31
Database Form

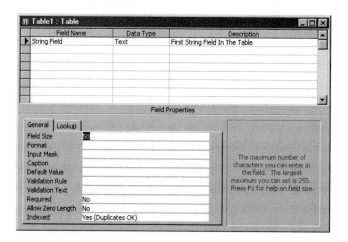

You can continue to add more fields in a similar manner. The choice of datatypes are shown in the following figure.

Figure 10.32
Different Datatypes

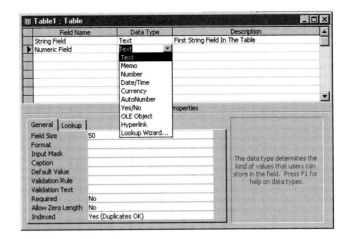

By selecting Number from the Data Type pull-down menu, you are presented with different size options within the Field Size property.

Figure 10.33
Numeric Field Added

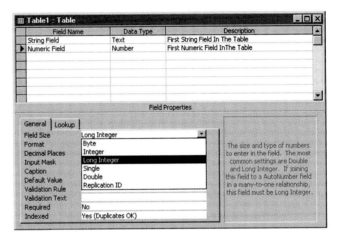

When you are finished adding all the fields, close the Design View. Because you didn't add a primary key (a unique index to improve efficiency), you will be presented with the following dialog box.

Figure 10.34
Database Form

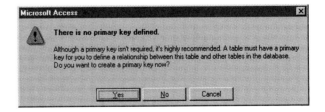

For now, do not create one. Simply click on the No button and the table will be created as in the following figure:

Figure 10.35
Database Form

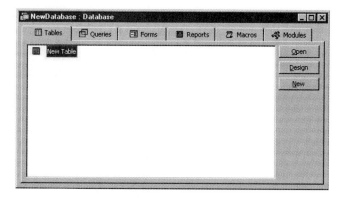

Using the Microsoft Visual Data Manager

While using Microsoft Access to create a database is easy, not every developer has access to Access (pardon the pun). For developers in this situation, Visual Basic comes with the Visual Data Manager.

The Visual Data Manager is fairly powerful and allows a developer to create and access databases through a graphical user interface. While there are a great many features of the Visual Data Manager, you will focus on how to create a database and a table for now. More information on the Visual Data Manager can be found in the MSDN.

Using the Visual Data Manager

Step 1: To access the Visual Data Manager, select Visual Data Manager from the Add Ins menu.

Figure 10.36
Microsoft's Visual Data
Manager

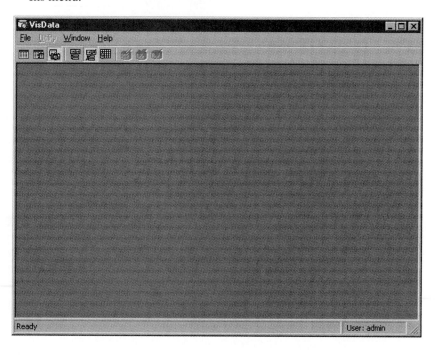

Step 2: The Visual Data Manager will allow a developer to access many data sources. To create a Microsoft Access database, select New from the File menu. A pop-up menu will appear. Select Microsoft Access from the pop-up menu. Another pop-up menu will appear. Select Version 7.0 MDB from the new pop-up and a dialog box will appear for you to save your new database with.

Figure 10.37
Selecting a Database Format

Figure 10.37
Selecting a Database Format

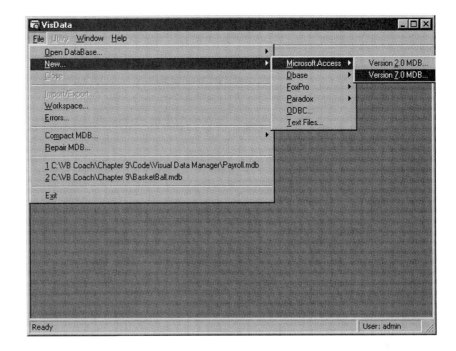

Step 3: When the new database is created, the next step is to add tables to it. The easiest way is to right-click over the Database window and select New Table from the pop-up menu.

Step 4: Specify a table name by placing it in the Table Name text box.

Step 5: Specify each field of the table, one at a time, by clicking on the Add Field button and filling in the following form and clicking on OK.

Figure 10.38
Adding First Text Field of
Size 20

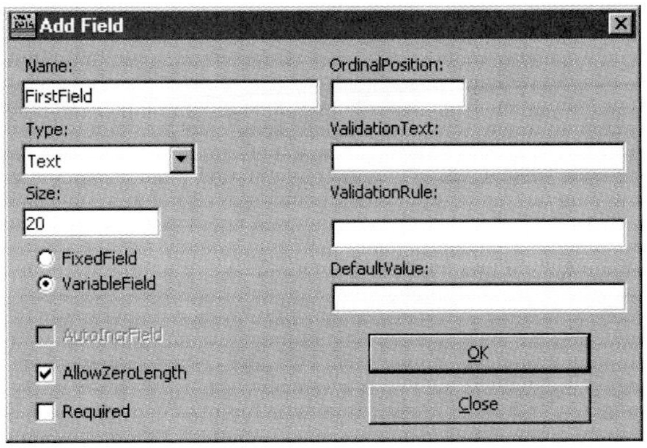

Step 6: Continue to create as many fields as you wish, and then click the Close command button. Your new fields will appear in the Table Structure window.

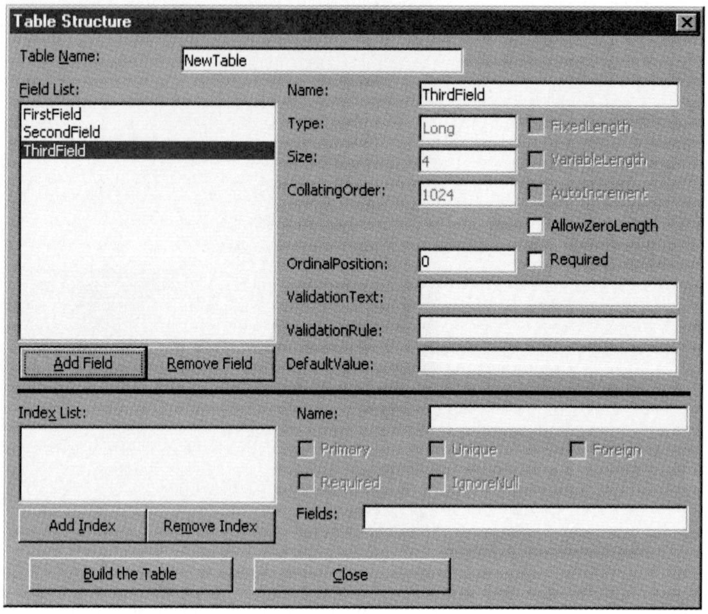

Figure 10.39
Completed Table
Specification

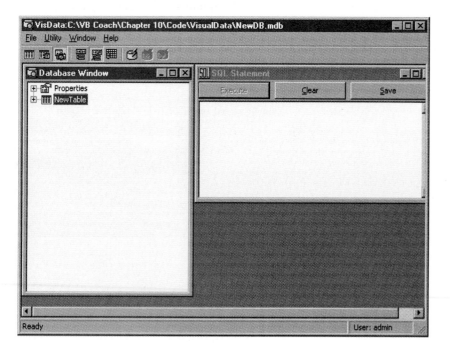

Step 7: Once your table is completely specified, click on the Build the Table command button to actually create your table.

Figure 10.40
New Table Showing in
Visual Data Manager

Answers to Chapter's Drills

Drill 10.1

The pattern of the buttons resembles that of a VCR control set. While many younger developers are familiar with these, how many of your parents know how to operate a VCR? I have always found it more intuitive to use another form of buttons.

Key Words and Key Terms

Database management system
A system that relates data together allowing structure and constraints, thus organizing the data into a more meaningful form.

Data control
A control that connects the form to a table in a database.

Data grid control
A control that allows the values in a grid to be bound directly to a table.

Data validation
The act of checking data to ensure that it is correct.

DB combo control
A control that allows the item selected from a combo box to be bound to a table. Additionally, the list of items presented can be loaded from a table.

Information
Data that has been organized so that it is meaningful.

Field
A single value in a record of data.

Record
A single unit of data composed of fields and stored in a table.

Table
A structure to store a collection of data, usually pertaining to a single entity.

Additional Exercises

Questions 1–3 are True/False.

1. To directly link a form and a table in a database, a developer uses a DB grid.

2. A data control can only connect to database management systems.

3. A data grid's column width cannot be set by the user.

4. Organize these terms from the smallest entity to the largest entity; largest being the one that contains the others.

   Field

   Database

   Record

   Table

5. Which term implies that the values stored in a database are organized in a meaningful manner: data or information?

6. List the data movement capabilities the user has from the data control placed on a form.

7. What happens if a `.MovePrevious` command is issued when you are at the first record in a table?

8. What happens if a `.MoveFirst` command is issued when you are at the first record in a table?

9. What happens if a `.MoveFirst` command is issued when you are at the last record in a table?

10. Can the `AbsolutePosition` of a table equal a negative number?

11. Correctly match the four terms with the four definitions:

Data Field	Sets a value that specifies the data control from which a control's list is filled
Data Source	Returns/sets a value that binds a control to a field in the current record.
List Field	Returns/sets the name of the field in the `RecordSet` object used to fill a control's list portion
Row Source	Sets a value that specifies the data control through which the current control is bound to a database

12. It is often useful to display the total number of records in the table as well as the current record number. Modify the case study so that this feature is added to the application. The new display should be updated whenever its value changes.

For questions 13 and 14 use the following file format:

Last Name	1–10	Games Played	31–35	Assists	46–50
First Name	11–20	Points	36–40	Position	51–60
Team	21–30	Rebounds	41–45		

13. Write an application that connects to the PlayerStats table in the `Basketball.mdb` database. Output all of the fields in the PlayerStats table into a fixed-format file.

14. Write an application that connects to the PlayerStats table in the `Basketball.mdb` database. The application should add a record for each line in a file, `Drafted.txt`, that contains the following information in a fixed-width format.

```
Hirsch      Michael    Sixers     22    420   32    100   Guard
MancoridisSpiros       Sixers     20    14    200   5     Center
Arnold      Rob        Sixers     18    220   110   57    Forward
```

15. Write an application that connects to the PlayerStats table in the `Basketball.mdb` database. The application should output in a message box the number of players who are forwards.

16. Write an application that connects to the PlayerStats table in the `Basketball.mdb` database. The application should output to a file, `HighScoringSixers.txt`, the players that are members of the Sixers who have more than 1,500 points.

17. Write an application that connects to the PlayerStats table in the `Basketball.mdb` database. The application should accept a player's name in a text box and output whether the user wishes to have either Points, Assists, or Rebounds displayed. The application should then search the database for that person and, if found, display the statistic in a message box. Otherwise, a message stating the player was not found should be displayed.

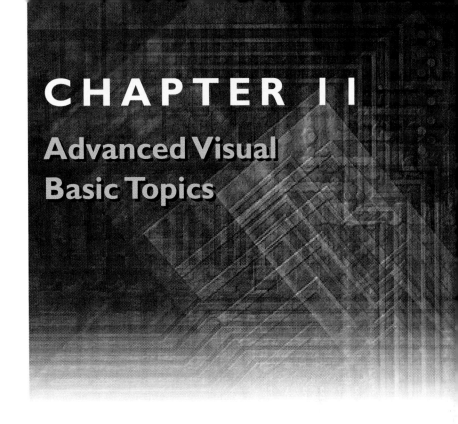

CHAPTER 11
Advanced Visual Basic Topics

CHAPTER OBJECTIVES

- Introduce the ADO data control
- Explain the syntax of the SQL SELECT statement
- Explain how to implement Drag and Drop
- Explain how to use the advanced graphics options

While the techniques you have learned so far allow you to create applications that accomplish a specific task, in this and the next chapter you will learn additional features of Visual Basic that allow your programs to operate with greater flexibility and a more professional look and feel.

11.1 The ADO (Advanced Data Object) Data Control

The default data control that you used in Chapter 9 is used when you first learn databases because of the ease of its implementation. Now that you are comfortable with many of the database concepts, we wish to introduce a "better" data control, the ADO data control.

With the **ADO data control** the developer has access to additional types of data and is given more flexibility in how to query that data.

Adding and Configuring a Data Control

Step 1: The ADO control is not one of the default controls in the toolbar, so you will have to add it. Select the Components option from the Project menu. When the Components window appears (Figure 11.1) select the Microsoft ADO Data Control 6.0. This will add the ADO control to the Control toolbar.

Figure 11.1
Adding ADO Data
Control

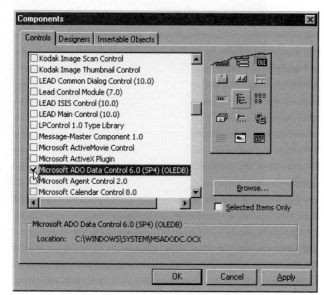

Figure 11.2
Updated Toolbar

Step 2: You add an ADO data control exactly as you would the standard
data control. Select the ADO data control from the toolbox and place it on
the form as in Figure 11.3.

Figure 11.3
ADO Control on a Form

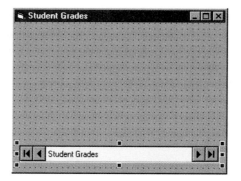

ADO allows a great deal of flexibility in what types of data sources you
can connect to. This makes connecting to the data source less straightforward
than with the standard data control. Therefore, when using an ADO control,
you will have to specify additional information to configure the control
properly.

Step 3: You must connect your ADO data control to your data source. You do this by
setting the `ConnectionString` property of the ADO data control. A
`ConnectionString` contains the information Visual Basic requires to connect an ADO data control to its data source. Click on the
`ConnectionString` property and the following window will appear.

Figure 11.4
Property Pages to Build
`ConnectionString`

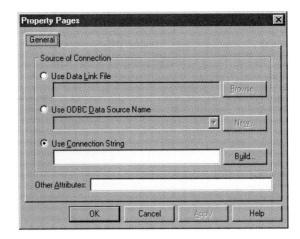

Step 4: Although it is possible to enter a `ConnectionString` directly, this is not recommended. It is far easier to allow Visual Basic to create the `ConnectionString` for you. You can do this by clicking on the Build button.

Figure 11.5
Select Microsoft Access as
Database

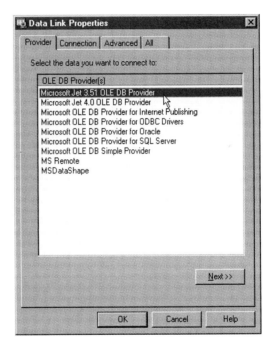

Step 5: Select the Microsoft Jet 3.51 OLE DB Provider from the Data Link Properties window. Your sources may be slightly different; it will depend upon what data sources you have on your machine.

TIP

If you wish to use Access 2000, you will need to select Microsoft Jet 4.0 OLE DB Provider.

Step 6: Click on the Next button and the Data Link Properties window will display the Connection tab.

Step 7: Now you must select the database file that you will connect to this control. By clicking on the **...** button, you can select the mdb from a File Open dialog box.

Figure 11.6
Setting the Database Name

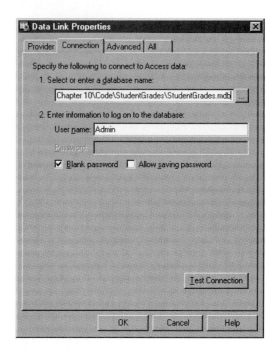

Step 8: After you have selected a file, you can see its path appear in the text box. To ensure that the connection works properly, click on the Test Connection button. After you determine everything works properly, click on the OK button to commit your changes.

Step 9: When you return to the Property Pages window, you will notice that the `ConnectionString` has been filled in.

Figure 11.7
Updated Property Pages

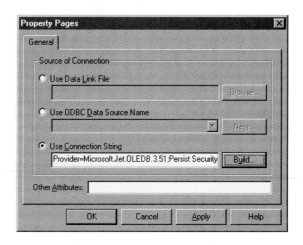

Step 10: Once the `ConnectionString` is set, you still must select the record source for your control. For now, set the control to use the `StudentGrades` table as the source. This requires setting the Command Type to `2 - adCmdTable`

and the Table Name to `StudentGrades`. Later you will learn about some of the other options.

Figure 11.8
Setting the Record Source

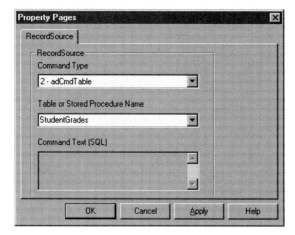

Once an ADO data control has been configured, it can be used basically in the same manner as the default control. So why add another control? Check out the next section and you will see one of the most important uses of the ADO control.

11.2 SQL SELECT

With the addition of the ADO control comes the capability to use a standard query language for manipulating databases. SQL (pronounced either "sequel" or "S-Q-L") is a standard series of statements that allows a programmer to manipulate a database in a concise and efficient manner. Although implementations of SQL can vary slightly from implementation to implementation, the syntax shown here should work in all cases.

The first SQL statement is `SELECT`. It allows the developer to retrieve data from a table or series of tables. Instead of showing you the complete syntax of the SQL `SELECT` statement, we will introduce portions of the statement at a time to aid in your complete understanding of the statement.

Simple Form of the SQL SELECT Statement

The syntax of the `SELECT` statement has many options. The simplest form of the syntax is as follows:

`SELECT` *FieldList* `FROM` *TableName*

`SELECT`: A keyword that indicates that this will be a `SELECT` SQL statement to retrieve data from a table.

`FieldList`: If the developer wishes only some of the fields of a table to be selected, the field list should be a list of the field names desired, with each separated by a comma.

`FROM`: A keyword that indicates the next part of the statement will be the `TableName` from which to retrieve the data.

`TableName`: The name of the table from which the data will be retrieved. The table must exist in the database that you selected when building your SQL statement.

Simple SELECT Statement Examples   For the following examples assume that the following table has been created:

Figure 11.9
StudentGrades Table
Definition

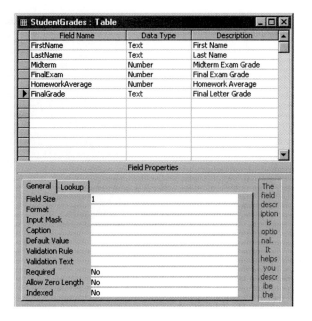

Problem: Retrieve all the student records.

SQL: SELECT * FROM StudentGrades

Although the SELECT statement could have been written as SELECT FirstName, LastName, MidTerm, FinalExam, HomeworkAverage, FinalGrade FROM StudentGrades, you employ a shortcut. The asterisk in a SELECT statement acts as a wildcard that will select all the fields in the table.

Figure 11.10
StudentGrades Records

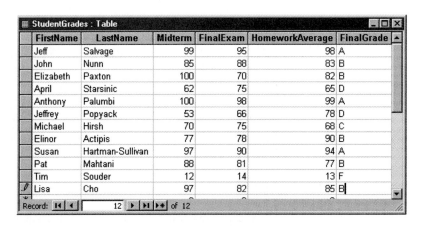

Problem: Retrieve only the first and last name of every student.

SQL: SELECT FirstName, LastName FROM StudentGrades

Figure 11.11
StudentGrades Records

Write the SELECT statement that will retrieve the last name and final grade of every student.

Adding Search Criteria to a SQL SELECT Statement

SQL SELECT statements allow the developer to add search conditions to the statement so that only records matching the search conditions are returned when the SELECT statement is executed.

The syntax to add a search condition is as follows:

SELECT *FieldList* FROM *TableName* [WHERE *SearchCondtions*]

WHERE: A keyword indicating that a search condition will be specified.

SearchConditions: A search condition for a SELECT statement does not vary much from the conditional expressions with which you are already familiar. The main difference is that usually the search condition will contain at least one field from a table. Just as with the earlier conditional expressions, conditional expressions within a SELECT statement can be combined using the logical operators of And and Or.

SELECT Statement Examples with Simple Search Criteria

Problem: Retrieve all the students' records that have a final grade of an A.

SQL: SELECT * FROM StudentGrades WHERE FinalGrade = "A"

Figure 11.12
StudentGrades Records

FirstName	LastName	Midterm	FinalExam	HomeworkAverage	FinalGrade
Jeff	Salvage	99	95	98	A
Anthony	Palumbi	100	98	99	A
Susan	Hartman-Sullivan	97	90	94	A

Record: 3 of 3

Problem: Retrieve the first and last name of all the students' records who have a midterm grade greater than 65.

SQL: SELECT FirstName, LastName FROM StudentGrades WHERE Midterm > 65

Figure 11.13
StudentGrades Records

DRILL 11.2

Write the SELECT statement that will retrieve the last name and final grade of every student with a final grade of an A or B.

DRILL 11.3

Write the SELECT statement that will retrieve all the students' records who failed the midterm. A failing midterm is a grade lower than 65.

SELECT Statement Examples with Simple Search Criteria

Problem: Retrieve all the students' records who have a final grade of an A, B, or C.

SQL: SELECT * FROM StudentGrades WHERE FinalGrade = "A" OR
FinalGrade="B" OR FinalGrade="C"

Figure 11.14
StudentGrades Records

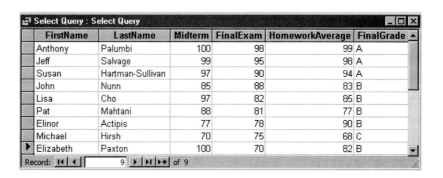

Problem: Retrieve all the students' records whose midterm and homework grades are a 90 or higher.

SQL: SELECT * FROM StudentGrades WHERE Midterm >=90 AND
HomeworkAverage >= 90

Figure 11.15
StudentGrades Records

DRILL 11.4

Write the SELECT statement that will retrieve the students' first and last names who received a B on the midterm. A B on the midterm is a grade of at least an 80 and no more than 89.

DRILL 11.5

Write the SELECT statement that will retrieve the all the students' records who have a failing grade for the midterm, final exam, or their homework average.

SELECT Statement Examples with Wildcards in the Search Criteria

Problem: Retrieve all the students' records whose last name starts with an S.

SQL: SELECT * FROM StudentGrades WHERE LastName LIKE "S%"

Another wildcard character is the percent sign. By using the percent sign in a String, as in the previous example, you are specifying that the records returned are all the records with a last name starting with the letter S.

Figure 11.16
StudentGrades Records

FirstName	LastName	Midterm	FinalExam	HomeworkAverage	FinalGrade
Jeff	Salvage	99	95	98	A
April	Starsinic	62	75	65	D
Tim	Souder	12	14	13	F

Record: 1 of 3

DRILL 11.6

Write the SELECT statement that will retrieve the first and last names of the students whose first name starts with the letter J.

Ordering the Records Returned by a SQL SELECT Statement

The SQL SELECT statement also allows you to specify the order in which the records are retrieved. You can order the results based on a list of fields that will sort the results.

```
SELECT FieldList FROM TableName [WHERE SearchCondtions] _
        [ORDER BY OrderList ASC or DESC]
```

ORDER BY: The keywords to indicate that the developer will specify at least one field to sort the results by.

OrderList: A field or list of fields separated by commas that specify the order that the records will be retrieved.

ASC or DESC: The keywords to indicate whether the results should be sorted in ascending (ASC) or descending (DESC) order. If this option is left off, the default order is ascending.

SELECT Statement Examples with an ORDER BY Clause

Problem: Retrieve all the students' records who have a final grade of an A, B, or C in descending order based on their final exam.

SQL: SELECT * FROM StudentGrades WHERE FinalGrade = "A" OR FinalGrade="B" OR FinalGrade="C" ORDER BY FinalExam DESC

Figure 11.17
StudentGrades Records

FirstName	LastName	Midterm	FinalExam	HomeworkAverage	FinalGrade
Anthony	Palumbi	100	98	99	A
Jeff	Salvage	99	95	98	A
Susan	Hartman-Sullivan	97	90	94	A
John	Nunn	85	88	83	B
Lisa	Cho	97	82	85	B
Pat	Mahtani	88	81	77	B
Elinor	Actipis	77	78	90	B
Michael	Hirsh	70	75	68	C
Elizabeth	Paxton	100	70	82	B

Record: 9 of 9

Problem: Retrieve all the students' records who failed the final exam but passed the midterm in ascending order based on their midterm. A passing grade is a grade of 65 or more.

SQL: SELECT * FROM StudentGrades WHERE FinalExam < 65 AND Midterm >= 65 ORDER BY Midterm ASC

No records are returned!

DRILL 11.7

Write the SELECT statement that will retrieve all the final exams greater than 90 and list the records in alphabetical order. Alphabetical order should be ascending by last name and then first name.

TIP

When comparing date values, date constants are coded with a # on either side of the date as in the following example:
SELECT * FROM Payroll WHERE Day > #3/10/2001#

Setting the Record Source

ADO will allow a developer to use a SQL statement as its record source instead of accessing a table directly. All that is required is to change the Command Type from 2 - adCmdTable to 1 - adCmdText and place the SQL statement in the Command Text (SQL) window.

Figure 11.18 shows this with the SQL statement Select * from StudentGrades.

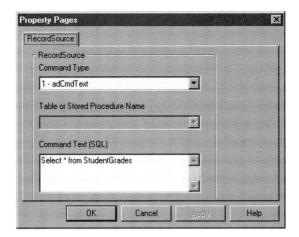

Figure 11.18
Using SQL as the
Record Source

Binding Controls to an ADO Data Control

An ADO data control by itself doesn't give you much power. Just as with the standard data control, an ADO data control is used by binding other controls to it. Fortunately, the mechanism for binding controls to an ADO control is the same as the method we introduced in Chapter 10.

In Figure 11.19, you see a simple form that displays students' names and their final grade. When users run this application, they can step through the students' names and their final grades. The controls operate identically to the standard data control.

Figure 11.19
Complete Application

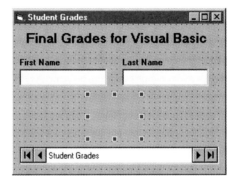

To create this application, you perform the following steps.

Create the Form

Step 1: Create a new project.
Step 2: Set the `Name` property of the form to `frmGrades`.
Step 3: Set the `Caption` property to `Student Grades`.

Add the Title Label

Step 1: Place a label control across the top of the form.
Step 2: Set the `Name` to `lblTitle`.
Step 3: Set the `Caption` to `Final Grades for Visual Basic`.
Step 4: Set the `Font` property to a Size of 14 and a Style of `Bold`.
Step 5: Set the `Alignment` property to `Center`.

Add the Ado Control

Step 1: Place an ADO data control across the top of the form.
Step 2: Set the `Caption` to `Student Grades`.

Step 3: Click on the `ConnectionString` property.
Step 4: Click on the `...` button that appears in the `ConnectionString` property window.
Step 5: Click on the Build button.
Step 6: Select Microsoft Jet 3.51 OLE DB Provider from the list of providers.
Step 7: Click on the Next button.
Step 8: Select the `StudentGrades.mdb` provided.
Step 9: Click on the OK button to commit your selection of the database.
Step 10: Click on the OK button to finish building the `ConnectionString`.
Step 11: Click on the `RecordSource` property.
Step 12: Click on the `...` button that appears in the `RecordSource` property window.
Step 13: Select `1- adCmdText` as the Command Type.
Step 14: Set the Command Text to `SELECT * FROM StudentGrades`.
Step 15: Click on the OK button to commit your record source.

Add the First Name Label

Step 1: Place a label control below the `lblTitle` label.
Step 2: Set the `Name` to `lblFirstName`.
Step 3: Set the `Caption` to `First Name`.

Add the First Name Text Box

Step 1: Place a text box control on the form below the `lblFirstName` label.
Step 2: Set the `Name` property of the control to `txtFirstName`.
Step 3: Erase the value in the `Text` property.
Step 4: Set the `DataSource` equal to the Ado Grades data control. The control should appear in the `DataSource` property window when you click on the down arrow button. If the control does not appear as in Figure 11.20, you did not configure your ADO data control properly.

Figure 11.20
Setting the Data Source

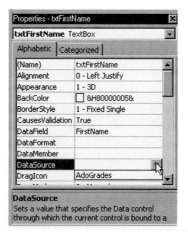

Step 5: Set the `DataField` property to `FirstName`. If the list of field names does not appear as in Figure 11.21, you did not configure the ADO properly or you did not set the data source properly in step 4.

Figure 11.21
Setting the Data Field

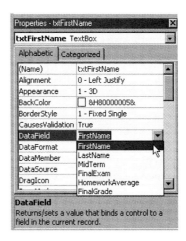

Add the Last Name Label

Step 1: Place a label control to the right of the `lblFirstName` label.
Step 2: Set the `Name` to `lblLastName`.
Step 3: Set the `Caption` to `Last  Name`.

Add the Last Name Text Box

Step 1: Place a text box control on the form below the `lblLastName` label.
Step 2: Set the `Name` property of the control to `txtLastName`.
Step 3: Erase the value in the `Text` property.
Step 4: Set the `DataSource` equal to the Ado Grades data control.
Step 5: Set the `DataField` property to `LastName`.

Add the Final Grade Label

Step 1: Place a label control to the right of the `lblFirstName` label.
Step 2: Set the `Name` to `lblLastName`.
Step 3: Set the `DataSource` equal to the Ado Grades data control.
Step 4: Set the `DataField` property to `FinalGrade`.
Step 5: Set the `Font` property to a Size of 48 and a Style of `Bold`.
Step 6: Set the `Alignment` property to `Center`.

T I P

Although we didn't mention it before, you can use a label control to display fields from a database in the same way that you use text boxes.

If you get through configuring all the previous steps, your application should appear as follows. In Figure 11.22, the initial record of the table is displayed. By clicking on the Next button of the ADO control, the second record is displayed as shown in Figure 11.23.

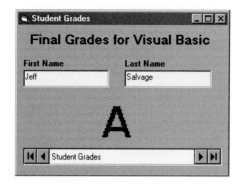

Figure 11.22 Initial Record Displayed

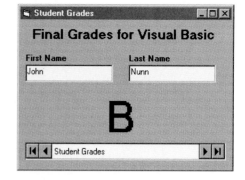

Figure 11.23 Second Record Displayed

Advanced Features of the SELECT Statement

When you write SQL statements, you must be careful about the amount of data that you return. Wherever possible, you should return the minimum amount of data required.

Consider the problem of totaling the payroll costs in your case study. Imagine you wished to display the total payroll cost for each department in the company.

This could be accomplished by writing a SQL statement to retrieve the Daily Pay and Department for every record in the database. Once the data is retrieved, you could loop through all of the records and add the Daily Pay associated with each record to a variable tracking the total pay for that department. When the last record is accounted for, you could display the value in each variable.

This method is extremely inefficient. If a database exists on a different computer than the one running the application, all of the data will have to travel over a computer network in order for it to be processed. A better approach would be to calculate the totals within the SQL statement. This will cause the data to be processed on the machine containing the data and will result in only the totals being passed to the application.

Fortunately, SQL provides you with a mechanism to accomplish this. By using the GROUP BY clause, it allows you to compress records together into a single record where the records have a column or columns in common.

Records can be grouped in many ways. Each field returned in the rows being grouped should have a function that specifies the method for grouping the individual fields of a record together. SQL provides you with a few functions that help you accomplish this.

In this example, you would want to total the Daily Pay of the grouped records, so you would use the SUM function.

The syntax for a SQL statement that uses a the GROUP BY clause is as follows:

```
SELECT FieldList with Grouping Functions FROM TableName _
    [WHERE SearchConditions] [ORDER BY OrderList ASC or DESC] [GROUP BY FieldList]
```

The SQL statement to total the payroll expenditures would then be

```
SELECT SUM([Daily Pay]), Department FROM payroll _
    GROUP BY Department ORDER BY Department
```

TIP

Tables can be created with spaces in the field names. If this occurs, you must enclose the field name in brackets [ ] as in the previous `SELECT` statement. Notice how Daily Pay is enclosed as follows: `[Daily Pay]`.

There is one problem with using the previous SQL statement. What is the name of the calculated value? It is better to use the `As` keyword and rename the field to a meaningful name.

To rename a field all that is required is to type `As` and then the new name after the function call in the SQL statement.

Therefore, if you wished to rename the results of the summing of the Daily Pay column as TotalDailyPay, you could do so with the following SQL statement:

```
SELECT SUM([Daily Pay]) AS TotalDailyPay, Department FROM payroll _
     GROUP BY Department ORDER BY Department
```

Payroll : Table

Employee ID	HoursWorked	Department	Day	Daily Pay
1	10	Management	3/11/01	$500.00
2	8	Processing	3/11/01	$120.00
3	6	Phone	3/11/01	$60.00
4	6	Sales	3/11/01	$150.00
1	30	Sales	1/11/01	$750.00
1	8	Management	3/11/01	$400.00
1	20	Sales	2/11/01	$500.00

Record: 6 of 7

Figure 11.24   Payroll Records

Group By Query : Sele...

TotalDailyPay	Department
$900.00	Management
$60.00	Phone
$120.00	Processing
$1,400.00	Sales

Record: 4

Figure 11.25   Payroll Query

For example, the $900.00 associated with Management in Figure 11.25 is the sum of $500.00 (Record 1) and $400.00 (Record 6) in Figure 11.24.

Just as you used the `Sum` function to calculate the total payroll for each department, you can also use other functions with SQL statements. They are:

`AVG(Select_Item)`	Averages a column of numeric data.
`COUNT(Select_Item)`	Counts the number of select items in a column.
`COUNT(*)`	Counts the number of rows in the query output.
`MIN(Select_Item)`	Determines the smallest value of `Select_Item` in a column.
`MAX(Select_Item)`	Determines the largest value of `Select_Item` in a column.
`SUM(Select_Item)`	Totals a column of numeric data.

DRILL 11.8

Write the `SELECT` statement that will retrieve the average hours worked for each department.

11.3 Drag and Drop

Since the first computer switch was set programming the first electronic computer, developers of computer applications have constantly quested for an intuitive interface for their applications. The first electronic computers required the physical setting of switches to achieve the desired results. In the 1980s computers were brought to the masses with the advent of the personal computer. However, users were required to remember cryptic commands to perform operations. The graphical user interface released the user from this burden. One of the really slick features of a GUI is the ability to perform a command by dragging one piece of the application to another piece.

This is used in Microsoft Word when you wish to move a piece of text from one location to another. Users can select the text they wish to move, cut it, move the mouse to the destination location, click on the destination position, and then paste it in place. However, the user can also select the text, drag it to its new location, and then drop it in place. The latter is usually more efficient.

By adding this functionality to your Visual Basic applications, you can develop applications that are more intuitive. In this chapter we will first show you how to develop a Drag and Drop–enabled application and then improve a previously developed application using Drag and Drop to simplify its use as well as its development. Believe it or not, the Drag and Drop version of the application can require less code than the traditionally developed application.

Drag and Drop Actions

Drag and Drop actions occur between a **Source** object and a **Target**. Observe Figure 11.26. Here you have used an image of an archer to symbolize the source object and the image of the bull's eye is your target.

Figure 11.26
Source and Target for a
Drag and Drop Application

Source   Target

You can view the Drag and Drop action that occurs between the source and target objects as three distinct actions.

Dragging the Source Toward the Target   When the source object is dragged towards the target object an icon of your choosing can be displayed instead of the default (a gray box) being displayed. Icons can be pre-selected from existing icons on your computer, or you can create an icon using an external graphics application.

In Figure 11.27, you see the icon of an arrow displayed for the cursor as the source object is dragged toward the target object.

TIP

Icon files end in .ico.

Drag an Object

Step 1: Move the mouse pointer over the source object.
Step 2: Click and hold down the left mouse button.
Step 3: While holding the left mouse button down, move the mouse in the direction of the target object.
Step 4: The icon will follow the motions of your mouse.

Figure 11.27
Dragging the Source toward
the Target for a Drag and
Drop Application

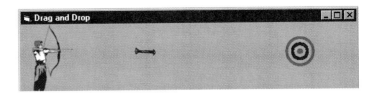

Dragging the Source Over the Target   It is possible to set the target object to execute code when the source object's icon is dragged over the target object. Figure 11.28 shows how the target object's picture can be changed to display another image when the bullet icon passes over the target object. This code is tied to the object's `DragOver` event.

Figure 11.28
Dragging Source over the
Target for a Drag and Drop
Application

Dropping the Source Object on the Target   When the left mouse button is released and the icon is over the target object, code can be executed. Figure 11.29 shows how the target object's picture can be changed to a hit target. This code is tied to the object's `DragDrop` event.

Figure 11.29
Dropping the Source on the
Target for a Drag and Drop
Application

Example: Shoot the Target

The following are the steps to follow and code to write to create the previous application.

Add Identification for Project and Form

Step 1: Set the project's `Name` property to `DragAndDrop`.
Step 2: Set the `Name` property of the form to `frmDragAndDrop`.
Step 3: Set the `Caption` property of the form to `Drag and Drop`.

Add Source Picture Box

Step 1: Place a picture box control to the left of the form.
Step 2: Set the `Name` property to `pctSource`.
Step 3: Set the `BorderStyle` property to 0 because you wish your images to appear without borders.
Step 4: Set the `Picture` property to ...`Chapter 11/Drag And Drop Example/Archer.jpg`.
Step 5: Set the `DragIcon` property to ...`Chapter 11/Drag And Drop Example/Arrow.ico`.

Add Target Picture Box

Step 1: Place a picture box control to the left of the form.

Step 2: Set the `Name` property to `pctTarget`.

Step 3: Set the `BorderStyle` property to 0 because you wish your images to appear without borders.

Step 4: Set the `Picture` property to ...`Chapter 11/Drag And Drop Example/BullsEye.jpg`.

Step 5: Set the `Picture` property to ...`Chapter 11/Drag And Drop Example/BullsEye.jpg`.

Step 6: Set the `DragMode` property to `1 - Automatic`.

 TIP

By setting the `DragMode` property to `1 - Automatic`, the object can be dragged around the form and interact with other objects that have their `DragOver` and `DragDrop` events coded.

Setting the DragOver Event of the Target Picture Box

Step 1: Right-click the mouse and select View Code from the pop-up menu.

Step 2: Select the `pctTarget` picture box control.

Step 3: Select the `DragOver` event. The following code appears:

```
Private Sub pctBullseye_DragOver(Source As Control, X As Single, Y As Single, _
                       State As Integer)


End Sub
```

Step 4: For now, you can ignore the parameters that are provided. Simply add the following code:

```
Private Sub pctBullseye_DragOver(Source As Control, X As Single, _
     Y As Single, State As Integer)

pctBullseye.Picture = LoadPicture _
     ("C:\VB Coach\Chapter 11\Code\Drag And Drop Example\DraggedOver.bmp")

End Sub
```

 TIP

The code entered in the `DragOver` event executes when a source object is dragged over the target object.

Setting the DragDrop Event of the Target Picture Box

Step 1: Right-click the mouse and select View Code from the pop-up menu.

Step 2: Select the `pctTarget` picture box control.

Step 3: Select the `DragDrop` event. The following code appears:

```
Private Sub pctBullseye_DragDrop(Source As Control, X As Single, Y As Single)
End Sub
```

Step 4: For now, you can ignore the parameters that are provided. Simply add the following code:

```
Private Sub pctBullseye_DragDrop(Source As Control, X As Single, Y As Single)
pctBullseye.Picture = LoadPicture("C:\VB Coach\Chapter 11\Code\ _
                Drag And Drop Example\HitBullseye.jpg")
End Sub
```

> **TIP**
>
> The code entered in the `DragDrop` event executes when a source object is dropped on the target object.

Removing the Source Picture Box

After the archer has fired, and the target struck with the arrow, it might be nice to remove the archer so that the police cannot find him or her.

You can remove the source's picture box in a number of ways. You might think of coding `pctSource.Visible = False` directly in the `pctTarget`'s `DragDrop` event. However, what would you do if you had multiple sources? Imagine creating an application with a gun, bow, and a tank. If all could hit the target, how could you code it easily? Simple, the `Source` parameter is actually a reference to the source object that was dropped on the target.

You can modify the `DragDrop` event of the target to contain the following code:

```
Private Sub pctBullseye_DragDrop(Source As Control, X As Single, _
        Y As Single)
pctBullseye.Picture = LoadPicture( _
        "C:\VB Coach\Chapter 11\Code\Drag And Drop Example\HitBullseye.jpg")
Source.Visible = False
End Sub
```

> **TIP**
>
> When the source object is dropped on the target object, all of the source object's properties are accessible from the `Source` parameter.

Example: Drag and Drop Number Puzzle

By combining the power of Drag and Drop with control arrays, you can create pretty slick applications. In Chapter 8, you created a number puzzle application that allowed you to move puzzle pieces around by clicking on command buttons. This interface should have felt a bit awkward. Instead of having to click on the piece you wish to move and then clicking on a direction, it would be far easier to just drag the puzzle piece to its new location.

The following three figures show how a puzzle piece can be dragged from one location to another. While the puzzle piece is being dragged, notice how a puzzle icon is displayed.

Figure 11.30   Before Move

Figure 11.31   During Move

Figure 11.32   After Move

The code to develop this application isn't more complicated than the version in Chapter 8. Actually, it's simpler.

Your new application does not require:

◆ Code to be processed from four command buttons.
◆ A current position to be tracked.
◆ A current piece to be highlighted.
◆ Checking to make sure that you don't move past the edge of the puzzle.

Therefore, you can process moving a piece in any direction by one routine, `pctGamePiece_DragDrop`. Because `pctGamePiece` is a control array of picture boxes, an index variable is added to the parameters of the `DragDrop` event. The `Index` parameter indicates the index of the picture box that the puzzle piece is dropped onto.

To determine whether a puzzle piece's move is valid, you must first determine if the destination piece is empty and then determine if you are moving the piece only one square.

Direction	Value
Left	1
Right	–1
Up	4
Down	–4

By subtracting the index of the source piece from the index of the destination piece, you can determine if the piece was moved only one position in a given direction.

Remember the following chart showing the indices of each position of the board? You can verify that the previous chart is correct by trying a few examples.

If you move left from position 6, the new position would be 7, which is 1 more than 6, so the chart is correct.

If you move right from position 6, the new position would be 5, which is 1 less than 6, so the chart is correct.

If you move down from position 6, the new position would be 10, which is 4 more than 6, so the chart is correct.

0	1	2	3
4	5	6	7
8	9	10	11
12	13	14	15

If you move up from position 6, the new position would be 2, which is 4 less then 6, so the chart is correct.

All other positions can be verified in the same manner.

The code for pctGamePiece_DragDrop follows:

```
Private Sub pctGamePiece_DragDrop(Index As Integer, Source As Control, _
                        X As Single, Y As Single)
Dim intIndexDiff As Integer

intIndexDiff = Index - Source.Index
If ((GamePieces(Index) = 0) And ((intIndexDiff = 1) Or _
    (intIndexDiff = -1) Or (intIndexDiff = 4) Or (intIndexDiff = -4))) Then

    'Move internal representation of new square to piece
    GamePieces(Index) = GamePieces(Source.Index)

    'Set internal representation of old square to blank
    GamePieces(Source.Index) = 0

    'Copy old piece to new location
    pctGamePiece(Index).Picture = pctGamePiece(Source.Index).Picture

    'Copy blank piece to old location
    pctGamePiece(Source.Index).Picture = _
            LoadPicture("c:\VB Coach\Chapter 8\Blank.jpg")
Else
    MsgBox "Invalid Destination Square"
End If
End Sub
```

The General Declarations section is almost identical. However, you no longer need the intCurrentPos variable.

```
Dim GamePieces(0 To 15) As Integer
```

The `cmdStart_Click` and `Form_Load` events as well as the `Initialize` subroutine are identical to their previous implementations.

11.4 Graphics

You are already familiar with displaying some graphics in your applications. The picture box control allows you to display a previously created image. While this gives you the capability to beautify your applications, its usefulness as a method of output is limited.

January:	$12,400
February:	$15,120
March:	$12,500
April:	$19,995
May:	$10,275
June:	$14,222
July:	$12,400
August:	$15,120
September:	$12,500
October:	$19,995
November:	$10,275
December:	$14,222

The power of graphical applications can really be exploited when you display data graphically instead of producing a text-based result.

Figure 11.33
Line Chart

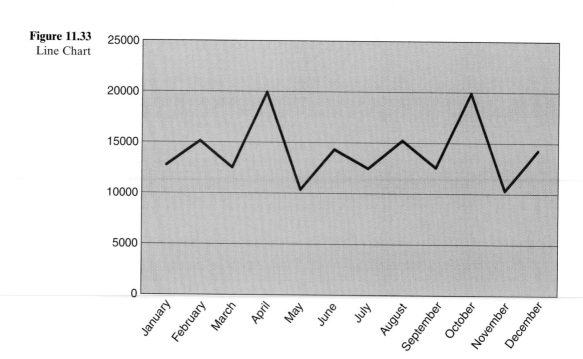

Figure 11.34
Bar Chart

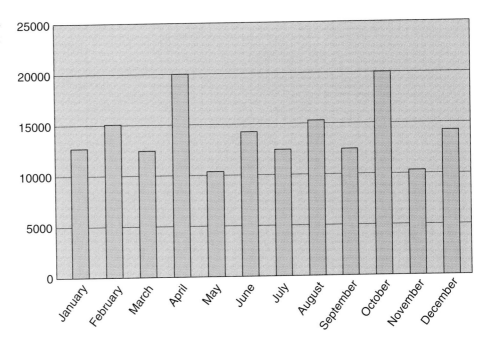

Imagine if you wished to display the sales data of a company for each month of the year. If the data were stored in a database, you could query the results and display them in a text box as follows:

While the previous method fulfills the function of displaying the information, it does not do an adequate job of portraying the annual sales. A far better way is to display the information in form of a line or bar chart. Observe Figures 11.33 and 11.34, which show the data represented in a line chart and bar chart, respectively.

However, before you can produce effective graphics as in the previous figures, you must learn the basics of coordinate systems and how to display them.

Defining a Coordinate System

Developing a chart with Visual Basic is similar to the methods you employ when creating a chart on pen and paper. Instead of graph paper, you will use a picture box. Instead of a pen, you will use picture box methods to draw lines and circles.

The first step in drawing a chart on paper is to draw your axis and determine the scale to use. Traditionally, you draw an axis as a straight line with a label. In high school, you often would draw an x-axis and a y-axis. The x-axis would be the horizontal line, whereas the y-axis would be the vertical line.

Picking the scale for each axis is very important. Probably the first scale you were introduced to was when you were shown the number line in grade school. The number line was basically an x-axis with 1-unit intervals. Observe Figure 11.35 where you demonstrate an x-axis number line with a lower bound of –3 and an upper bound of 3.

Figure 11.36 expands the concept by creating an x-axis and y-axis from –3 to 3.

Figure 11.35
X-axis from
–3 to 3

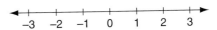

Figure 11.36
X- and Y-axes Combined

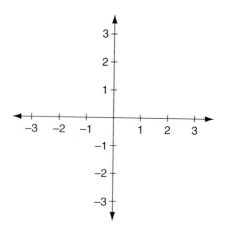

However, is this the proper scale for all applications? Clearly this would not be the case. Some charts require a much greater range of values, while others do not require negative data. Choosing the proper scale is very important to achieving a useful chart. Observe Figures 11.37, 11.38, and 11.39. The three charts display identical information, but each chart has a different scale for the range of values of the maximum and minimum sales for each month.

The choice of which is best might seem obvious, but it is not that clear cut a decision. Aesthetically, Figure 11.38 is the most appealing, but is it the best representation of the data? That is a question left for statisticians to argue over.

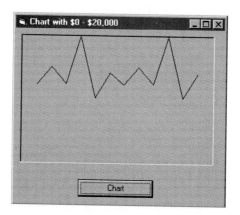

Figure 11.37   Range $0–$20,000

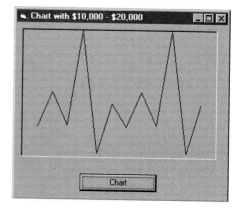

Figure 11.38   Range $10,000–$20,000

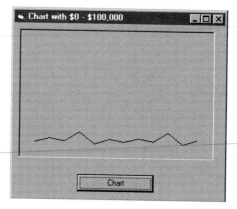

Figure 11.39   Range $0–$100,000

Figure 11.37 shows your results with a range of $0 to $20,000. However, because the minimum sales in a given month is never less than $10,000, more than half of the chart remains blank. This is a waste of display space.

Figure 11.38 shows your results with a range of $10,000 to $20,000. This is the most appropriate sized chart of the three. The lower and upper bounds of the displayed values matches closely to the range of values being displayed.

Figure 11.39 shows your results with a range of $0 to $100,000. While you may hope to sell $100,000 of merchandise in a single month, because you do not currently sell amounts that large, the extra display space requires too much space and flattens your chart so much that the differences from month to month become difficult to make out.

Setting the Coordinate System of a Picture Box   The syntax for setting a picture box's scale to the scale in Figure 11.40 is as follows:

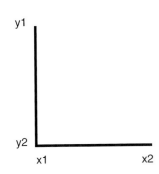

PictureBoxName.Scale($x1$, $y1$) – ($x2$, $y2$)

- $x1$ is the lower bound of the value displayed on the x-axis.
- $x2$ is the upper bound of the value displayed on the x-axis.
- $y2$ is the lower bound of the value displayed on the y-axis.
- $y1$ is the upper bound of the value displayed on the y-axis.

Figure 11.40
Setting the Scale for an Image

To set the scale of a picture box to $10,000 to $20,000 on the x-axis and 0 to 13 on the y-axis, use the following code.

```
pctOutput.Scale (10000, 13) - (20000, 0)
```

> **TIP**
>
> When setting the scale for a range of values it is always best to set the scale a little larger and smaller than the highest and lowest value you will display. This will give the chart a natural border, making it more aesthetically pleasing.

> **WARNING**
>
> When setting the scale for values like currency, do not include the dollar sign or commas in the specification of the scale. You will receive an error message.

Drawing a Line

Once a scale has been set, you are ready to learn how to draw a line in the picture box. The syntax for drawing a line in a picture box like the one in Figure 11.41 is as follows:

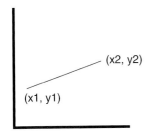

PictureBoxName.Line($x1$, $y1$) – ($x2$, $y2$)

$x1$— Is the coordinate along the x-axis of Point1.

$y1$— Is the coordinate along the y-axis of Point1.

$x2$— Is the coordinate along the x-axis of Point2.

$y2$— Is the coordinate along the y-axis of Point2.

By drawing multiple lines, one can draw simple figures as in Figure 11.42.

Figure 11.41
Drawing a Line from
($x1$, $y1$) to ($x2$, $y2$)

Figure 11.42
Simple Drawing of a Man

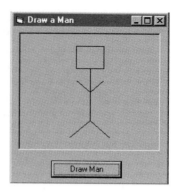

The code to produce it is as follows:

```
Private Sub cmdDrawMan_Click()

'Draw Head
pctOutput.Scale (0, 100)-(100, 0)
pctOutput.Line (40, 90)-(60, 90)
pctOutput.Line (60, 90)-(60, 70)
pctOutput.Line (60, 70)-(40, 70)
pctOutput.Line (40, 70)-(40, 90)

'Draw Body
pctOutput.Line (50, 70)-(50, 25)

'Draw Left Leg
pctOutput.Line (50, 50)-(40, 60)
pctOutput.Line (50, 50)-(60, 60)

'Draw Right Leg
pctOutput.Line (50, 25)-(35, 10)
pctOutput.Line (50, 25)-(65, 10)

End Sub
```

DRILL 11.9

Add code to draw a face in the previous figure.

Adding Color

When drawing figures, color can be a key element. Fortunately, Visual Basic allows you to set the color of your lines by simply adding a parameter to the `Line` method.

The syntax for drawing a line and specifying a color in a picture box is as follows:

PictureBoxName.`Line`(*x*1, *y*1) - (*x*2, *y*2), *vbCOLOR*

vbCOLOR: Can be any of the existing Visual Basic color constants

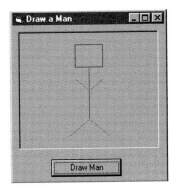

Figure 11.43 Colored Drawing of a Man

The code to produce it is as follows:

```
Private Sub cmdDrawMan_Click()

'Draw a Red Head
pctOutput.Scale (0, 100)-(100, 0)
pctOutput.Line (40, 90)-(60, 90), vbRed
pctOutput.Line (60, 90)-(60, 70), vbRed
pctOutput.Line (60, 70)-(40, 70), vbRed
pctOutput.Line (40, 70)-(40, 90), vbRed


'Draw a Blue Body
pctOutput.Line (50, 70)-(50, 25), vbBlue

'Draw a Yellow Left Leg
pctOutput.Line (50, 50)-(40, 60), vbYellow
pctOutput.Line (50, 50)-(60, 60), vbYellow


'Draw a Yellow Right Leg
pctOutput.Line (50, 25)-(35, 10), vbYellow
pctOutput.Line (50, 25)-(65, 10), vbYellow

End Sub
```

Drawing a Rectangle

Instead of simply drawing a line, by viewing the coordinates of the `Line` method slightly differently, you can use the `Line` method to draw a rectangle.

Listing the coordinates of two opposite corners of the rectangle can specify a rectangle. Observe Figure 11.44. By specifying Point1 as the starting coordinate and Point2 as the ending coordinate, you can specify the entire rectangle.

Figure 11.44
Specifying Coordinates for a
Rectangle

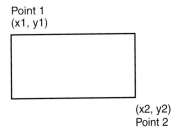

The syntax for drawing a rectangle is as follows:

PictureBoxName.Line(*x*1, *y*1) - (*x*2, *y*2), *vbCOLOR*, *Flag*

`Flag`: By adding the `Flag` parameter you indicate to Visual Basic to draw a rectangle.
If you place a B for the flag, the rectangle will be drawn as a series of lines.
However, if you place a BF for the flag, the rectangle will be filled in.

Observe the following code for drawing the head of your man by drawing a rectangle instead of four lines:

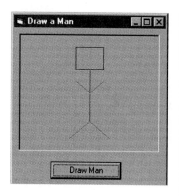

Figure 11.45 Head Drawn with Rectangle

```
Private Sub cmdDrawMan_Click()

pctOutput.Scale (0, 100)-(100, 0)

'Draw a Red Head as a rectangle that is not filled in
pctOutput.Line (40, 70)-(60, 90), vbRed, B

'Draw a Blue Body
pctOutput.Line (50, 70)-(50, 25), vbBlue

'Draw a Yellow Left Leg
pctOutput.Line (50, 50)-(40, 60), vbYellow
pctOutput.Line (50, 50)-(60, 60), vbYellow

'Draw a Yellow Right Leg
pctOutput.Line (50, 25)-(35, 10), vbYellow
pctOutput.Line (50, 25)-(65, 10), vbYellow

End Sub
```

Observe the following code for drawing the head of your man with a filled-in rectangle instead of an empty rectangle:

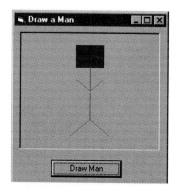

Figure 11.46 Head Drawn with Filled-in Rectangle

```
Private Sub cmdDrawMan_Click()

pctOutput.Scale (0, 100)-(100, 0)

'Draw a Red Head
pctOutput.Line (40, 70)-(60, 90), vbRed, BF

'Draw a Blue Body
pctOutput.Line (50, 70)-(50, 25), vbBlue

'Draw a Yellow Left Leg
pctOutput.Line (50, 50)-(40, 60), vbYellow
pctOutput.Line (50, 50)-(60, 60), vbYellow

'Draw a Yellow Right Leg
pctOutput.Line (50, 25)-(35, 10), vbYellow
pctOutput.Line (50, 25)-(65, 10), vbYellow

End Sub
```

Drawing a Circle

Your man probably isn't feeling too styling with a square head. By using the circle method, you can display circles as simply as you create rectangles.

Observe Figure 11.47. By specifying the center point of a circle and its radius, a circle can be created.

Figure 11.47
Specifying Coordinates for a
Circle

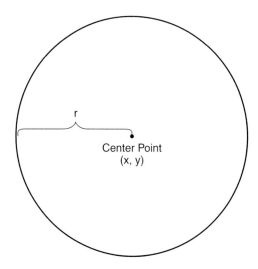

Remember, a radius is
half the size of the
diameter of a circle.

The syntax for drawing a circle is as follows:

PictureBoxName.Circle(*x*, *y*), *r*, *vbCOLOR*

Observe the following code for drawing the head of your man with a circle
instead of a rectangle:

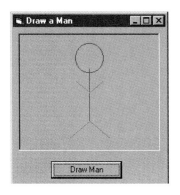

Figure 11.48   Man Drawn
with a Circle for a Head

```
Private Sub cmdDrawMan_Click()

pctOutput.Scale (0, 100)-(100, 0)

'Draw a Red Head as a Circle
pctOutput.Circle (50, 80), 10, vbRed

'Draw a Blue Body
pctOutput.Line (50, 70)-(50, 25), vbBlue

'Draw a Yellow Left Leg
pctOutput.Line (50, 50)-(40, 60), vbYellow
pctOutput.Line (50, 50)-(60, 60), vbYellow

'Draw a Yellow Right Leg
pctOutput.Line (50, 25)-(35, 10), vbYellow
pctOutput.Line (50, 25)-(65, 10), vbYellow

End Sub
```

Adding Text

The last building block you need to create meaningful charts is the capability to add
text to your figures. However, text cannot be added by issuing just one command. It's a
combination of three. You need to set the starting x and y coordinates of the text, and
then you can call a method to display the text at that position.

The syntax for displaying text is as follows:

```
PictureBoxName.CurrentX = XCoordinate
PictureBoxName.CurrentY = YCoordinate
PictureBoxName.Print "TEXT GOES HERE"
```

So to place the name of your man, Adam, as in Figure 11.49, you would use the following code:

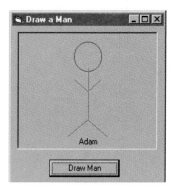

Figure 11.49 Adam with His Name Displayed

```
Private Sub cmdDrawMan_Click()

pctOutput.Scale (0, 100)-(100, 0)

'Draw a Red Head
pctOutput.Circle (50, 80), 10, vbRed

'Draw a Blue Body
pctOutput.Line (50, 70)-(50, 25), vbBlue

'Draw a Yellow Left Leg
pctOutput.Line (50, 50)-(40, 60), vbYellow
pctOutput.Line (50, 50)-(60, 60), vbYellow

'Draw a Yellow Right Leg
pctOutput.Line (50, 25)-(35, 10), vbYellow
pctOutput.Line (50, 25)-(65, 10), vbYellow

'Draw the name Adam over the man.
pctOutput.CurrentX = 44
pctOutput.CurrentY = 10
pctOutput.Print "Adam"
End Sub
```

Creating a Chart

You now have all the tools necessary to develop graphical charts of data values. The remainder of this section of the text will demonstrate how to create a static chart from values you have predetermined. However, the case study at the end of the chapter will show you how to use the techniques developed here as an output method for a database query.

Figure 11.50
Line Chart with Text

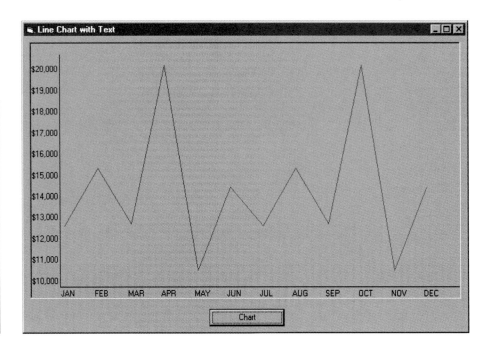

January:	$12,400
February:	$15,120
March:	$12,500
April:	$19,995
May:	$10,275
June:	$14,222
July:	$12,400
August:	$15,120
September:	$12,500
October:	$19,995
November:	$10,275
December:	$14,222

While the code to produce this chart is long, it is not very complex.

Declaring and Initializing Variables   The first step is to declare and initialize any local variables that are required. You need a variable to loop through the labels for the x-axis and y-axis. In addition, you declare an array to store the abbreviations for each month in the year. This will allow you to create a loop to output the labels.

```
Dim intCurrentY As Integer 'Counter used to track Y label
Dim intMonth As Integer 'Counter used to loop through months
Dim strMonths(0 To 11) As String 'Array to store month names

'Initialize Months
strMonths(0) = "JAN"
strMonths(1) = "FEB"
strMonths(2) = "MAR"
strMonths(3) = "APR"
strMonths(4) = "MAY"
strMonths(5) = "JUN"
strMonths(6) = "JUL"
strMonths(7) = "AUG"
strMonths(8) = "SEP"
strMonths(9) = "OCT"
strMonths(10) = "NOV"
strMonths(11) = "DEC"
```

Setting the Scale   The next step is to set the scale. You want to make sure that when you set the scale there is enough room to display all of the values in the chart as well as leave room for the labels. Because there are 12 months, you should set the range of months from 0 to 13. This will leave space on both sides of the chart. Because the sales figures range from about $10,000 to $20,000, you will set the scale from 9,000 to 21,000.

The Scale method is shown in the following code:

```
pctOutput.Scale (0, 21000)-(13, 9000)
```

Setting the Y-Axis   To draw the y-axis you must first draw a line where the axis will be. Then you need to draw the labels to the right of it. Because the range of values is roughly from $10,000 to $20,000, it seems natural to place a label every $1,000 starting at $10,000. Each label needs to be placed to the right of the y-axis, so the starting x coordinate of the text will be 0.01. The starting y coordinate can be the same value as the label. So, the label $10,000 will have a starting y coordinate of 10,000. The label $11,000 will have a starting y coordinate of 11,000, and so on.

The code to draw the y-axis and its labels is as follows:

```
'Draw y-axis
pctOutput.Line (0.85, 9500)-(0.85, 20500)


'Output the labels for the y-axis
pctOutput.CurrentX = 0.01

For intCurrentY = 10000 To 20000 Step 1000
   pctOutput.CurrentY = intCurrentY
   pctOutput.Print FormatCurrency(intCurrentY, 0)
Next intCurrentY
```

Setting the X-Axis   To draw the x-axis you must first draw a line where the axis will be. Then you need to draw the labels beneath it. Because each value is a monthly total, it is natural to label each interval as the month it represents. Each label should be centered under the point in the line representing that month's sales. Because you do not know how to center text, you will have to estimate the best location of the text. Therefore, each label will be placed 0.1 away from the center point. Also, each label needs to be slightly below the x-axis itself. Therefore the y coordinate of all the text will be 9,400. The x coordinate will be .9 for January, 1.9 for February, and so on. Finally, for each month you will display the three-letter abbreviation to simplify the centering of each month's name.

The code follows:

```
'Draw x-axis
pctOutput.Line (0.85, 9500)-(13, 9500)

'Draw Month Labels
For intMonth = 0 To 11
   pctOutput.CurrentY = 9400
   pctOutput.CurrentX = 0.9 + intMonth
   pctOutput.Print strMonths(intMonth)
Next intMonth
```

The last code you must write is to draw the actual line itself. The code requires drawing a point from one value to the next:

```
'Draw the line on the graph
pctOutput.Line (1, 12400)-(2, 15120), vbBlue
pctOutput.Line (2, 15120)-(3, 12500), vbBlue
pctOutput.Line (3, 12500)-(4, 19995), vbBlue
pctOutput.Line (4, 19995)-(5, 10275), vbBlue
pctOutput.Line (5, 10275)-(6, 14222), vbBlue
pctOutput.Line (6, 14222)-(7, 12400), vbBlue
pctOutput.Line (7, 12400)-(8, 15120), vbBlue
```

(continues)

(continued)

```
pctOutput.Line (8, 15120)-(9, 12500), vbBlue
pctOutput.Line (9, 12500)-(10, 19995), vbBlue
pctOutput.Line (10, 19995)-(11, 10275), vbBlue
pctOutput.Line (11, 10275)-(12, 14222), vbBlue
End Sub
```

◆ 11.5 Case Study

Problem Description   It's now time to put many of the advanced features of Visual Basic to work in one application. Since the first chapters of the text, you have been building a data entry payroll system. While data can be entered and viewed, it is helpful to have analysis tools to evaluate the data.

A useful analysis for the data that you have collected is the total payroll expenditures for each department over a specific period. This case study will display payroll totals for periods of 30, 60, or 90 days in a bar chart. The user will be able to select which total by dragging and dropping a 30, 60, or 90 icon onto the chart.

The application should look as follows:

Figure 11.51
Sketch of Payroll Charting
Application

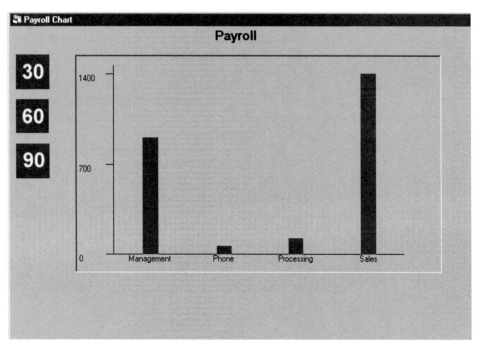

Problem Discussion   The application will utilize all of the advanced topics introduced in this chapter. The solution to this application can be thought of as three distinct problems:

First, you must develop the Drag and Drop interface so that you can select the proper range of dates to total payroll expenditures for.

Second, you must gather and total the data for the date range specified. You can accomplish this with an ADO data control and write SQL to limit the SQL and total the results.

Finally, you will utilize the advanced graphics to display the actual chart. However, displaying the results of a SQL query as a chart introduces a new problem. In the previous charting problems, the range of values was fixed before you wrote the code to display the chart. Because you are dynamically generating the values to chart, you do not know the possible ranges at the time the code is written. So, what should the proper range of value be for the chart? It is impossible to answer that question. Instead, you must dynamically assign the ranges based on the values returned from your SQL query. This will be explained in detail in the solution.

Problem Solution The first step is to place an ADO data control on the form and set the properties as follows:

Name: adoPayroll

CommandType: 1 - adCmdText

ConnectionString: Provider=Microsoft.Jet.OLEDB.3.51;Persist Security Info=False;Data Source=C:\VB Coach\Chapter 11\Code\Case Study\Payroll.mdb

RecordSource: Select * from Payroll

Visible: False

The code for the solution could be completely written in the DragDrop event. However, the length of the code would make it difficult to understand. Instead you will break the code into separate routines and functions to improve readability.

When one of the three images are dragged onto the pctChart picture box, the DragDrop event will execute.

The first step is to query the database and return the total pay for the time period specified. You can build a SQL statement that returns only records within the time period specified. To improve performance and simplify code, you can sum each department's payroll by grouping the results by department and using the SUM function on the Daily Pay column.

Once the SQL statement is built and executed, you can compute the range of values that you will display in the chart. Because the range of values can be from 0 to any positive currency value, you will have to determine the range of sums and set the y-axis accordingly.

This will be left to a separate function. Once the axis is drawn, you can draw a bar for each department's payroll totals.

```
Private Sub pctChart_DragDrop(Source As Control, X As Single, Y As Single)
Dim dteFirstDay As Date
Dim curManagement As Currency
Dim curPhone As Currency
Dim curProcessing As Currency
Dim curSales As Currency

Dim curMinValue As Currency
Dim curMaxValue As Currency
Dim curMinChartValue As Currency

'Compute the number of days to display data for
Select Case Source.Name
    Case "pctOneMonth"
        dteFirstDay = Date - 30
    Case "pctTwoMonths"
        dteFirstDay = Date - 60
    Case "pctThreeMonths"
        dteFirstDay = Date - 90
End Select
```

(continues)

(continued)

```
'Query database for new data
adoPayroll.RecordSource = "SELECT SUM([Daily Pay]) AS DailyPay, _
 Department FROM Payroll Where Day >= #" & CDate(dteFirstDay) _
 & "# GROUP BY Department ORDER BY Department"
adoPayroll.Refresh

'Gather totals for each department
adoPayroll.Recordset.MoveFirst
curManagement = adoPayroll.Recordset.Fields(0)

adoPayroll.Recordset.MoveNext
curPhone = adoPayroll.Recordset.Fields(0)

adoPayroll.Recordset.MoveNext
curProcessing = adoPayroll.Recordset.Fields(0)

adoPayroll.Recordset.MoveNext
curSales = adoPayroll.Recordset.Fields(0)

'Compute Min and Max Values
curMinValue = Min(curManagement, curPhone, curProcessing, curSales)
curMaxValue = Max(curManagement, curPhone, curProcessing, curSales)

'Draw Axis and labels for chart
curMinChartValue = DrawAxis(curMaxValue, curMinValue)

'Draw Management Bar
pctChart.Line (0.9, curMinChartValue)-(1.1, curManagement), vbBlue, BF

'Draw Phone Bar
pctChart.Line (1.9, curMinChartValue)-(2.1, curPhone), vbBlue, BF

'Draw Processing Bar
pctChart.Line (2.9, curMinChartValue)-(3.1, curProcessing), vbBlue, BF

'Draw Sales Bar
pctChart.Line (3.9, curMinChartValue)-(4.1, curSales), vbBlue, BF
End Sub
```

Because you do not know the range of values at the time you develop the application, drawing the axis and determining the proper scale is no trivial task.

You must determine range of values for the specific chart that you are attempting to display. If you displayed exactly the range of values for the chart, your chart would look cramped toward the edges. Therefore, you must add a fudge factor to allow for some space around the edges of the chart.

The first calculation is to determine the lower bound of the chart. Because payroll can only be positive, the absolute lower bound is 0. However, if you are charting values of $1,000,000 to $1,200,000 for each department, you might not want to display your values starting at 0. This would only show minor differences from department to department. Instead, you wish to display your values from a little below $1,000,000 to a little above $1,200,000.

Therefore, you compute your minimum chart value as 10 percent below the smallest value to display. If this value ends up being negative, you will use 0 instead.

The next step is to set the scale for the picture box. You need to set the scale slightly larger than the range of values you are going to display. You need the extra space for the labels you are going to place on the axis. The amount of space you add is another fudge factor, in this case you add 10 percent to the y-axis. The x-axis is a simpler calculation. Because you know that you are displaying four values, you can set the scale to display values from 0 to 5. This will leave you plenty of space for labels and the axis.

```
Private Function DrawAxis(curMaxValue As Currency, curMinValue As Currency) _
 As Currency

Dim curRange As Currency
Dim curMinChartValue As Currency
curRange = curMaxValue - curMinValue

'Compute Chart Minimum Value
curMinChartValue = Max2(curMinValue - curRange * 0.1, 0)

'Clear Previous Chart
pctChart.Cls

'Set scale of chart to just larger and smaller than the max and min values
pctChart.Scale (0, curMaxValue + curRange * 0.1)- _
             (5, curMinChartValue - curRange * 0.1)

'Draw X-Axis
pctChart.Line (0.5, curMinChartValue)-(4.5, curMinChartValue)

'Add Labels to X-Axis
pctChart.CurrentX = 0
pctChart.CurrentY = curMinChartValue
pctChart.Print curMinChartValue
pctChart.Line (0.4, curMinChartValue)-(0.5, curMinChartValue)

pctChart.CurrentX = 0
pctChart.CurrentY = curMaxValue
pctChart.Print curMaxValue
pctChart.Line (0.4, curMaxValue)-(0.5, curMaxValue)

pctChart.CurrentX = 0
pctChart.CurrentY = curMaxValue / 2
pctChart.Print curMaxValue / 2
pctChart.Line (0.4, curMaxValue / 2)-(0.5, curMaxValue / 2)


'Draw Y-Axis
pctChart.Line (0.5, curMinChartValue)-(0.5, curMaxValue + curRange * 0.05)

'Add Labels to Y-Axis
pctChart.CurrentY = curMinChartValue * 0.95
pctChart.CurrentX = 0.7
pctChart.Print "Management"
```

(continues)

(continued)

```
pctChart.CurrentX = 1.85
pctChart.CurrentY = curMinChartValue * 0.95
pctChart.Print "Phone"

pctChart.CurrentX = 2.75
pctChart.CurrentY = curMinChartValue * 0.95
pctChart.Print "Processing"

pctChart.CurrentX = 3.88
pctChart.CurrentY = curMinChartValue * 0.95
pctChart.Print "Sales"

'Return the Minimum Chart Value
DrawAxis = curMinChartValue

End Function
```

To simplify the other function's implementations, we have developed three functions to determine the maximum and minimum of a series of values.

The `Max2` function determines the maximum of two currency values:

```
Private Function Max2(curVal1 As Currency, curVal2 As Currency) As Currency
If (curVal1 > curVal2) Then
    Max2 = curVal1
Else
    Max2 = curVal2
End If
End Function
```

The `Max` function determines the maximum of four currency values:

```
Private Function Max(curVal1 As Currency, curVal2 As Currency, _
                 curVal3 As Currency, curVal4 As Currency) As Currency
If (curVal1 > curVal2) And (curVal1 > curVal3) And (curVal1 > curVal4) Then
    Max = curVal1
ElseIf (curVal2 > curVal3) And (curVal2 > curVal4) Then
    Max = curVal2
ElseIf (curVal3 > curVal4) Then
    Max = curVal3
Else
    Max = curVal4
End If
End Function
```

The `Min` function determines the minimum of four currency values:

```
Private Function Min(curVal1 As Currency, curVal2 As Currency, _
                 curVal3 As Currency, curVal4 As Currency) As Currency
If (curVal1 < curVal2) And (curVal1 < curVal3) And (curVal1 < curVal4) Then
    Min = curVal1
ElseIf (curVal2 < curVal3) And (curVal2 < curVal4) Then
    Min = curVal2
```

(continues)

(continued)

```
ElseIf (curVal3 < curVal4) Then
    Min = curVal3
Else
    Min = curVal4
End If
End Function
```

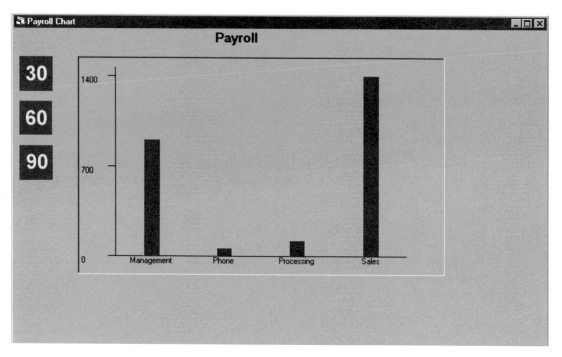

Figure 11.52 Final Application

Answers to Chapter's Drills

Drill 11.1

To select all the last names and the final grades of all the students, you will need to specify each field you desire in the results. The field name for a student's last name is `LastName`. The field name for a student's final grade is `FinalGrade`; therefore, the SQL statement required is

```
SELECT LastName, FinalGrade FROM StudentGrades
```

Drill 11.2

To select only the last names and the final grades of the students with a final grade of an A or B, you will need to specify each field you desire in the results. The field name for a student's last name is `LastName`. The field name for a student's final grade is `FinalGrade`. Additionally, because you are limiting the students who are returned by the query to only those with A's or B's in the final grade, you will require a `WHERE` clause that compares the final grade to an A or B. The SQL statement required is

```
SELECT LastName, FinalGrade FROM StudentGrades _
WHERE FinalGrade = "A" OR FinalGrade = "B"
```

Drill 11.3
Because you were not asked to limit the fields, you can use the asterisk operator to select all of the fields. However, you will need a WHERE clause to limit the records returned to those who failed the midterm. The SQL statement required is

```
SELECT * FROM StudentGrades WHERE MidtermGrade < 65
```

Drill 11.4
To select only the first and last names with midterm grade >80 and <89, you will need to specify each field you desire in the results. The field name for a student's first name is FirstName. The field name for a student's last name is LastName. Additionally, because you are limiting the students who are returned by the query to only those with a B for their midterm, you will require a WHERE clause that compares the midterm grade ≥80 and ≤89. The SQL statement required is

```
SELECT FirstName, LastName FROM StudentGrades _
WHERE MidtermGrade >= 80 AND MidtermGrade <=89
```

Drill 11.5
Because you were not asked to limit the fields, you can use the asterisk operator to select all the fields. However, you will need a WHERE clause because you wish to limit the records returned to those that failed either the midterm, final exam, or has a failing homework average. The SQL statement required is

```
SELECT * FROM StudentGrades _
WHERE MidtermGrade < 65 OR FinalExam <65 OR HomeworkAverage <65
```

Drill 11.6
To select only the first and last names with whose first name starts with the letter J, you will need to specify each field you desire in the results. The field name for a student's first name is FirstName. The field name for a student's last name is LastName. Additionally, because you are limiting the students who are returned by the query to only those whose first name starts with the letter J, you will need a WHERE clause uses the LIKE operator. Depending on whether you use Microsoft Access or another database, the SQL statement required is:

```
SELECT FirstName, LastName FROM StudentGrades WHERE FirstName LIKE "J*"
```

or

```
SELECT FirstName, LastName FROM StudentGrades WHERE FirstName LIKE "J%"
```

Drill 11.7
Because you were not asked to limit the fields, you can use the asterisk operator to select all of the fields. However, you will need a WHERE clause because you wish to limit the records returned to those who had a final exam grade of greater than 90. Additionally, because you are asked to sort the results, you need an ORDER BY clause to be added to the SQL statement. The SQL statement required is:

```
SELECT * FROM StudentGrades WHERE FinalExam > 90 ORDER BY LastName, FirstName
```

Drill II.8

Because you are asked to average the hours worked in each department, you must group the results by the `Department` field. Averaging the hours is as simple as using the `AVG` function on the `HoursWorked` field.

```
SELECT AVG([HoursWorked]) AS AverageHours, Department FROM Payroll _
GROUP BY Department ORDER BY Department
```

Drill II.9

You were asked to draw a face for the stick figure. There are many ways to draw a face; here's one possible solution:

Figure 11.53

Figure with a Face

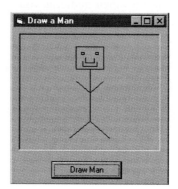

```
'Draw Face

'Draw Mouth
pctOutput.Line (45, 77)-(45, 73)
pctOutput.Line (45, 73)-(55, 73)
pctOutput.Line (55, 73)-(55, 77)

'Draw Nose
pctOutput.Line (47, 80)-(47, 76)
pctOutput.Line (47, 76)-(53, 76)
pctOutput.Line (53, 76)-(53, 80)

'Draw Left Eye
pctOutput.Line (44, 85)-(46, 85)
pctOutput.Line (46, 85)-(46, 83)
pctOutput.Line (46, 83)-(44, 83)
pctOutput.Line (44, 83)-(44, 85)

'Draw Right Eye
pctOutput.Line (56, 85)-(54, 85)
pctOutput.Line (54, 85)-(54, 83)
pctOutput.Line (54, 83)-(56, 83)
pctOutput.Line (56, 83)-(56, 85)
```

Key Words and Key Terms

ADO data control
A control to access databases and other data sources that works similarly to the standard data control, but allows greater flexibility.

ConnectionString
A specification for the ADO control to define the information required for communicating with a data source.

Circle
A method to draw a circle on a picture box.

CurrentX
An attribute containing the current x-axis position of a picture box.

CurrentY
An attribute containing the current y-axis position of a picture box.

Drag and Drop
An interface that allows actions to occur based on objects on a form being clicked on and dragged to other objects.

DragDrop
An event that is triggered when a Drag and Drop–enabled object is dropped on another object.

DragOver
An event that triggers when a Drag and Drop–enabled object is dragged over another object.

FROM
A keyword in the SQL statement that specifies the table the SQL statement will query from.

GROUP BY
Keywords in the SQL statement that combine records together to allow computations to be performed more efficiently.

Line
A method to draw a line on a picture box.

ORDER BY
Keywords in the SQL statement that specify the order the results are returned from the SQL statement.

Print
A method that will draw a text message on a picture box.

Scale
A method that sets the range of values to be displayed in a picture box.

SQL SELECT
An industry standard method for querying a database.

WHERE
A keyword in the SQL statement that specifies the conditions that will limit the query.

Additional Exercises

Questions 1–5 are True/False

1. The ADO control is the default data control in Visual Basic.
2. All implementations of SQL are exactly the same.
3. The only way to draw a rectangle is to issue four draw line commands.
4. Text cannot be drawn on a picture box.
5. Selecting records with SQL can be accomplished with the standard data control.

For questions 6–10, use the following table:

Figure 11.54
StudentGrades Table

FirstName	LastName	Midterm	FinalExam	HomeworkAverage	FinalGrade
Jeff	Salvage	99	95	98	A
John	Nunn	85	88	83	B
Elizabeth	Paxton	100	70	82	B
April	Starsinic	62	75	65	D
Anthony	Palumbi	100	98	99	A
Jeffrey	Popyack	53	66	78	D
Michael	Hirsh	70	75	68	C
Elinor	Actipis	77	78	90	B
Susan	Hartman-Sullivan	97	90	94	A
Pat	Mahtani	88	81	77	B
Tim	Souder	12	14	13	F
Lisa	Cho	97	82	85	B

StudentGrades : Table — Record: 12 of 12

6. Write a SQL SELECT statement that returns the homework averages in ascending order.

7. Write a SQL SELECT statement that returns all the midterm grades and the last names of the people who took them in descending order.

8. Write a SQL SELECT statement that returns all of Jeff Salvage's grades.

9. Write a SQL SELECT statement that returns the first and last name of the students whose first name starts with the letter "A."

10. Write a SQL SELECT statement that counts the number of A's for a final grade.

11. Write an application that contains a picture for the letters "A," "B," "C," "D," and "F." The application should allow the user to drag the picture to a grid where the student records with a final grade matching the grade contained on the picture dragged onto the grid is displayed.

12. You have all seen Web sites that display a thumbnail image and then when you click on it, it displays a larger image. Write an application that displays three smaller thumbnail images. Enable the images so that they can be dragged to a viewing screen. The application should display a larger version of the image when it is dropped on the viewing screen. The viewing screen will just be another picture box. The images for the application can be created in any graphics program.

13. Write an application that draws a truck using the `Line` and `Circle` commands.

Figure 11.55
Drawing of Truck

14. Write an application that charts three bars representing the average of the Midterm Exam, Final Exam, and Homework Average. The application should request the person's first and last name, query the table, and chart the results.

INTERVIEW

An Interview with Joe Hummel

Joe Hummel is a Computer Scientist specializing in traditional CS education as well as Windows-based technologies such as VB, COM, MTS/COM+, and .NET. He works as a trainer for DevelopMentor, and is a professor of Computer Science at Lake Forest College. Joe received bachelor degrees in Math and Computer Science from Allegheny College and his Masters in Computer Science from the University of Michigan. At the University of California, Irvine, he focused on programming language design and optimizing compilers, and received his Ph.D. in Computer Science. He is co-author of Addison-Wesley's *Effective Visual Basic: How to Improve Your VB/COM+ Applications.*

How did you become interested in computers?

I started programming in high school in the late 1970's on an old IBM mainframe, and it was just very exciting to be in control of such an expensive piece of hardware. Also, I found the logic of programming to be very comfortable, something I could do well, but it took a few years of college (and a year in graduate school!) before I truly understood what I was doing.

Aside from teaching, what kinds of projects are you working on?

My current project is another book: a definition of the new Visual Basic .NET programming language. Visual Basic has always lacked what I felt is a proper language reference manual. I'm trying to write that book for VB .NET.

What are some of the challenges of using VB .NET? Do you have any suggestions for overcoming them?

The biggest challenge is for existing VB6 users. VB .NET offers some significant additions to the language, and it's not always clear how to use these new features. For example, VB .NET now offers multi-threading. Should all your Apps be multi-threaded? Definitely not. Multi-threading is hard to get right, and only appropriate in certain situations (like a web server that has to respond to poten-

tially hundreds of client requests at the same time). As another example, VB .NET now has inheritance—when should this be used? Again, there's a time and a place, and it's not always obvious. Students with a good CS education will feel right at home in VB .NET, but the rest of us have lots to learn before we can use VB .NET safely and effectively.

Do you have any advice for students entering the computer field using VB?

Master the concepts, not where the semi-colons go. The language isn't important, it's the concepts: programming logic, data structures, algorithms, software design, user-interface design, concurrency, etc. To be successful in the workplace you'll need to master different operating systems and programming languages, and be able to learn new concepts quickly. If all you know is VB, make sure you branch out and learn more about real OOP (VB6 is not truly OO), database access via SQL, and whatever else you can about computer science. VB is not the be-all-end-all, it's just another language for expressing your thoughts, better in some cases and worse in others. I like using VB, but mostly because it's fun, not because it's the best language. VB .NET is a much better language than VB6, but it still shouldn't be the only language in your repertoire.

CHAPTER 12

Wrapping Up Your Application

CHAPTER
OBJECTIVES

◆ Explain how to create menus using the Menu Editor

◆ Introduce multiform applications

◆ Explain the difference between standard multiform applications and MDI

◆ Revisit global variables

◆ Introduce object-oriented concepts

12.1 Creating Menus Using the Menu Editor

By now, you are more than familiar with menus. Menus are present in almost every application making commonly used options available to the user.

Observe Figure 12.1, showing the menu for VB and the submenu and separator bars.

Figure 12.1
Visual Basic Menu and
Submenu

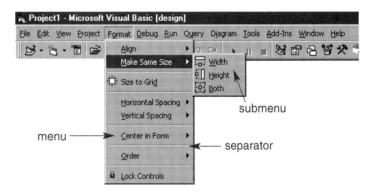

To produce a menu, Visual Basic provides a graphical tool to assist their creation. It is called the Menu Editor and is available from the Tools menu.

Figure 12.2
Menu Editor

Example: Simple Menu Application

Menus can be used to provide an easy way to access an application's commonly used functions. To focus on your understanding of the operation of a menu, we will keep the example as simple as possible.

Your application will display a label and a picture that show a racewalking competition. The application will contain two menus, one to modify the picture and one to modify the label.

The application should have menu items to add a border to the picture and another menu item to remove it.

The Label menu will contain a menu item that will increase the size of the font in the label and another menu item to reduce the size of the font in the label. Additionally, the menu items will be created to set the color of the text to black, blue, or red.

Your menus for the application would look as follows:

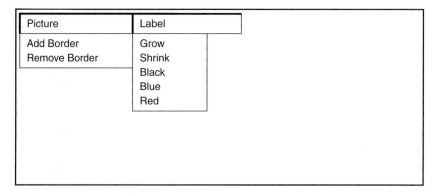

Building an Application with a Menu

Step 1: To create a menu for a form, the form must be active. Then select Menu Editor from the Tools menu. The Menu Editor shown in Figure 12.2 will appear.

Step 2: At a minimum to create a menu for your application, you need to specify a title for the menu and then specify the properties of each individual item under that menu.

Step 3: To title your menu, type the text you wish displayed as the menu title in the Caption text box.

Step 4: Add &Picture as the title of the first menu.

Notice that you used an ampersand in front of the word `Picture`. Just as
you used the ampersand as a keyboard shortcut on command buttons, you can
use it here to indicate that the Picture menu can be accessed by pressing the
<ALT> key and then the <P> key to allow a keystroke access of the menu
item.

Selecting a key combination from the Shortcut drop-down box on the Menu Editor
can also create shortcuts. A different shortcut can be created for each menu item.
Two menu items, regardless of whether they are on the same menu, should not be
assigned the same shortcut keys.

Step 5: Just as all controls in Visual Basic have a name, so should menus. Name your
Picture menu `mnuPicture` by typing `mnuPicture` in the Name text box.

Figure 12.4
Menu Editor with Picture
Menu Specified

Step 6: You need to add the menu items that belong to the Picture menu. To associate
menu items with a menu, you need to first click on the Next button so that the
Menu Editor moves from the current menu to a space to create either a new
menu or menu items.

Then, by clicking on the right arrow button, you indicate to the Menu
Editor that the item is not a new menu, but a menu item belonging to the
Picture menu. See Figure 12.7, where the ellipsis acts as a placeholder for your
first menu item.

Figure 12.5
First Item of Picture Menu
Ready to be Specified

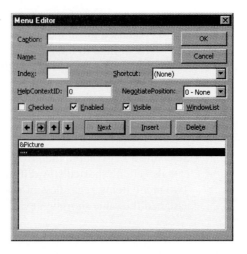

Step 7:   You now can specify the menu item in a similar fashion to your specification of the menu title. You need to specify a Caption and Name for the menu item. In this case they will be **&Add Border** and **mnuAddBorder**, respectively.

Figure 12.6
Specification of the First
Menu Item of the Picture
Menu

Step 8:   You can add the second menu item in the same manner. Click on the Next button and fill in **&Remove Border** and **mnuRemoveBorder** for the Caption and Name of this menu item.

Figure 12.7
Specification of the Second
Menu Item of the Picture
Menu

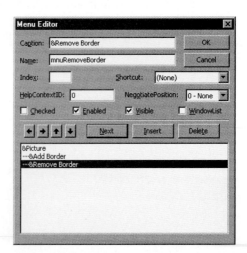

WARNING

You do not need to press the right arrow key again. The Menu Editor will remember that you are working on the Picture menu until you specify otherwise.

Step 9:   With the first menu specified, you now must specify a title of the second menu. However, before you can, you must press the Next button followed by pressing the left arrow button. The left arrow button will return the Menu Editor to the first level. Notice how the ellipsis has disappeared.

Figure 12.8
Specification of the
Second Menu

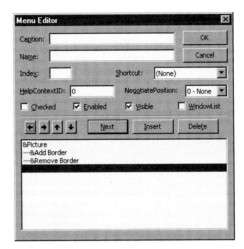

Step 10:   Add &Label and mnuLabel to specify the new menu.

Figure 12.9
Specification of the
Label Menu

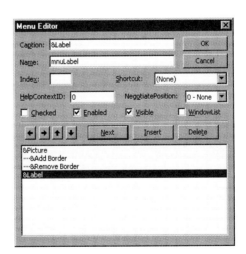

Step 11:   You can now specify the first menu item of the Label menu. First, you click on the Next button. Then, you must once again click on the right arrow button to indicate that you are adding menu items and not a menu. You need to specify a Caption and Name for the menu item. In this case the names will be &Grow and mnuGrow, respectively.

Figure 12.10
Specification of the First
Menu Item of the Label
Menu

Step 12: You can add the remaining menu items in the same manner. Click on the Next button and fill in &Shrink and mnuShrink for the Caption and Name of this menu item. Repeat this process for &Black and mnuBlack, B&lue and mnuBlue, and &Red and mnuRed.

Figure 12.11
Specification of the Second
Menu Item of the Label
Menu

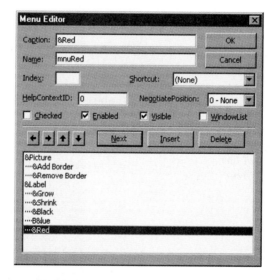

You are now complete with creating the "shell" of your menu; however, you still must specify the code that will execute when the individual menu items are selected.

Specifying Code to Execute

Each menu item has a Click event for which you can specify code to accomplish whatever the purpose of the menu item is.

Step 1: By clicking on the menu and then the menu item you desire, you will call up the Click event code for that menu item. Observe how in Figure 12.12 you click on the Picture menu and then Add Border and then Figure 12.13 appears.

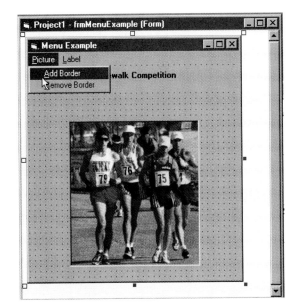

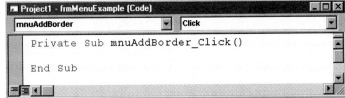

Figure 12.12 Entering Menu Item `Click` Event Code

Figure 12.13 Menu Item `Click` Event Code

Step 2: Now you can just add your code to set a border around your picture:

```
Private Sub mnuBorder_Click()
pctRacing.BorderStyle = 1
End Sub
```

Step 3: To add the code to the menu item `mnuRemoveBorder`, you could also select the control from the pull-down as shown in Figure 12.14.

Figure 12.14
New Coding Options

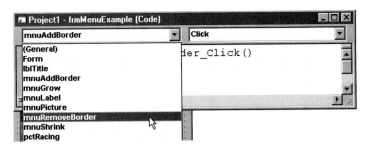

Step 4: Add your code as you did in step 2.

```
Private Sub mnuRemoveBorder_Click()
pctRacing.BorderStyle = 0
End Sub
```

Step 5: Repeat the method you prefer for `mnuGrow`, `mnuShrink`, `mnuBlack`, `mnuBlue`, and `mnuRed`.

```
Private Sub mnuGrow_Click()
lblTitle.Font.Size = Str(Val(lblTitle.Font.Size) + 2)
End Sub
```

(continues)

(continued)

```
Private Sub mnuShrink_Click()
lblTitle.Font.Size = Str(Val(lblTitle.Font.Size - 2))
End Sub

Private Sub mnuBlack_Click()
lblTitle.ForeColor = vbBlack
End Sub

Private Sub mnuBlue_Click()
lblTitle.ForeColor = vbBlue
End Sub

Private Sub mnuRed_Click()
lblTitle.ForeColor = vbRed
End Sub
```

When you are done, the application will look as follows:

Figure 12.15
Simple Menu Application

TIP

The `Click` event is actually the only event that can be associated with a menu item.

Adding a Separator Line

As menu controls grow in size, it is often helpful to divide them into groups of common functionality by separator lines. In the previous example the number of items in the Label menu already contains five items. Imagine if you added additional colors like yellow and magenta. A separator line would be helpful to divide the menu items to change the size of the font from those that change the color of the font.

Figure 12.16 shows the use of a separator line and the additional menu items:

Figure 12.16
Menu with Separator Line

Adding a Separator Line

To add a separator line, follow these simple steps:

Step 1: Click on the menu item below the menu item you wish the separator line to appear under. In this case, click on the mnuBlack menu item.

Step 2: Fill in the Caption with a hyphen.

Step 3: Because all menu items require a Name, use mnuSeparator1.

Figure 12.17
Menu Editor with
Separator Line

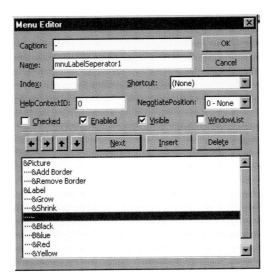

TIP

If you have more than one separator, remember that all names must be unique. Additional separators should be named mnuSeparator2, mnuSeparator3, and so on.

Adding a Submenu

Although a separator line is a good way of breaking up a large menu, at some point too many menu items under one menu becomes cumbersome. A submenu is an excellent way to combat this.

Observe the Label menu in Figures 12.18 and 12.19. It shows two submenus. The first shows the menu items related to changing the size of the font and the second shows the menu items related to changing the color of the font.

Figure 12.18
Change Size Submenu

TIP

The triangle on each of the Label menu items indicates a submenu exists. This is placed there automatically when the submenus are created.

Figure 12.19
Change Color

TIP

Notice that the S in Change Size and the S in Shrink are both shortcuts. This will work even though they use the same letter, because one is a menu item and the other is a submenu item.

Creating a Submenu

Step 1: You must create the menu item that will contain the submenu. Such a menu item is created in the same manner as any other menu item. The one difference is in the naming convention that you will follow. When a submenu is named, it should include the parent menu as part of the name. In this case, you add `Change &Size` and `mnuLabelChangeSize` for the `Caption` and `Name` properties.

Step 2: Because the submenu items are already created, a minimum of effort is required to associate the menu items as submenus. First, you must associate the individual submenu items with their menu item. By clicking on the menu item, `mnuGrow`, and then clicking on the right arrow button, the menu item will be shifted to the right. This symbolizes that the menu item now belongs to a submenu of the previous menu item. Additionally, change the name from `mnuGrow` to `mnuLabelGrow`.

Step 3: This process can be repeated for the other submenu items. Your final menu specification should look like Figure 12.20.

Figure 12.20
Complete Submenu
Specification

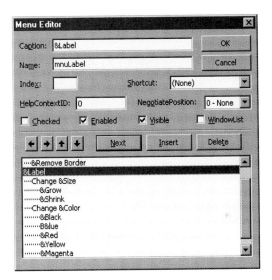

While it may seem trivial, you should always use the proper naming conventions. The effort to maintain your applications will be greatly reduced.

12.2 Multiple Form Applications

All of the applications you have developed so far have been limited to a single form. This limits the functionality of your applications. As you begin to explore the possibilities of multiple form applications, you will first start with a simple application that does not consider the many issues that arise when you use applications with more than one form. Then, after you are comfortable with the new functionality, you will address the concerns that arise from the use of multiple forms.

Showing Another Form

To open another form from the current form is a simple matter. The syntax is as simple as

FormName`.Show`

If you wish to show the form `frmDemographics` from the command button `cmdDemographics`, you would type:

```
Private Sub cmdDemographics_Click()
frmDemographics.Show
End Sub
```

TIP

Form_Load is called before Form_Activate.

When a form is called, two events are called: `Form_Load` and `Form_Activate`. `Form_Load` is called the first time a form is loaded into memory. `Form_Activate` is called each time the form is displayed.

Code can be placed in either event handler, however, care should be taken so that the code you add executes at the proper time.

Hiding or Unloading a Form

Once a form has been loaded, you can make the form disappear in two ways. If you want the form to merely disappear from the screen, but still remain in memory, use the `Hide` event. The syntax for hiding a form is as follows:

FormName`.Hide`

Therefore, if you wish to hide the form `frmDemographics` from the command button `cmdHide`, you would type:

```
Private Sub cmdHide_Click()
frmDemographics.Hide
End Sub
```

TIP

Visual Basic provides a shortcut that allows you a great deal of flexibility. Instead of having to type the name of the form you wish to hide, you can use the `Me` object. `Me` refers to the form the user has focus upon. By using `Me` instead of the form name, it allows the code to be simpler. Therefore, you could use the code `Me.Hide` to hide the active form regardless of the name of the form.

The other option for removing a form is to remove it both from the screen and the computer's memory. This is accomplished with the `Unload` command. When a form is unloaded, unless the information that was entered into it is saved elsewhere, it will be lost. The syntax for unloading a form is as follows:

`Unload` *FormName*

TIP

When we say that we remove it from the computer's memory, we are referring to the computer's RAM. The form is not actually removed from the computer's hard drive.

Therefore, if you wish to hide the current form from the command button cmdUnload, you would type:

```
Private Sub cmdUnload_Click()
Unload Me
End Sub
```

TIP

If a form is unloaded from memory and then loaded again, the form's Form_Load and Form_Activate events will execute. However, if a form is hidden, when the form is re-shown, only the Form_Activate event will execute.

Example: Personnel Information

Now that you can create an application with more than one form, you can increase the amount of information you can gather in a single application. For simplicity, you will create an application that gathers personnel information, but it will not save the information anywhere. The case study at the end of the chapter will demonstrate that.

Your application will contain three forms: frmPersonnel, frmDemographics, and frmFinancial. Each will contain different information about a person working for a company. The first form that the user will be presented with is frmPersonnel:

Figure 12.21
Personnel Information

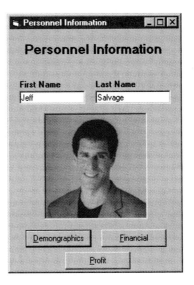

The personnel form is the main form of your application. It is the form that will be presented to the user when the application starts. From it, you will be able to call both the demographic and financial forms. These forms will be displayed when the cmdDemographics or cmdFinancial command buttons are clicked. The code for these command button follows:

```
Private Sub cmdDemographics_Click()
frmDemographics.lblTitle.Caption = "Demographics for " + _
Trim(txtFirstName.Text) & " " & Trim(txtLastName.Text)
frmDemographics.Show
End Sub

Private Sub cmdFinancial_Click()
frmFinancial.lblTitle.Caption = "Financials for " + _
Trim(txtFirstName.Text) & " " & Trim(txtLastName.Text)
frmFinancial.Show
End Sub
```

The `cmdProfit` button will display a message box containing information from the additional forms of the application. We will explain the code for this at the end of the example.

> ## WARNING
>
> You must create this form first when developing your application. By default, the first form created will be the first form shown to the user. As a developer you can change this; we will explain that feature later in the chapter.

The demographics form, shown in Figure 12.22, will contain information pertaining to an individual's demographic information.

Figure 12.22
Demographic Information

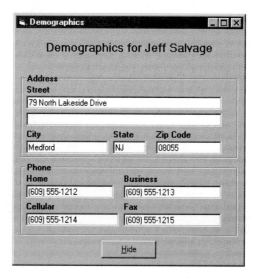

In addition to the demographic information that the user will enter on this form, notice that we have displayed information from the `frmPersonnel` form (my name) and added the `cmdHide` command button.

The `cmdHide` command button will allow the user to remove the form from the computer screen without removing it from the computer's memory. However, if the close window button is clicked, the form will not only be removed from the computer screen, but it will be unloaded from the computer's memory.

The code form the `cmdHide` command button is as follows:

```
Private Sub cmdHide_Click()
Me.Hide
End Sub
```

The financial form, shown in Figure 12.23, will contain information pertaining to an individual's financial information.

Figure 12.23
Financial Information

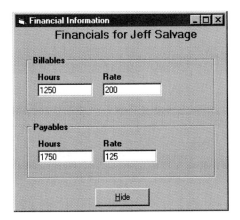

Your financial form contains text boxes to enter the amount of hours and rate an individual billed and worked. Typically, consultants may work more hours than they can bill. Additionally, consultants will be billed out at a higher rate than they are getting paid.

The code form the `cmdHide` command button for `frmFinancial` is the same as for `frmDemographics`:

```
Private Sub cmdHide_Click()
Me.Hide
End Sub
```

With this information, you can calculate the profit a company makes for an individual. The `cmdProfit` command button on the `frmPersonnel` form will display the profit amount as well as the individual's name and phone number in a message box. It will look like the following figure:

Figure 12.24
Profit Message Box

The code for the `cmdProfit` command button is as follows:

```
Private Sub cmdProfit_Click()
MsgBox Trim(txtFirstName.Text) & " " & Trim(txtLastName.Text) & _
" Net Profit is " &
Str(Val(frmFinancial.txtBillableHours.Text) * _
    Val(frmFinancial.txtBillableRate.Text) - _
    Val(frmFinancial.txtPayableHours.Text) * _
    Val(frmFinancial.txtPayableRate.Text)) & _
" he can be reached at " & frmDemographics.txtHomePhone, vbOKOnly, "Profit"
End Sub
```

Using Form_Load or Form_Activate in Your Application

By placing the code to set the `lblTitle` label in the `Form_Activate` event, you can simplify the calling of the form `frmDemographics`.

```
Private Sub cmdDemographics_Click()
frmDemographics.Show
End Sub
```

The code in `Form_Activate` requires you to refer to the text boxes of the `frmPersonnel` form, but this is not complicated.

```
Private Sub Form_Activate()
lblTitle.Caption = "Demographics for " + Trim(frmPersonnel.txtFirstName.Text) & _
" " & Trim(frmPersonnel.txtLastName.Text)
End Sub
```

The same can be done for the financial form.

Do you think it would matter if you placed the code in `Form_Load` instead of `Form_Activate`? Even though they both execute before the form is loaded, you must place the code in `Form_Activate` if you want your form to execute properly.

If your code was placed in `Form_Load`, the first time the form was displayed everything would work fine. However, if you chose to go back to the personnel form and change the person's name, when you returned to the demographics form, the changes to the person's name would not be displayed. Try it yourself!

What to Do When the First Form Created Isn't the First Form to Be Displayed

When you created your applications, you made sure that you created the form that you wished to be displayed as the default form of the application first.

However, this is not always a practical solution. Therefore, Visual Basic allows you to manually set the form to be displayed.

Step 1: Open the Project Properties window by selecting Project Properties from the Project menu.

Step 2: Select the form that you wish to be the first form executed. Figure 12.25 shows the pull-down menu where you can select any of the forms in the project as the startup form (found in the Startup Object drop-down box).

Figure 12.25
Startup Object

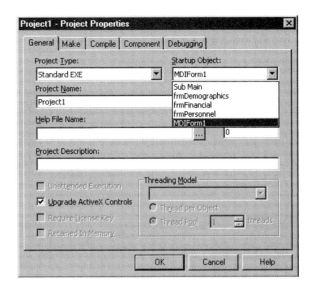

Global Variables

In Chapter 3, we mentioned that variables could be declared so that they are visible throughout the entire application. Variables of this nature are called global. Global variables are declared with the **Public** keyword and must be declared in a **module**. A module is a Visual Basic file with code and a .bas extension, but no visual interface.

A module can be created by selecting Add Module from the Project menu. Visual Basic will give the module a default name, which you can rename by changing the Name property in the properties window of the module. Observe in Figure 12.26 the module CommonCode.

Figure 12.26
Startup Object

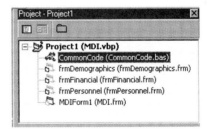

Once you have created a module, you can place code inside that can be shared by all forms in your application.

Therefore, declaring variables in the CommonCode module you just created, would declare them as global to the entire program. The code follows:

```
Public intCounter As Integer
```

WARNING

It is not enough just to declare a variable in the module in order for it to be global. It also must be declared with a Public keyword. If a variable is declared with the Public keyword but not in a module or a variable is declared in the module but not with a Public keyword, it will not be considered global.

12.3 **Multiple Document Interface (MDI)**

Although the multiform application you just developed is an improvement over the single-formed applications you previously developed, it does not behave in the same manner as some multiform windows applications with which you are familiar.

Applications like Microsoft Word are enclosed in a single parent form with child forms contained within it. Observe Figure 12.27, which shows your previous application developed as an MDI application. Notice how the MDI form contains the three other forms that you created.

The choice of using MDI over the previous multiform implementation is mainly one of style and is easy to implement.

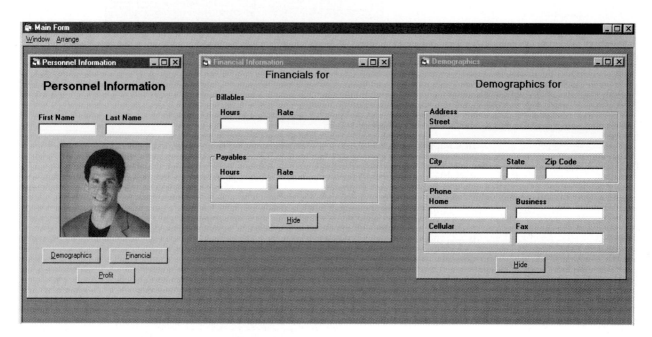

Figure 12.27   MDI Application

> **TIP**
>
> While the child forms in your example do not require different menus, it is possible to create an application where the child windows are associated with different menus. If an application is designed this way, the menu associated with the active child window is active in the parent window.

Creating MDI Documents

An MDI application is created by adding an MDI form to a project and specifying that the supporting forms are child forms.

To add an MDI form to an application, simply click on Add MDI Form in the Project menu. A new MDI form will appear in the project window. Because only one MDI form can exist for a project, once you add an MDI form to the project, the option on the Project menu is removed and replaced with the Remove MDI Form option.

The next step is to set the `MDIChild` property of three forms you will make children to the MDI form. All that is required is that you set the `MDIChild` property to `True` on each form.

The last step in creating your MDI application is to add a menu to the MDI window (Figure 12.28). There is really no difference between an MDI application's menu and a single document interface (SDI) application's menu. However, usually an MDI application's menu will include the options to arrange the windows either by cascading them, arranging them horizontally, or arranging them vertically.

Figure 12.28
Menu for your MDI
Application

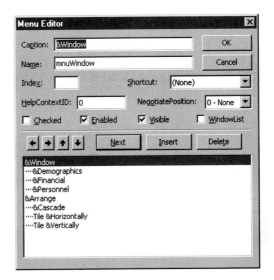

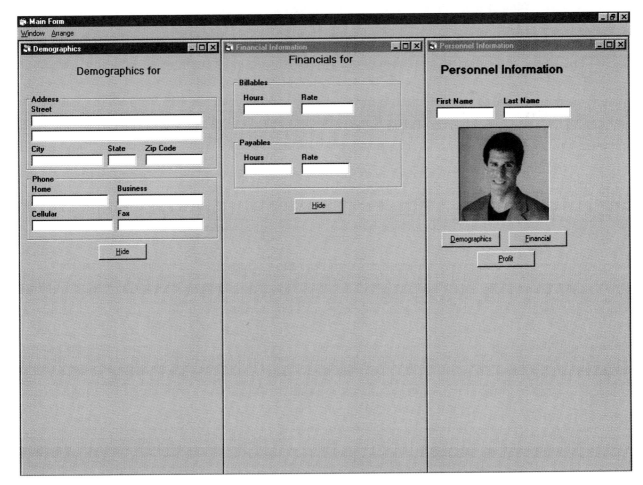

Figure 12.29 Forms Tiled Vertically

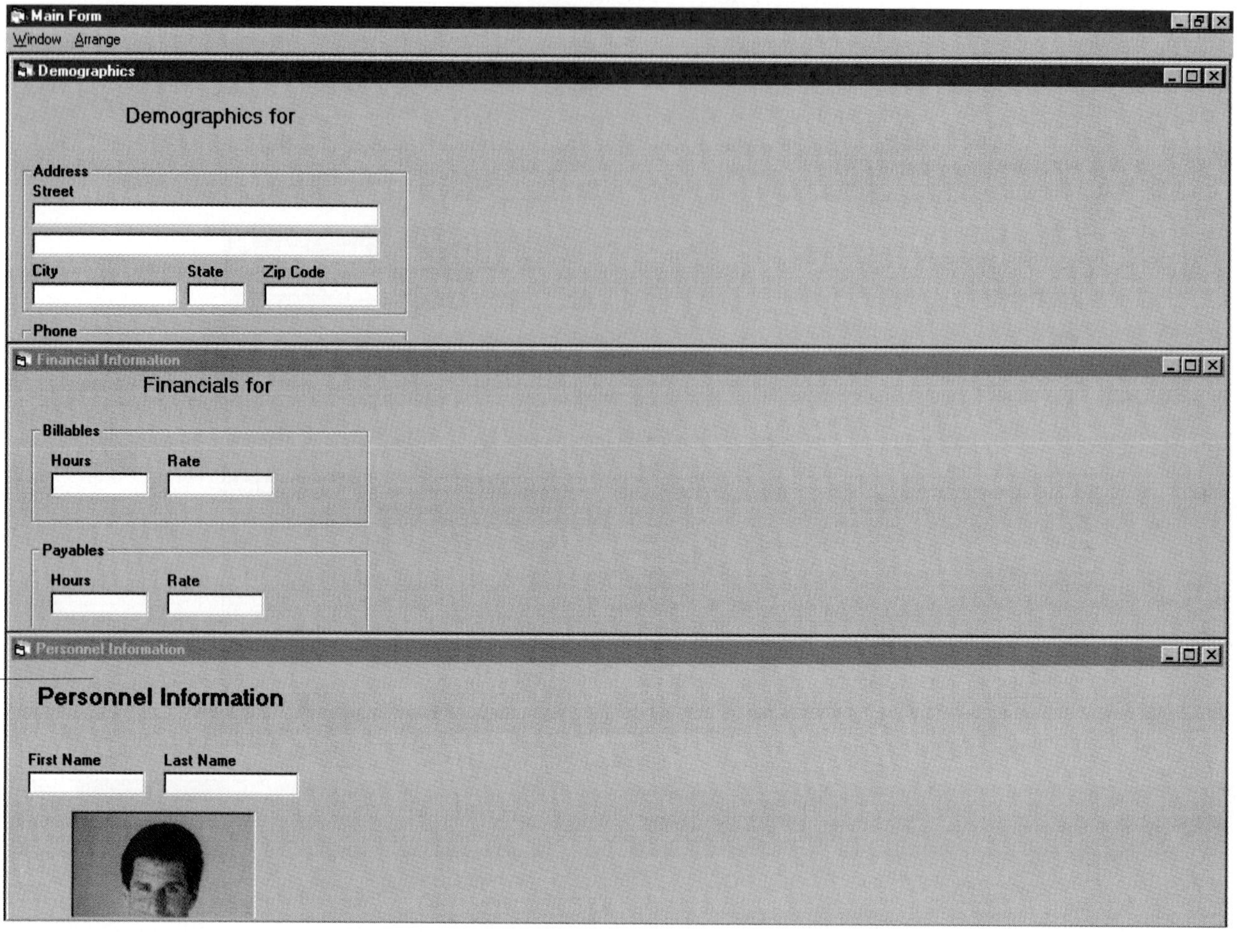

Figure 12.30   Forms Tiled Horizontally

To arrange the child windows as in Figures 12.29–12.31, you must call the Arrange event from the MDI form as in the following syntax:

```
MDIFormName.Arrange vbCascade
```

or

```
MDIFormName.Arrange vbTileHorizontal
```

or

```
MDIFormName.Arrange vbTileVertical
```

Therefore, the code for the menu events is as follows:

```
Private Sub mnuDemographics_Click()
frmDemographics.Show
End Sub
Private Sub mnuFinancial_Click()
frmFinancial.Show
End Sub
```

(continues)

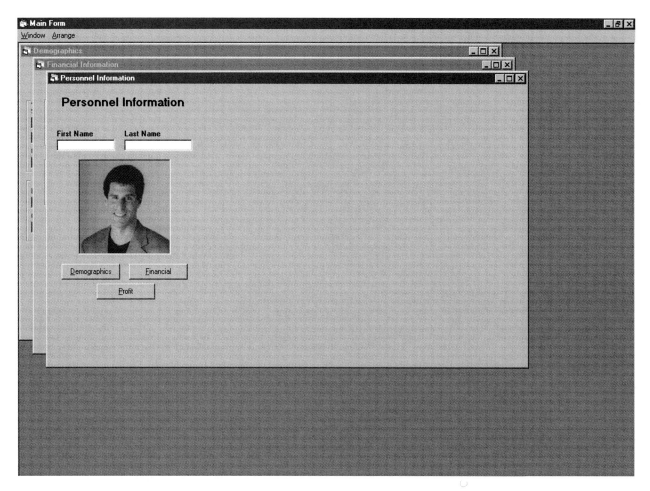

Figure 12.31 Forms Cascaded

(continued)

```
Private Sub mnuPersonnel_Click()
frmPersonnel.Show
End Sub
Private Sub mnuCascade_Click()
MDIForm1.Arrange vbCascade
End Sub
Private Sub mnuTileHorizontally_Click()
MDIForm1.Arrange vbTileHorizontal
End Sub
Private Sub mnuVertically_Click()
MDIForm1.Arrange vbTileVertical
End Sub
```

12.4 Object-Oriented Development Concepts

Many computer languages throw the term object-oriented programming around, but what is it? A *real* object-oriented programming language supports three basic concepts: **encapsulation**, **polymorphism**, and **inheritance**.

Confused? Most people are. So, instead of delving straight into a confusing array of terms and concepts, let's take a step back for a discussion about real-world objects.

Then once you have the concept, you will relate the terms of object-oriented programming to the analogy. This will provide a good parallel to introduce many confusing terms.

A Real-World Example

Let's discuss an object that everyone is familiar with, a TV. If I asked you to explain exactly how a TV works could you do it? Could you explain every detail of how a show is broadcast and displayed? I doubt it. I certainly cannot; however, that does not stop me from watching the latest episode of *Buffy the Vampire Slayer*.

How about another question; how is a TV built? Well, I can't tell you all the details of that either, but somewhere someone has designed a set of blueprints that specifically outline the necessary parts and their configuration. These blueprints would specify the internal and external characteristics that define how the TV would operate.

There are a great many variations in television design. TVs now come in different shapes, sizes, method of display, and the list goes on and on. If I had a set of blueprints for the latest 65" HDTV, I would have the information required to build a great TV, but I couldn't watch Buffy staking vampires on the blueprint.

However, if someone created a TV from those specifications and placed it in front of me, I would be ready to watch whatever show I wanted.

Of course, the TV probably would not come set to the exact station that I wanted when I received it. Nor would it probably be set to the volume level and brightness that I desired. Does this mean that I will have to go through the blueprints and determine the exact inner workings of the TV to change some of it settings? Of course not, because the TV comes with an interface in the form of a remote control. This interface allows the user to set certain of the TV's characteristics to specific values.

Object-Oriented Concepts

Just as real-world objects need specifications to detail the design of an object, so do **objects** that you will develop in Visual Basic. In Visual Basic you use a **class** to describe the properties and actions associated with an object in the same manner as a blueprint describes the properties and functionality of a TV. You may think of a class as a combination of a user-defined type and the functions/subroutines that are declared to execute on the user-defined type.

A class contains fields and functions as you are used to, however, when referring to them within a class, the terminology changes. Instead of referring to the individual data elements of a user-defined type as the fields, in a class you refer to them as **properties**. Just as you do not have access to the inner workings of a TV, a developer should not allow access to the properties of a class except by specific routines that the developer creates. These routines will no longer be referred to as functions, but as **methods** of the class.

Just as the blueprint for a TV does not serve as a functioning TV, a class does not serve as a functioning version of the item you are creating. The class must be *built* just as your TV is assembled. When you wish to create a functioning version of the class, you must create an **object**. While the computer does not have an assembly line to create an object, it does have to allocate the memory required for the object and initialize any variables. This process of creating an object from a class is known as **instantiating** an object.

So now that you are familiar with a few object-oriented terms, the question remains, how object-oriented is Visual Basic? Let's look at the three terms introduced earlier and see if Visual Basic implements some or all of them.

Encapsulation

During the course of the day, you are used to using many real-word objects without concerning yourself with the details of how they work internally. You use these objects with an interface that restricts your use to predefined tasks.

As in your earlier example, a television has a series of controls on the outside for the viewer to turn it on or off, change the channel, and adjust the picture. You are restricted from making other changes to the television by the box that surrounds it.

Encapsulation enables the programmer designing the class to dictate what types of operations are permissible upon a class without permitting other programmers access to the inner workings of the class. In essence, the class designer allows other programmers to have the complexity of a class hidden and ensure that other programmers can only use the class in ways intended by the programmer designing the class.

Objects like text boxes, combo boxes, or check boxes were all used by you without your knowledge of their internal workings. The properties and events that you accessed only allowed you to manipulate the objects in ways predetermined by the developers of the objects.

Imagine if you had an `Integer` variable that was supposed to represent the minute portion of a time. You would not want to the value to be beyond the range of 0–59. An integer could be between the range –32,768 to 32,767. By providing control over these issues, classes provide a user-interface over your data.

Polymorphism

Let's revisit your real-world television example. There are many types of televisions. Currently you can choose from a black and white, color, HDTV, picture tube, LCD, or projection television. While all of these televisions have different features, they are all commonly referred to as TVs. These TVs have many of the same functions, even though these functions might operate differently from set to set.

Try switching the channels on a bunch of different sets. Do they all do the same thing? The channel up button/switch will generally move to the next channel. However, depending upon the set, any of the following actions can occur:

◆ The television is set to the next numerical channel above the current one.
◆ The television is set to the next valid channel above the current one.
◆ The television is set to the next numerical channel above the current one and it briefly displays the new channel number.

While there are many other possibilities, you get the idea.

The concept of having one name but a different behavior depending upon the object it belongs to is known as polymorphism. You are already familiar with polymorphism in Visual Basic. Many of the controls that you have built your applications from have properties, methods, or events with the same name but take on a slightly different meaning from control to control.

Inheritance

One of the keys to efficient development of applications is the capability to reuse the code that you previously developed. One way programmers accomplish this is to "cut and paste" code from one project to another. A better method, inheritance, is to build new classes from previous ones without modifying the original code.

Often when you develop a class, you realize after developing it that you may need another class that is very similar. Beginner programmers will copy the original class, make any changes necessary, and rename the old class. Although this works in the short term, it is problematic. Imagine if you have created many classes using this method. Then after using the new classes in various programs, you discover that there was a bug in the original code. Now you must go back and modify the code in all the classes you copied the bug into. With inheritance, if you modify the original class, all the classes based on that change will be updated automatically.

The other problem, although not quite as severe, is that you waste a lot of unnecessary disk space by having multiple copies of the source code each time you copy it.

A simple example of using inheritance is to create a class called `Person`. A person would have the properties like first name, last name, address, city, state, zip, and phone number.

If you then wanted to develop a `Student` class, by inheriting the properties of the class `Person`, you can simply add the properties specific to being a student: major, GPA, total credits, and so on.

Unfortunately, Visual Basic Version 6.0 does not support inheritance. However, Visual Basic .NET will.

Creating Your Own Classes

To create a class, you must add a `Class` module to the application. To do so, select Add Class Module from the Project menu. Figure 12.32 will appear.

Figure 12.32
Add Class Module

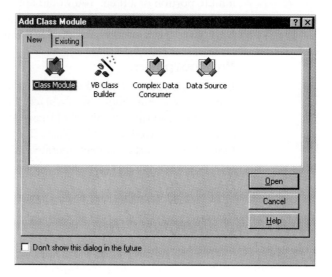

When creating a class, you should always give it a name. Its file extension will be `.cls`. You can name a class by changing the `Name` property in the Property window. Once the module is created and properly named, creating a class is a combination of specifying what properties your class will store and what methods will be performed upon these properties.

When designing a class it is important to follow as many of the principles of object-oriented development as possible. Therefore, all properties should be declared as private to the class and only accessible through methods that give access to the properties in ways intended by the developer of the class.

Declaring properties is no different than declaring variables, however an "m" is added to the prefix to indicate that the property is declared inside a class.

Declaring methods is no different than declaring functions and subroutines, however, note that they will have access to the properties defined for the class.

Example: Student Class

Let's create a `Student` class that should contain the first and last names of the student. Additionally, you should track the midterm grade, final exam grade, major, and social security number for the student.

Because good class programming follows the concepts of object-oriented development, you should not allow information to be accessed without calling the proper methods. Therefore, you will create methods to access and set each data value contained within the class. However, we will add one caveat. The student's social security number and grades will only be accessible with a password. Therefore, you will also store a valid password within the `Student` class.

Step I: Create a new class module by clicking on Add Class Module in the Project menu.

Step 2: Rename the class to Student by changing the Name property to Student.

Step 3: Declare the properties for the class using the following code:

```
Option Explicit

Private mstrFirstName As String
Private mstrLastName As String
Private mstrMajor As String
Private mintMidterm As Integer
Private mintFinalExam As Integer
Private mstrPassword As String
Private mstrSSN As String
```

Step 4: The first method that you will create initializes the required properties of a student. These properties include the first and last names, social security number, major, and a password.

```
Public Sub InitializeStudent(strFirstName As String, strLastName As String, _
strSSN As String, strMajor As String, strPassword As String)
If (Len(mstrPassword) > 0) Then
  MsgBox "The password is already set"
Else
  mstrFirstName = strFirstName
  mstrLastName = strLastName
  mstrSSN = strSSN
  mstrMajor = strMajor
  mstrPassword = strPassword
End If
End Sub
```

Notice that you check whether the password has already been set. It would not be a very useful class if someone could reset all the values by simply recalling InitializeStudent.

Step 5: You need to create methods to access the private data values contained in the class.

There are two ways of doing this. You could write methods called SetMidterm, SetFinalExam, and so on as you do in the following code:

```
Public Sub SetMidterm(intMidterm As Integer, strPassword As String)
If (mstrPassword = strPassword) Then
  mintMidterm = intMidterm
Else
  MsgBox "Invalid Password"
End If
End Sub

Public Sub SetFinalExam(intFinalExam As Single, strPassword As String)
If (mstrPassword = strPassword) Then
  mintFinalExam = intFinalExam
Else
  MsgBox "Invalid Password"
End If
End Sub
```

However, Visual Basic allows you to create special methods for accessing and setting properties. The property methods `Let` and `Get` will allow you to create methods so that the developer can set and access the properties of your class in the same manner as you have with the properties of controls and other objects in Visual Basic.

You have implemented three `Get` methods that require a password to return the midterm grade, final exam grade, or social security number. You have also implemented three `Get` methods that return the first and last names as well as the student's major.

```
Property Get intFinalExam(strPassword As String) As Integer
If (mstrPassword = strPassword) Then
    intFinalExam = mintFinalExam
Else
   MsgBox "Invalid Password"
End If
End Property

Property Get intMidterm(strPassword As String) As Integer
If (mstrPassword = strPassword) Then
    intMidterm = mintMidterm
Else
   MsgBox "Invalid Password"
End If
End Property

Property Get intSSN(strPassword As String) As String
If (mstrPassword = strPassword) Then
    intSSN = mintSSN
Else
   MsgBox "Invalid Password"
End If
End Property

Property Get strFirstName() As String
strFirstName = mstrFirstName
End Property

Property Get strLastName() As String
strLastName = mstrLastName
End Property

Property Get strMajor() As String
strMajor = mstrMajor
End Property
```

Step 6: You now must create four methods to allow the setting of the first name, last name, major, and social security number. These properties can be set using a `Let` method, which will allow the developer to set these properties as you would any predefined property.

```
Property Let strFirstName(strFirstName As String)
mstrFirstName = strFirstName
End Property
```

(continues)

(continued)

```
Property Let strLastName(strLastName As String)
mstrLastName = strLastName
End Property

Property Let strMajor(strMajor As String)
mstrMajor = strMajor
End Property

Property Let strSSN(strSSN As String)
mstrSSNName = strSSN
End Property
```

Step 7: To set the midterm and final exam grades you are going to require a password. Unfortunately, when you wish to pass a parameter to set a property, you must create methods in the traditional way. Here are the methods to set the midterm and final exam grades:

```
Public Sub SetMidterm(intMidterm As Integer, strPassword As String)
If (mstrPassword = strPassword) Then
  mintMidterm = intMidterm
Else
  MsgBox "Invalid Password"
End If
End Sub

Public Sub SetFinalExam(intFinalExam As Single, strPassword As String)
If (mstrPassword = strPassword) Then
  mintFinalExam = intFinalExam
Else
  MsgBox "Invalid Password"
End If
End Sub
```

By creating methods for setting the midterm and final exam that require a password, you prevent properties from being accessed that should not be accessed without the proper password.

Creating an Object from a Class

The simplest way to create an object is to use the New keyword. By using the following syntax you may create an object from a class defined in your project.

```
Dim ObjectName As New ClassName
```

Therefore, to create an object called Jeff in your Student class, you would use the following code:

```
Dim Jeff As New Student
```

 TIP

When you create a new class in your project, it will appear as one of the objects that can be created as you declare a variable.

Figure 12.33
Class Listed in Type Ahead
Pop-Up Menu

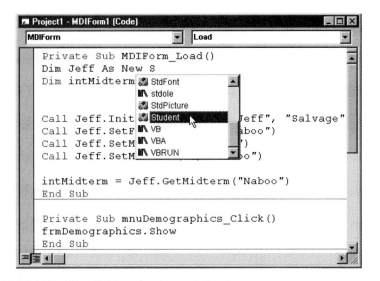

Observe the following code that declares an object called Jeff, initializes the object, and sets/accesses its properties.

```
Dim Jeff As New Student
Dim intMidterm As Integer

'Initialize the Object
Call Jeff.InitializeStudent("Jeff", "Salvage", "999-99-9999",
     "Computer Science", "Naboo")

'Set the Final Exam Grade
Call Jeff.SetFinalExam(99, "Naboo")

'Attempt to set the Midterm Grade
Call Jeff.SetMidterm(99, "XYZ")

'Set the Midterm Grade
Call Jeff.SetMidterm(99, "Naboo")

'Change the First Name
Jeff.strFirstName = "Jeffrey"


'Retrieve the Midterm Grade
intMidterm = Jeff.intMidterm("Naboo")
```

◆ 12.5 Case Study

Problem Description   Your last case study will be to combine different forms that you previously created into a single application. You will create one application that combines the database form for entering payroll data with the charting program that graphs the history of the payroll.

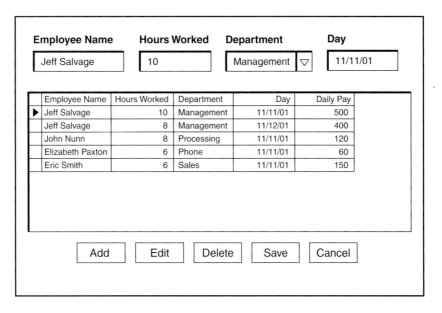

Figure 12.34 MDI Application with Data Entry Form Active

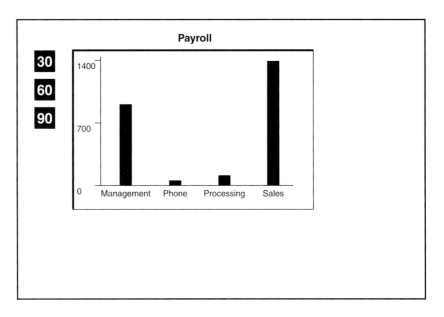

Figure 12.35 MDI Application with Charting Form Active

Problem Discussion When creating a multiform application, you must decide whether you are going to create an MDI application or not. If you do not then you can create a new project, add a form and a menu, and add the previously created forms to the project.

However, if you create an MDI application, you should resave your previously created forms to another name, as you will be modifying the properties to indicate that they are MDI child windows.

For your solution, you will create an MDI application.

Problem Solution   Very little code is required to solve this problem. You must first create a new project and add an MDI form.

Add to the form the following menu.

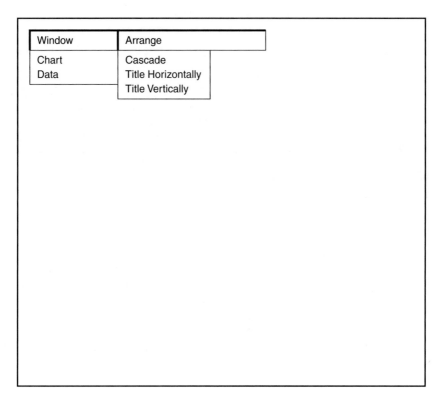

Figure 12.36   Sketch of the Menu

The Window menu should contain two menu items: `mnuData` and `mnuChart`. The code for them simply calls the form associated with each menu item:

```
Private Sub mnuChart_Click()
frmPayrollChart.Show
End Sub

Private Sub mnuData_Click()
frmPayroll.Show
End Sub
```

The Arrange menu should contain three menu items: `mnuCascade`, `mnuTileHorizontal`, and `mnuTileVertical`. The code for them is identical to the code you created for the other MDI applications you have developed.

```
Private Sub mnuCascade_Click()
MDIForm1.Arrange vbCascade
End Sub

Private Sub mnuTileHorizontally_Click()
MDIForm1.Arrange vbTileHorizontal
End Sub

Private Sub mnuTileVertical_Click()
MDIForm1.Arrange vbTileVertical
End Sub
```

With the MDI form and menu created, all that remains is to set the `MDIChild` attribute on the forms `frmPayroll` and `frmPayrollChart` to `True`.

Error Trapping

When writing Visual Basic applications, it is best to try to prevent or anticipate all run-time errors from occurring. Although user input can be validated and controls can be enabled or disabled in context, all errors cannot always be specifically checked and handled properly.

During the course of developing your applications, it is safe to say that you probably have run an application with an error from time to time. When the error occurs, a Visual Basic error message is displayed. Although developers understand these messages, they are sometimes confusing to users. Additionally, depending upon what type of error occurs, a determination can be made as to whether to terminate the application or allow the user to continue.

To use the built-in error handling, you combine two concepts: Setting the error handler and executing the error handler.

To set an error handler, use the following syntax:

```
On Error GoTo ErrorHandler
```

To handle the error handler, you need a label that matches the name of the error handler.

```
ErrorHandler:
    Code goes here
```

You can create different error handlers to cover different situations. It is better to attempt to localize your error handlers than to try to write one giant error handler to cover all possible programs for an entire application.

If you want to switch error handlers, all that is required is to execute another `On Error GoTo` statement with the name of a different error handler.

If you want to switch off an error handler that you have set, but not turn another one on, use the following statement:

```
On Error GoTo 0
```

After you have executed your error handler code, you have three main choices to determine what happens to your application.

If the error is one that can be corrected by the error handler, then you may wish to execute the following statement to try to execute the original code that caused the error.

```
Resume
```

If you issue a `Resume` statement and the error occurs again, you will be thrown back to the error handler.

Another option is to resume execution at the statement after the one that caused the error. This can be accomplished by executing the statement

```
Resume Next
```

If you determine in the error handler that the error is too severe to continue, you can always stop execution of the application with the `End` statement.

```
End
```

Observe the following example, which demonstrates a possible error trapping routine for performing a calculation that computes the average sales commission for a sales person for the summer months.

Notice that you check for common errors like overflow. You could also add other errors like divide by zero by using a `Select Case` statement on the different error codes.

```vb
Private Sub cmdCompute_Click()
Dim intAverageCommission As Integer
Dim intJuneSales As Integer
Dim intJulySales As Integer
Dim intAugustSales As Integer
Dim intPeriod As Integer


intJuneSales = 0
intJulySales = 0
intAugustSales = 0
intPeriod = 0

'Set values here


On Error GoTo Err_Calculation
intAverageCommission = (intJuneSales + intJulySales + intAugustSales) / shtPeriod

MsgBox Str(intAverageSales)

Err_Calculation:
If (Err.Number = 6) Then 'Overflow
        MsgBox "An error has occurred because the commission calculation was" _
            "too large to be stored."
Else
    MsgBox "An unknown error has occurred"
End If
End Sub
```

Visual Basic .NET Alert

Although the error handling introduced here will continue to work in VB .NET, VB .NET has greatly improved the capabilities of error handling. When switching to VB .NET, take the time to learn the new method of error handling.

Key Words and Key Terms

Arrange
A method on an MDI form that allows its child windows to be automatically arranged with it.

Cascade
An option of the `Arrange` method that arranges the child windows within each window slightly overlapping the others.

Class
A template for creating objects. A template may be thought of as combining a user-defined type with functions and procedures in one construct.

Encapsulation
Restricting the access of data from programmers.

Form_Activate
An event that is triggered when a form is displayed. It is triggered directly after the `Form_Load` event.

Form_Load
An event that is triggered when a form is displayed for the first time. It is triggered directly before the `Form_Activate` event.

Get
A special method used to access the properties in a class.

Hide
A method that causes a form to no longer to display, although it will not unload the form from the computer's memory.

Inheritance
The capability to create a class from an existing class.

Let
A special method used to set the properties in a class.

MDI
A multiple document interface.

Me
A reference to the current object.

Menu
An object that allows frequently used operations to be accessed in a user-friendly manner.

Method
A function or subroutine defined within a class.

New
A keyword used to create an object from a class.

Object
The instantiation of a class.

Polymorphism
The concept of using a single name for different behaviors depending upon the object to which it belongs.

Submenu

A menu that pops up from an existing menu.

SDI

Single document interface, an application that has only one form open at a time.

Show

A method that loads and displays a form.

Tile horizontally

An option of the `Arrange` method that arranges the child windows within each window from top to bottom.

Tile vertically

An option of the `Arrange` method that arranges the child windows within each window side by side.

Unload

A command that causes a form to no longer be displayed. This method will also remove the form from the computer's memory.

Additional Exercises

Questions 1–5 are True or False.

1. More than one menu can be associated with a single form.

2. A menu item has many events associated with it.

3. In an MDI application, the first form created will be the first form to be displayed. This cannot be changed.

4. A `Let` method cannot accept additional parameters other than the one needed to set the property.

5. Only one `on error` routine can exist in an application at a time.

6. Describe in your own words why critics of Visual Basic 6.0 claim that it is not truly object-oriented.

7. Are all multiple form applications considered MDI applications? Explain why or why not.

8. Write a class called `Employee`. It should have properties of `FirstName`, `LastName`, `Salary`, `Position`, `Password`, and `YearsOfEmployement`. It should have `Property` methods to set and access the `FirstName`, `LastName`, `Position`, and `YearsOfEmployeement` properties. There should also be a method to initialize all of the parameters. A method should exist to set the salary that requires a password. A method should exist to give an employee a raise. It should require a password.

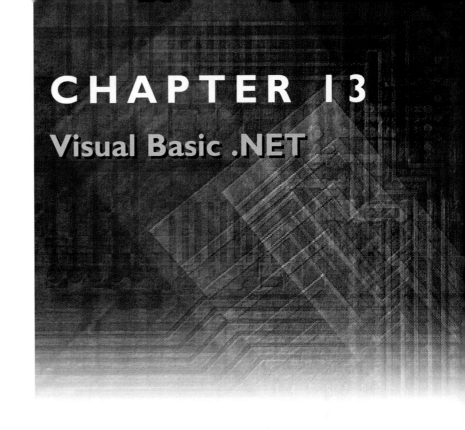

CHAPTER 13
Visual Basic .NET

- Introduce the concepts of Visual Basic .NET

- Explain the differences between Visual Basic 6.0 and Visual Basic .NET

- Explain the reasons for switching from Visual Basic 6.0 to Visual Basic .NET

You might have heard that Microsoft is coming out with a new version of Visual Basic called **Visual Basic .NET**. Microsoft has given Visual Basic a new name as opposed to just calling it Visual Basic 7.0 because this is much more than a simple upgrade. Different upgrades to Visual Basic have added new features to the programming language. With each upgrade came a certain amount of pain when the way things used to work changed. However, time proved the healer of all wounds as developers adapted to the new versions and learned to exploit their new features. With this upgrade, more than just the language and development environment are changing. Microsoft is making sweeping changes to the entire development architecture. Although in the future many texts will be written on these numerous changes, this chapter will present a primer of the key information so that you can start learning Visual Basic .NET now.

You will leverage the knowledge already gained from learning Visual Basic 6.0. Topics are presented in this chapter in the same order you encountered them as you worked through the text to this point. We will highlight the various changes to each major category of the Visual Basic language and introduce any new features so that you can maximize your productivity in Visual Basic .NET in the least amount of time. Stay tuned, because the Visual Basic .NET Coach will be available with a more complete explanation and examples.

13.1 What Is Visual Basic .NET?

What a question. It is hard to answer without explaining the bigger picture. Visual Basic .NET is one of a number of programming environments designed to work with the new .NET architecture.

The New Environment

You might ask yourself, why would a simple upgrade of a development environment require so many changes? The answer requires some knowledge outside of the scope of what you have learned about developing applications. So far, the applications you have developed have been simple. They were run on the computer that they were developed upon. However, when you deploy applications, many files are installed along with the main executable. If you have installed various applications on your computer, I am sure you have experienced the pains of incompatibility as one application interferes with another. The new .NET framework solves this problem.

One Development Environment

As you learn more programming languages, you must learn a completely different development environment. With the .NET framework, all the programs use the same integrated development environment. This makes switching languages far simpler.

A Common Set of Objects

The .NET framework doesn't end there. When we discussed Visual Basic's object-oriented capabilities, we said that it fell short of being a true object-oriented language. Visual Basic .NET is completely object-oriented. It incorporates all the characteristics of a true object-oriented language. However, with all of these object-oriented capabilities, you now are going to want to program with them. More importantly, you are going to want to use objects that have already been created.

Although you are already familiar with some objects, like the command button, text box, label, and so on, with a true object-oriented language the number of objects that can be included are limitless. So imagine you are programming in Visual Basic for some time, and you get used to the built-in objects and develop hundreds more. Then suddenly you have to program in another language. If you didn't have access to all the classes you were familiar with and had developed, you would have to start over completely. Another key benefit of the .NET framework is that the same objects are available regardless of the development language you choose. Furthermore, the other languages in the .NET framework can access any objects developed in any language. The benefits of such a relationship between environments should be obvious.

Another issue when you switch languages is that each language may interpret variable types differently. As someone who teaches multiple languages simultaneously it has always been annoying to have to remember the exact range of an `Integer` for the language that I am teaching at that moment. With the .NET framework all the types of variables and classes that are included are basically the same.

Sounds great doesn't it? Ah, but all this does not come without a price.

13.2 Issues with Converting to Visual Basic .NET

Wouldn't it be great if you got all of this added functionality and could still could develop your applications in the same manner as before? Although many of the keywords that you have grown accustomed to are still in place, many have also gone away or are no longer recommended for use.

To ensure that all of the new features work with all of the languages in the .NET framework, compromises had to be made. At first these compromises will seem annoying. However, in the long run these changes will make developing applications much simpler.

At the center of these issues is that with the additional power of a true object-oriented language, a new programming methodology must be mastered. This is no small task. One of the benefits of Visual Basic 6.0 and its predecessors was that it was relatively simple to develop an application with little or no previous programming experience. Now with the addition of true object-oriented development, the initial learning curve will be slightly steeper than before.

Shortly we will go into great detail about the changes you will have to make to adapt to developing in the Visual Basic .NET environment. You may feel like it's too steep a hill to climb. Many people felt this way when Visual Basic made radical changes between versions 3.0 and 4.0; however, over time developers realized that the new functionality is worth the time required to adapt. As you develop applications with Visual Basic .NET, you will come to realize that it was worth the effort.

Although many people will not port their existing Visual Basic 6.0 applications to Visual Basic .NET, clearly the future is going in the .NET arena and as the .NET world stabilizes, new applications should be developed with it. Eventually, support for Visual Basic 6. 0 will disappear and Visual Basic .NET will be considered the standard.

This chapter is not intended to teach you every feature of Visual Basic .NET, nor is it designed to teach object-oriented methodologies. Instead, it will be designed to teach you how to start to develop in Visual Basic .NET based on the knowledge you have gained from reading the first 12 chapters of this text.

We will follow the same sequence of information the text has introduced you to up to this point, and go over the biggest hurdles you will have in developing similar applications with Visual Basic .NET, as well as a few nifty new features. By September 2002, the Visual Basic .NET Coach will be published and it will cover all of these topics and more in great detail.

13.3 Your First VB .NET Applications

The first step in creating an application with Visual Basic .NET is to familiarize yourself with the main components of the new Integrated Development Environment.

Step I: When Visual Basic .NET is started, the familiar startup window is replaced with Figure 13.1. The new startup window is actually a home page for the application. Notice that it now has an Internet-like interface.

       Even with this new interface, you can still see that the major options previously presented are still available to you. These include

     ◆ Recently used projects
     ◆ The capability to open projects not listed in the recent projects
     ◆ An option to create new projects

Additionally, links are provided to other resources.

Figure 13.1
Home Page

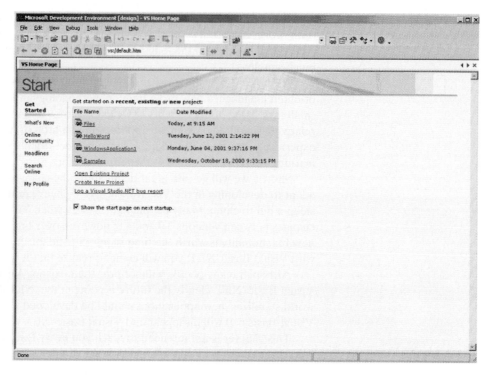

Step 2: The very first time that you run Visual Basic .NET, you will be presented with Figure 13.2. This window will allow you to personalize the settings of Visual Studio .NET as a whole. Because the same IDE is used for more than one language, you will wish to set the profile to Visual Basic as we have.

Once these features are set, this screen will not automatically appear. If you need to revisit it, you can select My Profile from the Home Page and change any of these values.

Figure 13.2
My Profile Page

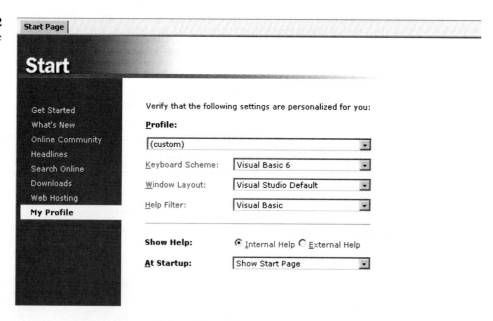

Step 3: If you select Create New Project from the Home Page, the New Project window will appear. Although you have the option to create a great variety of projects, for now, you will stick to the Windows application. To create a new

Windows application for Visual Basic, make sure Visual Basic Projects is selected from the Project Types and Windows Application is selected from the Templates.

With these options selected, all that remains is to specify a Name and Location for the new project. A directory for your files, with the name of your application, will be created for you.

Figure 13.3
New Project Window

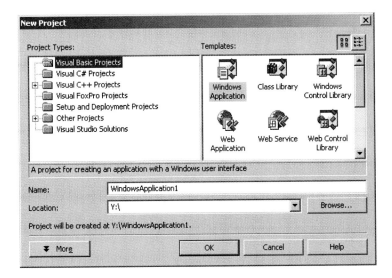

Step 4: At first glance, the IDE doesn't appear that different, but a great many things have changed.

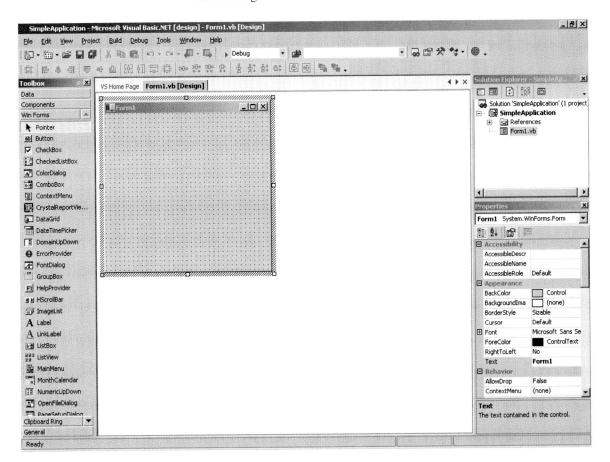

Figure 13.4 New Integrated Development Environment

Figure 13.5
New Toolbox

If we start by looking at our toolbox, we will notice many minor differences.

1 Each control listed now contains the icon for the control and the name of the control to the right of it.
2 There are a great many more default controls in the Toolbox.
3 Some of the controls that you are familiar with are renamed (i.e. command button is now called a button, a frame is now called a group box).
4 Along with the form controls are other controls. These additional controls are gouped and can be selected by clicking on their group name.
5 When the number of controls is greater than can be displayed inthe toolbox, an arrow appears so that you can scroll down the list.

Figure 13.6   Solution Explorer

While the new Solution Explorer will display more information than its predecessor the Project Explorer, there is very little difference to use for now.

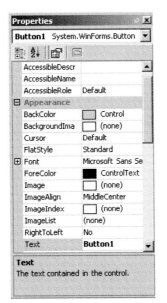

The Properties window looks almost identical and it functions pretty similar as well. In fact all it really had done to it was a minor face-lift.

One of the coolest of the face-lifts is the ability to expand and collapse areas of the Property window. Notice the small plus symbol next to the Font in Figure 13.7. By clicking on it, it will expand the Properties Window to show you all of the properties related to Fonts.

Likewise, if a minus symbol appears next to property, as it does in the Appearance group, then the user can click on it to make all of the properties in that group disappear.

Figure 13.7   New Toolbox

So at this point, you are feeling pretty confident that you can develop in this new environment. There aren't too many changes, and those that have been made appear to be cosmetic, right? Oh, you are in for a little surprise.

Let's add a button to the form. Although it has a different name, I can add it either by dragging and dropping the control from the toolbox to the form or double-clicking on the control from the toolbox.

Okay, that was painless. Let's now look at the code by double-clicking on the button you just added. See Figure 13.8.

If I were Robin, I would be saying "Holy code generation, Batman!" What's the deal with that? We mentioned earlier that Visual Basic .NET is completely object-oriented. This is your first sign of it. For now, ignore most of what you are seeing. Suffice to say it is code that will have meaning later.

If you wanted to add code to the button's `Click` event, you could do so in the same manner as before.

There are a few changes to how you deal with individual controls. In my opinion, they are good changes, although they may cause some confusion at first.

Did it ever bother you that when you set the text in a text box you use the `Text` property, but when you set the text to display in a label you set the `Caption` property? Well it bothered me, so I guess the gods at Microsoft listened.

The `Caption` property has gone away and been replaced with the `Text` property for label controls. Other changes like this have been made in various controls.

Your best plan of attack is to first try the old way. If it works, great, if not you will know because the property will not appear in the type ahead combo box that appears when you are coding with a defined control.

If the old property does not exist, you can look at the other properties that appear in the combo box or you can use the built-in help.

Figure 13.8
Initial Code for Your
Application

The help features in Visual Basic .NET are greatly improved. By clicking on the Help menu you can see the many options that are available to you. If you selected the Index submenu item, you could choose to look up the control with which you are having difficulty.

Figure 13.9
Help Window

By double-clicking on the Button Class, you are presented with Figure 13.10.

Figure 13.10
Button Help

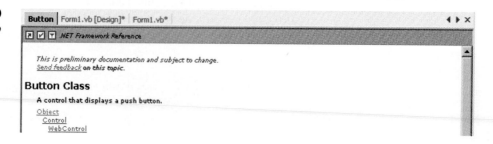

Although the entire window is not shown in Figure 13.10, you can see that additional information about the control is displayed. What you may not have noticed is that Visual Basic .NET did not open a new window, as would be the case in Visual Basic 6.0. Instead, it opened a new tab to the existing project window.

Notice the three tabs at the top of Figure 13.10. The first, Button, is the active one and shows the Button's help information. The second, Form1.vb [Design], contains the actual physical design of the form. The third, Form1.vb*, contains the code. This intuitive interface will allow you to switch back and forth between the three windows without having to close any of them.

One final note; we mentioned earlier in the text not to use the default properties. The reason is they will not work in Visual Basic .NET.

Re-creating Your First Application

Your first application, in Chapter 2, was "The Lady or the Tiger." Remember, it involved two doors that could be opened. One revealed a tiger, whereas the other revealed a young maiden. The application, shown in Figure 13.11, appears almost identically when created with Visual Basic .NET.

Figure 13.11
New Version of Application

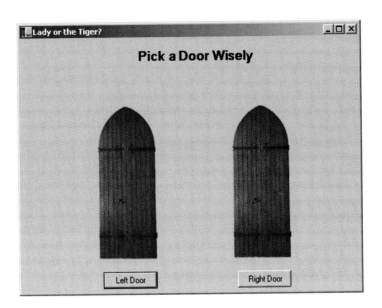

To create this application, follow similar steps to the ones in Chapter 2.

Step 1: Change the text that appears in the form's title bar from the default text to "Lady or the Tiger." In Visual Basic 6.0, this would require changing the `Caption` property; however, in Visual Basic .NET, you change the `Text` property.

 TIP

Remember the `Caption` property has been renamed to the `Text` property in many constructs.

Step 2: Add a label across the center of the form. Change the `Name` property of the label control to `lblTitle`.

Step 3: Change the `Text` property of the `lblTitle` label to `Lady or the Tiger`.

Step 4: Add a picture box control for the left door and change the `Name` property of the control to `pctLeftDoor`.

Step 5: Click on the `Image` property and select the `Door.jpg` file so that the door is initially displayed in the picture box control.

Step 6: Add a picture box control for the right door and change the `Name` property of the control to `pctRightDoor`.

Step 7: Click on the `Image` property and select the `Door.jpg` file so that the door is initially displayed in the picture box control.

Step 8: Add a button control for the left door and change the `Name` property of the control to `cmdLeftDoor`.

Step 9: Double-click on the `cmdLeftDoor` button control and add the following code to add the functionality required when the left door is selected:

```
Protected Sub cmdLeftDoor_Click(ByVal sender As Object, _
                            ByVal e As System.EventArgs)
    pctLeftDoor.Image = Image.FromFile("Y:\SimpleApp2\Lady.gif")
    lblTitle.Text = "Innocent"
End Sub
```

The code is similar to the code from the Version 6.0 application. However, now you set the `Image` property instead of the `Picture` property. Also, instead of calling the `LoadPicture` function, you now call the method `FromFile` from the `Image` object.

The final difference is you change the `Text` attribute instead of the `Caption` attribute of the `lblTitle` label control.

Step 10: Add a Button control for the left door and change the `Name` property of the control to `cmdLeftDoor`.

Step 11: Double-click on the `cmdRightDoor` button control and add the following code to add the functionality required when the left door is selected:

```
Protected Sub cmdRightDoor_Click(ByVal sender As Object, _
                            ByVal e As System.EventArgs)
    pctRightDoor.Image = Image.FromFile("Y:\SimpleApp2\Tiger.gif")
    lblTitle.Text = "Guilty"
End Sub
```

That's it. You are now ready to run your first application. Click on the Save icon in the main toolbar to save the work that you have done and press <F5> to run the application.

13.4 Performing Operations and Storing the Result
Changes to Data Types

With the advent of multiple languages working under a common architecture, each language must use the same data types. Therefore, Visual Basic .NET was required to change a few of the data types you are already familiar with and add a few that you are not.

Size	VB 6.0	VB .NET
16-bit Integer	Integer	Short
32-bit Integer	Long	Integer
64-bit Integer	Not available	Long
	Currency	Decimal
	Variant	Object
	Did not exist	Char

Change in Scope for Dim Statement

Hopefully, you heeded our warning in Chapter 3 and declared all of the variables required for a routine at the beginning of the routine. This would be true for all local variables whether you were declaring them in a function, subroutine, event, or method.

In Visual Basic 6.0, if you didn't heed the warning, the variable was visible to the entire routine anyway. However, the warning was given because in Visual Basic .NET, this will no longer work.

Observe the two declarations of the Max function. If you declared intMaximumValue as in Visual Basic 6.0, in the new Visual Basic .NET environment, it would only be visible to the code within the If block that it was declared. This would lead to an error that could have been avoided by simply coding your local variable declarations first.

Visual Basic 6.0

```
Private Function Max(ByVal intVal1 As Integer, ByVal intVal2 As Integer) _
            As Integer
    If (intVal1 > intVal2) Then
        Dim intMaximumValue As Integer
        intMaximumValue = intVal1
    Else
        intMaximumValue = intVal2
    End If

    Max = intMaximumValue
End Function
```

Visual Basic .NET

```
Private Function Max(ByVal intVal1 As Integer, ByVal intVal2 As Integer) _
            As Integer
    Dim intMaximumValue As Integer

    If (intVal1 > intVal2) Then
        intMaximumValue = intVal1
    Else
        intMaximumValue = intVal2
    End If

    Return intMaximumValue
End Function
```

You may think this is an annoying change, but it is done to empower the developer to have maximum control over when variables and objects go in and out of scope.

A Quick Shortcut

Visual Basic .NET gives you a shortcut when you know the initial value you wish to set the variable to at the time of its declaration.

If you want to initialize a variable to a value, you just assign it to the right of the declaration. Observe how you declare an `Integer` called `intValue` to 1 in the following code:

```
Dim intValue As Integer = 1
```

Changes to Operators

VB .NET has introduced a few operators that, although not earth-shattering in their impact, are a really nice addition.

How often have you wanted to add, subtract, multiply, or divide a number to an existing variable and store the result back in the variable? For me, it happens pretty often and I was always frustrated that Visual Basic did not have the shortcut operators other languages like C++ provide.

My frustration ends with the addition of the following operators to Visual Basic .NET. See the following chart to showing the addition of many of the new operators. If you choose to ignore the new feature, the old method will work the same way.

Operation	VB 6.0	VB .NET
Addition	`intVar = intVar + 1`	`intVar += 1`
Subtraction	`intVar = intVar - 1`	`intVar -= 1`
Division	`intVar = intVar / 1`	`intVar /= 1`
Multiplication	`intVar = intVar * 1`	`intVar *= 1`
String concatenation	`strVar = strVar & "New Text"`	`strVar &= "New Text"`

Comments

The use of comments is basically the same in Visual Basic .NET. The only exception is the warning we gave in Chapter 3. You cannot continue a comment on the next line simply by using a continuation character as in the following example.

```
'This is the first line of a comment _
This is meant to be the second line of the comment
```

In Visual Basic .NET you would need to write the comment as follows:

```
'This is the first line of a comment
'This is meant to be the second line of the comment
```

13.5 Decision Making
Changes to the Conditional Operators

In Visual Basic 6.0 a conditional statement evaluated every subexpression regardless if it were necessary. To improve performance, Visual Basic .NET no longer evaluates conditional statements in this manner. Now, as soon as a conditional expression's evaluation can be determined, the evaluation of that expression terminates without evaluating the remainder of the expression.

Imagine you have an expression in one of the following forms:

Expression 1: `True Or False`

Expression 2: `True Or True`

Expression 3: `False And True`

Expression 4: `False And False`

In Expression 1 and Expression 2, when the first subexpression evaluates to `True`, there is no reason evaluate the second subexpression. Whether the second subexpression evaluates to `False` or `True`, the entire expression evaluates to `True`. So why bother evaluating it?

In Expression 3 and 4, when the first subexpression evaluates to `False`, there is no reason to evaluate the second subexpression. Whether the second subexpression evaluates to `True` or `False`, the entire expression evaluates to `False`. So again, why bother evaluating it?

You may think that this is only a minor issue of performance, but it can have an effect on how your applications execute. If you didn't follow our advice earlier and coded your conditional statements with function calls or other side effects, they may not function the way you thought.

Now if the function or side effect is in the part of the conditional statement that is not called, the function will not be call and the side effect will not occur.

Changes to the Value of True

In Visual Basic 6.0 it is possible to compare a Boolean value or the result of a comparison expression to the keywords of `True` or `False`. In Visual Basic 6.0 it is also possible to compare a `True` value to –1 and a `False` value to 0. This should be avoided, because the value of `True` may change to 1 in VB .NET. Therefore, always use the constants `True` and `False` when you want to compare for `True` and `False` values.

13.6 Subroutines, Functions, and Events
Parameter Passing

Although by appearance it doesn't look like there are major changes in the way functions, subroutines, and events are handled, appearances can be deceiving.

In Visual Basic 6.0, most arguments are passed by reference by default. In Visual Basic .NET, they are passed by value.

```
Private Sub FirstRoutine()
Dim intValue As Integer
intValue = 1
Call SecondRoutine(intValue)
End Sub


Private Sub SecondRoutine(intArgument As Integer)
intArgument = 0
End Sub
```

If the previous code were executed in Visual Basic 6.0, because `intValue` is passed by reference, when the argument is changed to 0, so would `intValue`. However, in Visual Basic .NET when `intValue` is passed, a copy of the variable is passed, so the original is unaffected by the changes made to it in `SecondRoutine`.

To ensure that your parameters are passed by reference when you want them to be, use the `ByRef` keyword. So you could change the declaration of the `SecondRoutine` subroutine to the following to ensure that it behaves the same way it did in Visual Basic 6.0.

```
Private Sub SecondRoutine(ByRef intArgument As Integer)
intArgument = 0
End Sub
```

Function's Return Value

In Visual Basic 6.0 you could assign the return value to the name of the function. This is a very odd behavior. Most languages use a `Return` statement that allows a function to pass back a value to the calling routine. Observe the old versus new way of returning values from functions.

VB 6.0

```
Private Function Max(intVal1 As Integer, intVal2 As Integer) As Integer
  If (intVal1 > intVal2) Then
      Max = intVal1
  Else
      Max = intVal2
  End If
End Function
```

VB .NET

```
Private Function Max(ByVal intVal1 As Integer, ByVal intVal2 As Integer) _
                As Integer
  If (intVal1 > intVal2) Then
      Return intVal1
  Else
      Return intVal2
  End If
End Function
```

Calling a Subroutine

In the past there were two recommended method for calling a subroutine.

Method 1 Call *SubroutineName* (*Argument List*)

Method 2 *SubroutineName Argument List*

The problem was that Visual Basic 6.0 also let you, even though you shouldn't use a third method.

Method 3 *SubroutineName* (*Argument List*)

This doesn't seem like a big deal, but in Visual Basic 6.0 most parameters were passed by reference. By adding the parentheses, it forces an evaluation of the arguments and passes them by value. If any side effects were supposed to occur in the subroutine, they would be forgotten. This inconsistency would lead to potential errors in the way applications execute.

Visual Basic .NET will allow you to use either Method 1 or Method 3. However, since Visual Basic .NET defaults to pass by value, it is not a problem. Furthermore, if you specify `ByRef` as the method of passing arguments, Method 3 will function properly.

If you attempt to use Method 2, Visual Basic .NET will automatically place the parentheses in place for you. So in essence, Method 2 will be converted to Method 3.

13.7 Repetition

Very little has actually changed in the realm of repetition in Visual Basic .NET. In fact, the only real change is to a looping construct you did not even bother to introduce. The `While/Wend` construct will basically do the same thing that `Do While/Loop` construct will. In Visual Basic .NET the new `While` construct is `While/End While`. However, you can continue to use the old `Do While/Loop` construct.

13.8 Arrays and User-Defined Types
Array Indices Change

In order for arrays in Visual Basic .NET to be compatible with the other languages in the .NET framework, the arrays in Visual Basic must start with a lower bound of 0.
Therefore, when an array is declared as

```
Dim intValues(10) As Integer
```

It will allocate an array with indexes from 0 to 9. The old syntax allowing the specification of an upper and lower bound is no longer supported.

A new shortcut has been introduced that simplifies the initialization of arrays. Now you can specify an array and its initial values all in one statement. Observe an array of strings that have been initialize to the starting players for the Philadelphia 76ers.

```
Dim strSixers() As String = {"Iverson", "Matumbo", "Lynch", "Jones", "McKee"}
```

Control Arrays

Control arrays go away in VB .NET. Their functionality can be reproduced with the use of objects.

User-Defined Types Replaced with Structures

Visual Basic 6.0's user-defined types have gone away. But fret not; they are replaced with a construct with an almost identical syntax. A structure is identical to a user-defined type except instead of the keyword `Type`, you now use the keyword `Structure`. Instead of the keywords `End Type`, you now use the keywords `End Structure`.

VB 6.0

```
Type Student
    strFirstName As String
    strLastName As String
    strMajor As String
    sngGPA As Single
    sngCredits As Single
End Type
```

VB .NET

```
Structure Student
    strFirstName As String
    strLastName As String
    strMajor As String
    sngGPA As Single
    sngCredits As Single
End Structure
```

One last difference that affects the use of user-defined types is that before you used fixed-length `Strings`; in Visual Basic .NET, `Strings` are defined without a maximum length limit.

13.9 Files

The reading and writing to files in Visual Basic .NET uses a completely different model from Visual Basic 6.0. Although the steps necessary to open, read, write, and close files are different, they are not overly complicated.

The major reason for having to learn a new method is the concept that everything in Visual Basic .NET should be an object. Files in Visual Basic .NET are implemented using a series of objects.

Although you have not explored the creation of objects yet, this does not stop you from using previously created objects.

Visual Basic .NET uses the classes `FileStream`, `StreamWriter`, and `StreamReader` to access files. To access these classes, you must include the namespace `System.IO` with an `Include` statement at the beginning of your file.

Although there are many options for the use of these objects, we will introduce a very simplified approach to writing and reading fixed-width files. Examine the following code:

```
Dim fs As New FileStream("y:\log.txt", FileMode.Open, FileAccess.Read)

Dim intCount As Integer
Dim r As New StreamReader(fs)

Dim strValue As String

Do While (r.Peek() <> -1)
    strValue = r.ReadLine()

    ' Do Something with the strValue

Loop

r.Close()
fs.Close()
```

Step 1: You create and initialize a `FileStream` object. The first parameter is the file path to the file that you are opening. The second parameter specifies the action upon opening the file. This can be either `Append`, `Create`, `CreateNew`, `Open`, `OpenOrCreate`, or `Truncate`. In your case, you want to open an existing file, so you will use the `Open` keyword. The second paragraph indicates the action(s) that will be performed upon the file once it is open. This can be either `Read`, `ReadWrite`, or `Write`.

Step 2: With the `FileStream` object created and opened to the file that you are reading, the next step is to use the `StreamReader` object to allow you to read an entire line of text at a time. You can do this with the statement: `Dim r as New StreamReader(fs)`. That creates a stream called `r` to the file that was opened with the `fs FileStream`.

Step 3: Once the `StreamReader` is created, you need to set up a loop to read each line of input from the file. However, you must check to ensure that you do not read past the end of the file. You can use `StreamReader`'s `Peek` method to check if the next character in the file is the end of file character. Unfortunately, a simple constant is not available, so you must check against the value –1.

Step 4: To perform the actual reading of data, you can use the `ReadLine` method of the `StreamReader` class. It returns a `String` with the contents of the next line of data in the text file.

Step 5: Once the data is read into a `String`, you can do anything you like with it.

Step 6: Finally, when you have reached the end of the file, you must close both the `StreamReader` and `FileStream` using the `Close` method.

Outputting data to a file is very similar. Observe the following code that writes five statements to the file `Output.dat`.

```
Dim fs As New FileStream("y:\Output.dat",
FileMode.OpenOrCreate, FileAccess.Write)
Dim w As New StreamWriter(fs)

w.WriteLine("Sixers didn't win it all this year")
w.WriteLine("but there is always next year")
w.WriteLine("We have to thank them for a great season")
w.WriteLine("They played tough")
w.WriteLine("and we are all proud of them")

w.Close()
fs.Close()
```

Step I: The first step for writing to a file is almost the same as reading from it. The only difference is that you will choose the `OpenOrCreate FileMode` and `Write FileAccess` methods instead of the ones selected for reading.

Step 2: Instead of creating a `StreamReader` to read data, you create a `StreamWriter` object to assist you with writing the data.

Step 3: Once the `StreamWriter` is instantiated, you can write `Strings` to the file using the `WriteLine` method that writes a `String` to a separate line. Otherwise, you can use the `Write` method that writes a `String` to the current line.

Step 4: Again, you must close both the `StreamWriter` and `FileStream` using the `Close` method.

I3.I0 Real Object-Oriented Development

Although previous versions of Visual Basic contained objects, many of the features commonly associated with object-oriented languages were lacking. Most noticeably absent was the capability to create one class of object and then to be able to create another class from the original class. This form of reuse is a must if a language is going to call itself object-oriented.

Visual Basic .NET's object-oriented capabilities are excellent. Everything in Visual Basic .NET is considered an object. Although this may seem like a purist approach, it gives the developer great power. When everything is an object, it allows you to create new objects from the existing objects. Therefore, if the objects that come with Visual Basic .NET do not meet your needs, you do not have to start from scratch. Instead, you can start with an object that contains the majority of the functionality you require and create a new object that inherits the original object's functionality, but also contains the additional information.

One of the coolest features is that Visual Basic .NET does not only allow you to code classes with inheritance, but also you can inherit visually. Visual Inheritance allows the developer to inherit forms and controls to create new forms and controls. The possibilities are endless.

In it simplest application, imagine a company decides that all of it applications and forms should contain the company copyright and logo. Without inheritance, the company would probably create a form with the logo and copyright message and place it in a central location for developers to copy. If the logo changes, or the copyright date increments to the next year, the copy of the form would be updated, the developers would need to be informed to get the new copy, and the form would either have to have the logo and copyright moved to every application that used it, or each application would have to have all of the forms information copied onto the new form. That's a lot of work and that's just a small example.

Fret not; with Visual Inheritance you could create the form that all forms were to model and then tell Visual Basic that you wish to create a form based on the original form. With Visual Inheritance, if you make a change to the original form, all that is required is that you rebuild your applications and the applications will automatically update themselves to reflect any changes to the base form.

To create a form that inherits its properties from a previous existing form, like the one just discussed, you should following these steps:

Step 1: Select Add Inherited Form from the Project menu.
Step 2: Select Open from the dialog box that appears.

Figure 13.12
Add New Item—Inherited
Form

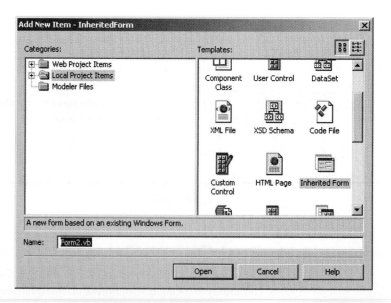

Step 3: Select Inherited Form from the Templates. Change the `Name` of the form from `Form2.vb` to the name you wish your new form to be called. You will use `DerivedForm` for this example. Click on the Open button. The following dialog box will appear:

Figure 13.13
Select Form to Inherit From

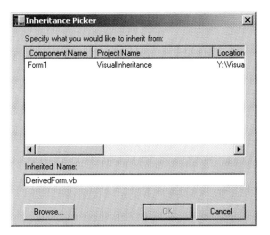

Step 4: Select `Form1` as the form you wish to base your new form on. Click on the OK button and your new form should appear and look similar to the base form that you created it from.

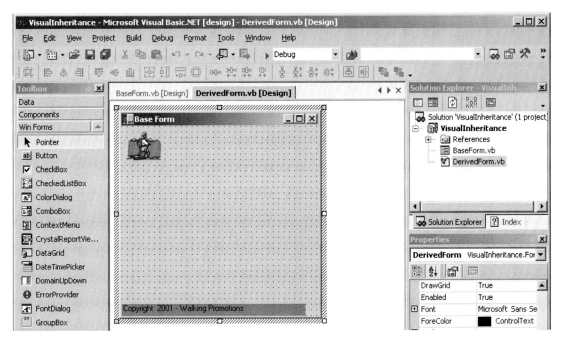

Figure 13.14   Derived Form

Visual Inheritance does not just apply to inheriting cosmetic changes like logos and copyright information. It applies to any controls or code that you include in a base class/object. Although you won't code this example, it's worth mentioning to show you the power of Visual Inheritance. Imagine if your company tracked information relating to different types of people. You could have employees, customers, suppliers, and so on. For each group of people you would track some information that would be the same regardless of the group the person belonged to, and some information that would be different.

Ideally, the information that is in common with all groups should be defined in one place. Imagine if you created a single form containing the common demographic data for people. You could create a form with controls to gather the person's first name, middle initial, last name, street address, city, state, zip code, email address, and so on. Then additional forms could inherit from this form the basic information and add the information pertinent to the specific group they belonged to. The code associated with the basic information could also be contained in the base form and added to the derived forms.

This allows you to modify the basic demographic information in one place and again have it propagate through all the company's applications with a minimum of effort. It wasn't that long ago that companies were not tracking email addresses. Then there was a time where some applications would and some would not. Visual Inheritance is an excellent way to enforce uniformity across a company.

Inheritance in Code

Just as Visual Inheritance is handy to facilitate code reuse, so is utilizing inheritance with code. With a minor change in syntax from Visual Basic 6.0, you can create classes and objects that inherit from one another.

A base class is defined primarily the same way any other class in Visual Basic 6.0 was, with a few exceptions.

◆ In Visual Basic 6.0, there were separate `Property Get` and `Set` statements; in Visual Basic .NET you will learn how to code `Property` statements as a single statement that contains both the `Get` and `Set` code.

◆ Previously, you used either the `Private` or `Public` keyword to determine the scope of a property; now you add the `Protected` keyword. The `Protected` keyword is used when you wish to define an attribute to be visible to derived classes. If one attempts to access an attribute in a base class from a derived class that is defined with a `Private` scope, it will not be accessible from methods in the derived class.

◆ If you wish to allow a method in the base class to be rewritten by a derived class, you must add the **Overridable** keyword to the base class method definition.

◆ When you wish to define a new class that is derived from a base class, you must use the keyword `Inherits` as well as the name of the base class.

◆ Although Visual Basic 6.0 allowed a basic constructor, its usefulness was limited by its inability to accept parameters. This restriction is removed in Visual Basic .NET. Not only can you pass parameters, but also you can set up more than one constructor if you wish different types of parameters to be passed.

Clock/Alarm Clock Example

The easiest way to reinforce all of these new ideas is to show a simple class and then show how to create a derived class from that class.

Imagine if you wished to create a class that would store the information for a clock, display the current time, and allow the time to be incremented by one second at a time. Although your `Clock` class will not keep actual time and increment time automatically, it will serve as an excellent example to demonstrate many of the new constructs you have just discussed.

After you have implemented a `Clock` class, you will then implement an `AlarmClock` class. The `AlarmClock` class will function in a similar manner to the `Clock` class, however, it will add the functionality of an alarm to the class. This will require storing the time the alarm could be set for and whether the alarm is set or not. It will also require allowing the user to set the alarm.

For simplicity, your clock will keep military time and should track hours, minutes, and seconds. Therefore, you will need three attributes, all of which will be stored as `Integers`. Each of these attributes will be `Protected` in scope because you wish to allow them to be accessible by derived classes.

To define a class and all of its attributes and methods, enclose all of the contents using the following syntax:

```
Public Class Clock
    Properties Go Here

    Property Get/Set Statements go here

    Methods Go Here
End Class
```

Although it is not required to list the properties first, and then the property `Get`/`Set` statements, and finally the methods, it is a good convention to follow.

When you declare a class that will act as a base class for derived classes, initially there appears to be no difference. Observe how the your `Clock` class is defined with the same syntax you are already familiar with:

```
Public Class Clock
```

Next you must declare any properties required for your base class. Remember, if you wish the properties to be visible in the derived classes, you must use the `Protected` keyword to define the scope.

```
    Protected mintHour As Integer
    Protected mintMinute As Integer
    Protected mintSecond As Integer
```

Next you must create any `Get`/`Set` statements required for the new properties. Remember, the syntax has changed slightly from Visual Basic 6.0:

```
    Public Property Hour() As Integer
        Get
            Return mintHour
        End Get
        Set
            mintHour = value
        End Set
    End Property
    Public Property Minute() As Integer
        Get
            Return mintMinute
        End Get
        Set
            mintMinute = value
        End Set
    End Property
    Public Property Second() As Integer
        Get
            Return mintSecond
```

(continues)

(continued)

```
        End Get
        Set
            mintSecond = value
        End Set
    End Property
```

By convention, it is a good practice to list all of the constructors before listing any additional methods.

In your implementation you are going to code two constructors. The first will be the default constructor that will accept no parameters. It will initialize the clock to 12:00.

```
    Public Sub New()
        mintHour = 12
        mintMinute = 0
        mintSecond = 0
    End Sub
```

The second constructor will accept parameters for the hour, minute, and second to initialize your clock. All parameters must be present in order for this constructor to be called.

```
Public Sub New(ByVal intH As Integer, ByVal intM As Integer, _
            ByVal intS As Integer)
    mintHour = intH
    mintMinute = intM
    mintSecond = intS
End Sub
```

To create more than one constructor, each constructor that you create must contain a different combination of types for the parameter list. This means that you can have one constructor with a parameter list of an `Integer` and a `String`, and another constructor with a parameter list of a `String` and an `Integer`, but you cannot have two constructors with an `Integer` and a `String` in the same order. The name that you give the parameters does not affect this situation.

The next method to implement is to display the time. The implementation is fairly straightforward. You wish to display the time in an H:M:S format. You can use the `Integer` class's method `.ToString` to perform the type conversion to convert the `Integer` to a `String` for purposes of display. Although the old function would work, it is good practice to get used to using the new methods.

Finally, because this method will be overridden in the derived class, you add the keyword `Overridable` to the method definition. The code follows:

```
    Public Overridable Function Time() As String
    Return mintHour.ToString & ":" & mintMinute.ToString & _
        ":" & mintSecond.ToString
    End Function
```

The final method, `Increment`, must also be declared as `Overridable`. It will increment the time by one second. When you increment the seconds by one second, you must check if the total number of seconds equals 60. If it does, you must set the seconds back to 0 and increment the total number of minutes. If the number of minutes now equals 60, you must set the total number of minutes to 0 and increment the total number of hours by 1. Finally if the total number of hours equals 24, you reset the total number of hours to 0. The code follows:

```
Public Overridable Sub Increment()
    mintSecond += 1
    If (MintSecond = 60) Then
        mintSecond = 0
        mintMinute += 1
        If (mintMinute = 60) Then
            mintMinute = 0
            mintHour = mintHour + 1
            If mintHour = 24 Then
                mintHour = 0
            End If
        End If
    End If
End Sub
End Class
```

Once the base class has been defined, most of the work is already done. The goal in creating the `AlarmClock` class is to rewrite the least amount of code possible from the `Clock` class.

When you think about it, the properties for the `Clock` class are all required in the `AlarmClock` class. Although you need additional properties to store the alarm time and whether or not the alarm is set, you can simply add them to the new class.

As far as new methods are concerned you will have to create a `SetAlarm` method as well as a `ShutAlarm` method to set and shut off the alarm. Where things get tricky is when you wish to modify the behavior of methods that already exist.

A perfect case is the `Time` method. Most alarm clocks will somehow signal that its alarm is set. For your class, when the `Time` method is called, you will display an asterisk next to the time when the alarm is set. Although you could rewrite the entire `Time` method, it would be a waste of code. It would also create a maintenance issue if you ever wished to change the way a time is displayed. As a golden rule, code should only be written once.

Visual Basic .NET gives you complete control of the situation so that you can call the `Time` method in the base class and add the code you require in the derived class.

First, you must declare the derived method using the keyword `Overrides`. The syntax for declaring a method that overrides a base class's method is as follows:

```
Public Overrides Function MethodName(Parameter List) As Return Type
Public Overrides Sub MethodName(Parameter List)
```

To use the functionality of a base class's method, use the following syntax of code to explicitly call the method wherever you wish it to be called in the new method.

MyBase . OriginalMethod

With this information, you can now code your derived class. First let's declare `AlarmClock` as a class that inherits the properties and methods of the `Clock` class:

```
Public Class AlarmClock
    Inherits Clock
```

Next you must declare any additional properties required for your derived class.

```
Private mintAlarmHour As Integer
Private mintAlarmMinute As Integer
Private mintAlarmSecond As Integer
Private mblnAlarmSet As Boolean
```

Next you must create any Get/Set statements required for the new properties.

```
Public Property AlarmHour() As Integer
    Get
        Return mintAlarmHour
    End Get
    Set
        mintAlarmHour = value
    End Set
End Property

Public Property AlarmMinute() As Integer
    Get
        Return mintAlarmMinute
    End Get
    Set
        mintAlarmMinute = value
    End Set
End Property

Public Property AlarmSecond() As Integer
    Get
        Return mintAlarmSecond
    End Get
    Set
        mintAlarmSecond = value
    End Set
End Property
```

Sometimes when you create a derived class you must create a new constructor. This happens when you need to initialize any of the new properties defined for the derived class or if the derived class behaves differently than the base class.

In this case, you are going to want to initialize the alarm in the clock to be off. Although you could also initialize the time the alarm is set to, you will not because you will set the alarm time when you turn the alarm on.

Because the only new functionality of your constructor is to set `mintAlarmSet` to `False`, you should not re-create all of the work done by the base class's constructor; instead you should call the base classes constructor and pass it all of the parameters it requires. Then you can simply set `mintAlarmSet` to `False` and your constructor would look as follows:

```
Public Sub New(ByVal intH As Integer, ByVal intM As Integer, _
        ByVal intS As Integer)
    MyBase.New(intH, intM, intS)
    mblnAlarmSet = False
End Sub
```

As with the constructor, your `Increment` method shared functionality between the base case and the derived class. You wish the `Increment` method to add a second to the clock, as it did in the base class. However, then you wish it to compare the current clock time to the alarm's time. If they are the same, you will pop up a message box indicating the alarm has rung.

To implement this functionality, explicitly call the base class's `Increment` method and then perform the check comparing the base class's properties to the derived class's properties. Because you declared the base class's properties with a `Protected` scope, they are directly accessible in the derived class.

```
Public Overrides Sub Increment()
    MyBase.Increment()
    If (mintAlarmHour = mintHour) And (mintAlarmMinute = mintAlarmMinute) _
        And (mintAlarmSecond = mintAlarmSecond) And (mblnAlarmSet = True) Then
            MsgBox("ALARM")
    End If
End Sub
```

The implementation of the `SetAlarm` method is straightforward. This method does not exist in the base class, so it does not contain the `Overrides` keyword. The contents of the method simply set the attributes for the alarm time to the values passed as parameters as well as setting the alarm to on by setting the `mintAlarmSet` attribute to `True`.

```
Public Sub SetAlarm(ByVal intH As Integer, ByVal intM As Integer, _
                ByVal intS As Integer)
        mintAlarmHour = intH
        mintAlarmMinute = intM
        mintAlarmSecond = intS
        mintAlarmSet = True
End Sub
```

The implementation of the `ShutAlarm` method is straightforward. This method does not exist in the base class, so it does not contain the `Overrides` keyword. The contents of the method simply set the attribute `mintAlarmSet` to `False`.

```
Public Sub ShutAlarm()
    mblnAlarmSet = False
End Sub

Public Overrides Function Time() As String
    If (mblnAlarmSet = True) Then
        Return MyBase.Time() & " *"
    Else
        Return MyBase.Time()
    End If
End Function
End Class
```

Instantiating and Dereferencing Objects

When you define a class, all that you have accomplished is creating a model for declaring objects. To create an object of a class you must instantiate it. In Visual Basic 6.0 you instantiated objects with the `Set` keyword. In Visual Basic .NET, the `Set` keyword goes away. Instead, you can use the following syntax:

```
Dim objName As New ClassName()
```

The statement will declare and instantiate an object called `objName` of the class `ClassName`. If you do not wish to declare and instantiate an object in the same statement, you can separate them. Sometimes this is desirable because you may not require the object in all cases and it would be a waste of resources to allocate it early. Why then should you declare the object early? Remember that variables in Visual Basic .NET are visible only in the scope of the code they are declared. Therefore, if you declared it exactly where you needed it, it might not be visible to the rest of the code. The syntax for declaring and instantiating an object separately is as follows:

```
Dim objName As ClassName
'Other code goes here
objName = New ClassName()
```

To dereference an object, you simply set the object to `Nothing`. This is shown in the following syntax:

```
ObjName = Nothing
```

TIP

Visual Basic .NET uses non-deterministic deallocation of resources due to its use of garbage collection. This means that even though you set an object to `Nothing`, you cannot be sure when the destructor is called and the entire object is deallocated. However, you still must dereference objects so that the garbage collector can deallocate the object when it deems necessary.

13.11 Graphics

The way you draw on a form in Visual Basic .NET is completely different from Visual Basic 6.0. However, the new methods for drawing give you more control and capabilities than you previously had. Although the initial method of using the `Graphics` class will seem very different, you will see that once you get the basics, you can explore the vast number of objects and methods with your intuition and Visual Basic's type ahead feature.

By including the `System.Drawing` namespace you will have access to numerous classes that when used together allow you to draw directly on a form.

We'll introduce these features by showing you how to create a drawing similar to the one of the man named Adam in Chapter 11. To create it, you will need to create a couple of objects to allow you to draw the types of figures you desire.

Step 1: You must create a **Graphics** object and the instantiate it. This is done by declaring a `Graphics` object and then calling a `CreateGraphics` method from the form.

You can declare the `Graphics` object using the following code:

```
Dim grfGraphics As Graphics
```

Because you will include the statement `Imports System.Drawing`, you do not need to preface `Graphics` with `System.Drawing.` each time you refer to it.

To instantiate the object, you have to call the `CreateGraphics` method of the form. The easiest way to do this is to refer to the form using the `Me` keyword.

```
grfGraphics = Me.CreateGraphics
```

Step 2: Once the `Graphics` object is created, you need to declare and instantiate a `Pen` object. A `Pen` object will be used to draw with the `Graphics` object. With the `Pen` object you will select a color. You will notice as you type the code that many more predefined colors are available than in Visual Basic 6.0.

To create a `Pen` object, use the following code:

```
Dim penOurPen as New Pen(Color.Red)
```

With the `Pen` object created, you can now draw with the `Graphics` object. Let's start by drawing the circular head. The easiest way to do this is to use the `Ellipse` method of the `Graphics` object. It takes a `Pen` as the first parameter and then the x and y locations of the upper-left corner of a rectangle that bounds the circle/ellipse that you are drawing. The final two parameters are the length and width of the bounding rectangle.

Therefore, the code to draw the head would be as follows:

```
grfGraphics.DrawEllipse(penOurPen, 50, 50 , 40, 40)
```

Step 3: To draw the body, you need to draw a straight line. The `Graphics` object contains a method `DrawLine` that will allow you to do this. However, to re-create Adam as closely as possible, you must change the color of the pen to blue. This is easily accomplished with the following code:

```
penOurPen.Color = Color.Blue
```

Step 4: Now you must draw the line. This is accomplished using the `DrawLine` method in the following code:

```
grfGraphics.DrawLine(penOurPen, 70, 90, 70, 15)
```

Step 5: You can follow the same procedure to draw the arms and legs. In the original drawing, Adam's arms and legs were yellow, so you must change the color of the pen to yellow. This is accomplished with the following code:

```
penOurPen.Color = Color.Yellow
```

Step 6: Now you can draw the left and right arms with the following code:

```
grfGraphics.DrawLine(penOurPen, 70, 150, 55, 105)
grfGraphics.DrawLine(penOurPen, 70, 150, 85, 105)
```

Step 7: To add legs, since they are the same color, you do not have to change the `Pen` object. You can simply use the following code to draw the two lines representing the legs:

```
grfGraphics.DrawLine(penOurPen, 70, 150, 45, 170)
grfGraphics.DrawLine(penOurPen, 70, 150, 95, 170)
```

Step 8: The last step to re-create your drawing is to add the text to the figure. However, in Visual Basic .NET, it's not as simple as in Visual Basic 6.0. In Visual Basic .NET you have much more control over the text you display. You can control the font and the brush that you draw it with. Although we will only select a simple brush, you can select textured brushes that allow you to draw with a pattern contained in a bitmap file.

To create a simple brush and font object and then display the text "Adam," use the following code:

```
Dim bshAdam as SolidBrush
Dim fntAdam as Font

BshAdam = New SolidBrush(System.Drawing.Color.Black)
FntAdam = New Font("Times", 10)
GrfGraphics.DrawString("Adam", fntAdam, bshAdam, 55, 180)
```

Step 9: Although you are done creating the image as it was in Chapter 11, I thought it would be interesting to show you the `DrawRectangle` method. You will use it to create feet for Adam. Big feet.

The `DrawRectangle` method takes two parameters: a `Pen` and a `Rectangle`. You already have a `Pen` created, so you only need to create a `Rectangle` object. However, to create a `Rectangle` object you need a `Point` object and a `Size` object. Observe the following code that shows how it all works together:

```
'Draw Feet
Dim rctFoot As Rectangle
Dim pntFoot As Point
Dim szeFoot As Size

szeFoot = New Size(20, 10)

'Left Foot
pntFoot = New Point(25, 160)
rctFoot = New Rectangle(pntFoot, szeFoot)
grfGraphics.DrawRectangle(penOurPen, rctFoot)

'Right Foot
pntFoot = New Point(95, 160)
rctFoot = New Rectangle(pntFoot, szeFoot)
grfGraphics.DrawRectangle(penOurPen, rctFoot)


'Draw Adam Text
Dim bshAdam As SolidBrush
Dim fntAdam As Font

bshAdam = New SolidBrush(System.Drawing.Color.Black)
fntAdam = New Font("Times", 10)
grfGraphics.DrawString("Adam", fntAdam, bshAdam, 55, 180)
```

The final image would look as follows:

Figure 13.15
Drawing of Adam

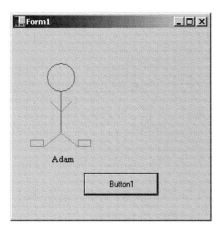

13.12 Improved Error Handling

Although Visual Basic 6.0 gave you the capability to handle errors, the lack of structure of the `On Error Goto` statement was a point of weakness when compared with languages like C++. In Visual Basic .NET an improved, more standard, method is introduced.

The new `Try`, `Catch`, `Finally` block structure allows Visual Basic .NET programmers to code error handling local to the code that it checks for errors. Instead of writing a single error handler for a large area of code, the new method can be used to trap errors against specific areas of your code.

The syntax of the new structure is as follows:

```
Try
    'Code to check for error
Catch When Err.Number = ErrorNumber
    'Code to handle specific error
Catch When Err.Number = Another ErrorNumber
    'Code to handle other specific error
Catch
    'Code to handle the all other errors
Finally
    'Code to execute directly after
End Try
```

Imagine if you had to perform a calculation between a series of `Short` variables to output the average commission a salesperson makes per month over the summer. The calculation might be coded as follows:

```
shtAverageCommission = (shtJuneSales +  shtJulySales + _
                shtAugustSales) / shtPeriod
```

The calculation adds the sales of the months June, July, and August and then divides them by the variable storing the number of months in the period.

There are two very obvious possible sources of error. First, remember that a `Short` variable can have a maximum value of 32,767. If the addition of all three months is greater than 32,767 you could get an overflow error.

You also have to worry that the variable `shtPeriod` is not equal to zero or you will get a divide by zero error when performing the calculation.

The answer to these problems is to place the code inside a `Try` block as follows:

```
Try
    'Code to check for error
    shtAverageCommission = (shtJuneSales +  shtJulySales + _
                    shtAugustSales) / shtPeriod
Catch When Err.Number = 1
    'Code to handle OverFlow
    MessageBox "An overflow occurred when adding the sum" & _
            shtJuneSales.ToString & " and " _
            shtJulySales.ToString & " and " _
            shtAugustSales.ToString _

Catch When Err.Number = Another ErrorNumber
    'Code to handle divide by zero
    MessageBox "The number of months was zero when computing" & _
            "the average summer commission"
Catch
    MessageBox "An " & Err.Description & _
            " error occurred when computing the average summer commission"
Finally
    'Code to execute directly after
End Try
```

TIP

Although the old method of `On Error Goto` can still be used, it should be avoided.

13.13 Data Handling

Although I would love to be able to summarize all the changes in data handling in a few scant pages, it is impossible. The changes made to data handling will give you a great deal of control over how you interact with a data source, but they require a lot of information to create a useful application. We will leave that to the Visual Basic .NET Coach.

Key Words and Key Terms

+=

A new operator that adds the value to the right of the operator with the variable on the left and stores the result in the variable on the left.

−=

A new operator that subtracts the value to the right of the operator from the variable on the left and stores the result in the variable on the left.

*=

A new operator that multiplies the value to the right of the operator with the variable on the left and stores the result in the variable on the left.

/=

A new operator that divides the value to the right of the operator into the variable on the left and stores the result in the variable on the left.

&=

A new operator that concatenates the `String` to the right of the operator to the `String` on the left and stores the result in the `String` on the left.

Button

A new control that replaces the command button control.

Catch

A statement to attempt to handle an error defined within a `Try` block.

Char

A new data type that stores a single character.

CreateGraphics

A method called to instantiate a `Graphics` object.

FileStream

An object to handle file input and output.

Graphics

An object to give the developer access to many graphical routines.

Group box

A new control the replaces the frame control.

Include

The keyword to associate other files with the project.

Nothing

The keyword to set an object to so that it will be disposed of.

Overridable

The keyword that indicates a method can be overridden by a derived class.

Overrides

The keyword that indicates a method is overriding the base class's method.

Pen

An object used to draw with a `Graphics` object.

Protected

A new classification of scope to indicate that an item is visible to classes that are inherited from the class in which it is defined.

Short

A new data type that stores a 16-bit `Integer`.

Short circuit evaluation

The method Visual Basic .NET uses to evaluate conditional expressions in which it only evaluates as much of the expression as necessary.

Solutions Explorer

A new tool that replaces the Project Explorer.

StreamReader

An object to assist in reading data from a file.

StreamWriter

An object to assist in writing data to a file.

Structure

A replacement for user-defined types.

Try

The start of a block of code that will be protected by an error handler.

Visual Basic .NET

The new version of Visual Basic.

INTERVIEW

An Interview with Michael Iem

Michael Iem is currently a Visual Basic Product Manager for the .NET Developer Solutions Group at Microsoft Corporation headquarters. Michael graduated from Purdue University where he received a Bachelor of Science in Engineering. Prior to joining Microsoft, Michael spent nine years at Tandem Computers as a Senior Consultant specializing in Client Server. In April of 1996, Michael joined Microsoft Consulting Services Advanced Technology Group (MCSAT), where he project managed Microsoft's Internet banking server, then moved to product manager of BackOffice Server and authored its Performance Characterization and Reliability white papers. A Microsoft Certified Systems Engineer, Michael is a regular speaker at industry events such as Microsoft TechEd and the Professional Developers Conference.

How did you become interested in computers?

My dad bought me a TI 55 programmable Calculator and asked me, "If I gave you a penny a day and doubled it for 30 days how much money would you have?" I think I was in 6th grade. When I got to high school I bought an HP 41 calculator that was programmable and that got me programming.

Which person in the computer industry has inspired you most?

Bill Gates. He had a vision of how personal computers would change people's lives and give everyone equal access to information. He stuck with his dream even when people thought he was crazy. I admire people who have conviction and work toward seeing their vision a reality.

What does your current position at Microsoft entail?

I do technical presentations, demos, as well as marketing activities like press meetings, product positioning, etc. I am considered a Tech Champ.

What makes Visual Basic .NET better than its predecessor and other programming languages?

Visual Basic .NET has some great new features that make it a first class language on .NET. Free Threading, Inheritance, and Structured Exception Handling, to name a few. Developers using Visual Basic .NET have full access to the .NET Framework. The product just rocks!

I personally like the ability to build Web Forms and XML Web services with Visual Basic .NET and use the One Click Hosting feature from the start page to host that content and services for free with Visual Studio .NET Beta 2. I also like the new features in Windows forms like anchoring, docking, and in place menu editor. I have always wanted to build applications for my Pocket PC and now I can with the Mobile Internet Toolkit.

What kinds of projects are you currently working on?

At the moment I am focused on the .NET Developer Training Tour. A 26-city Roadshow using our best third-party trainers and CTECs to deliver two intense days of .NET Training. Signup, it is a life changing experience.

What advice do you have for students using VB?

With Visual Basic .NET you now have the most productive tool for building .NET Windows and web applications. Get started today with Beta 2 to start building the coolest, most compelling Windows, web and XML web services to do things that people never dreamed possible before. The only thing stopping you is your imagination.

APPENDIX A
ASCII
Character Set

0	null '\0'	22	syn	44	comma	66	B	88	X	110	n
1	soh	23	etb	45	minus	67	C	89	Y	111	o
2	stx	24	can	46	period	68	D	90	Z	112	p
3	etx	25	em	47	/	69	E	91	[	113	q
4	end transmission	26	sub	48	0	70	F	92	\	114	r
5	enquire	27	escape	49	1	71	G	93	]	115	s
6	acknowledge	28	fs	50	2	72	H	94	^	116	t
7	ring a bell '\a'	29	gs	51	3	73	I	95	underscore	117	u
8	backspace '\b'	30	rs	52	4	74	J	96	back quote	118	v
9	tab '\t'	31	us	53	5	75	K	97	a	119	w
10	new line '\n'	32	blank	54	6	76	L	98	b	120	x
11	vertical tab '\v'	33	!	55	7	77	M	99	c	121	y
12	form feed '\f'	34	"	56	8	78	N	100	d	122	z
13	carriage return '\r'	35	#	57	9	79	O	101	e	123	{
14	so	36	$	58	:	80	P	102	f	124	|
15	si	37	%	59	;	81	Q	103	g	125	}
16	dle	38	&	60	<	82	R	104	h	126	~
17	dc1	39	single quote	61	=	83	S	105	i	127	delete
18	dc2	40	(	62	>	84	T	106	j		
19	dc3	41	)	63	?	85	U	107	k		
20	dc4	42	*	64	@	86	V	108	l		
21	nak	43	+	65	A	87	W	109	m		

APPENDIX B
Visual Basic Trappable Errors

Code	Message
3	Return without GoSub
5	Invalid procedure call
6	Overflow
7	Out of memory
9	Subscript out of range
10	This array is fixed or temporarily locked
11	Division by zero
13	Type mismatch
14	Out of string space
16	Expression too complex
17	Can't perform requested operation
18	User interrupt occurred
20	Resume without error
28	Out of stack space
35	Sub, Function, or Property not defined
47	Too many DLL application clients
48	Error in loading DLL
49	Bad DLL calling convention
51	Internal error
52	Bad file name or number
53	File not found
54	Bad file mode
55	File already open
57	Device I/O error
58	File already exists
59	Bad record length
61	Disk full
62	Input past end of file
63	Bad record number
67	Too many files

Code	Message
68	Device unavailable
70	Permission denied
71	Disk not ready
74	Can't rename with different drive
75	Path/File access error
76	Path not found
91	Object variable or With block variable not set
92	For loop not initialized
93	Invalid pattern string
94	Invalid use of Null
97	Can't call Friend procedure on an object that is not an instance of the defining class
98	A property or method call cannot include a reference to a private object, either as an argument or as a return value
298	System DLL could not be loaded
320	Can't use character device names in specified file names
321	Invalid file format
322	Can't create necessary temporary file
325	Invalid format in resource file
327	Data value named not found
328	Illegal parameter; can't write arrays
335	Could not access system registry
336	ActiveX component not correctly registered
337	ActiveX component not found
338	ActiveX component did not run correctly
360	Object already loaded

Code	Message
361	Can't load or unload this object
363	ActiveX control specified not found
364	Object was unloaded
365	Unable to unload within this context
368	The specified file is out of date. This program requires a later version
371	The specified object can't be used as an owner form for Show
380	Invalid property value
381	Invalid property-array index
382	Property Set can't be executed at run time
383	Property Set can't be used with a read-only property
385	Need property-array index
387	Property Set not permitted
393	Property Get can't be executed at run time
394	Property Get can't be executed on write-only property
400	Form already displayed; can't show modally
402	Code must close topmost modal form first
419	Permission to use object denied
422	Property not found
423	Property or method not found
424	Object required
425	Invalid object use
429	ActiveX component can't create object or return reference to this object
430	Class doesn't support Automation
432	File name or class name not found during Automation operation
438	Object doesn't support this property or method
440	Automation error
442	Connection to type library or object library for remote process has been lost
443	Automation object doesn't have a default value
445	Object doesn't support this action
446	Object doesn't support named arguments
447	Object doesn't support current locale setting
448	Named argument not found

Code	Message
449	Argument not optional or invalid property assignment
450	Wrong number of arguments or invalid property assignment
451	Object not a collection
452	Invalid ordinal
453	Specified DLL function not found
454	Code resource not found
455	Code resource lock error
457	This key is already associated with an element of this collection
458	Variable uses a type not supported in Visual Basic
459	This component doesn't support the set of events
460	Invalid Clipboard format
461	Specified format doesn't match format of data
480	Can't create AutoRedraw image
481	Invalid picture
482	Printer error
483	Printer driver does not support specified property
484	Problem getting printer information from the system. Make sure the printer is set up correctly
485	Invalid picture type
486	Can't print form image to this type of printer
520	Can't empty Clipboard
521	Can't open Clipboard
735	Can't save file to TEMP directory
744	Search text not found
746	Replacements too long
31001	Out of memory
31004	No object
31018	Class is not set
31027	Unable to activate object
31032	Unable to create embedded object
31036	Error saving to file
31037	Error loading from file

BIBLIOGRAPHY

BRADLEY, JULIA CASE. *Programming in Visual Basic 6.0.* McGraw Hill, 1999.

HARRIGER, ALKA R. *Introduction to Computer Programming with Visual Basic 6.0.* Que Education and Training, 1999.

HOLLIS, BILLY AND ROCKFORD LHOTKA. *VB.NET Programming with the Public Beta.* Wrok Press, 2001.

KERMAN, MITCHELL. *Computer Programming Fundamentals with Applications in Visual Basic 6.0.* Addison-Wesley, 2000.

MSDN Magazine. February 2001, Vol. 16, No 2. Microsoft, 2001.

MSDN Magazine. July 2001, Vol. 16, No 7. Microsoft, 2001.

SCHNEIDER, DAVID. *An Introduction to Programming Using Visual Basic 6.0.* Prentice Hall, 1999.

Visual Basic Programmer's Journal. February 2001, Vol 11, No 2.

ZAK, DIANE. *Programming with Microsoft Visual Basic 6.0.* Course Technologies, 1999.

INDEX